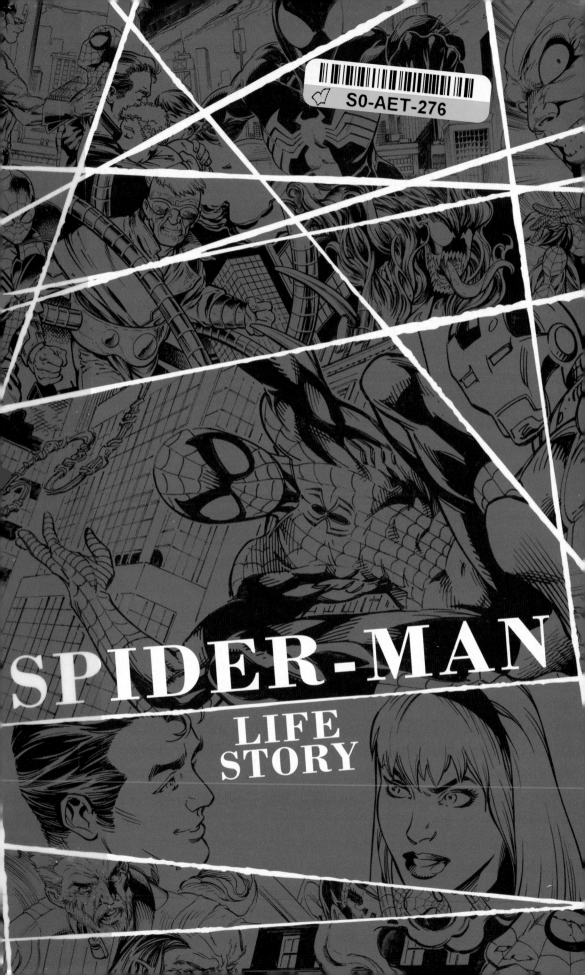

SPIDER-MAN

LIFE STORY

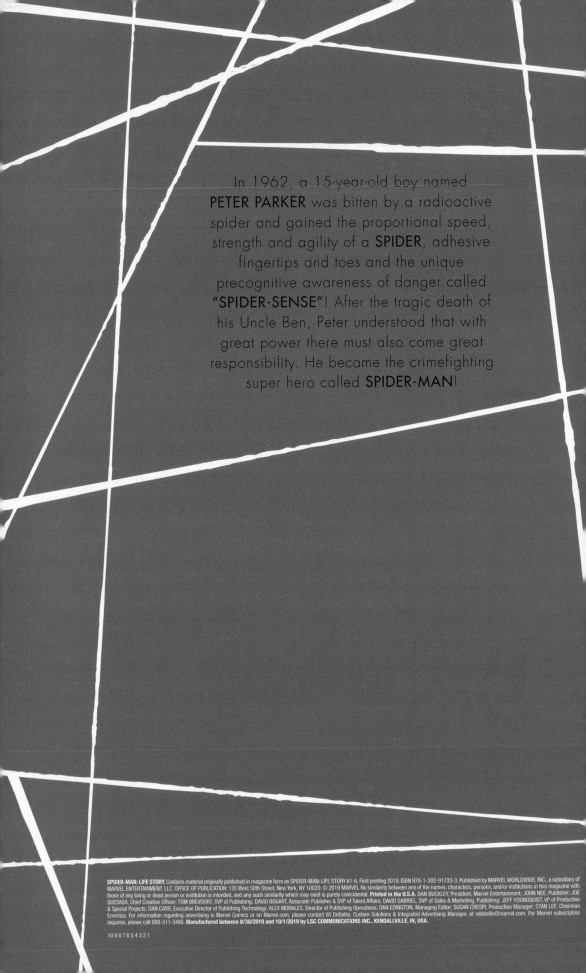

In 1962, a 15-year-old boy named
PETER PARKER was bitten by a radioactive
spider and gained the proportional speed,
strength and agility of a **SPIDER**, adhesive
fingertips and toes and the unique
precognitive awareness of danger called
"SPIDER-SENSE"! After the tragic death of
his Uncle Ben, Peter understood that with
great power there must also come great
responsibility. He became the crimefighting
super hero called **SPIDER-MAN**!

SPIDER-MAN: LIFE STORY. Contains material originally published in magazine form as SPIDER-MAN: LIFE STORY #1-6. First printing 2019. ISBN 978-1-302-91733-3. Published by MARVEL WORLDWIDE, INC., a subsidiary of MARVEL ENTERTAINMENT, LLC. OFFICE OF PUBLICATION: 135 West 50th Street, New York, NY 10020. © 2019 MARVEL No similarity between any of the names, characters, persons, and/or institutions in this magazine with those of any living or dead person or institution is intended, and any such similarity which may exist is purely coincidental. **Printed in the U.S.A.** DAN BUCKLEY, President, Marvel Entertainment; JOHN NEE, Publisher; JOE QUESADA, Chief Creative Officer; TOM BREVOORT, SVP of Publishing; DAVID BOGART, Associate Publisher & SVP of Talent Affairs; DAVID GABRIEL, SVP of Sales & Marketing, Publishing; JEFF YOUNGQUIST, VP of Production & Special Projects; DAN CARR, Executive Director of Publishing Technology; ALEX MORALES, Director of Publishing Operations; DAN EDINGTON, Managing Editor; SUSAN CRESPI, Production Manager; STAN LEE, Chairman Emeritus. For information regarding advertising in Marvel Comics or on Marvel.com, please contact Vit DeBellis, Custom Solutions & Integrated Advertising Manager, at vdebellis@marvel.com. For Marvel subscription inquiries, please call 888-511-5480. **Manufactured between 8/30/2019 and 10/1/2019 by LSC COMMUNICATIONS INC., KENDALLVILLE, IN, USA.**

10 9 8 7 6 5 4 3 2 1

SPIDER-MAN LIFE STORY

CHIP ZDARSKY
WRITER

MARK BAGLEY
PENCILER

JOHN DELL (#1, #3, #5) &
ANDREW HENNESSY (#2, #4, #6)
INKERS

FRANK D'ARMATA
COLORIST

VC's TRAVIS LANHAM
LETTERER

CHIP ZDARSKY
COVER ART

SHANNON ANDREWS BALLESTEROS
ASSISTANT EDITOR

ALANNA SMITH
ASSOCIATE EDITOR

TOM BREVOORT
EDITOR

SPIDER-MAN CREATED BY **STAN LEE** & **STEVE DITKO**

JENNIFER GRÜNWALD
COLLECTION EDITOR

CAITLIN O'CONNELL
ASSISTANT EDITOR

KATERI WOODY
ASSOCIATE MANAGING EDITOR

MARK D. BEAZLEY
EDITOR, SPECIAL PROJECTS

JEFF YOUNGQUIST
VP PRODUCTION & SPECIAL PROJECTS

ADAM DEL RE WITH **CHIP ZDARSKY**
BOOK DESIGNER

DAVID GABRIEL
SVP PRINT, SALES & MARKETING

SVEN LARSEN
DIRECTOR, LICENSED PUBLISHING

C.B. CEBULSKI
EDITOR IN CHIEF

JOE QUESADA
CHIEF CREATIVE OFFICER

DAN BUCKLEY
PRESIDENT

ALAN FINE
EXECUTIVE PRODUCER

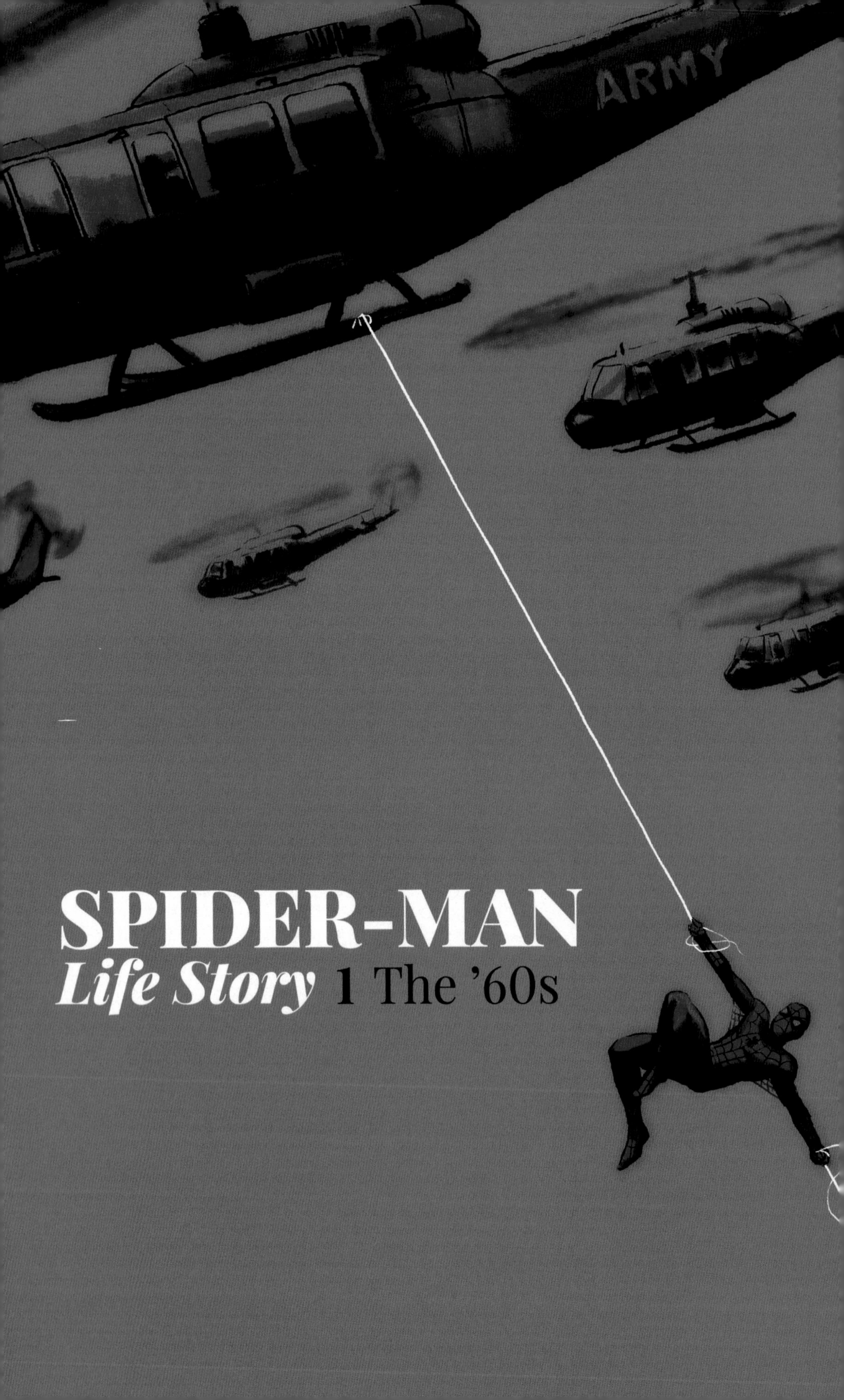
ARMY

SPIDER-MAN
Life Story 1 The '60s

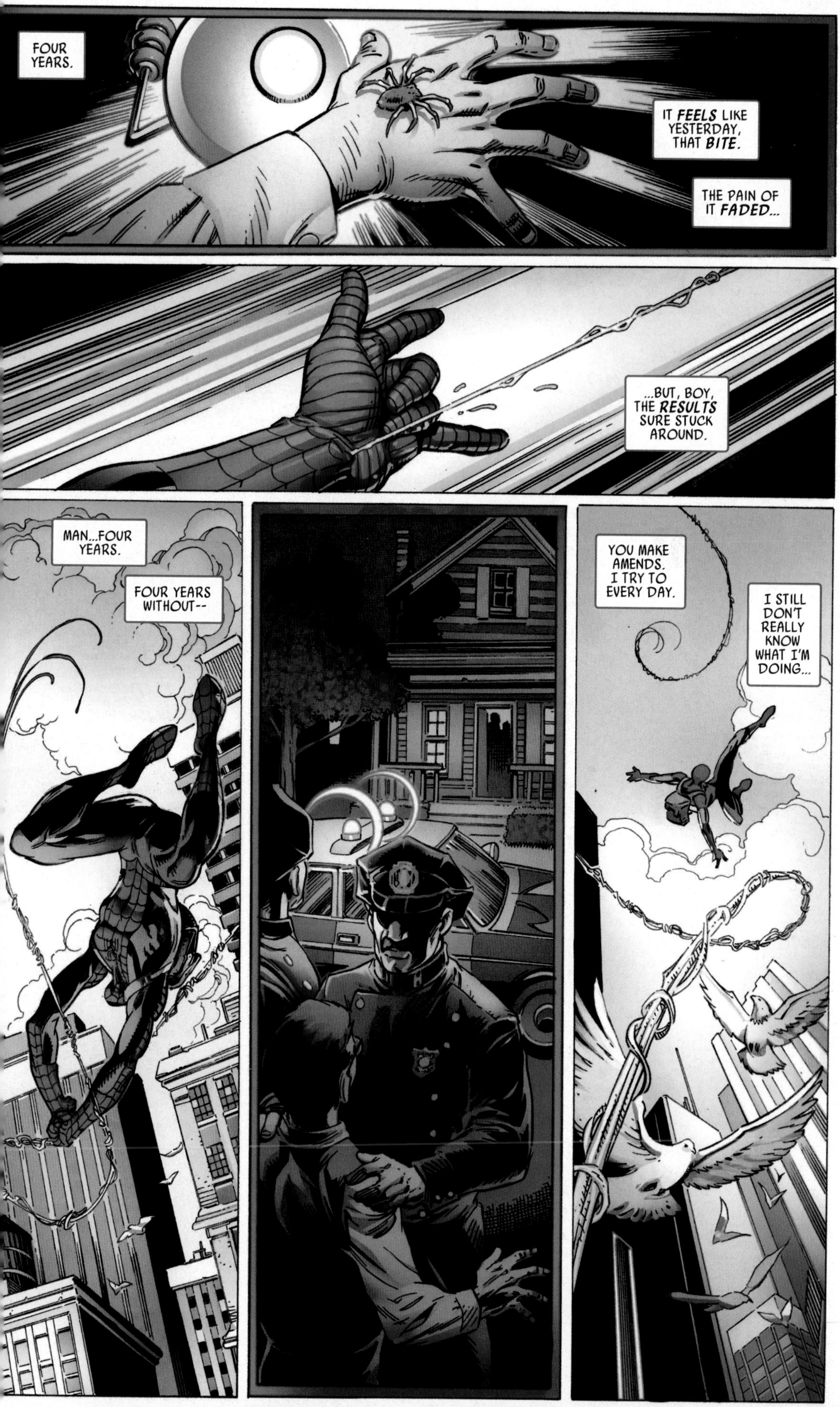
FOUR YEARS.
IT FEELS LIKE YESTERDAY, THAT BITE.
THE PAIN OF IT FADED...
...BUT, BOY, THE RESULTS SURE STUCK AROUND.
MAN...FOUR YEARS.
FOUR YEARS WITHOUT--
YOU MAKE AMENDS. I TRY TO EVERY DAY.
I STILL DON'T REALLY KNOW WHAT I'M DOING...

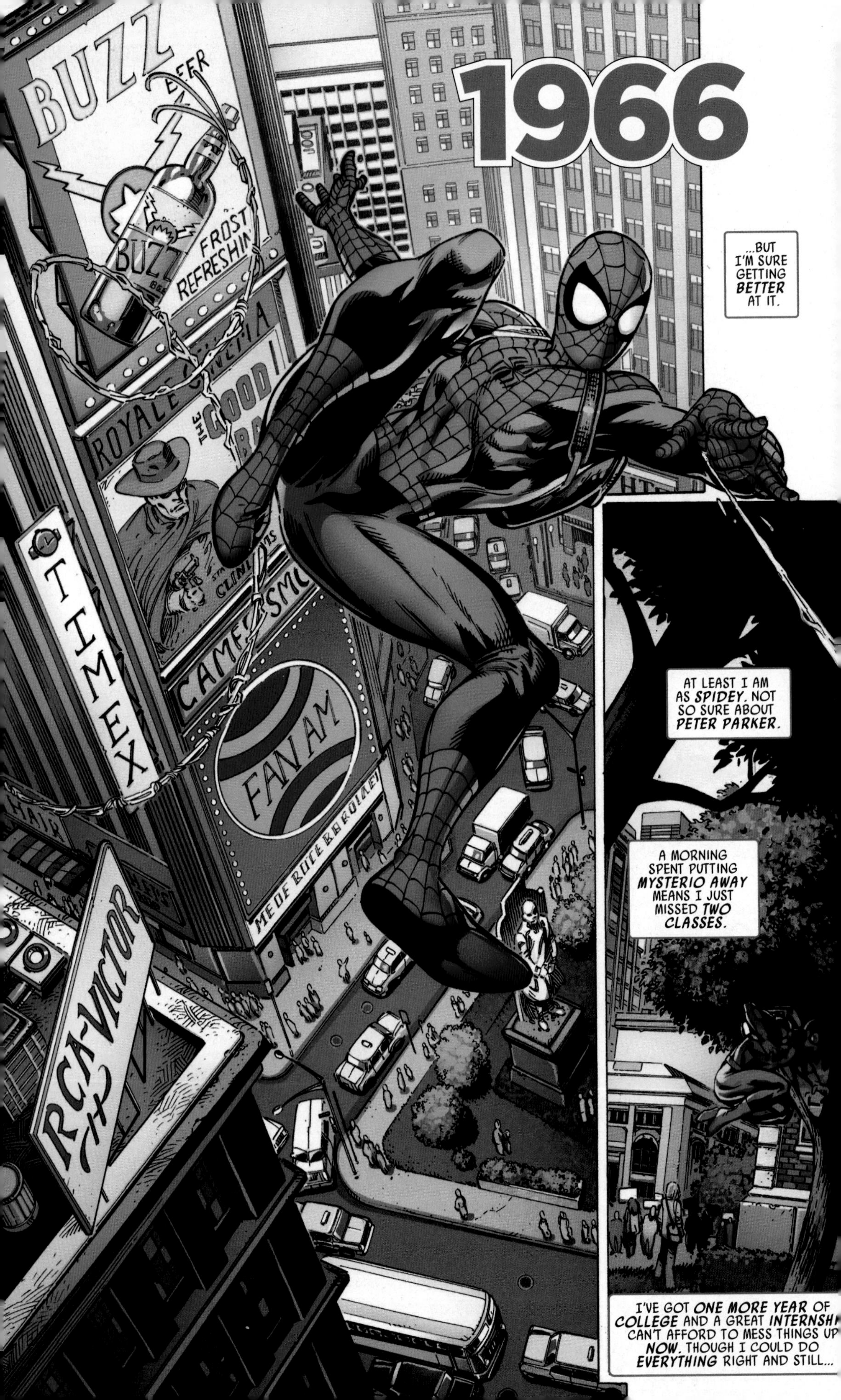
1966
...BUT I'M SURE GETTING BETTER AT IT.
AT LEAST I AM AS SPIDEY. NOT SO SURE ABOUT PETER PARKER.
A MORNING SPENT PUTTING MYSTERIO AWAY MEANS I JUST MISSED TWO CLASSES.
I'VE GOT ONE MORE YEAR OF COLLEGE AND A GREAT INTERNSHI CAN'T AFFORD TO MESS THINGS UP NOW. THOUGH I COULD DO EVERYTHING RIGHT AND STILL...
BUZZ
FROST REFRESHIN
ROYALE CINEMA
TIMEX
PAN AM
RCA-VICTOR

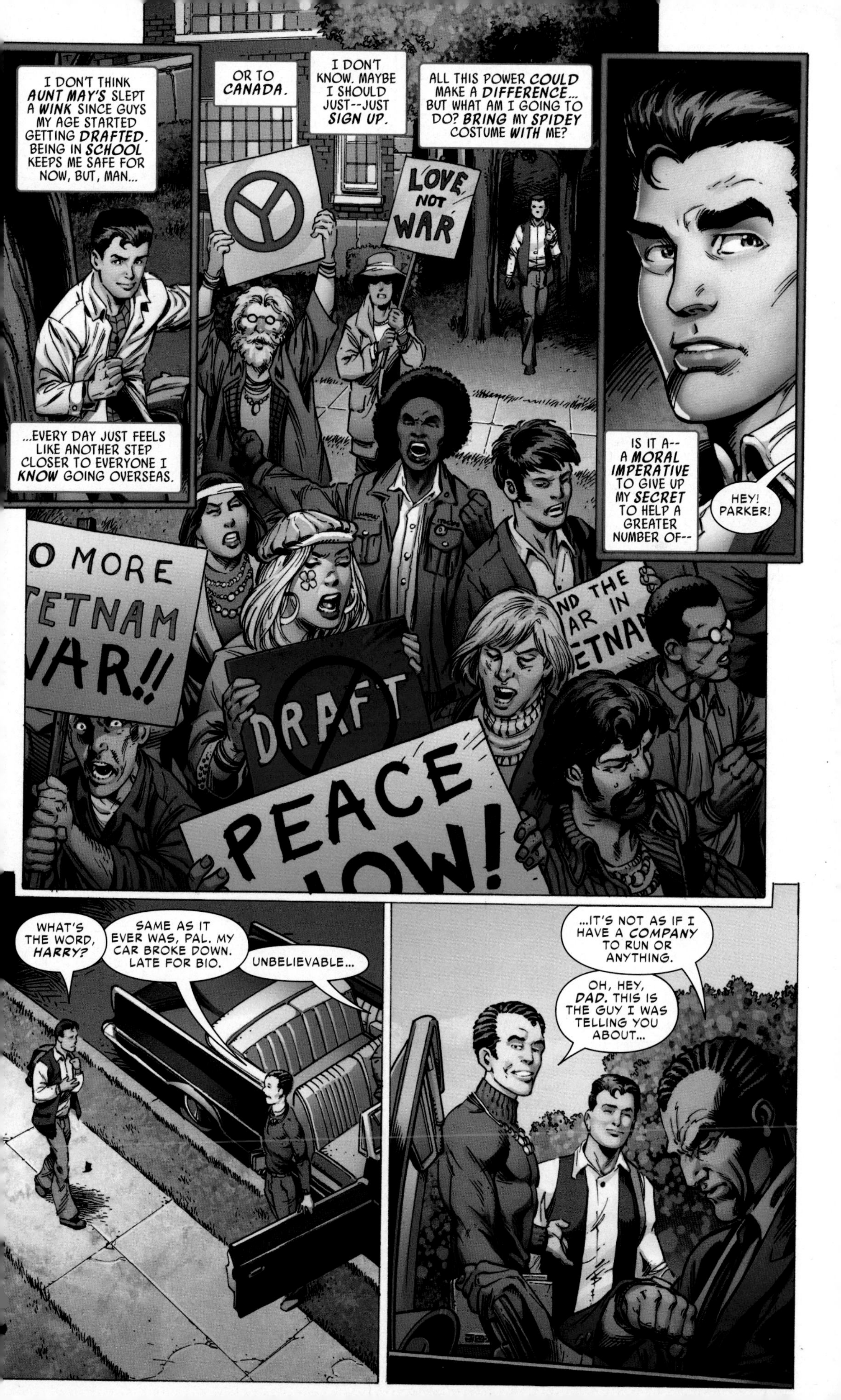

I DON'T THINK AUNT MAY'S SLEPT A WINK SINCE GUYS MY AGE STARTED GETTING DRAFTED. BEING IN SCHOOL KEEPS ME SAFE FOR NOW, BUT, MAN...
...EVERY DAY JUST FEELS LIKE ANOTHER STEP CLOSER TO EVERYONE I KNOW GOING OVERSEAS.
OR TO CANADA.
I DON'T KNOW. MAYBE I SHOULD JUST--JUST SIGN UP.
ALL THIS POWER COULD MAKE A DIFFERENCE... BUT WHAT AM I GOING TO DO? BRING MY SPIDEY COSTUME WITH ME?
LOVE NOT WAR
IS IT A-- A MORAL IMPERATIVE TO GIVE UP MY SECRET TO HELP A GREATER NUMBER OF--
HEY! PARKER!
O MORE ETNAM AR!!
DRAFT
ND THE AR IN ETNA
PEACE
WHAT'S THE WORD, HARRY?
SAME AS IT EVER WAS, PAL. MY CAR BROKE DOWN. LATE FOR BIO.
UNBELIEVABLE...
...IT'S NOT AS IF I HAVE A COMPANY TO RUN OR ANYTHING.
OH, HEY, DAD. THIS IS THE GUY I WAS TELLING YOU ABOUT...

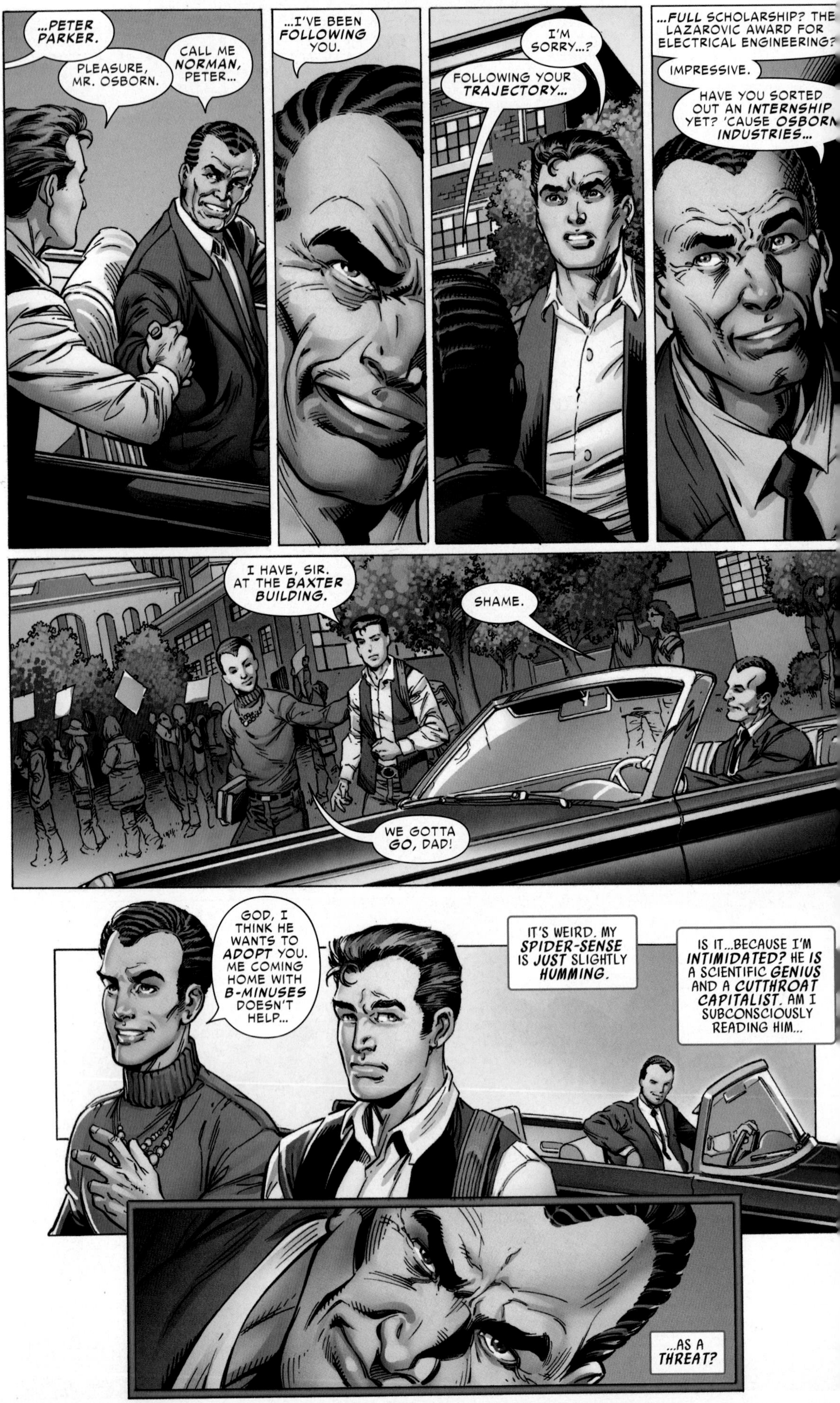

...PETER PARKER.
PLEASURE, MR. OSBORN.
CALL ME NORMAN, PETER...
...I'VE BEEN FOLLOWING YOU.
I'M SORRY...?
FOLLOWING YOUR TRAJECTORY...
...FULL SCHOLARSHIP? THE LAZAROVIC AWARD FOR ELECTRICAL ENGINEERING?
IMPRESSIVE.
HAVE YOU SORTED OUT AN INTERNSHIP YET? 'CAUSE OSBORN INDUSTRIES...
I HAVE, SIR. AT THE BAXTER BUILDING.
SHAME.
WE GOTTA GO, DAD!
GOD, I THINK HE WANTS TO ADOPT YOU. ME COMING HOME WITH B-MINUSES DOESN'T HELP...
IT'S WEIRD. MY SPIDER-SENSE IS JUST SLIGHTLY HUMMING.
IS IT...BECAUSE I'M INTIMIDATED? HE IS A SCIENTIFIC GENIUS AND A CUTTHROAT CAPITALIST. AM I SUBCONSCIOUSLY READING HIM...
...AS A THREAT?

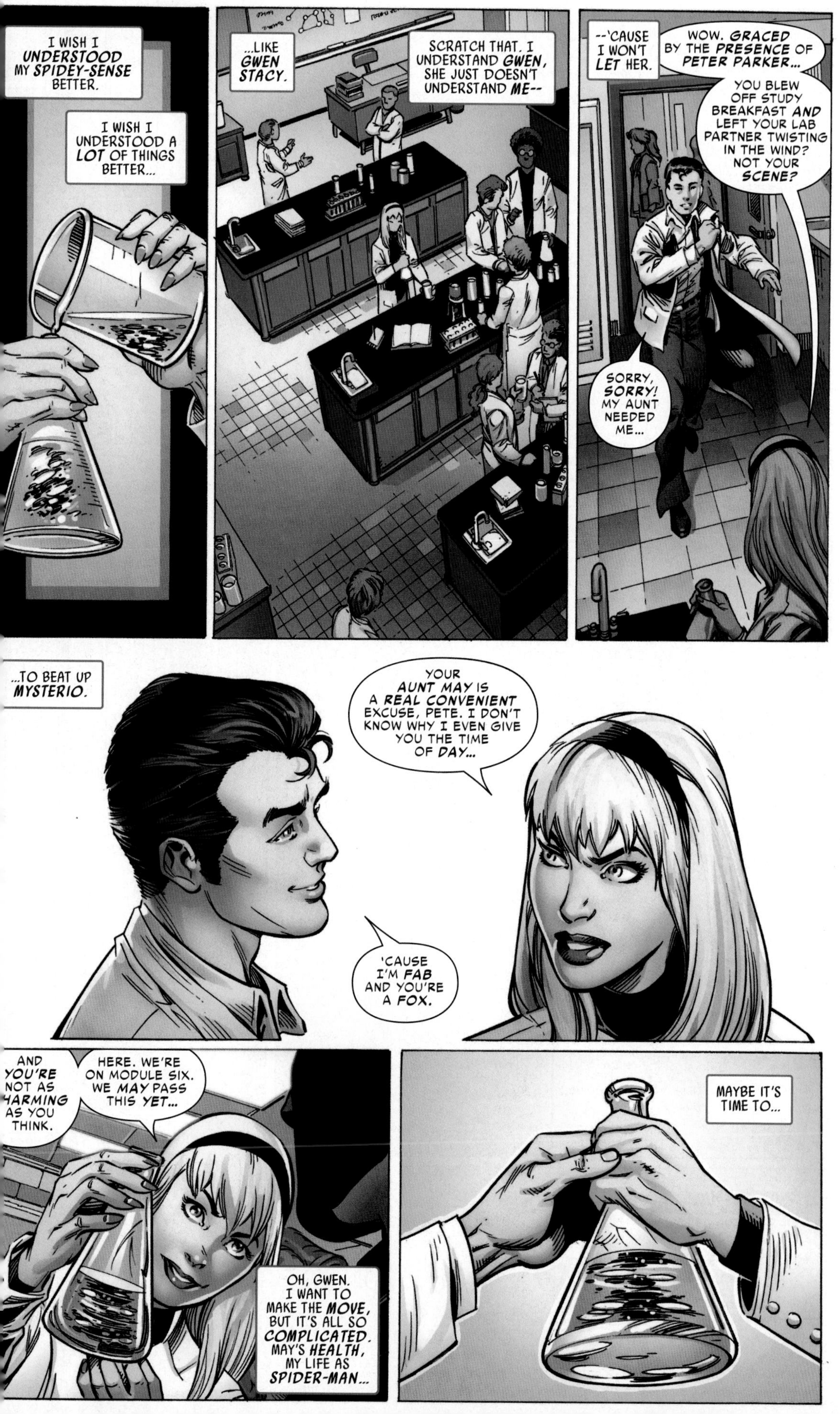
I WISH I UNDERSTOOD MY SPIDEY-SENSE BETTER.
I WISH I UNDERSTOOD A LOT OF THINGS BETTER...
...LIKE GWEN STACY.
SCRATCH THAT. I UNDERSTAND GWEN, SHE JUST DOESN'T UNDERSTAND ME--
--'CAUSE I WON'T LET HER.
WOW. GRACED BY THE PRESENCE OF PETER PARKER...
YOU BLEW OFF STUDY BREAKFAST AND LEFT YOUR LAB PARTNER TWISTING IN THE WIND? NOT YOUR SCENE?
SORRY, SORRY! MY AUNT NEEDED ME...
...TO BEAT UP MYSTERIO.
YOUR AUNT MAY IS A REAL CONVENIENT EXCUSE, PETE. I DON'T KNOW WHY I EVEN GIVE YOU THE TIME OF DAY...
'CAUSE I'M FAB AND YOU'RE A FOX.
AND YOU'RE NOT AS HARMING AS YOU THINK.
HERE. WE'RE ON MODULE SIX. WE MAY PASS THIS YET...
OH, GWEN. I WANT TO MAKE THE MOVE, BUT IT'S ALL SO COMPLICATED. MAY'S HEALTH, MY LIFE AS SPIDER-MAN...
MAYBE IT'S TIME TO...

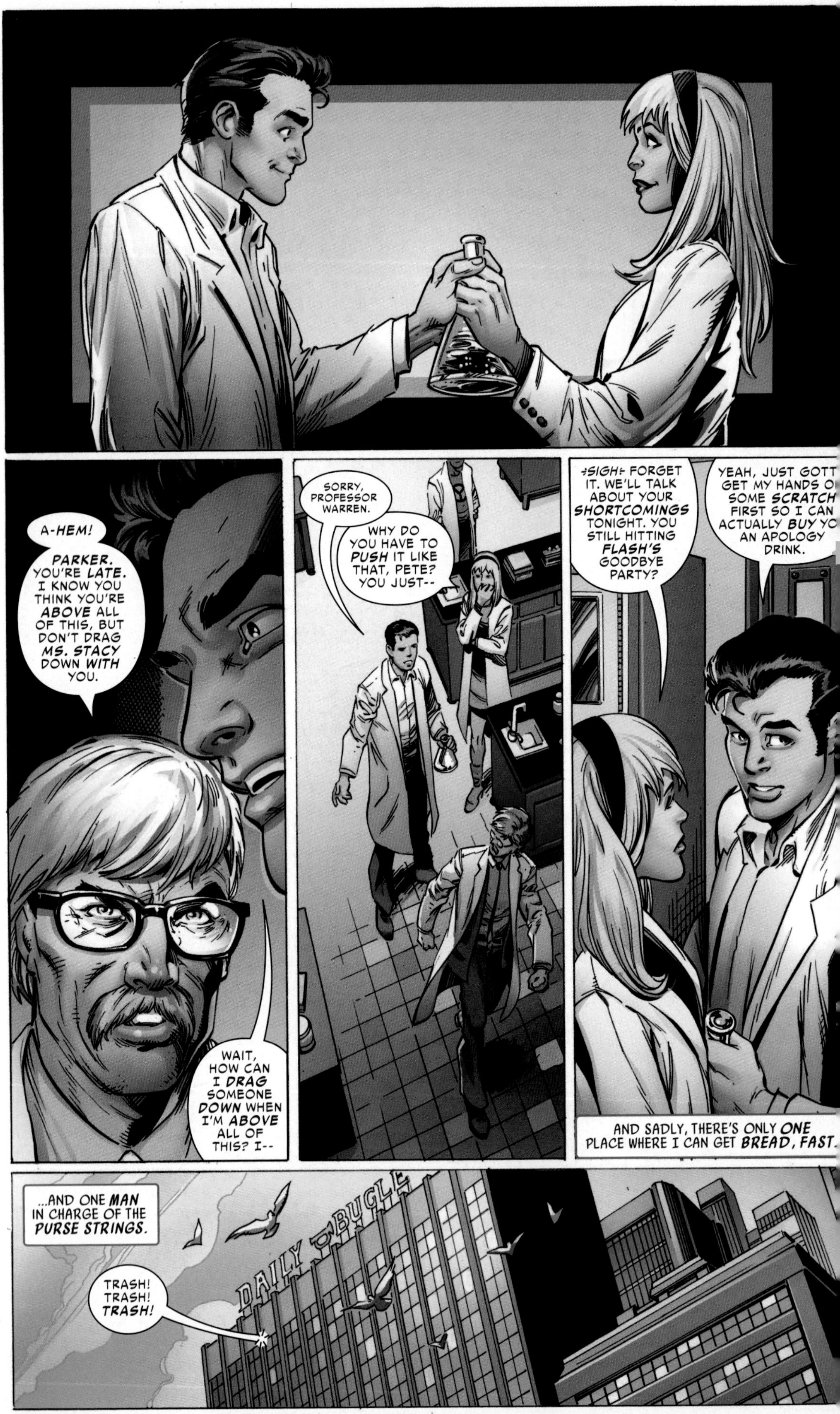
A-HEM!
PARKER. YOU'RE LATE. I KNOW YOU THINK YOU'RE ABOVE ALL OF THIS, BUT DON'T DRAG MS. STACY DOWN WITH YOU.
WAIT, HOW CAN I DRAG SOMEONE DOWN WHEN I'M ABOVE ALL OF THIS? I--
SORRY, PROFESSOR WARREN.
WHY DO YOU HAVE TO PUSH IT LIKE THAT, PETE? YOU JUST--
=SIGH= FORGET IT. WE'LL TALK ABOUT YOUR SHORTCOMINGS TONIGHT. YOU STILL HITTING FLASH'S GOODBYE PARTY?
YEAH, JUST GOTT GET MY HANDS O SOME SCRATCH FIRST SO I CAN ACTUALLY BUY YO AN APOLOGY DRINK.
AND SADLY, THERE'S ONLY ONE PLACE WHERE I CAN GET BREAD, FAST.
...AND ONE MAN IN CHARGE OF THE PURSE STRINGS.
DAILY BUGLE
TRASH! TRASH! TRASH!

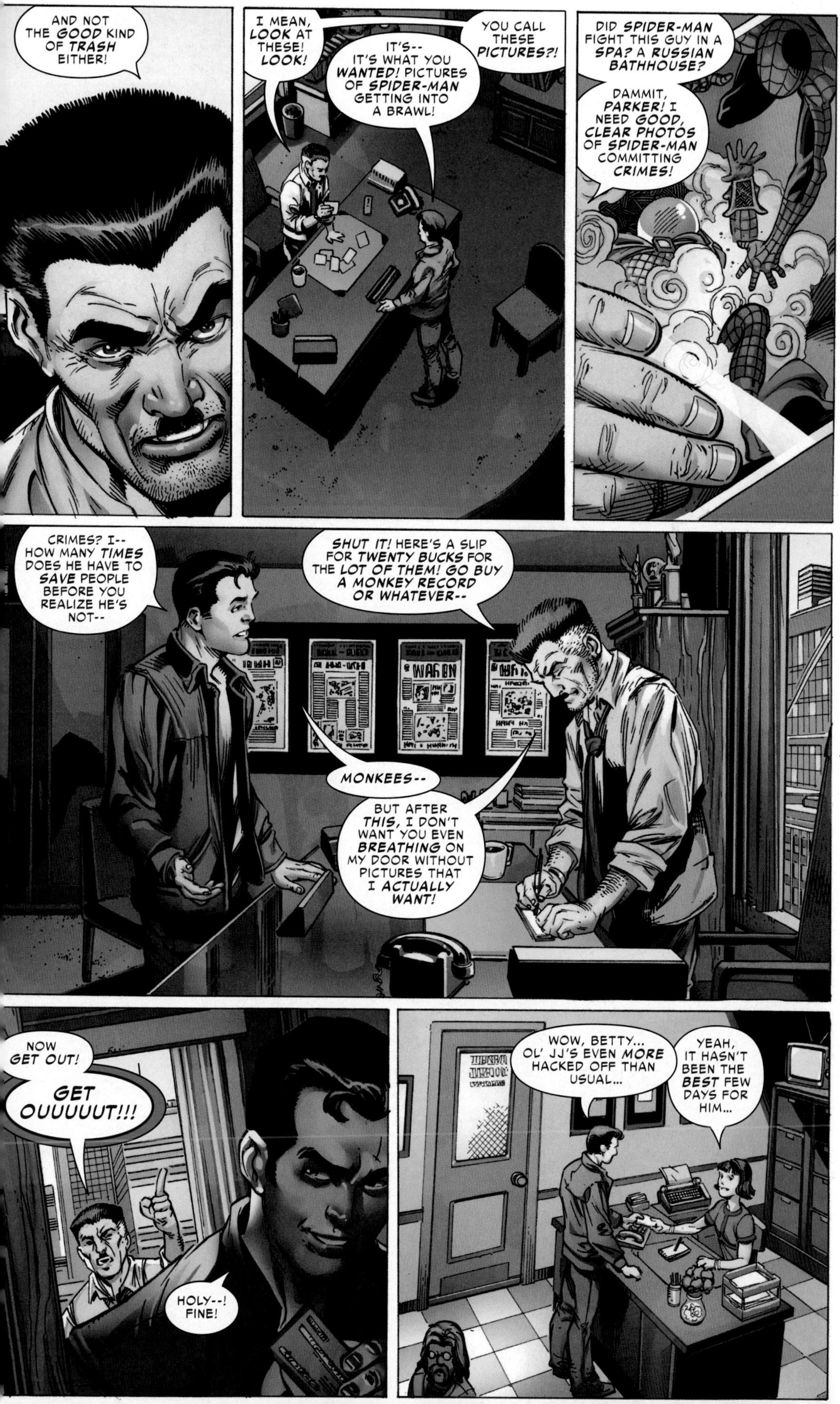

AND NOT THE GOOD KIND OF TRASH EITHER!
I MEAN, LOOK AT THESE! LOOK!
YOU CALL THESE PICTURES?!
IT'S-- IT'S WHAT YOU WANTED! PICTURES OF SPIDER-MAN GETTING INTO A BRAWL!
DID SPIDER-MAN FIGHT THIS GUY IN A SPA? A RUSSIAN BATHHOUSE?
DAMMIT, PARKER! I NEED GOOD, CLEAR PHOTOS OF SPIDER-MAN COMMITTING CRIMES!
CRIMES? I-- HOW MANY TIMES DOES HE HAVE TO SAVE PEOPLE BEFORE YOU REALIZE HE'S NOT--
SHUT IT! HERE'S A SLIP FOR TWENTY BUCKS FOR THE LOT OF THEM! GO BUY A MONKEY RECORD OR WHATEVER--
MONKEES--
BUT AFTER THIS, I DON'T WANT YOU EVEN BREATHING ON MY DOOR WITHOUT PICTURES THAT I ACTUALLY WANT!
NOW GET OUT!
GET OUUUUUT!!!
HOLY--! FINE!
WOW, BETTY... OL' JJ'S EVEN MORE HACKED OFF THAN USUAL...
YEAH, IT HASN'T BEEN THE BEST FEW DAYS FOR HIM...

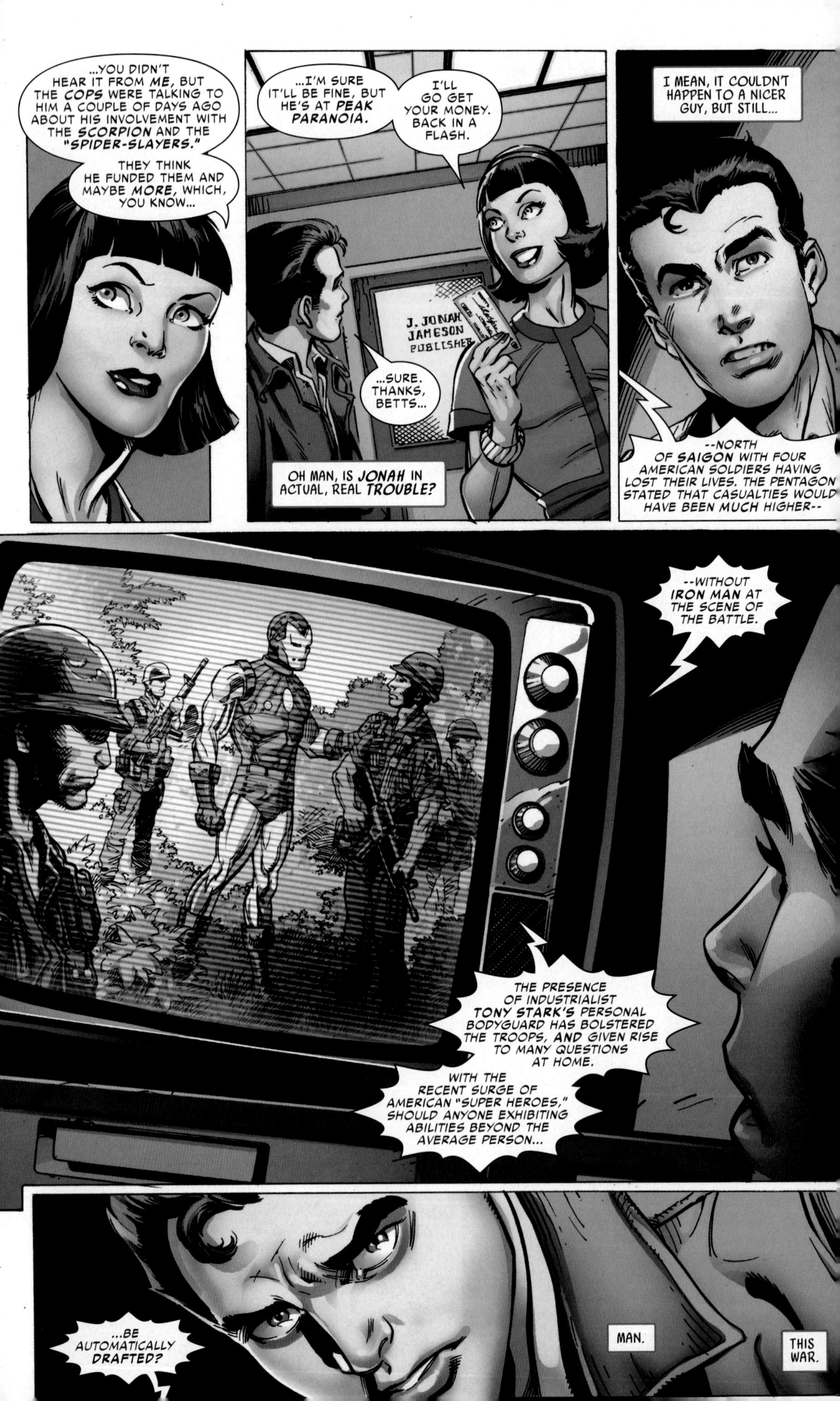

...YOU DIDN'T HEAR IT FROM ME, BUT THE COPS WERE TALKING TO HIM A COUPLE OF DAYS AGO ABOUT HIS INVOLVEMENT WITH THE SCORPION AND THE "SPIDER-SLAYERS."
THEY THINK HE FUNDED THEM AND MAYBE MORE, WHICH, YOU KNOW...
...I'M SURE IT'LL BE FINE, BUT HE'S AT PEAK PARANOIA.
I'LL GO GET YOUR MONEY. BACK IN A FLASH.
J. JONAH JAMESON PUBLISHER
...SURE. THANKS, BETTS...
OH MAN, IS JONAH IN ACTUAL, REAL TROUBLE?
I MEAN, IT COULDN'T HAPPEN TO A NICER GUY, BUT STILL...
--NORTH OF SAIGON WITH FOUR AMERICAN SOLDIERS HAVING LOST THEIR LIVES. THE PENTAGON STATED THAT CASUALTIES WOULD HAVE BEEN MUCH HIGHER--
--WITHOUT IRON MAN AT THE SCENE OF THE BATTLE.
THE PRESENCE OF INDUSTRIALIST TONY STARK'S PERSONAL BODYGUARD HAS BOLSTERED THE TROOPS, AND GIVEN RISE TO MANY QUESTIONS AT HOME.
WITH THE RECENT SURGE OF AMERICAN "SUPER HEROES," SHOULD ANYONE EXHIBITING ABILITIES BEYOND THE AVERAGE PERSON...
...BE AUTOMATICALLY DRAFTED?
MAN.
THIS WAR.

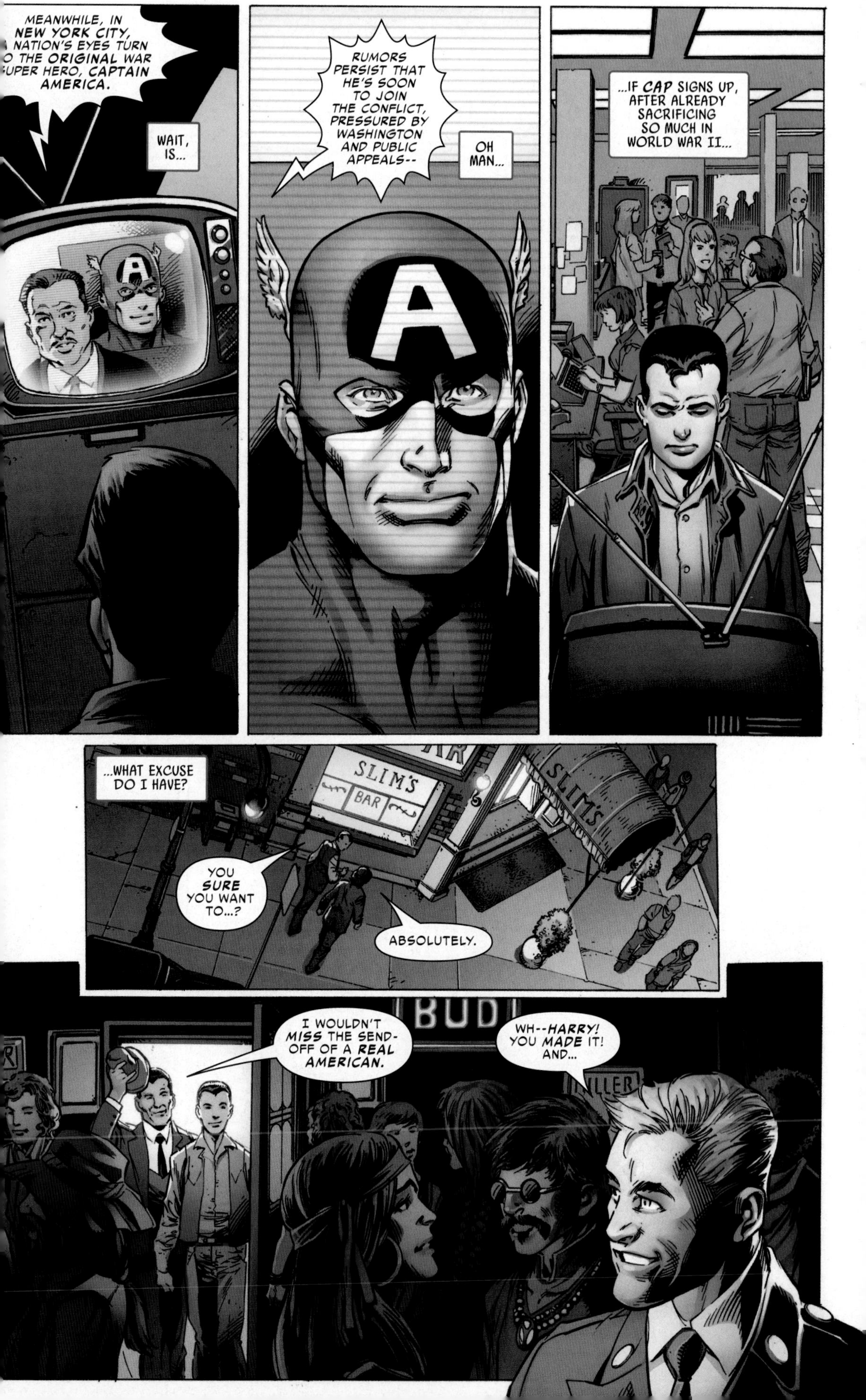
MEANWHILE, IN NEW YORK CITY, A NATION'S EYES TURN TO THE ORIGINAL WAR SUPER HERO, CAPTAIN AMERICA.
WAIT, IS...
RUMORS PERSIST THAT HE'S SOON TO JOIN THE CONFLICT, PRESSURED BY WASHINGTON AND PUBLIC APPEALS--
OH MAN...
...IF CAP SIGNS UP, AFTER ALREADY SACRIFICING SO MUCH IN WORLD WAR II...
...WHAT EXCUSE DO I HAVE?
SLIM'S BAR
SLIM'S
YOU SURE YOU WANT TO...?
ABSOLUTELY.
BUD
I WOULDN'T MISS THE SEND-OFF OF A REAL AMERICAN.
WH--HARRY! YOU MADE IT! AND...

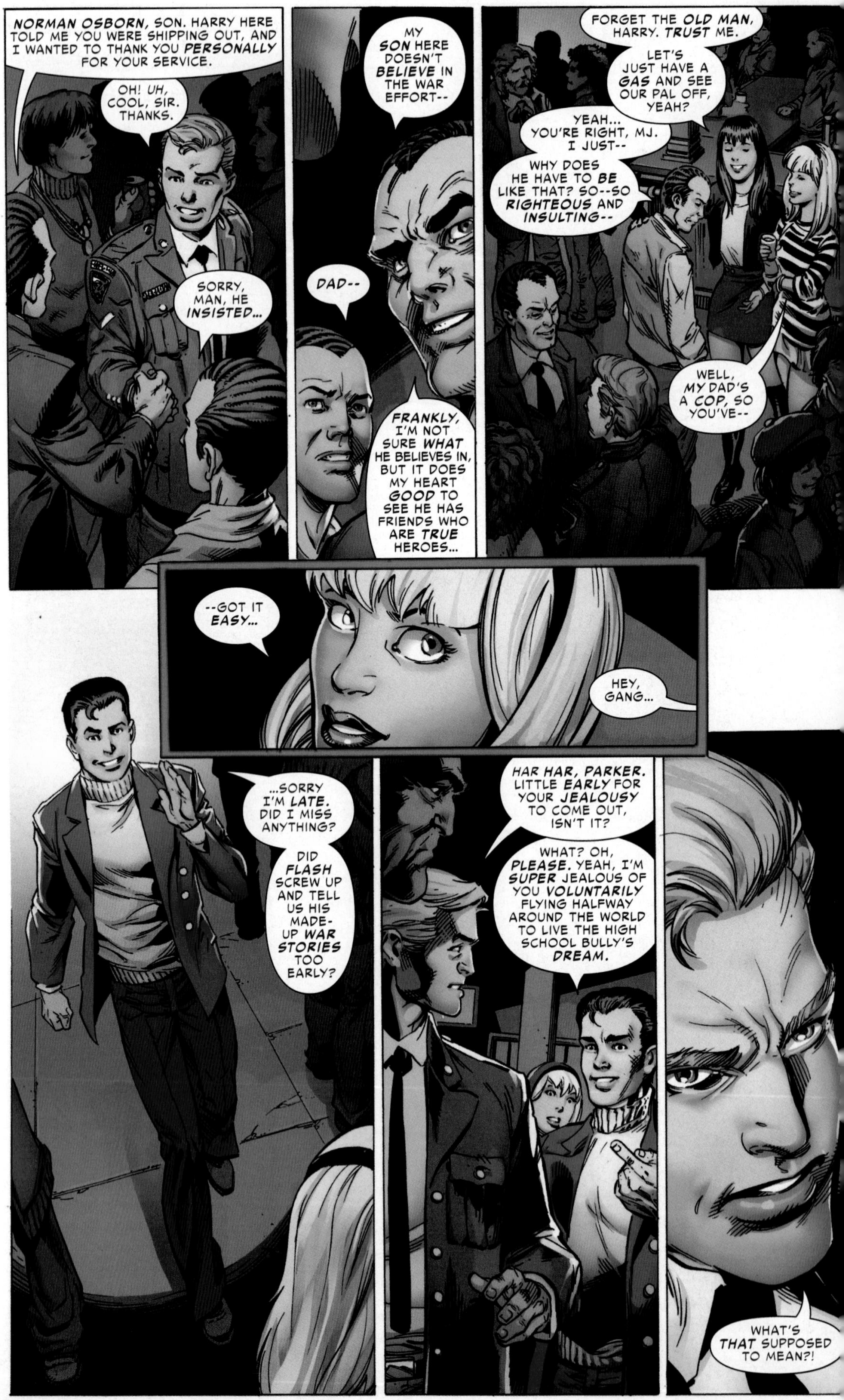
NORMAN OSBORN, SON. HARRY HERE TOLD ME YOU WERE SHIPPING OUT, AND I WANTED TO THANK YOU PERSONALLY FOR YOUR SERVICE.
OH! UH, COOL, SIR. THANKS.
SORRY, MAN, HE INSISTED...
MY SON HERE DOESN'T BELIEVE IN THE WAR EFFORT--
DAD--
FRANKLY, I'M NOT SURE WHAT HE BELIEVES IN, BUT IT DOES MY HEART GOOD TO SEE HE HAS FRIENDS WHO ARE TRUE HEROES...
FORGET THE OLD MAN, HARRY. TRUST ME.
LET'S JUST HAVE A GAS AND SEE OUR PAL OFF, YEAH?
YEAH... YOU'RE RIGHT, MJ. I JUST--
WHY DOES HE HAVE TO BE LIKE THAT? SO--SO RIGHTEOUS AND INSULTING--
WELL, MY DAD'S A COP, SO YOU'VE--
--GOT IT EASY...
HEY, GANG...
...SORRY I'M LATE. DID I MISS ANYTHING?
DID FLASH SCREW UP AND TELL US HIS MADE-UP WAR STORIES TOO EARLY?
HAR HAR, PARKER. LITTLE EARLY FOR YOUR JEALOUSY TO COME OUT, ISN'T IT?
WHAT? OH, PLEASE. YEAH, I'M SUPER JEALOUS OF YOU VOLUNTARILY FLYING HALFWAY AROUND THE WORLD TO LIVE THE HIGH SCHOOL BULLY'S DREAM.
WHAT'S THAT SUPPOSED TO MEAN?!

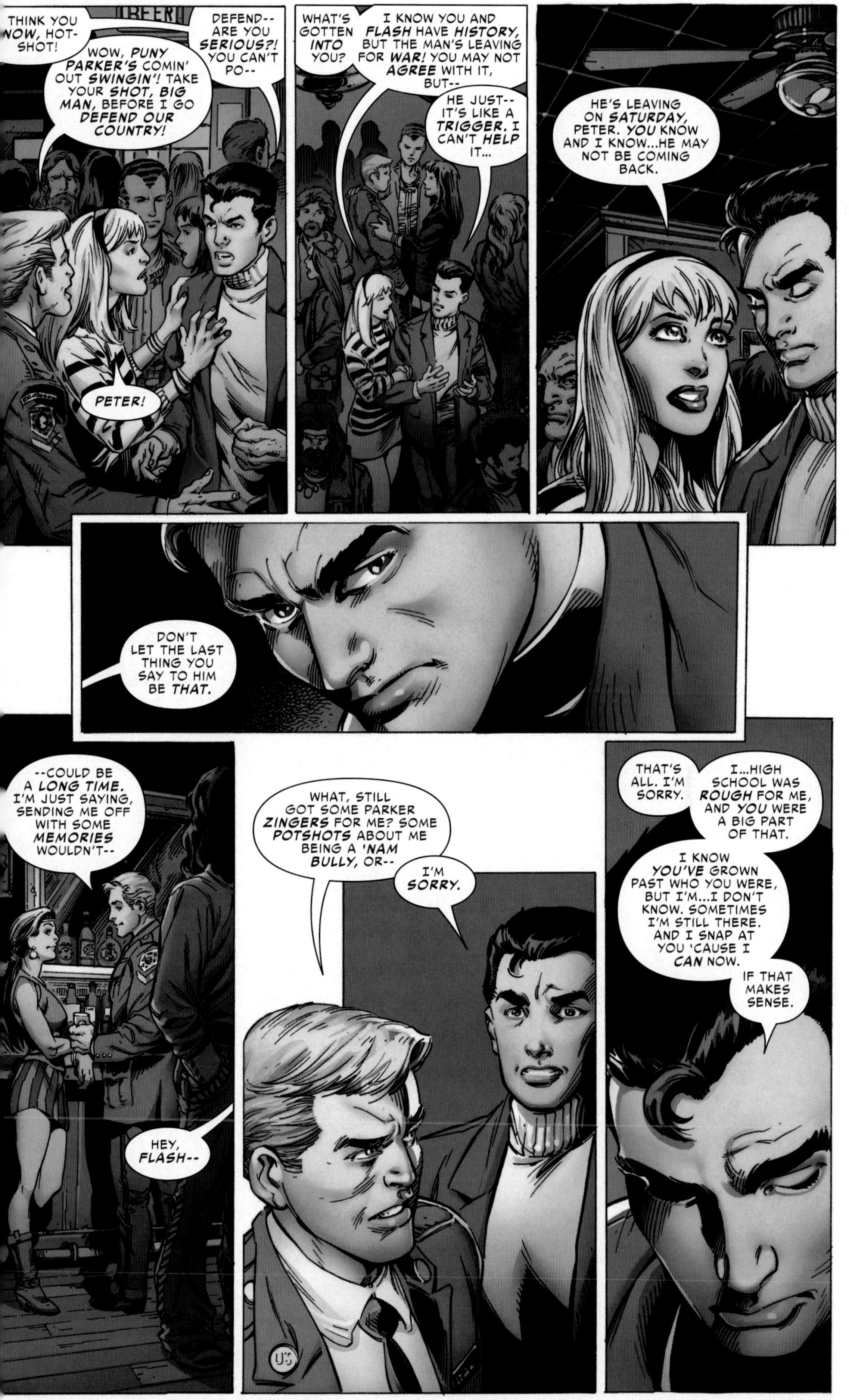
THINK YOU NOW, HOT-SHOT!
WOW, PUNY PARKER'S COMIN' OUT SWINGIN'! TAKE YOUR SHOT, BIG MAN, BEFORE I GO DEFEND OUR COUNTRY!
DEFEND-- ARE YOU SERIOUS?! YOU CAN'T PO--
PETER!
WHAT'S GOTTEN INTO YOU?
I KNOW YOU AND FLASH HAVE HISTORY, BUT THE MAN'S LEAVING FOR WAR! YOU MAY NOT AGREE WITH IT, BUT--
HE JUST-- IT'S LIKE A TRIGGER. I CAN'T HELP IT...
HE'S LEAVING ON SATURDAY, PETER. YOU KNOW AND I KNOW...HE MAY NOT BE COMING BACK.
DON'T LET THE LAST THING YOU SAY TO HIM BE THAT.
--COULD BE A LONG TIME. I'M JUST SAYING, SENDING ME OFF WITH SOME MEMORIES WOULDN'T--
HEY, FLASH--
WHAT, STILL GOT SOME PARKER ZINGERS FOR ME? SOME POTSHOTS ABOUT ME BEING A 'NAM BULLY, OR--
I'M SORRY.
THAT'S ALL. I'M SORRY.
I...HIGH SCHOOL WAS ROUGH FOR ME, AND YOU WERE A BIG PART OF THAT.
I KNOW YOU'VE GROWN PAST WHO YOU WERE, BUT I'M...I DON'T KNOW. SOMETIMES I'M STILL THERE. AND I SNAP AT YOU 'CAUSE I CAN NOW.
IF THAT MAKES SENSE.

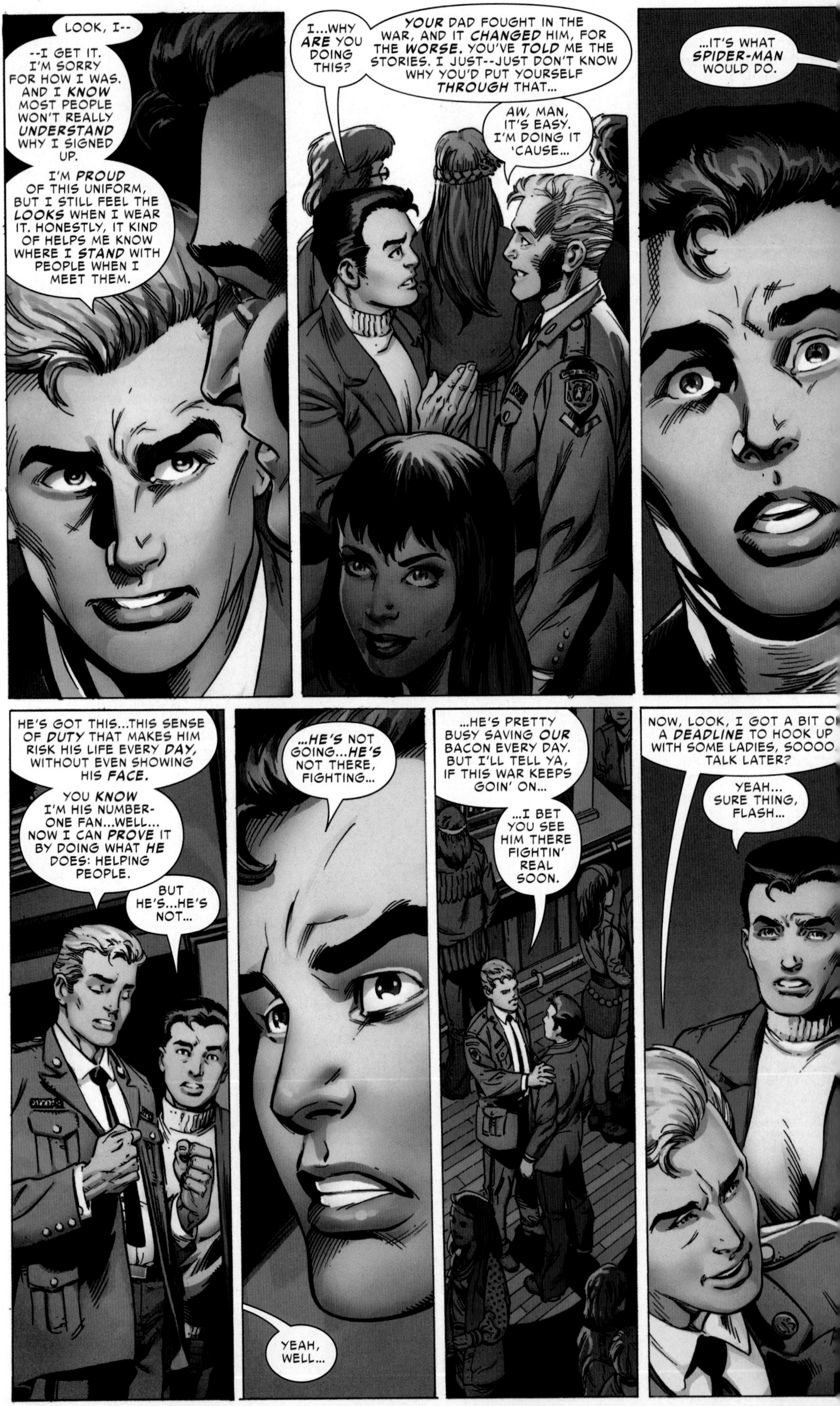
LOOK, I--
--I GET IT. I'M SORRY FOR HOW I WAS. AND I KNOW MOST PEOPLE WON'T REALLY UNDERSTAND WHY I SIGNED UP.
I'M PROUD OF THIS UNIFORM, BUT I STILL FEEL THE LOOKS WHEN I WEAR IT. HONESTLY, IT KIND OF HELPS ME KNOW WHERE I STAND WITH PEOPLE WHEN I MEET THEM.
I...WHY ARE YOU DOING THIS?
YOUR DAD FOUGHT IN THE WAR, AND IT CHANGED HIM, FOR THE WORSE. YOU'VE TOLD ME THE STORIES. I JUST--JUST DON'T KNOW WHY YOU'D PUT YOURSELF THROUGH THAT...
AW, MAN, IT'S EASY. I'M DOING IT 'CAUSE...
...IT'S WHAT SPIDER-MAN WOULD DO.
HE'S GOT THIS...THIS SENSE OF DUTY THAT MAKES HIM RISK HIS LIFE EVERY DAY, WITHOUT EVEN SHOWING HIS FACE.
YOU KNOW I'M HIS NUMBER-ONE FAN...WELL... NOW I CAN PROVE IT BY DOING WHAT HE DOES: HELPING PEOPLE.
BUT HE'S...HE'S NOT...
...HE'S NOT GOING...HE'S NOT THERE, FIGHTING...
YEAH, WELL...
...HE'S PRETTY BUSY SAVING OUR BACON EVERY DAY. BUT I'LL TELL YA, IF THIS WAR KEEPS GOIN' ON...
...I BET YOU SEE HIM THERE FIGHTIN' REAL SOON.
NOW, LOOK, I GOT A BIT O A DEADLINE TO HOOK UP WITH SOME LADIES, SOOOO TALK LATER?
YEAH... SURE THING, FLASH...

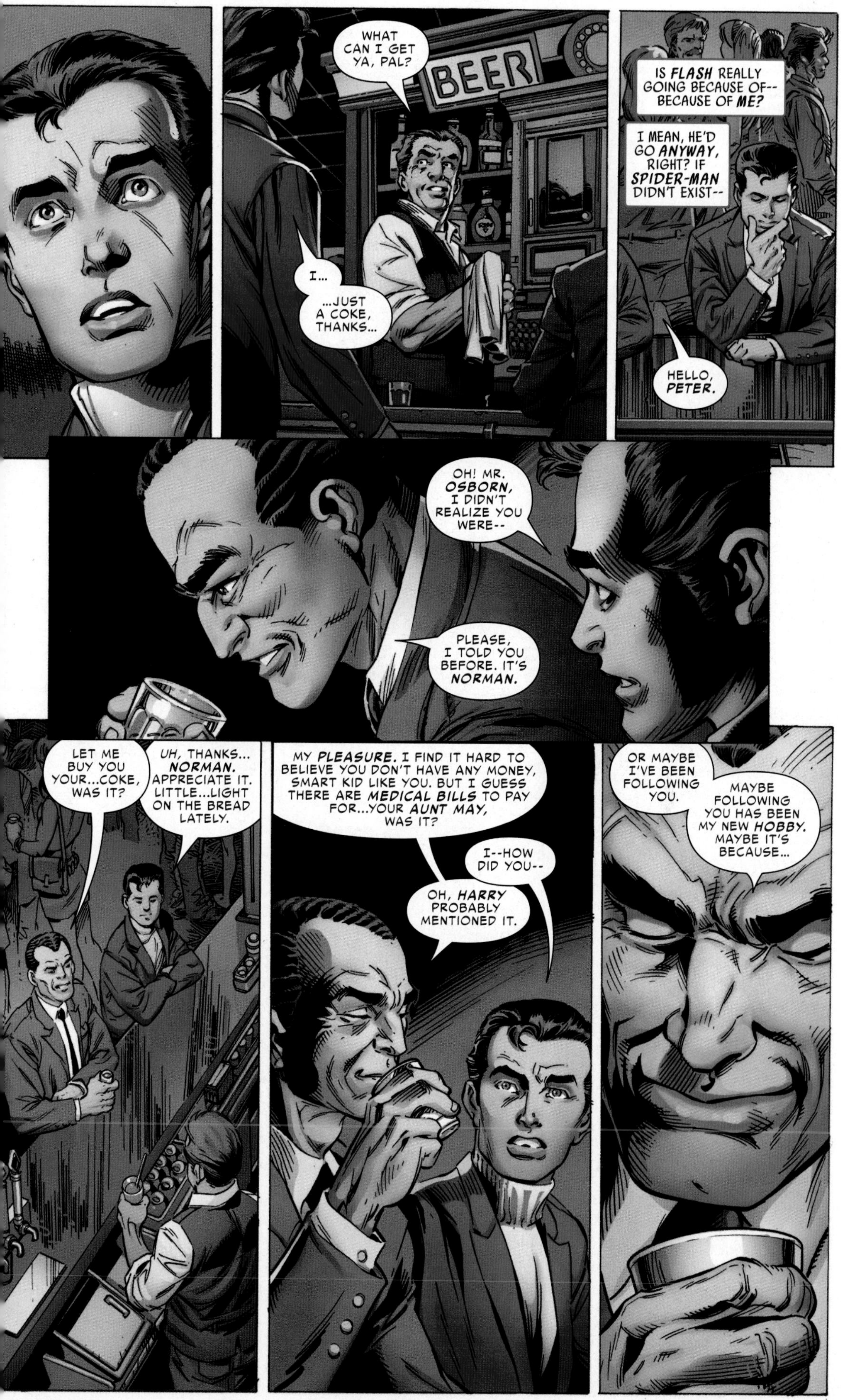
WHAT CAN I GET YA, PAL?
I...
...JUST A COKE, THANKS...
IS FLASH REALLY GOING BECAUSE OF-- BECAUSE OF ME?
I MEAN, HE'D GO ANYWAY, RIGHT? IF SPIDER-MAN DIDN'T EXIST--
HELLO, PETER.
OH! MR. OSBORN, I DIDN'T REALIZE YOU WERE--
PLEASE, I TOLD YOU BEFORE. IT'S NORMAN.
LET ME BUY YOU YOUR...COKE, WAS IT?
UH, THANKS... NORMAN. APPRECIATE IT. LITTLE...LIGHT ON THE BREAD LATELY.
MY PLEASURE. I FIND IT HARD TO BELIEVE YOU DON'T HAVE ANY MONEY, SMART KID LIKE YOU. BUT I GUESS THERE ARE MEDICAL BILLS TO PAY FOR...YOUR AUNT MAY, WAS IT?
I--HOW DID YOU--
OH, HARRY PROBABLY MENTIONED IT.
OR MAYBE I'VE BEEN FOLLOWING YOU.
MAYBE FOLLOWING YOU HAS BEEN MY NEW HOBBY. MAYBE IT'S BECAUSE...

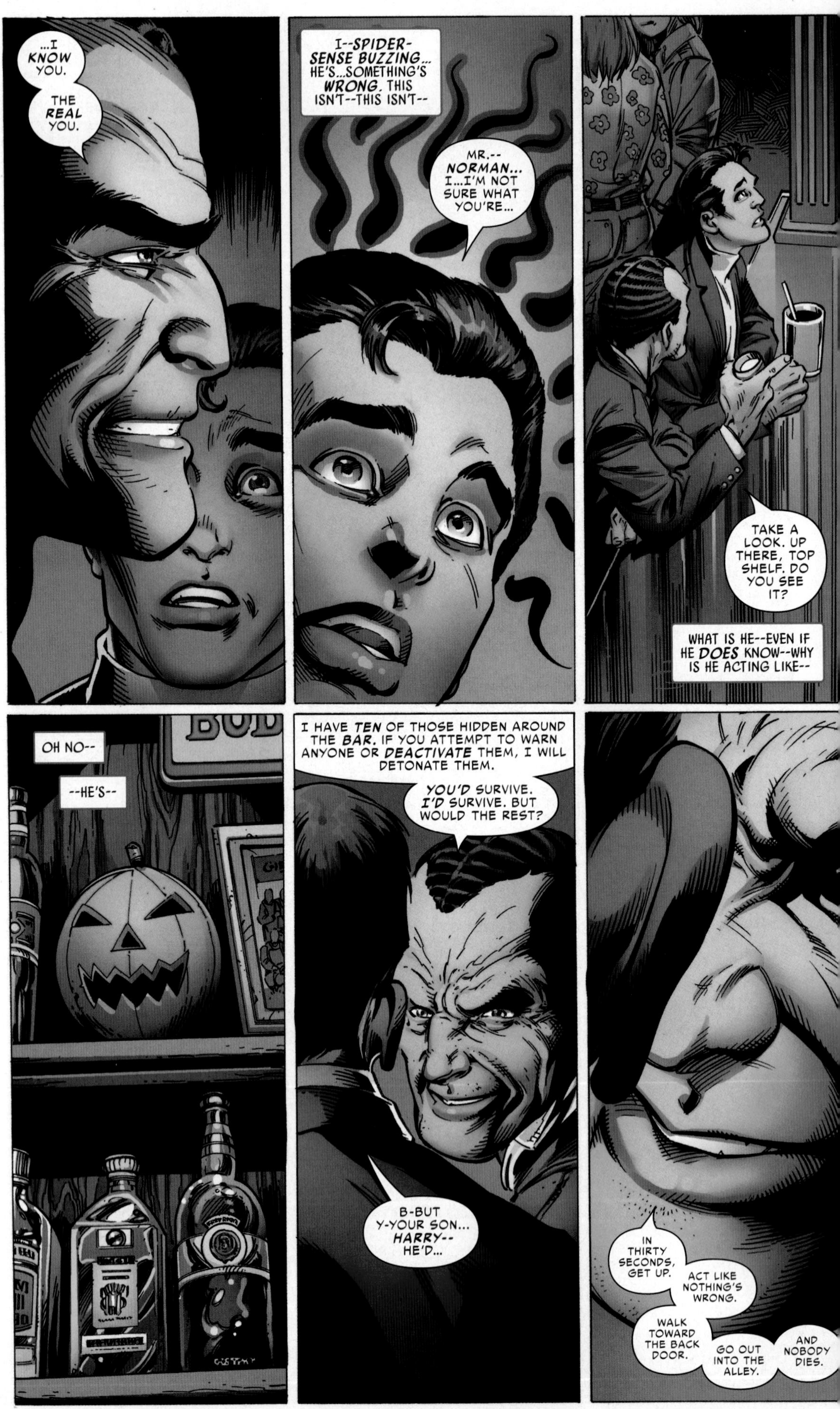

...I KNOW YOU.
THE REAL YOU.
I--SPIDER-SENSE BUZZING... HE'S...SOMETHING'S WRONG. THIS ISN'T--THIS ISN'T--
MR.--NORMAN... I...I'M NOT SURE WHAT YOU'RE...
TAKE A LOOK. UP THERE, TOP SHELF. DO YOU SEE IT?
WHAT IS HE--EVEN IF HE DOES KNOW--WHY IS HE ACTING LIKE--
OH NO--
--HE'S--
I HAVE TEN OF THOSE HIDDEN AROUND THE BAR. IF YOU ATTEMPT TO WARN ANYONE OR DEACTIVATE THEM, I WILL DETONATE THEM.
YOU'D SURVIVE. I'D SURVIVE. BUT WOULD THE REST?
B-BUT Y-YOUR SON... HARRY-- HE'D...
IN THIRTY SECONDS, GET UP.
ACT LIKE NOTHING'S WRONG.
WALK TOWARD THE BACK DOOR.
GO OUT INTO THE ALLEY.
AND NOBODY DIES.

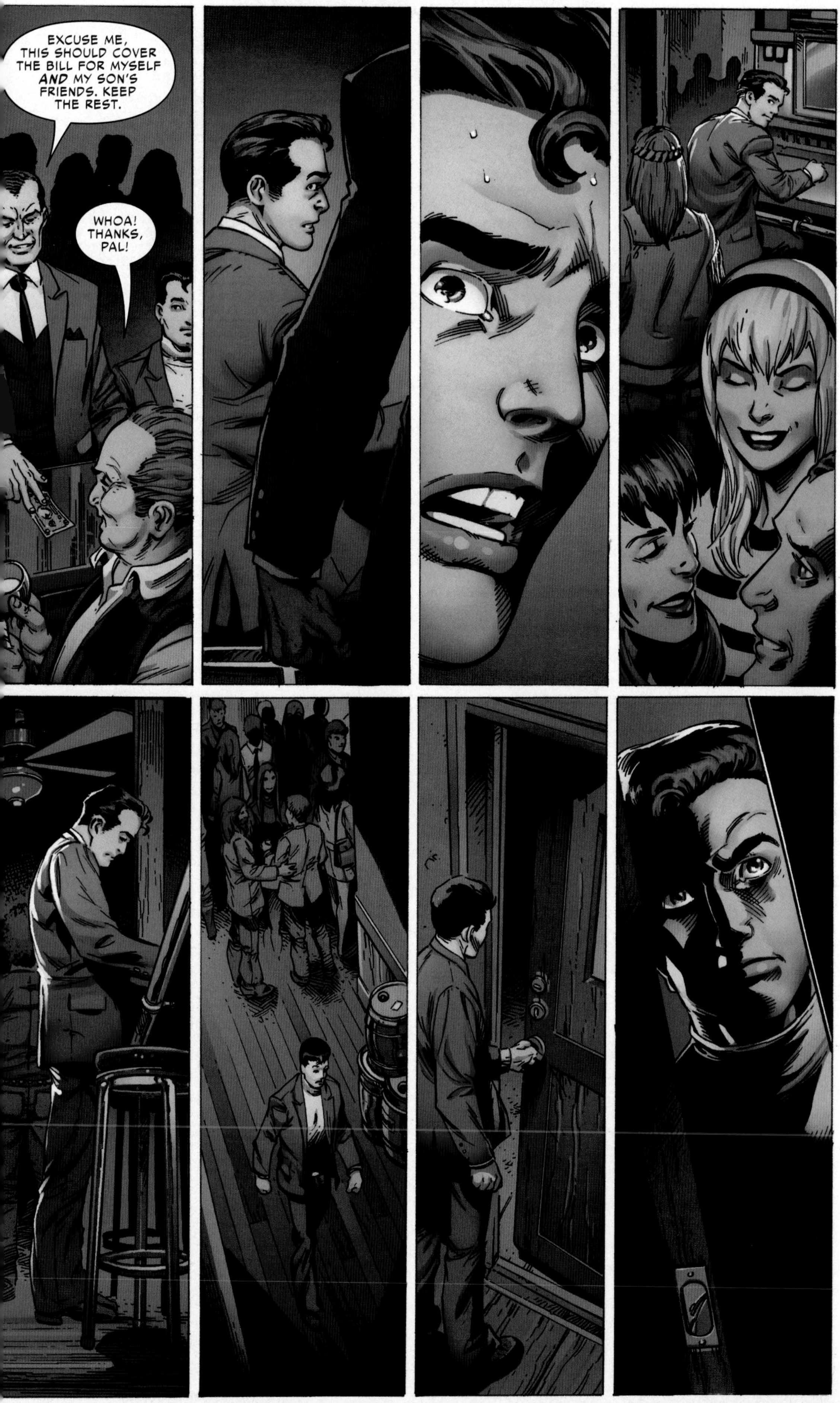
EXCUSE ME, THIS SHOULD COVER THE BILL FOR MYSELF *AND* MY SON'S FRIENDS. KEEP THE REST.
WHOA! THANKS, PAL!

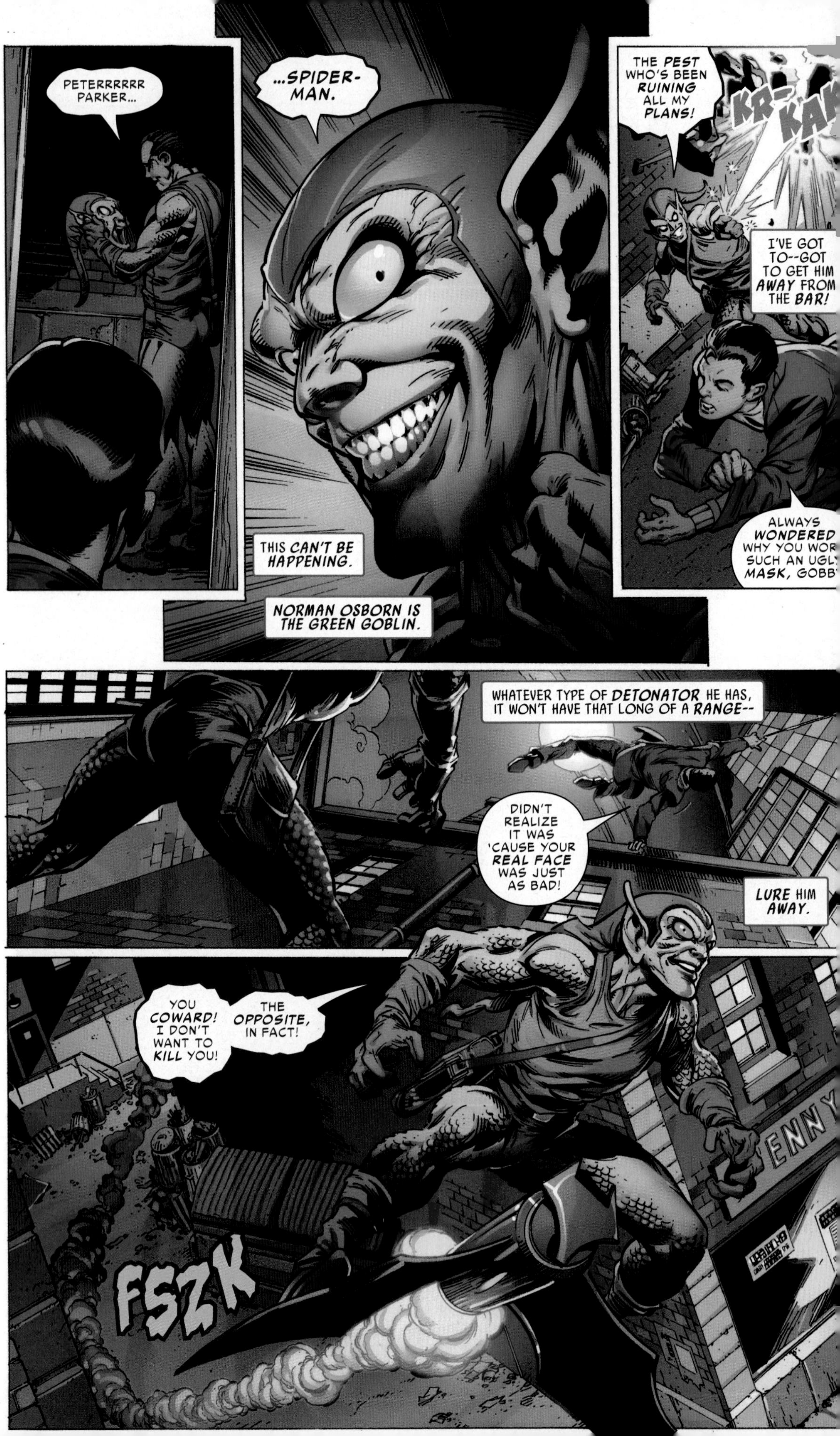
PETERRRRRR PARKER...
...SPIDER-MAN.
THIS CAN'T BE HAPPENING.
NORMAN OSBORN IS THE GREEN GOBLIN.
THE PEST WHO'S BEEN RUINING ALL MY PLANS!
KR-KAK!
I'VE GOT TO--GOT TO GET HIM AWAY FROM THE BAR!
ALWAYS WONDERED WHY YOU WOR SUCH AN UGL MASK, GOBB
WHATEVER TYPE OF DETONATOR HE HAS, IT WON'T HAVE THAT LONG OF A RANGE--
DIDN'T REALIZE IT WAS 'CAUSE YOUR REAL FACE WAS JUST AS BAD!
LURE HIM AWAY.
YOU COWARD! I DON'T WANT TO KILL YOU!
THE OPPOSITE, IN FACT!
FSZK

FZAK
FZAK
FZAK

NH!

...ARE WE...ARE WE *FAR* ENOUGH AWAY?

IS *FLASH* SAFE...

DAILY BUGLE
THE NEWS
AND ONLY
THE NEWS

...GWEN...

TAK TAK
FSZZZZ--

-ZZZ-
-ZZZ-

NO--

SKRA-KOOM

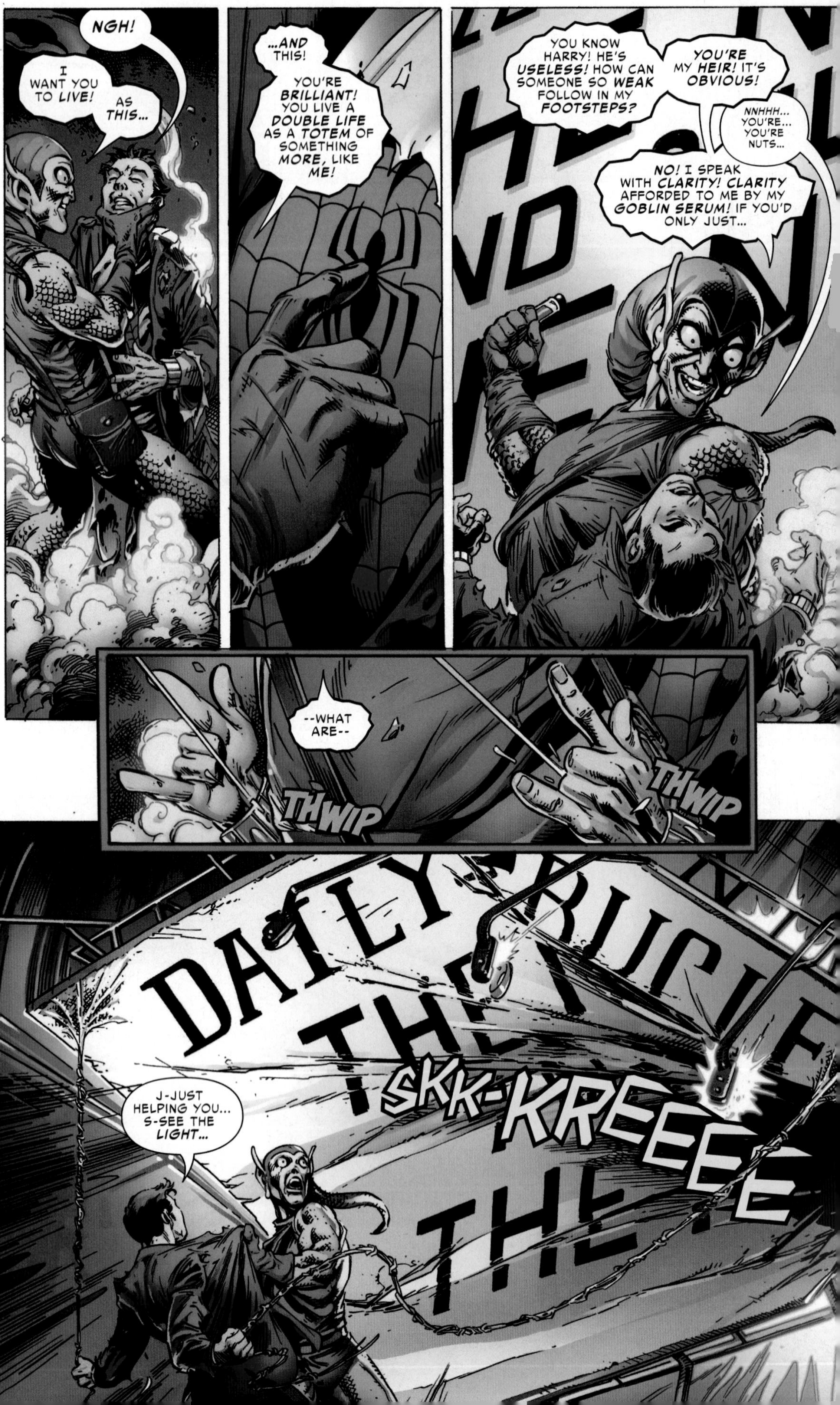
NGH!
I WANT YOU TO LIVE!
AS THIS...
...AND THIS!
YOU'RE BRILLIANT! YOU LIVE A DOUBLE LIFE AS A TOTEM OF SOMETHING MORE, LIKE ME!
YOU KNOW HARRY! HE'S USELESS! HOW CAN SOMEONE SO WEAK FOLLOW IN MY FOOTSTEPS?
YOU'RE MY HEIR! IT'S OBVIOUS!
NNHHH... YOU'RE... YOU'RE NUTS...
NO! I SPEAK WITH CLARITY! CLARITY AFFORDED TO ME BY MY GOBLIN SERUM! IF YOU'D ONLY JUST...
--WHAT ARE--
THWIP
THWIP
DAILY
J-JUST HELPING YOU... S-SEE THE LIGHT...
SKK-KREEEE

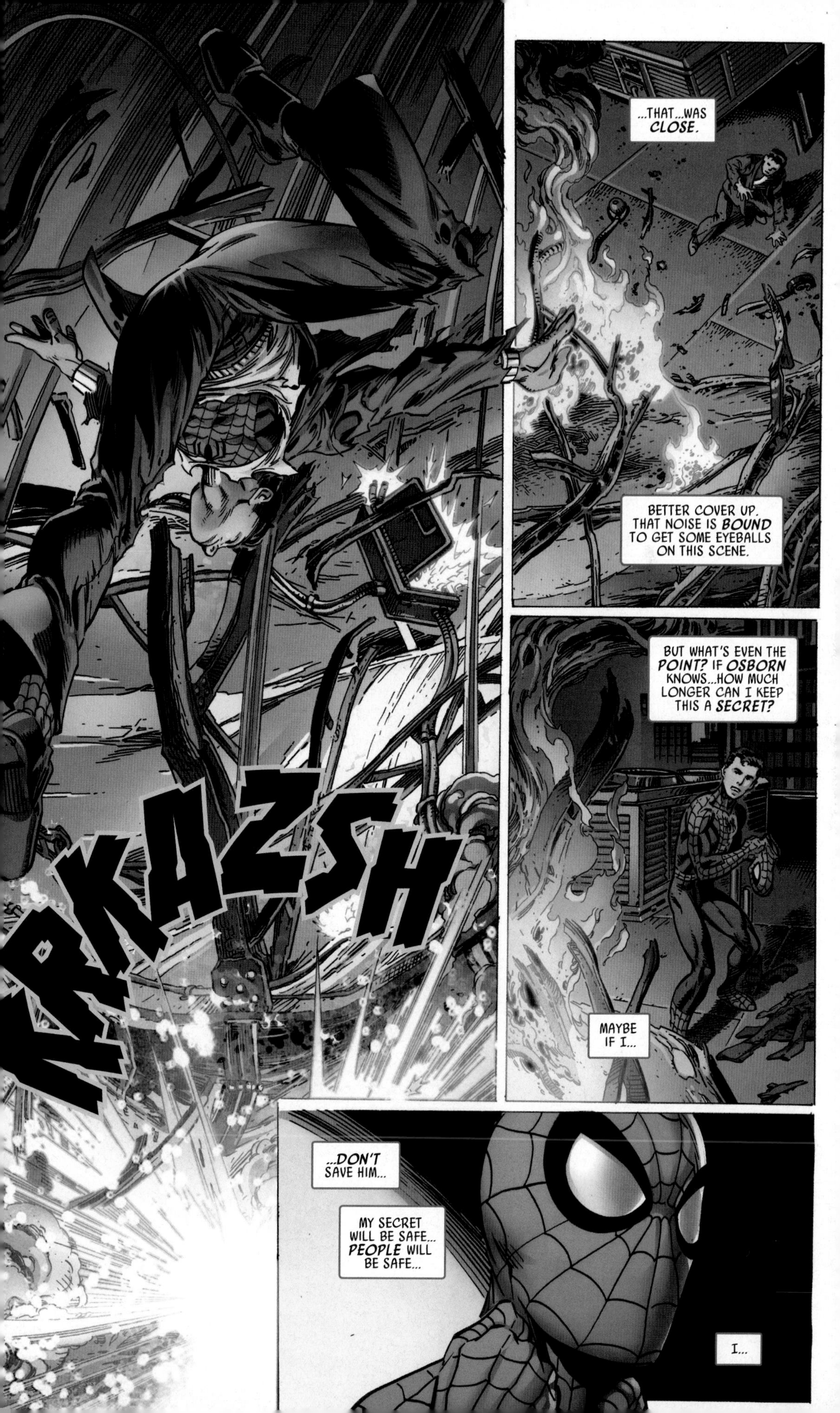

KRAZSH
...THAT...WAS CLOSE.
BETTER COVER UP. THAT NOISE IS BOUND TO GET SOME EYEBALLS ON THIS SCENE.
BUT WHAT'S EVEN THE POINT? IF OSBORN KNOWS...HOW MUCH LONGER CAN I KEEP THIS A SECRET?
MAYBE IF I...
...DON'T SAVE HIM...
MY SECRET WILL BE SAFE... PEOPLE WILL BE SAFE...
I...

...DAMN IT.

ALL RIGHT, OSBORN. IT'S OVER.

I'M GOING TO MAKE SURE YOU ROT IN PRISON, EVEN IF IT MEANS--

...WHAT... SPIDER-MAN?

...WHAT'S...WHAT'S HAPPENING...

WAIT, IS HE...?

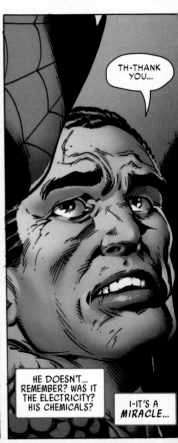

TH-THANK YOU...

HE DOESN'T... REMEMBER? WAS IT THE ELECTRICITY? HIS CHEMICALS?

I-IT'S A MIRACLE...

...A MIRACLE...

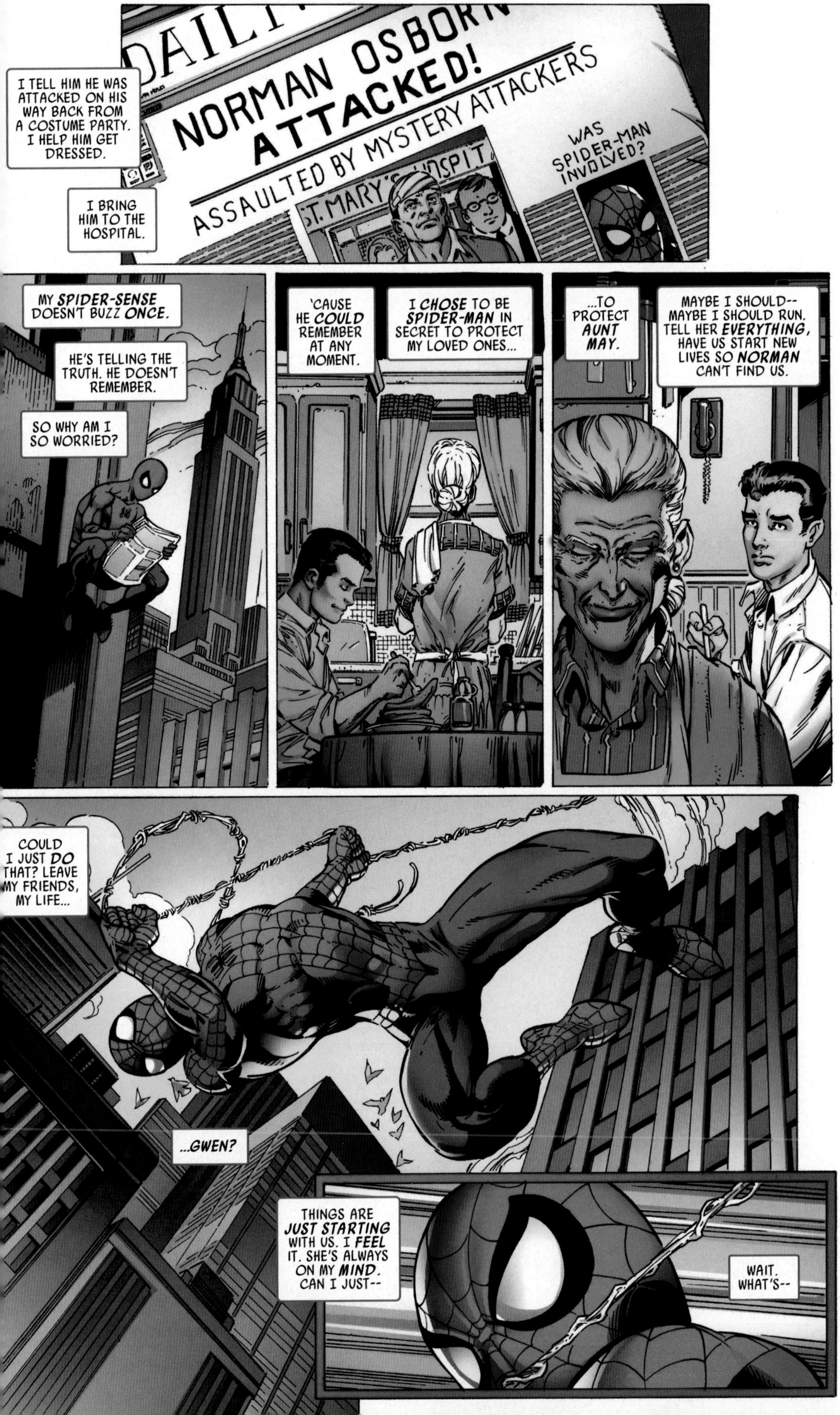
DAILY
NORMAN OSBORN ATTACKED!
ASSAULTED BY MYSTERY ATTACKERS
ST. MARY'S HOSPIT
WAS SPIDER-MAN INVOLVED?
I TELL HIM HE WAS ATTACKED ON HIS WAY BACK FROM A COSTUME PARTY. I HELP HIM GET DRESSED.
I BRING HIM TO THE HOSPITAL.
MY SPIDER-SENSE DOESN'T BUZZ ONCE.
HE'S TELLING THE TRUTH. HE DOESN'T REMEMBER.
SO WHY AM I SO WORRIED?
'CAUSE HE COULD REMEMBER AT ANY MOMENT.
I CHOSE TO BE SPIDER-MAN IN SECRET TO PROTECT MY LOVED ONES...
...TO PROTECT AUNT MAY.
MAYBE I SHOULD-- MAYBE I SHOULD RUN. TELL HER EVERYTHING, HAVE US START NEW LIVES SO NORMAN CAN'T FIND US.
COULD I JUST DO THAT? LEAVE MY FRIENDS, MY LIFE...
...GWEN?
THINGS ARE JUST STARTING WITH US. I FEEL IT. SHE'S ALWAYS ON MY MIND. CAN I JUST--
WAIT. WHAT'S--

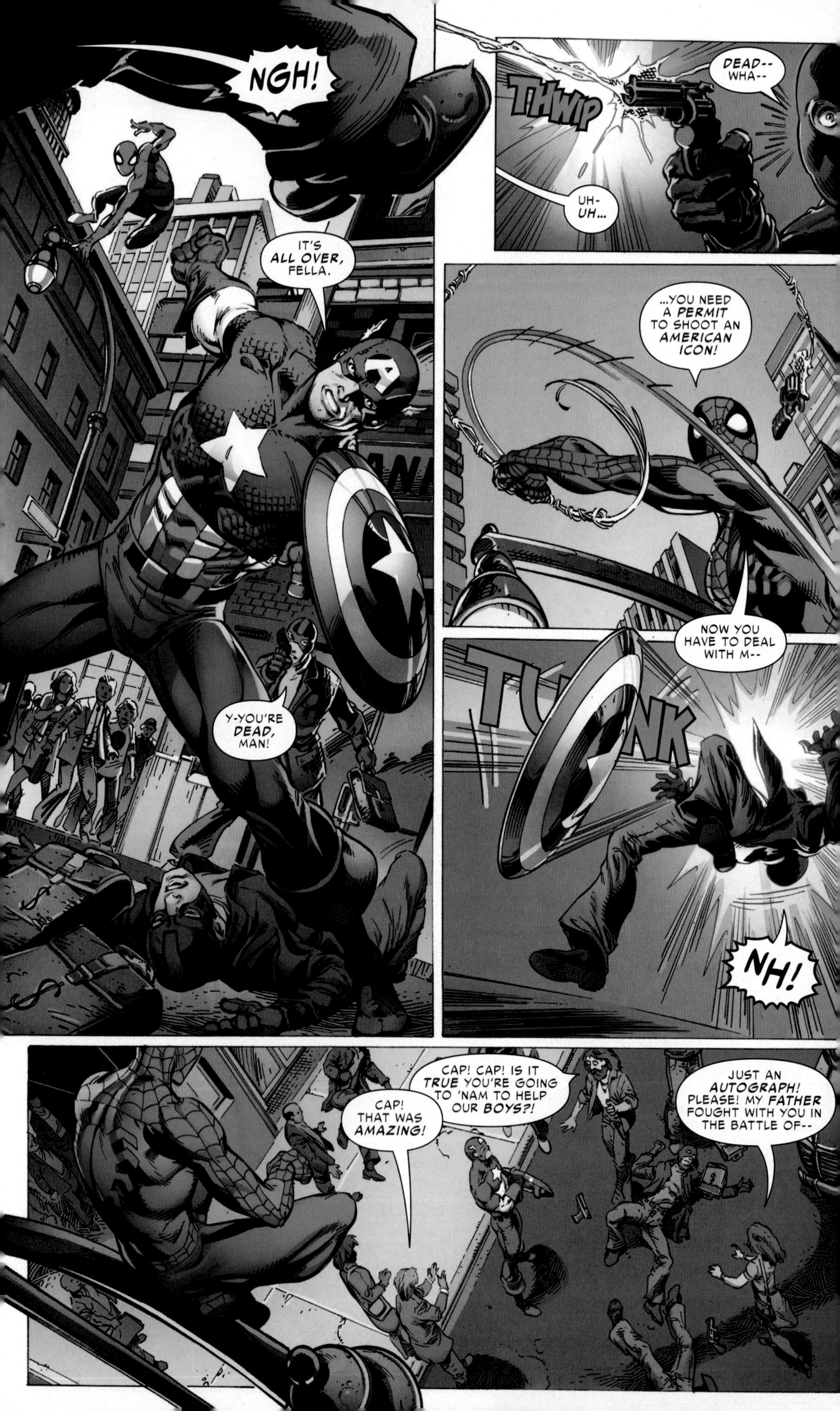
NGH!
IT'S ALL OVER, FELLA.
Y-YOU'RE DEAD, MAN!
THWIP
DEAD-- WHA--
UH-UH...
...YOU NEED A PERMIT TO SHOOT AN AMERICAN ICON!
NOW YOU HAVE TO DEAL WITH M--
TUNK
NH!
CAP! THAT WAS AMAZING!
CAP! CAP! IS IT TRUE YOU'RE GOING TO 'NAM TO HELP OUR BOYS?!
JUST AN AUTOGRAPH! PLEASE! MY FATHER FOUGHT WITH YOU IN THE BATTLE OF--

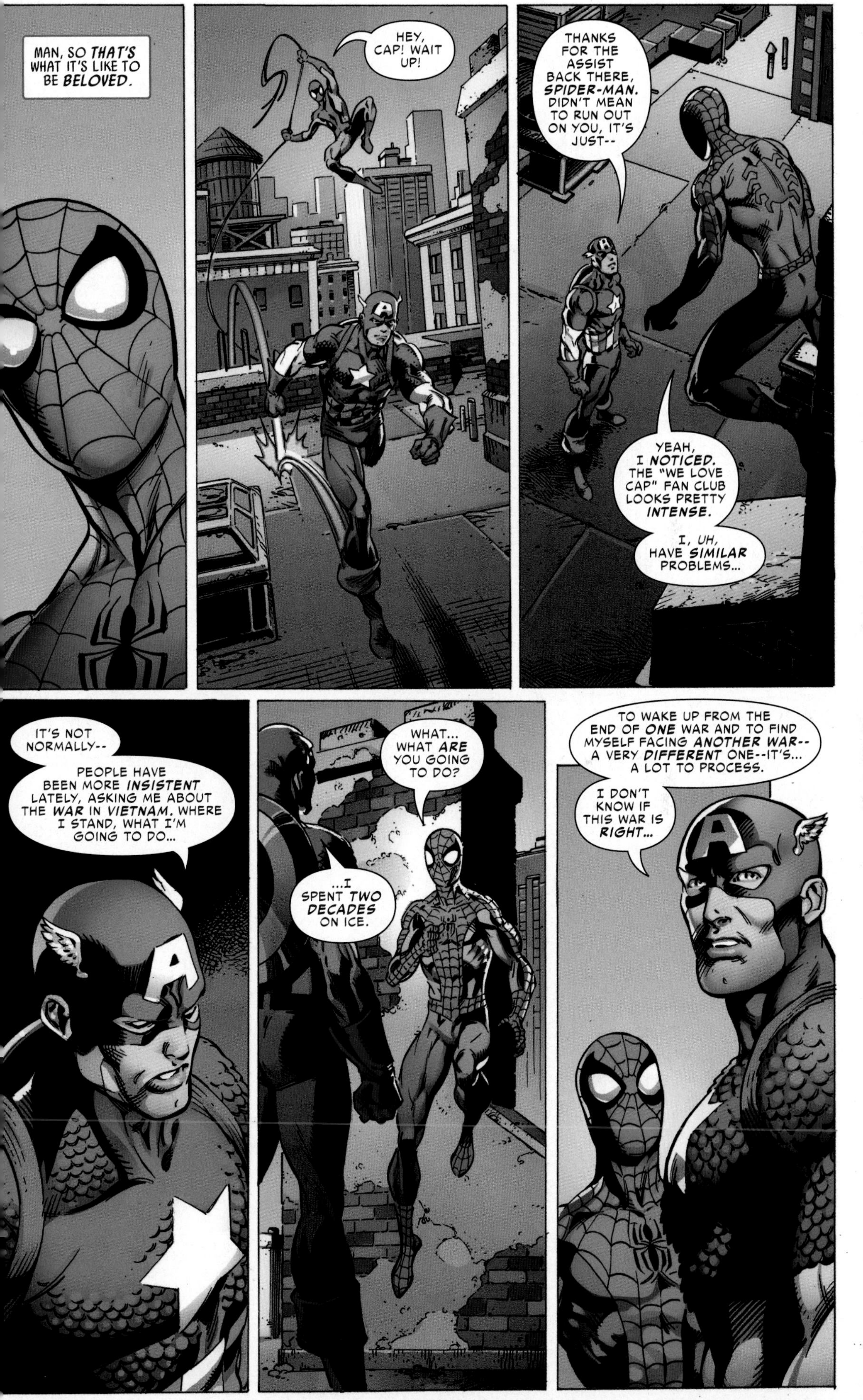

MAN, SO THAT'S WHAT IT'S LIKE TO BE BELOVED.
HEY, CAP! WAIT UP!
THANKS FOR THE ASSIST BACK THERE, SPIDER-MAN. DIDN'T MEAN TO RUN OUT ON YOU, IT'S JUST--
YEAH, I NOTICED. THE "WE LOVE CAP" FAN CLUB LOOKS PRETTY INTENSE.
I, UH, HAVE SIMILAR PROBLEMS...
IT'S NOT NORMALLY--
PEOPLE HAVE BEEN MORE INSISTENT LATELY, ASKING ME ABOUT THE WAR IN VIETNAM. WHERE I STAND, WHAT I'M GOING TO DO...
WHAT... WHAT ARE YOU GOING TO DO?
...I SPENT TWO DECADES ON ICE.
TO WAKE UP FROM THE END OF ONE WAR AND TO FIND MYSELF FACING ANOTHER WAR-- A VERY DIFFERENT ONE--IT'S... A LOT TO PROCESS.
I DON'T KNOW IF THIS WAR IS RIGHT...

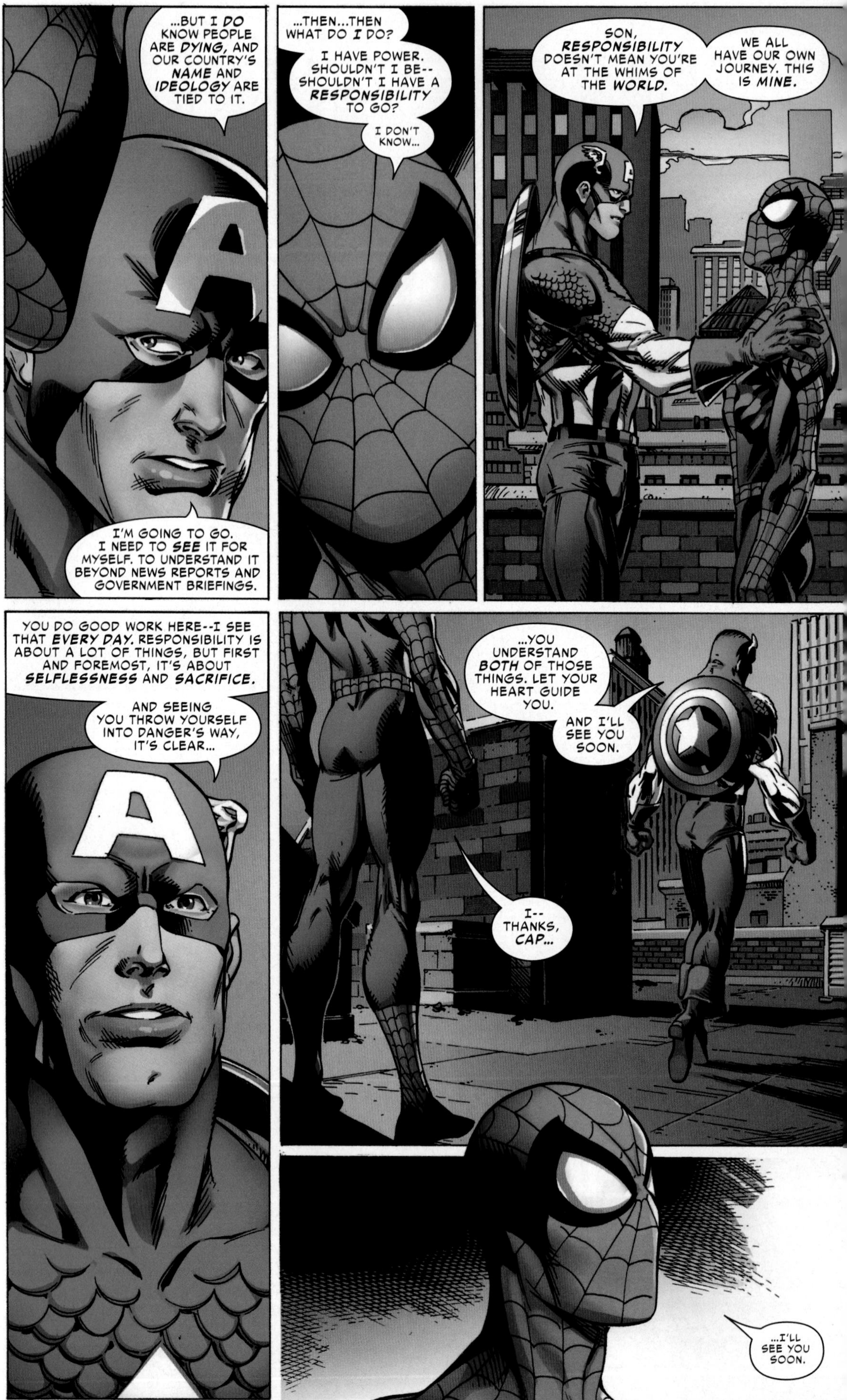
...BUT I DO KNOW PEOPLE ARE DYING, AND OUR COUNTRY'S NAME AND IDEOLOGY ARE TIED TO IT.
I'M GOING TO GO. I NEED TO SEE IT FOR MYSELF. TO UNDERSTAND IT BEYOND NEWS REPORTS AND GOVERNMENT BRIEFINGS.
...THEN...THEN WHAT DO I DO?
I HAVE POWER. SHOULDN'T I BE-- SHOULDN'T I HAVE A RESPONSIBILITY TO GO?
I DON'T KNOW...
SON, RESPONSIBILITY DOESN'T MEAN YOU'RE AT THE WHIMS OF THE WORLD.
WE ALL HAVE OUR OWN JOURNEY. THIS IS MINE.
YOU DO GOOD WORK HERE--I SEE THAT EVERY DAY. RESPONSIBILITY IS ABOUT A LOT OF THINGS, BUT FIRST AND FOREMOST, IT'S ABOUT SELFLESSNESS AND SACRIFICE.
AND SEEING YOU THROW YOURSELF INTO DANGER'S WAY, IT'S CLEAR...
...YOU UNDERSTAND BOTH OF THOSE THINGS. LET YOUR HEART GUIDE YOU.
AND I'LL SEE YOU SOON.
I-- THANKS, CAP...
...I'LL SEE YOU SOON.

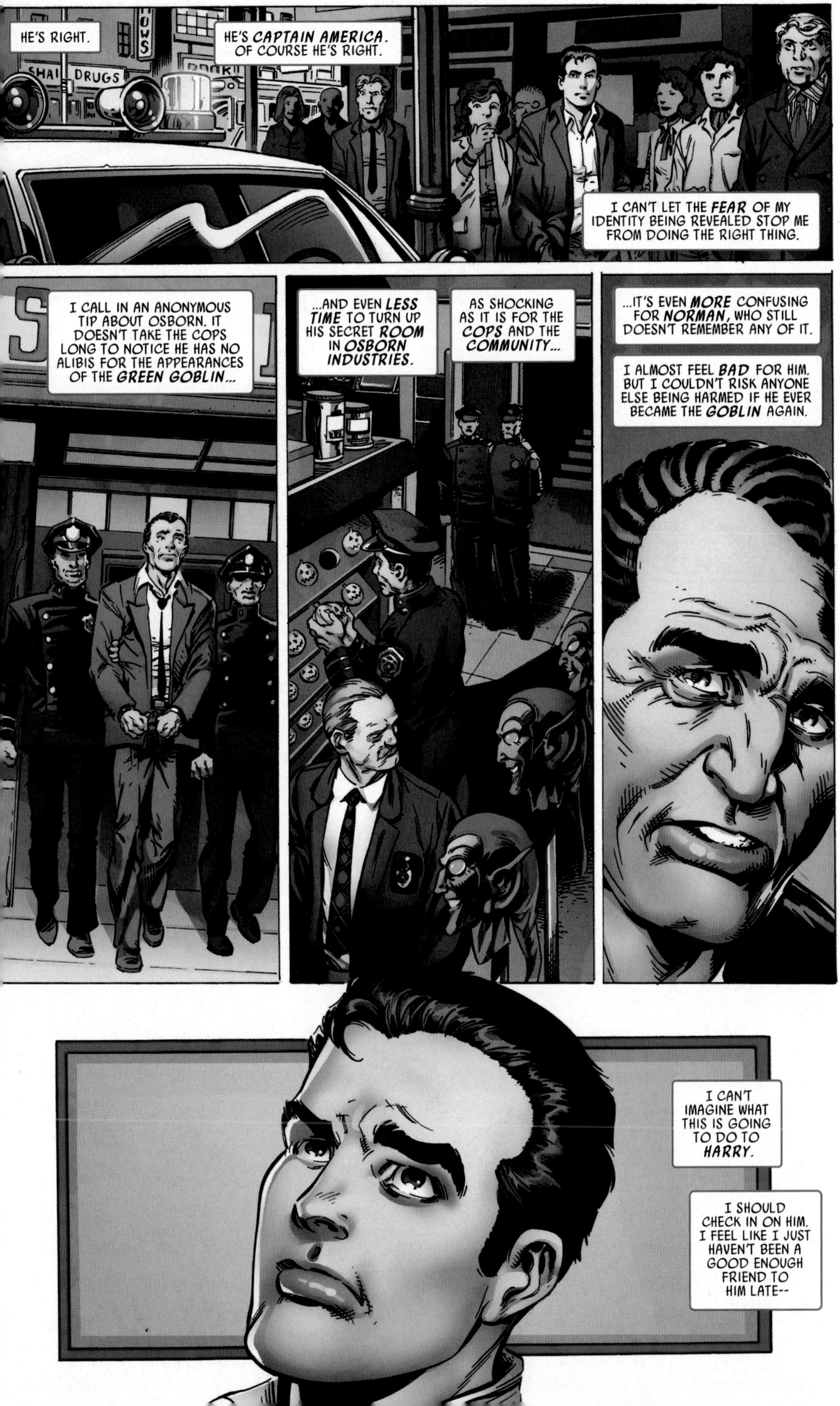

SHAI
DRUGS
HE'S RIGHT.
HE'S *CAPTAIN AMERICA.* OF COURSE HE'S RIGHT.
I CAN'T LET THE *FEAR* OF MY IDENTITY BEING REVEALED STOP ME FROM DOING THE RIGHT THING.
I CALL IN AN ANONYMOUS TIP ABOUT OSBORN. IT DOESN'T TAKE THE COPS LONG TO NOTICE HE HAS NO ALIBIS FOR THE APPEARANCES OF THE *GREEN GOBLIN...*
...AND EVEN *LESS TIME* TO TURN UP HIS SECRET *ROOM* IN *OSBORN INDUSTRIES.*
AS SHOCKING AS IT IS FOR THE *COPS* AND THE *COMMUNITY...*
...IT'S EVEN *MORE* CONFUSING FOR *NORMAN,* WHO STILL DOESN'T REMEMBER ANY OF IT.
I ALMOST FEEL *BAD* FOR HIM. BUT I COULDN'T RISK ANYONE ELSE BEING HARMED IF HE EVER BECAME THE *GOBLIN* AGAIN.
I CAN'T IMAGINE WHAT THIS IS GOING TO DO TO *HARRY.*
I SHOULD CHECK IN ON HIM. I FEEL LIKE I JUST HAVEN'T BEEN A GOOD ENOUGH FRIEND TO HIM LATE--

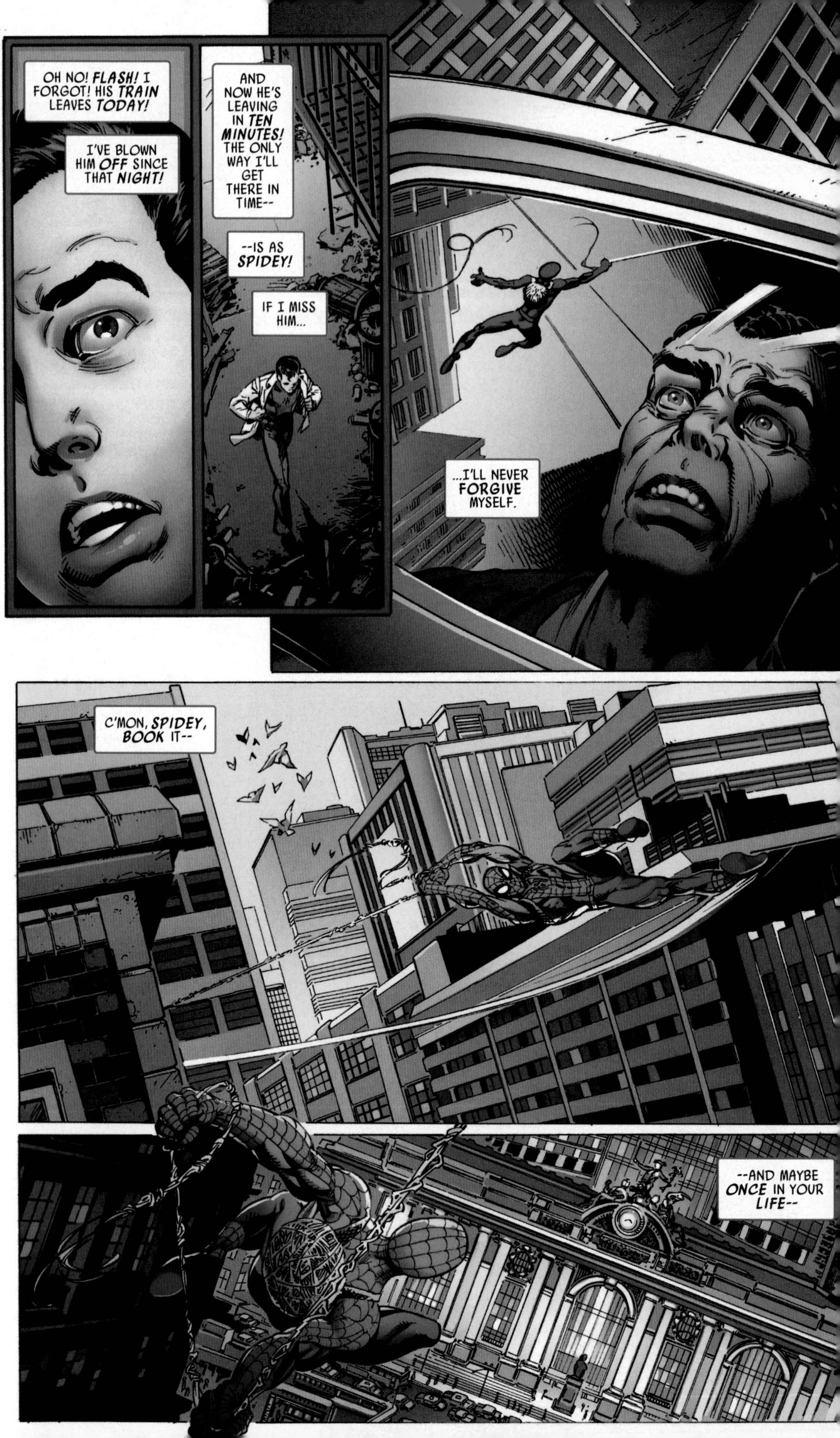
OH NO! FLASH! I FORGOT! HIS TRAIN LEAVES TODAY!
I'VE BLOWN HIM OFF SINCE THAT NIGHT!
AND NOW HE'S LEAVING IN TEN MINUTES! THE ONLY WAY I'LL GET THERE IN TIME--
--IS AS SPIDEY!
IF I MISS HIM...
...I'LL NEVER FORGIVE MYSELF.
C'MON, SPIDEY, BOOK IT--
--AND MAYBE ONCE IN YOUR LIFE--

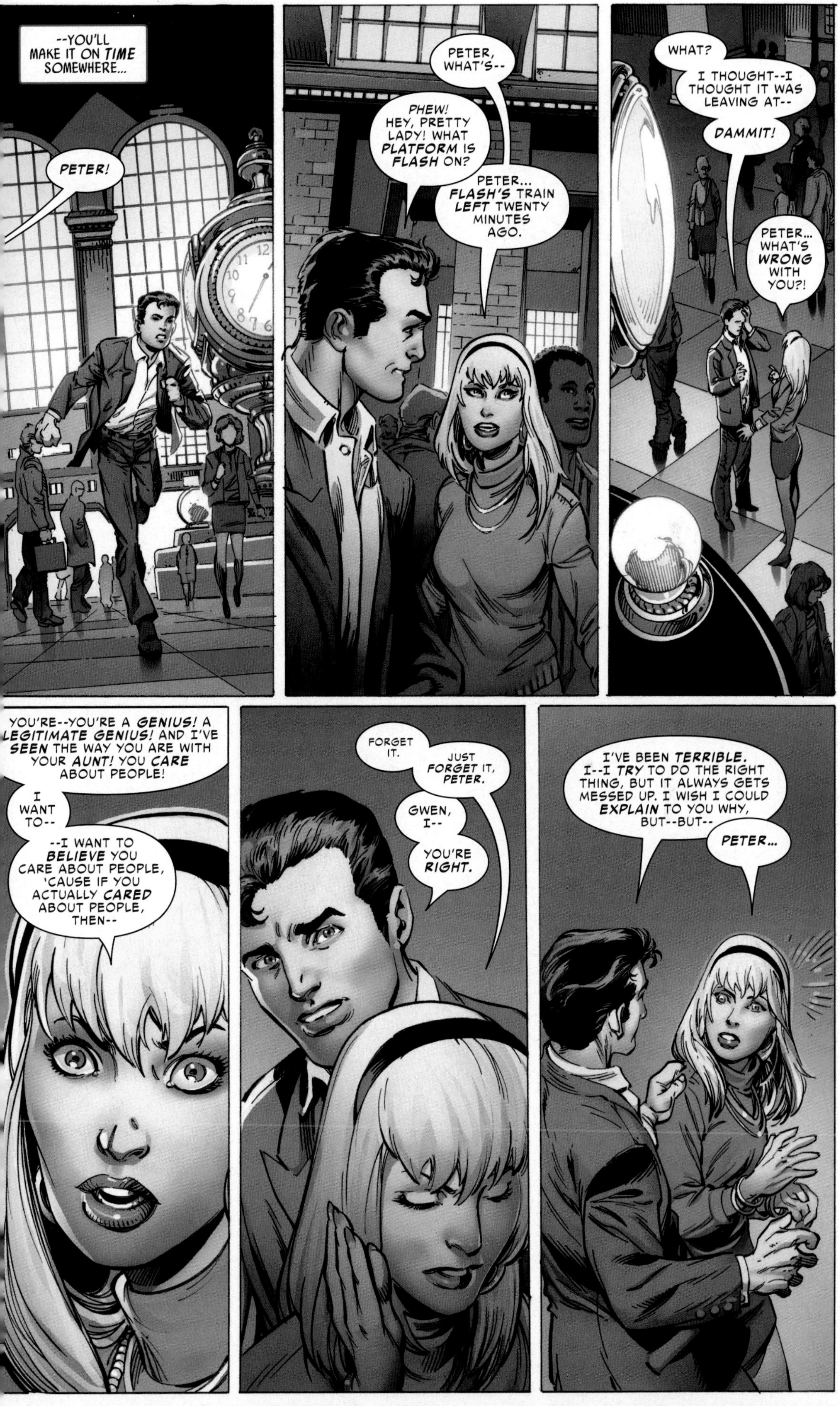
--YOU'LL MAKE IT ON TIME SOMEWHERE...
PETER!
PETER, WHAT'S--
PHEW! HEY, PRETTY LADY! WHAT PLATFORM IS FLASH ON?
PETER... FLASH'S TRAIN LEFT TWENTY MINUTES AGO.
WHAT?
I THOUGHT--I THOUGHT IT WAS LEAVING AT--
DAMMIT!
PETER... WHAT'S WRONG WITH YOU?!
YOU'RE--YOU'RE A GENIUS! A LEGITIMATE GENIUS! AND I'VE SEEN THE WAY YOU ARE WITH YOUR AUNT! YOU CARE ABOUT PEOPLE!
I WANT TO--
--I WANT TO BELIEVE YOU CARE ABOUT PEOPLE, 'CAUSE IF YOU ACTUALLY CARED ABOUT PEOPLE, THEN--
FORGET IT.
JUST FORGET IT, PETER.
GWEN, I--
YOU'RE RIGHT.
I'VE BEEN TERRIBLE. I--I TRY TO DO THE RIGHT THING, BUT IT ALWAYS GETS MESSED UP. I WISH I COULD EXPLAIN TO YOU WHY, BUT--BUT--
PETER...

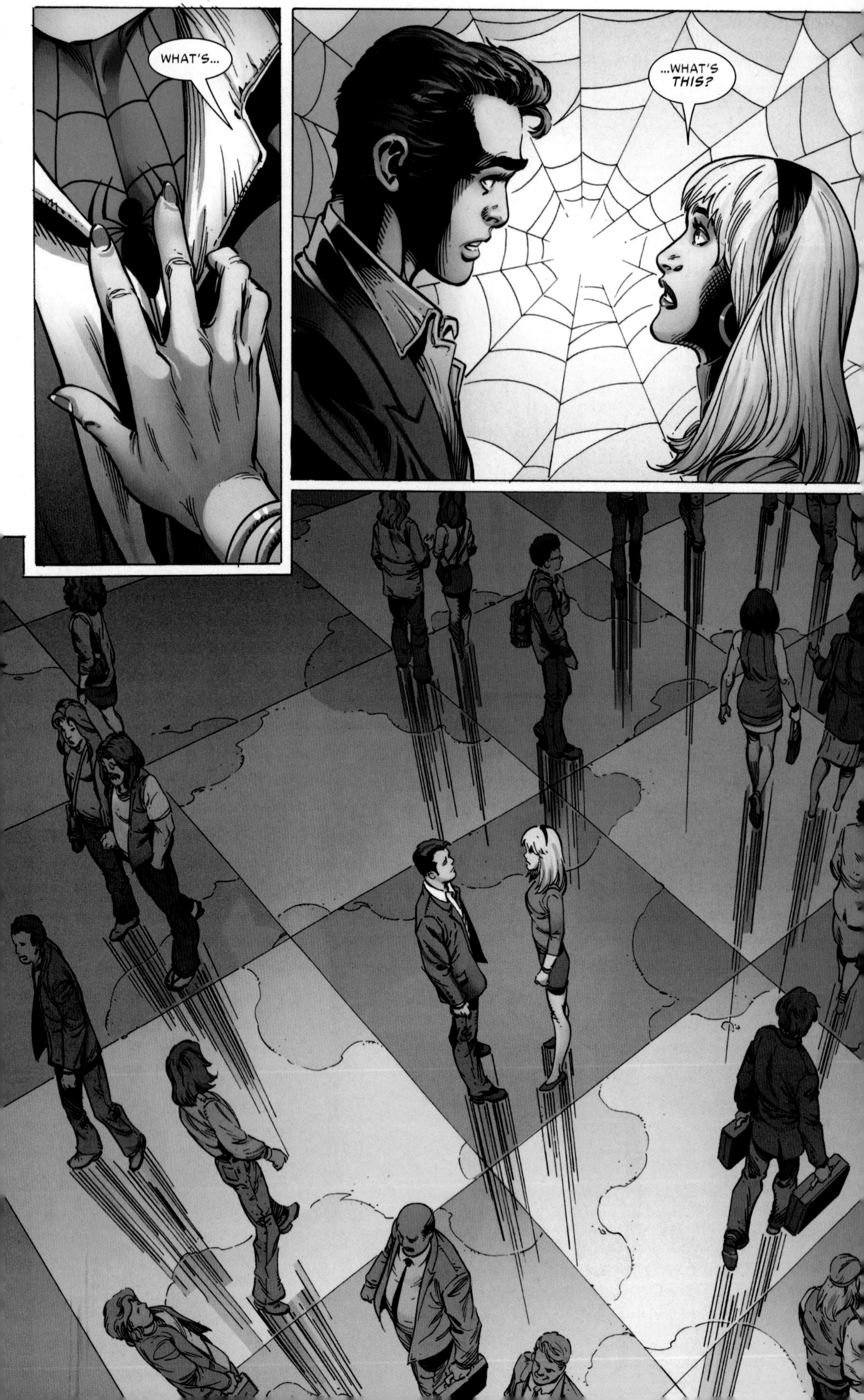
WHAT'S...
...WHAT'S THIS?

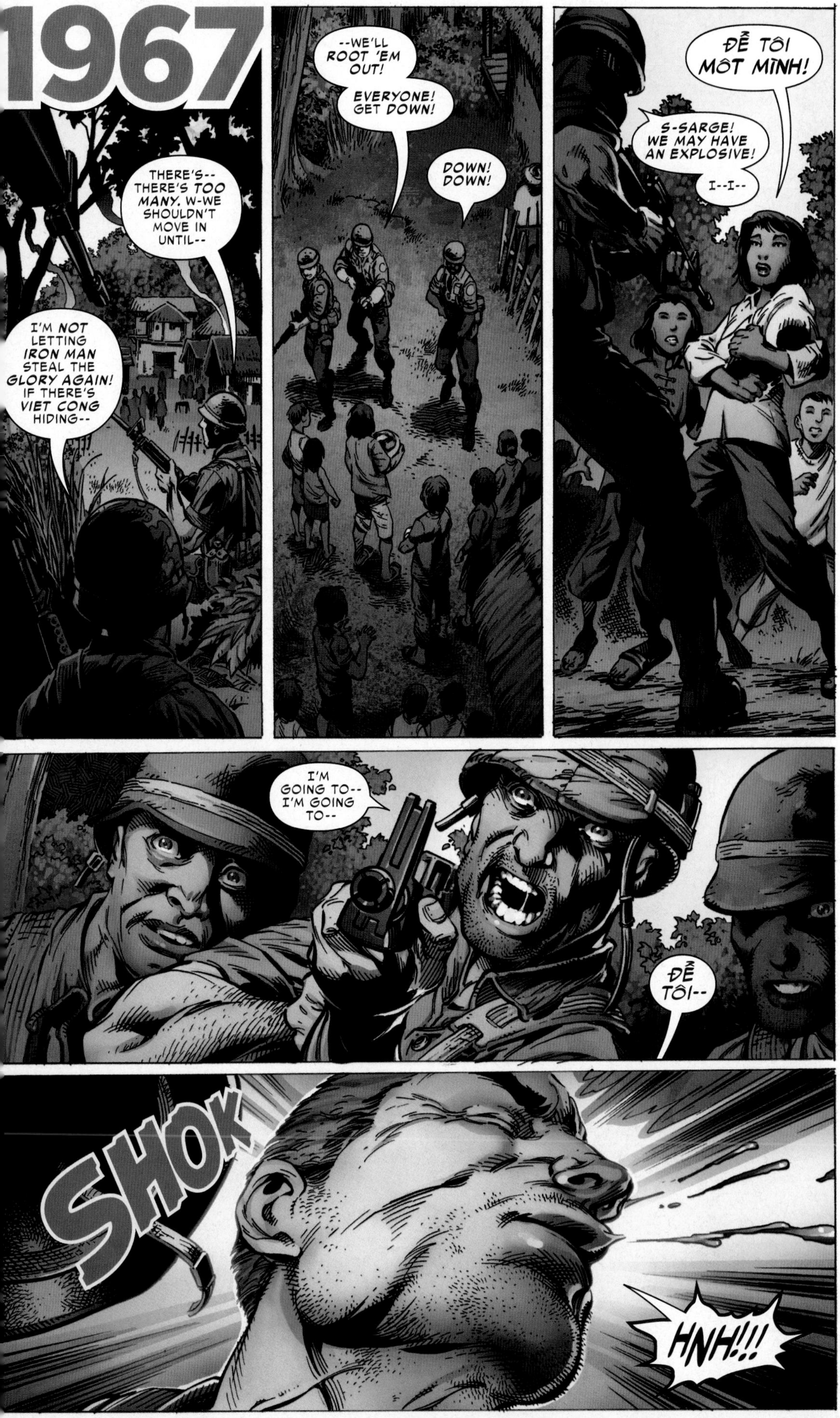
1967
THERE'S-- THERE'S TOO MANY. W-WE SHOULDN'T MOVE IN UNTIL--
I'M NOT LETTING IRON MAN STEAL THE GLORY AGAIN! IF THERE'S VIET CONG HIDING--
--WE'LL ROOT 'EM OUT!
EVERYONE! GET DOWN!
DOWN! DOWN!
ĐỂ TÔI MỘT MÌNH!
S-SARGE! WE MAY HAVE AN EXPLOSIVE!
I--I--
I'M GOING TO-- I'M GOING TO--
ĐỂ TÔI--
SHOK
HNH!!!

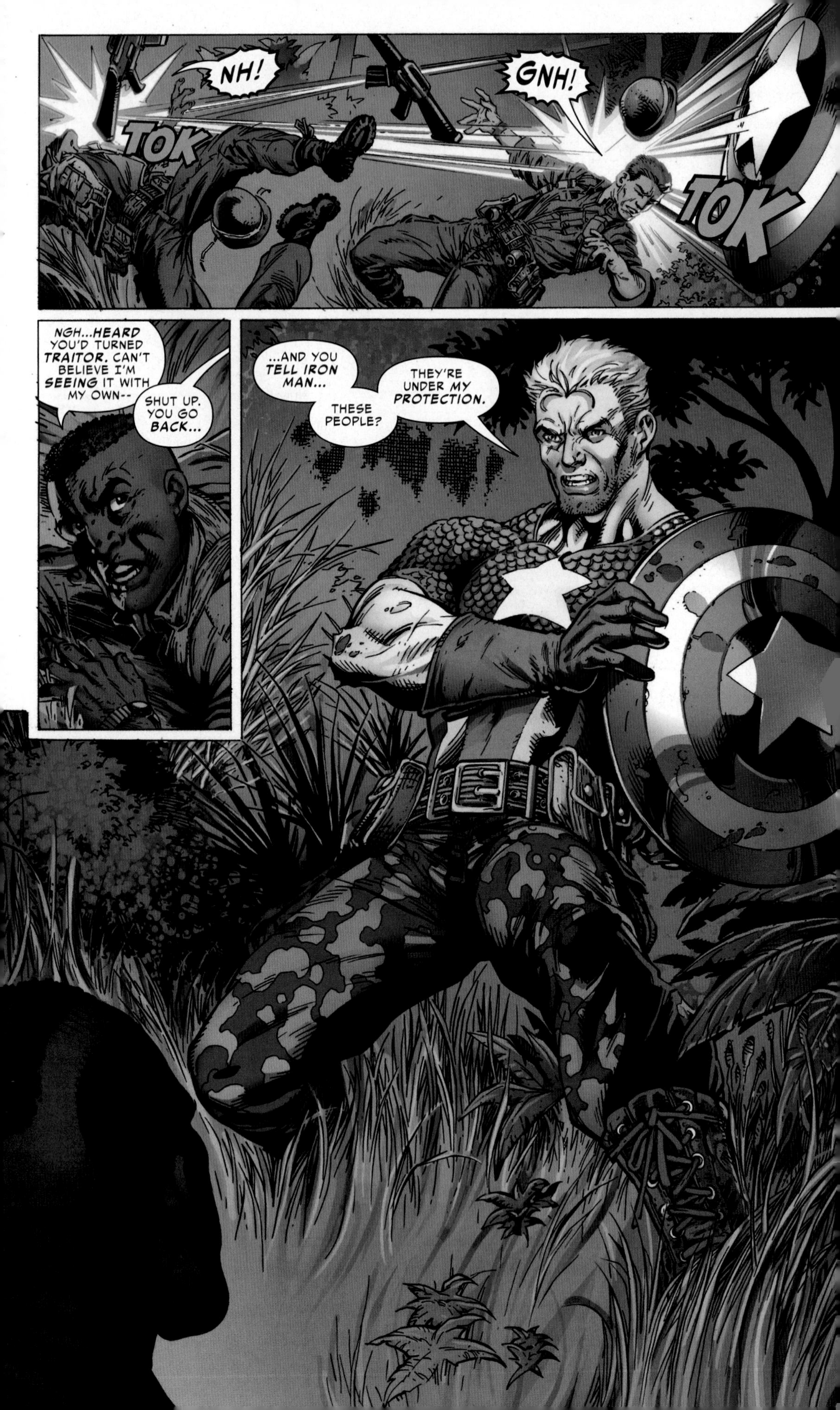
NH!
TOK
GNH!
TOK
NGH...HEARD YOU'D TURNED TRAITOR. CAN'T BELIEVE I'M SEEING IT WITH MY OWN--
SHUT UP. YOU GO BACK...
...AND YOU TELL IRON MAN...
THESE PEOPLE?
THEY'RE UNDER MY PROTECTION.

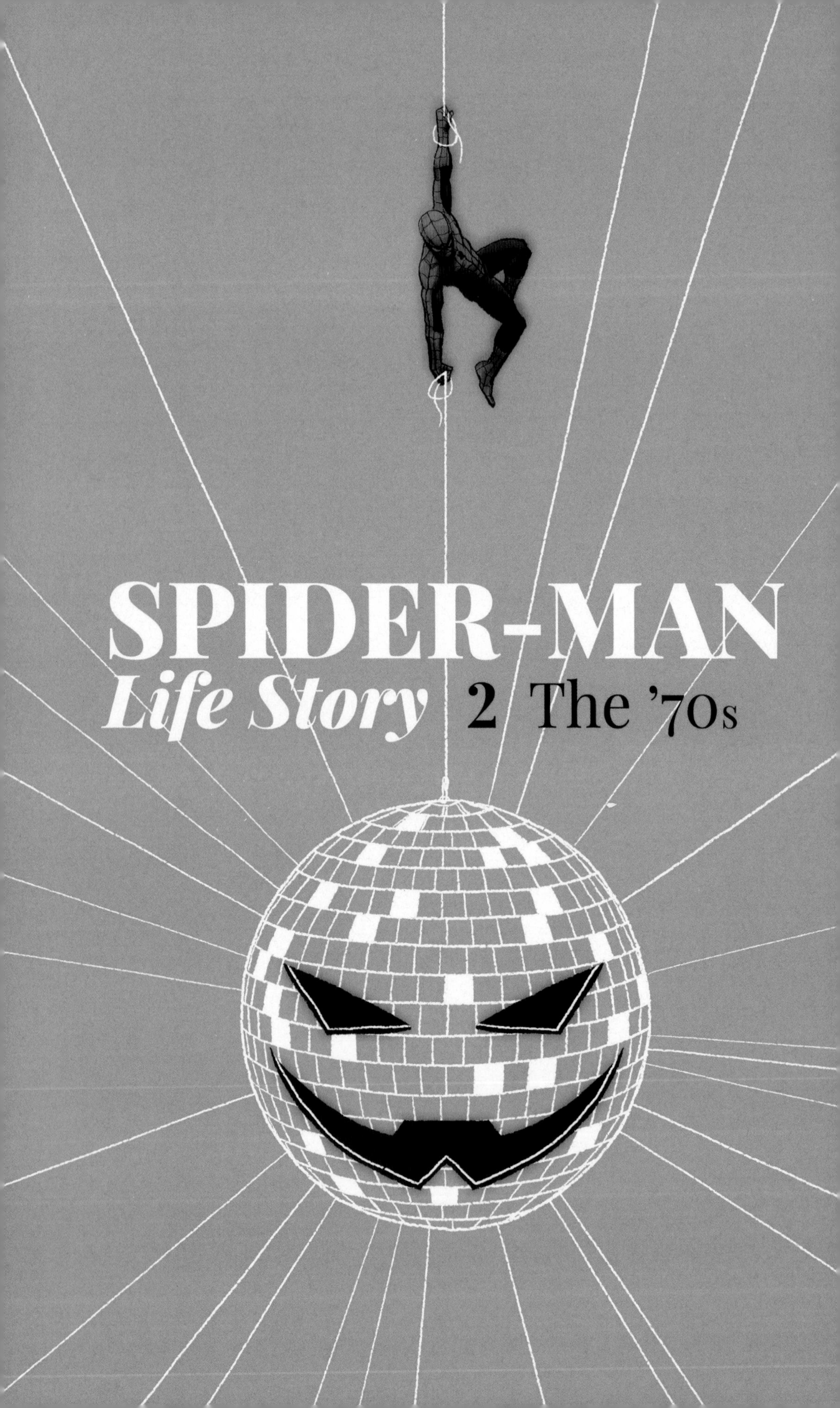
SPIDER-MAN
Life Story 2 The '70s

...AND *HARRY*, WELL, HE'S IN *CHARGE* NOW.

I THINK HE'S *HAPPY?* IT'S HARD TO TELL. RUNNING HIS DAD'S BUSINESS ISN'T *EASY*, BUT I THINK HE'S FOUND HIS PLACE...

SPEAKING OF: REMEMBER PROFESSOR WARREN? HE *LEFT* THE UNIVERSITY, STARTED HIS OWN *BIO-ENGINEERING COMPANY.* CUTTING-EDGE STUFF, MAN.

GWEN WENT TO WORK FOR HIM, ACTUALLY. *CHIEF BIOLOGIST*, IF YOU CAN BELIEVE IT.

IT'S A GOOD THING I HAVE A HEALTHY *EGO*, 'CAUSE HAVING MY *WIFE* MAKE *MORE* THAN ME RAISES A FEW EYEBROWS, I TELL YOU...

YOU DON'T MIND IT WHEN *PAYDAY* COMES AROUND...

HONEY! I THOUGHT YOU WERE--

SKIPPED OUT EARLY. FIGURED I'D FIND YOU HERE.

ANNIVERSARY OF HIS DEATH, YOUR UNREASONABLE PARKER GUILT...

...I COULD HAVE SAVED HIM, GWEN. I KNOW IT.

IT'S...IT ALL FEELS *HARDER* WHEN EVERYTHING IS CLICKING INTO *PLACE.* WHEN WE'RE DOING WELL, WHEN WE'RE ALL *HAPPY.*

HOW CAN WE BE *HAPPY?* HOW CAN ANY OF US WHEN--

PETER, I LOVE YOU.

YOU'RE *ALLOWED* TO BE *HAPPY.* THE WORLD IS--THE WORLD ALWAYS GIVES UP CHALLENGES AND SADNESS. IT'S *NEVER* IN SHORT SUPPLY.

BUT YOU *CAN'T* LET IT DRIVE YOU. THE DEAD DON'T WANT YOU TO WALLOW. THEY WANT YOU TO *LIVE*...

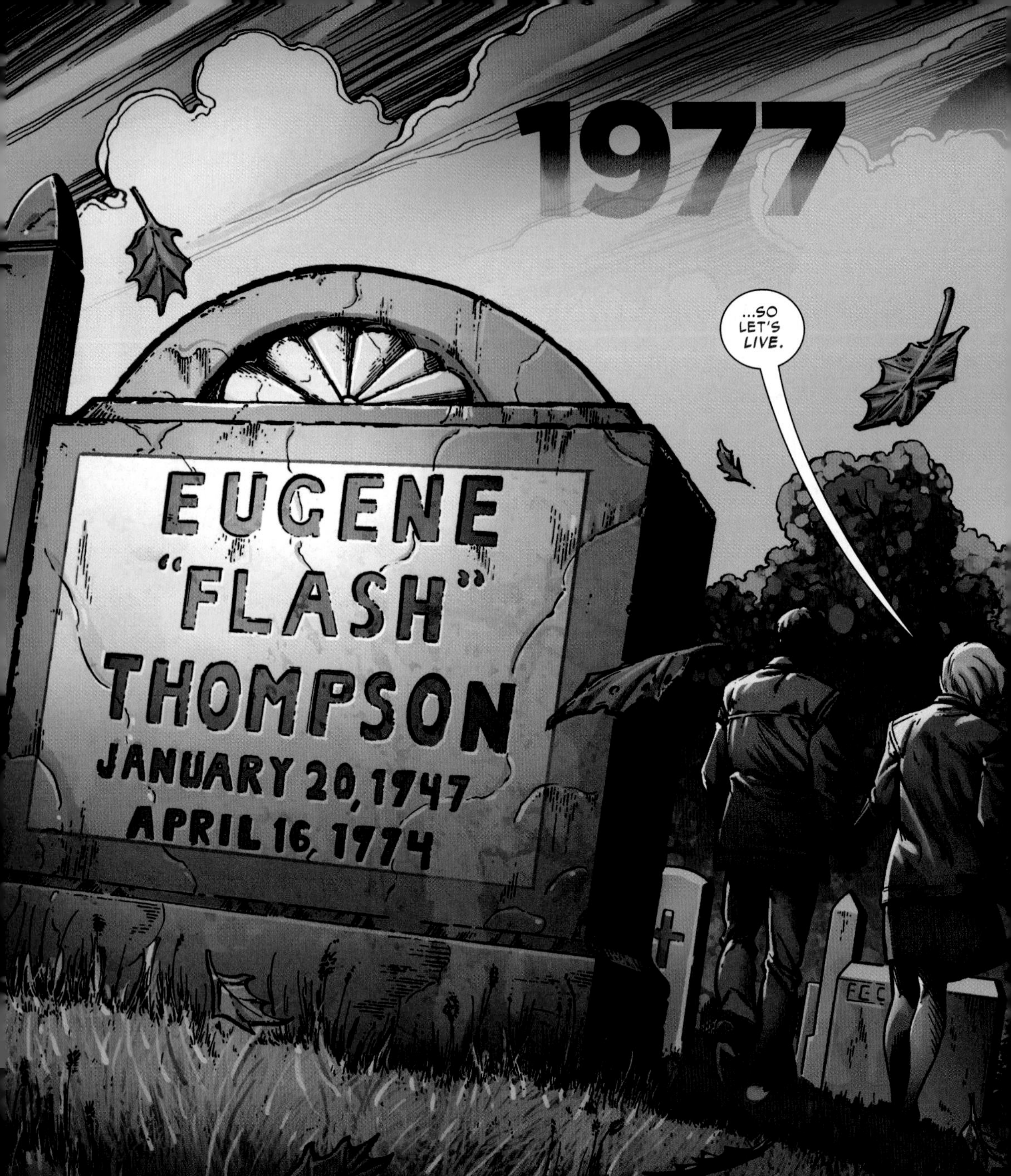
1977
EUGENE "FLASH" THOMPSON
JANUARY 20, 1947
APRIL 16, 1974
...SO LET'S *LIVE*.
F.C.C

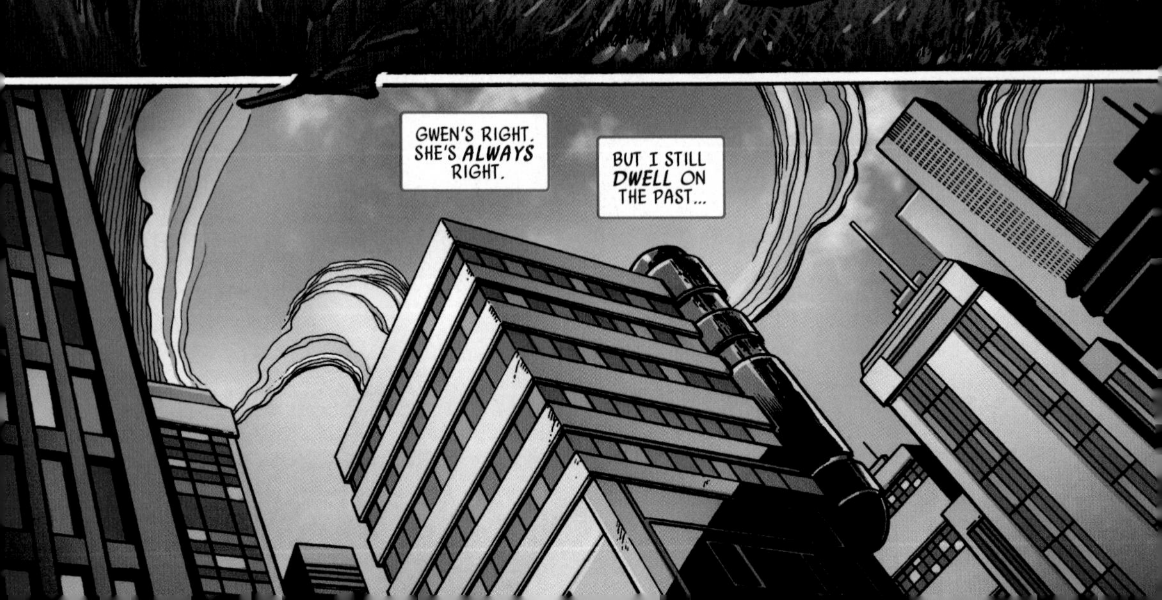
GWEN'S RIGHT. SHE'S *ALWAYS* RIGHT.
BUT I STILL *DWELL* ON THE PAST...

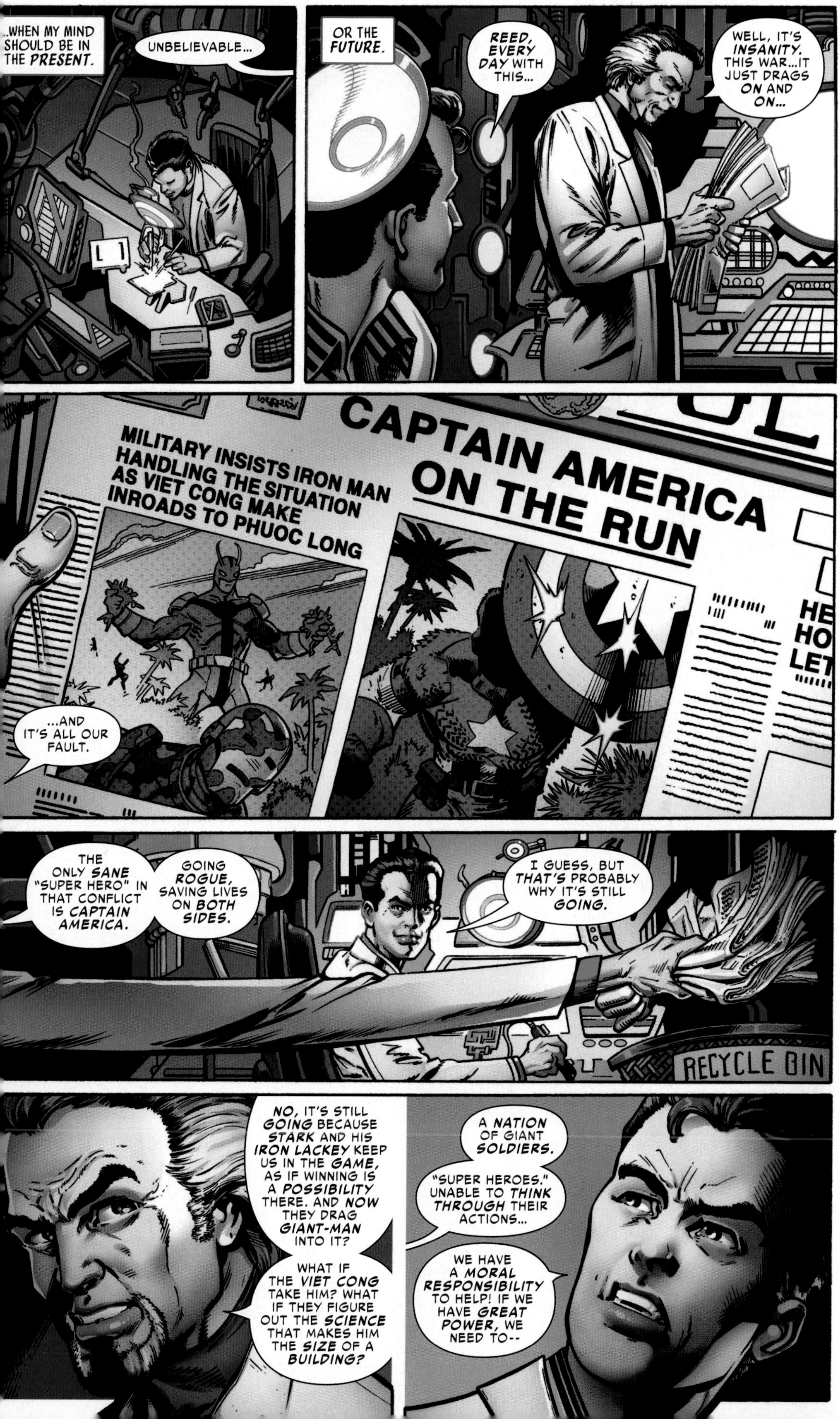
..WHEN MY MIND SHOULD BE IN THE PRESENT.
UNBELIEVABLE...
OR THE FUTURE.
REED, EVERY DAY WITH THIS...
WELL, IT'S INSANITY. THIS WAR...IT JUST DRAGS ON AND ON...
CAPTAIN AMERICA ON THE RUN
MILITARY INSISTS IRON MAN HANDLING THE SITUATION AS VIET CONG MAKE INROADS TO PHUOC LONG
...AND IT'S ALL OUR FAULT.
THE ONLY SANE "SUPER HERO" IN THAT CONFLICT IS CAPTAIN AMERICA.
GOING ROGUE, SAVING LIVES ON BOTH SIDES.
I GUESS, BUT THAT'S PROBABLY WHY IT'S STILL GOING.
RECYCLE BIN
NO, IT'S STILL GOING BECAUSE STARK AND HIS IRON LACKEY KEEP US IN THE GAME, AS IF WINNING IS A POSSIBILITY THERE. AND NOW THEY DRAG GIANT-MAN INTO IT?
WHAT IF THE VIET CONG TAKE HIM? WHAT IF THEY FIGURE OUT THE SCIENCE THAT MAKES HIM THE SIZE OF A BUILDING?
A NATION OF GIANT SOLDIERS.
"SUPER HEROES." UNABLE TO THINK THROUGH THEIR ACTIONS...
WE HAVE A MORAL RESPONSIBILITY TO HELP! IF WE HAVE GREAT POWER, WE NEED TO--

GENTLEMEN. ALWAYS WITH THE DEBATES.

OTTO OCTAVIUS. HARD TO BELIEVE HE WAS TRYING TO MURDER ME A FEW YEARS AGO.

WE DO GOOD WORK HERE. THE FUTURE FOUNDATION IS FINALLY CHANGING THE WORLD FOR THE BETTER.

MOBILE COMMUNICATIONS! ADVANCED PROSTHETICS! SAFE DIMENSIONAL TRAVEL! THESE ARE THINGS TO BE PROUD OF!

BUT AFTER HIS HEART ATTACK, HE REALIZED THERE WAS MORE TO LIFE THAN ACCUMULATING WEALTH AND POWER...

BUT YOU ALWAYS INSIST ON CHASTISING OTHERS FOR THE PATHS THEY'VE TAKEN.

I TOOK A SIMILAR PATH UNTIL YOU OFFERED ME THIS CHANCE. AND I FOUND MAY...

THAT ALSO HELPED. NOW HE'S "UNCLE OTTO." OF ALL THE THINGS I'VE HAD TO GET USED TO OVER THE YEARS, THAT ONE IS THE HARDEST...

...BUT OTTO KNOWS HOW TO BRING REED OUT OF HIS FUNKS, WHEREAS I JUST GET RILED UP THINKING ABOUT SOME OF HIS INVENTIONS THAT HE HOARDS...

HE HAS HIS REASONS. BUT THE MORE I LOOK AT THE WORLD...

NIXON RESIGNING... THE WAR STILL GOING...

I JUST KEEP THINKING...

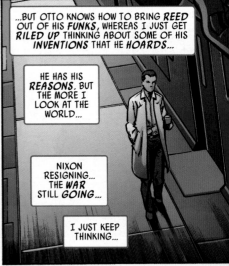

...SHOULDN'T WE DO MORE?

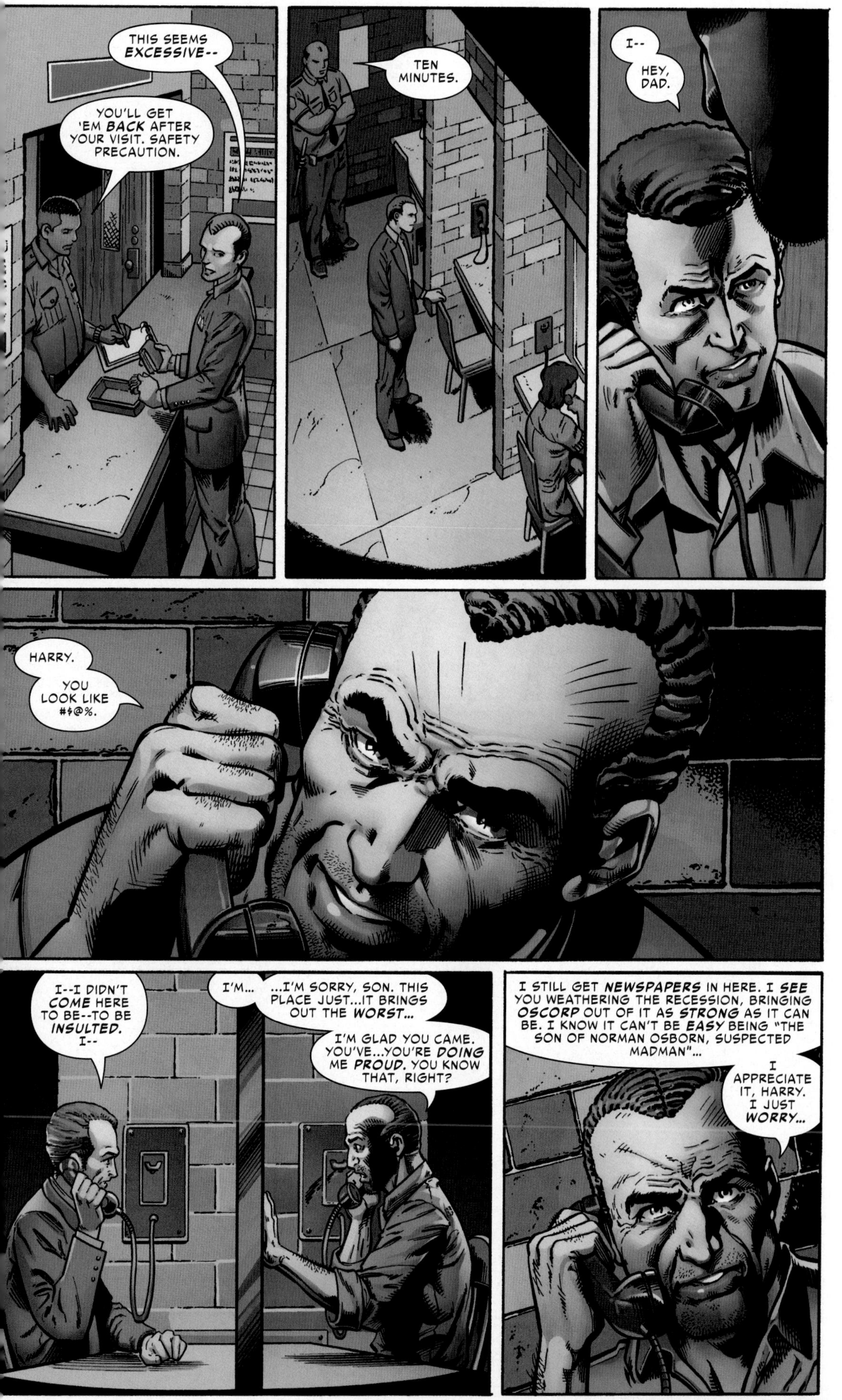
THIS SEEMS EXCESSIVE--
YOU'LL GET 'EM BACK AFTER YOUR VISIT. SAFETY PRECAUTION.
TEN MINUTES.
I--
HEY, DAD.
HARRY.
YOU LOOK LIKE #$@%.
I--I DIDN'T COME HERE TO BE--TO BE INSULTED. I--
I'M...
...I'M SORRY, SON. THIS PLACE JUST...IT BRINGS OUT THE WORST...
I'M GLAD YOU CAME. YOU'VE...YOU'RE DOING ME PROUD. YOU KNOW THAT, RIGHT?
I STILL GET NEWSPAPERS IN HERE. I SEE YOU WEATHERING THE RECESSION, BRINGING OSCORP OUT OF IT AS STRONG AS IT CAN BE. I KNOW IT CAN'T BE EASY BEING "THE SON OF NORMAN OSBORN, SUSPECTED MADMAN"...
I APPRECIATE IT, HARRY. I JUST WORRY...

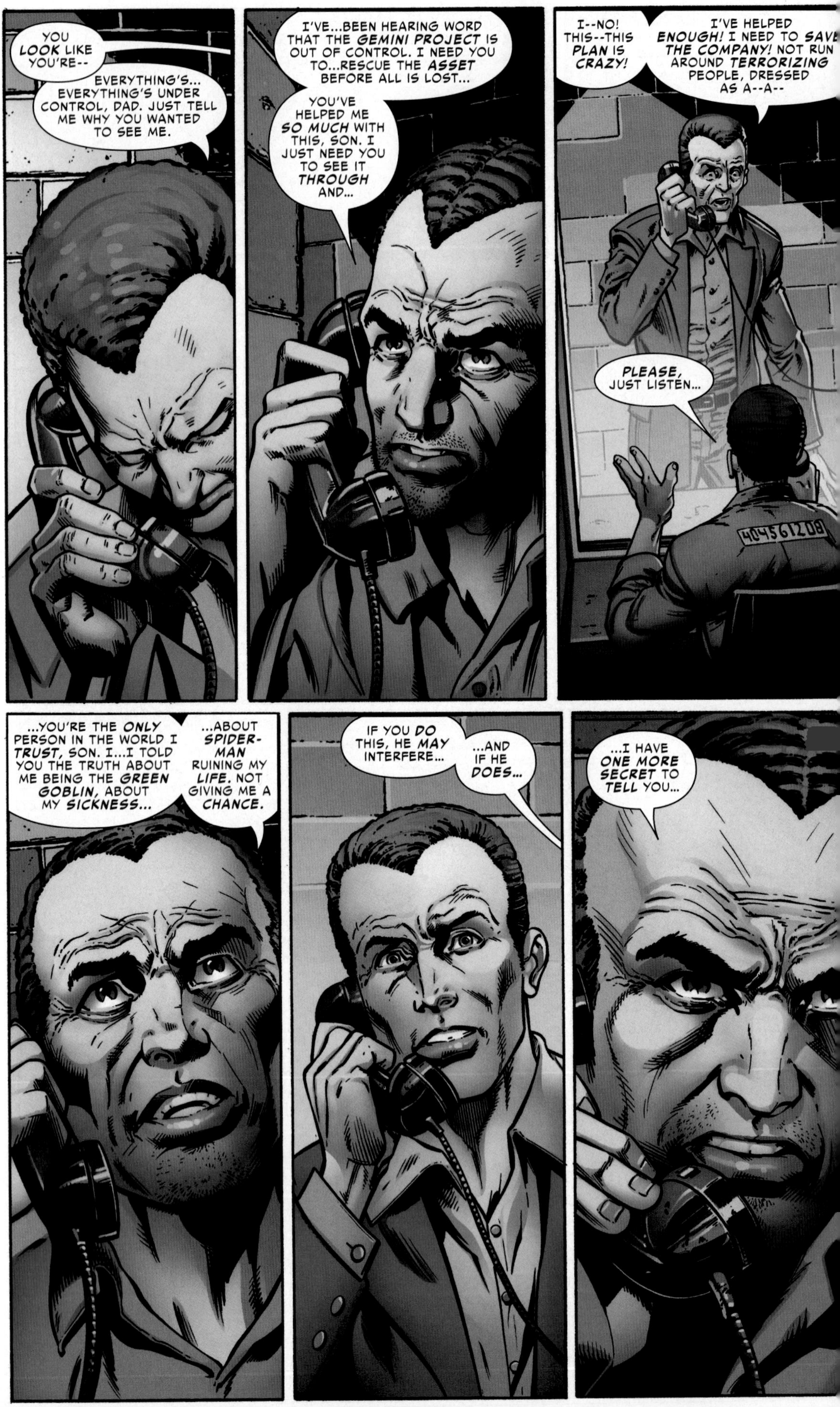

YOU LOOK LIKE YOU'RE--
EVERYTHING'S... EVERYTHING'S UNDER CONTROL, DAD. JUST TELL ME WHY YOU WANTED TO SEE ME.
I'VE...BEEN HEARING WORD THAT THE GEMINI PROJECT IS OUT OF CONTROL. I NEED YOU TO...RESCUE THE ASSET BEFORE ALL IS LOST...
YOU'VE HELPED ME SO MUCH WITH THIS, SON. I JUST NEED YOU TO SEE IT THROUGH AND...
I--NO! THIS--THIS PLAN IS CRAZY!
I'VE HELPED ENOUGH! I NEED TO SAVE THE COMPANY! NOT RUN AROUND TERRORIZING PEOPLE, DRESSED AS A--A--
PLEASE, JUST LISTEN...
4045612O8
...YOU'RE THE ONLY PERSON IN THE WORLD I TRUST, SON. I...I TOLD YOU THE TRUTH ABOUT ME BEING THE GREEN GOBLIN, ABOUT MY SICKNESS...
...ABOUT SPIDER-MAN RUINING MY LIFE. NOT GIVING ME A CHANCE.
IF YOU DO THIS, HE MAY INTERFERE...
...AND IF HE DOES...
...I HAVE ONE MORE SECRET TO TELL YOU...

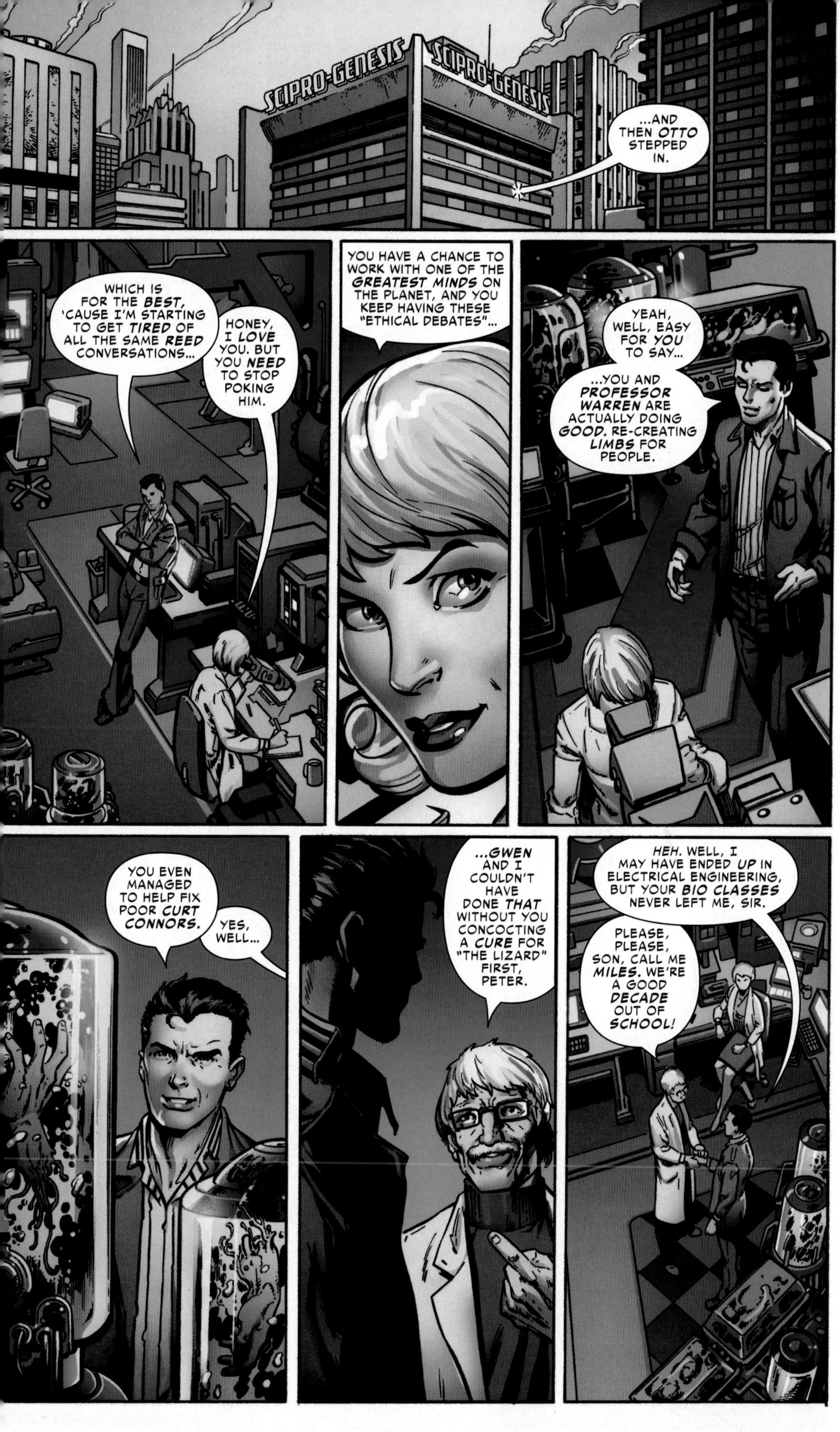
SCIPRO-GENESIS
SCIPRO-GENESIS
...AND THEN OTTO STEPPED IN.
WHICH IS FOR THE BEST, 'CAUSE I'M STARTING TO GET TIRED OF ALL THE SAME REED CONVERSATIONS...
HONEY, I LOVE YOU. BUT YOU NEED TO STOP POKING HIM.
YOU HAVE A CHANCE TO WORK WITH ONE OF THE GREATEST MINDS ON THE PLANET, AND YOU KEEP HAVING THESE "ETHICAL DEBATES"...
YEAH, WELL, EASY FOR YOU TO SAY...
...YOU AND PROFESSOR WARREN ARE ACTUALLY DOING GOOD. RE-CREATING LIMBS FOR PEOPLE.
YOU EVEN MANAGED TO HELP FIX POOR CURT CONNORS.
YES, WELL...
...GWEN AND I COULDN'T HAVE DONE THAT WITHOUT YOU CONCOCTING A CURE FOR "THE LIZARD" FIRST, PETER.
HEH. WELL, I MAY HAVE ENDED UP IN ELECTRICAL ENGINEERING, BUT YOUR BIO CLASSES NEVER LEFT ME, SIR.
PLEASE, PLEASE, SON, CALL ME MILES. WE'RE A GOOD DECADE OUT OF SCHOOL!

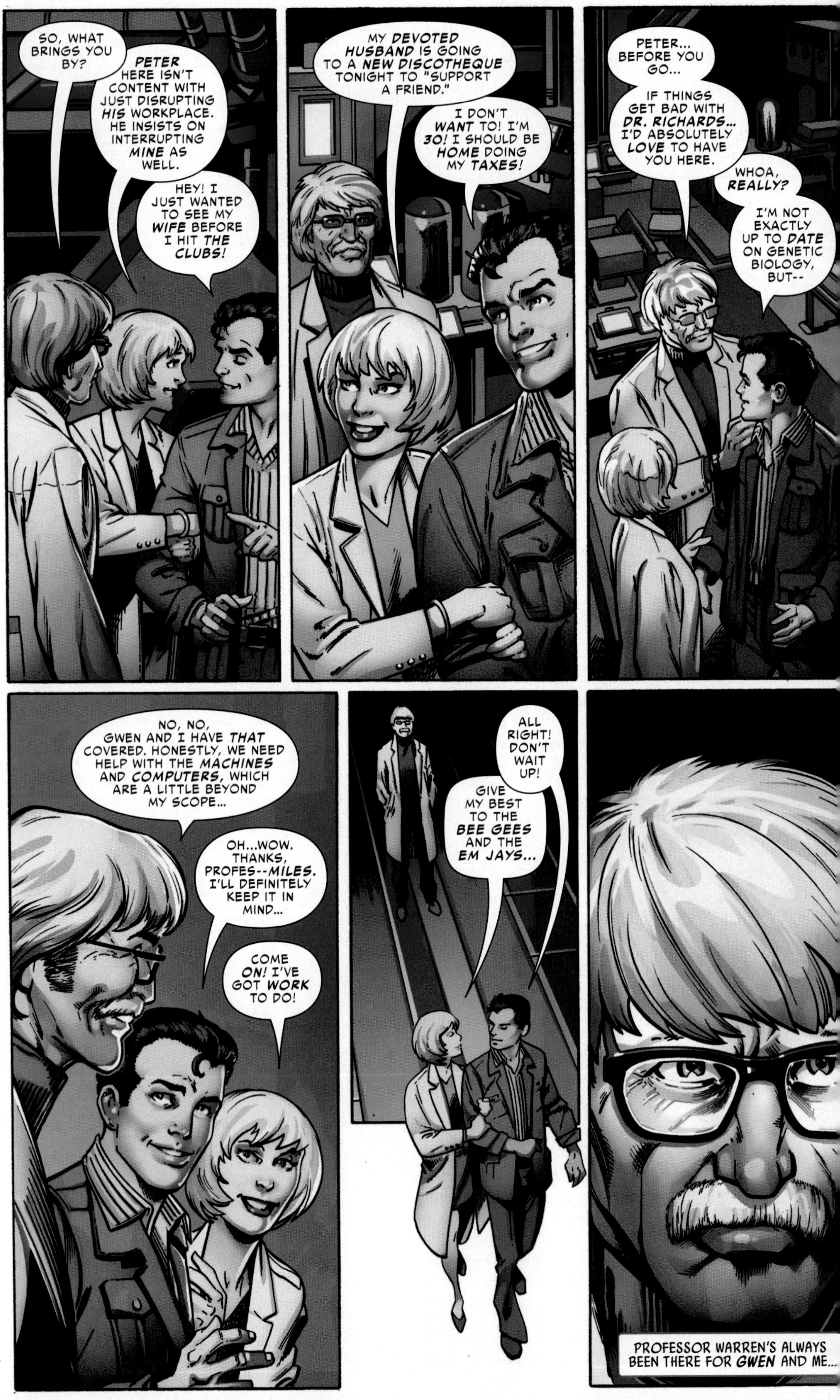
SO, WHAT BRINGS YOU BY?
PETER HERE ISN'T CONTENT WITH JUST DISRUPTING HIS WORKPLACE. HE INSISTS ON INTERRUPTING MINE AS WELL.
HEY! I JUST WANTED TO SEE MY WIFE BEFORE I HIT THE CLUBS!
MY DEVOTED HUSBAND IS GOING TO A NEW DISCOTHEQUE TONIGHT TO "SUPPORT A FRIEND."
I DON'T WANT TO! I'M 30! I SHOULD BE HOME DOING MY TAXES!
PETER... BEFORE YOU GO...
IF THINGS GET BAD WITH DR. RICHARDS... I'D ABSOLUTELY LOVE TO HAVE YOU HERE.
WHOA, REALLY?
I'M NOT EXACTLY UP TO DATE ON GENETIC BIOLOGY, BUT--
NO, NO, GWEN AND I HAVE THAT COVERED. HONESTLY, WE NEED HELP WITH THE MACHINES AND COMPUTERS, WHICH ARE A LITTLE BEYOND MY SCOPE...
OH...WOW. THANKS, PROFES--MILES. I'LL DEFINITELY KEEP IT IN MIND...
COME ON! I'VE GOT WORK TO DO!
ALL RIGHT! DON'T WAIT UP!
GIVE MY BEST TO THE BEE GEES AND THE EM JAYS...
PROFESSOR WARREN'S ALWAYS BEEN THERE FOR GWEN AND ME...

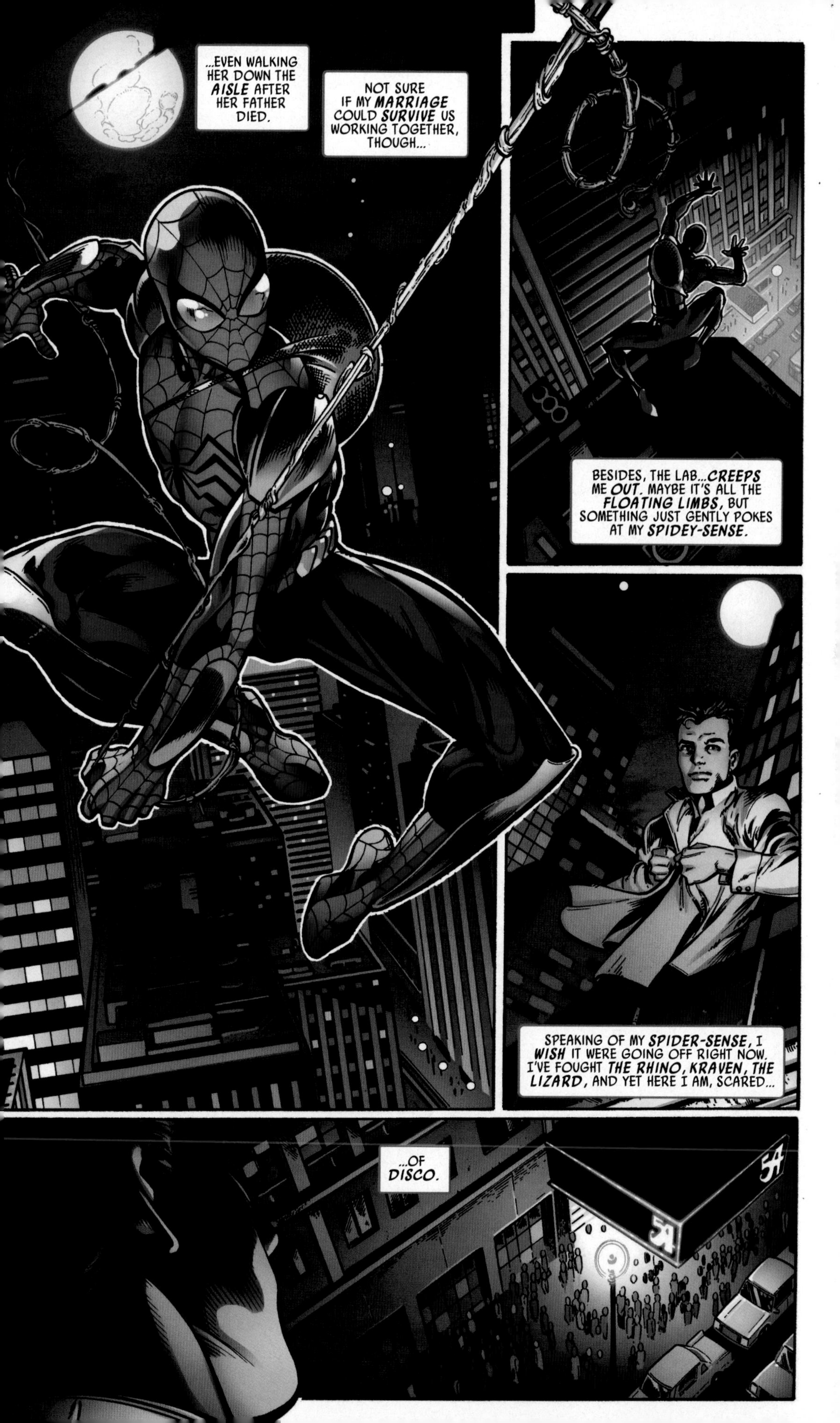

...EVEN WALKING HER DOWN THE AISLE AFTER HER FATHER DIED.
NOT SURE IF MY MARRIAGE COULD SURVIVE US WORKING TOGETHER, THOUGH...
BESIDES, THE LAB...CREEPS ME OUT. MAYBE IT'S ALL THE FLOATING LIMBS, BUT SOMETHING JUST GENTLY POKES AT MY SPIDEY-SENSE.
SPEAKING OF MY SPIDER-SENSE, I WISH IT WERE GOING OFF RIGHT NOW. I'VE FOUGHT THE RHINO, KRAVEN, THE LIZARD, AND YET HERE I AM, SCARED...
...OF DISCO.
54
54

JUST SUCK IT UP, PETE...AT LEAST YOU WERE ON THE LIST...

MR. PARKER?

PLEASE, YOU'RE EXPECTED IN THE VIP SECTION...

OH. OF...OF COURSE...

I ALWAYS FORGET THAT HARRY IS, LIKE, CRAZY RICH.

AND IF HARRY IS CRAZY RICH, SO IS HIS FIANCÉE...

...MARY JANE WATSON.

PETEYYYY!..

UH, HEY, MJ. DID I MISS YOUR SET?

OH GOD NO! I DON'T HIT THE DJ BOOTH UNTIL MIDNIGHT!

MIDNIGHT?! OH MAN, I DON'T THINK I CAN LAST THAT LONG! THIS ISN'T-- ISN'T REALLY MY SCENE...

HAHA! WHEN DID YOU GET SO OLD?!

I'VE ALWAYS BEEN OLD! PUT A BEATLES 45 ON AND I'M FINE...

UNBELIEVABLE! JUST GIVE SOMETHING NEW A CHANCE FOR ONCE!

YEAH, YEAH...WHERE'S HARRY?

OL' HARRY DIDN'T QUITE GET THE UPPERS/ DOWNERS COMBO RIGHT...

OH MAN...

IT'S FINE. JUST MEANS I DON'T H TO BABYSIT HIM NIGHT AND LIST TO HIS STUPID HIGH-FINANCE TALES.

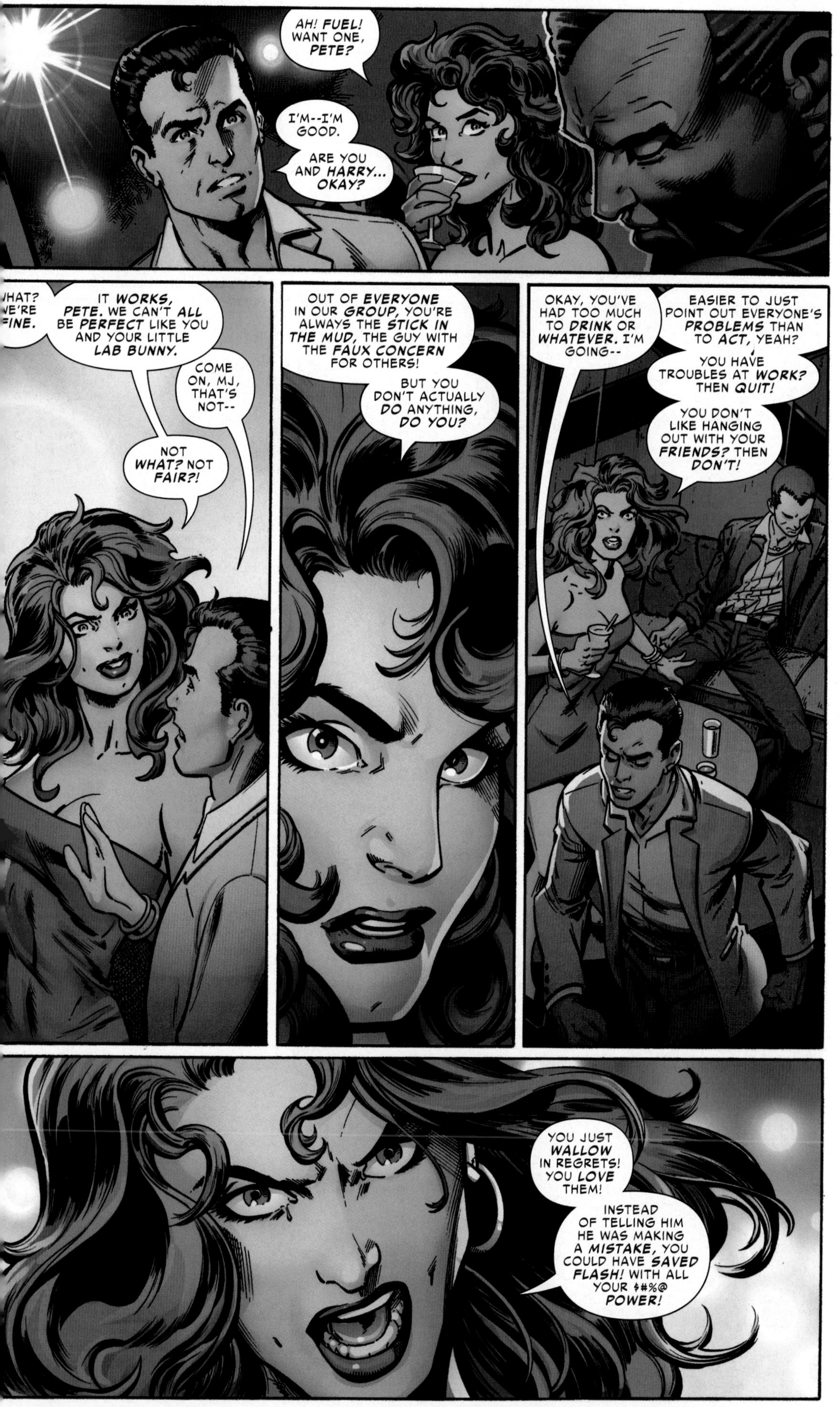
AH! FUEL! WANT ONE, PETE?
I'M--I'M GOOD.
ARE YOU AND HARRY... OKAY?
WHAT? WE'RE FINE.
IT WORKS, PETE. WE CAN'T ALL BE PERFECT LIKE YOU AND YOUR LITTLE LAB BUNNY.
COME ON, MJ, THAT'S NOT--
NOT WHAT? NOT FAIR?!
OUT OF EVERYONE IN OUR GROUP, YOU'RE ALWAYS THE STICK IN THE MUD, THE GUY WITH THE FAUX CONCERN FOR OTHERS!
BUT YOU DON'T ACTUALLY DO ANYTHING, DO YOU?
OKAY, YOU'VE HAD TOO MUCH TO DRINK OR WHATEVER. I'M GOING--
EASIER TO JUST POINT OUT EVERYONE'S PROBLEMS THAN TO ACT, YEAH?
YOU HAVE TROUBLES AT WORK? THEN QUIT!
YOU DON'T LIKE HANGING OUT WITH YOUR FRIENDS? THEN DON'T!
YOU JUST WALLOW IN REGRETS! YOU LOVE THEM!
INSTEAD OF TELLING HIM HE WAS MAKING A MISTAKE, YOU COULD HAVE SAVED FLASH! WITH ALL YOUR $#%@ POWER!

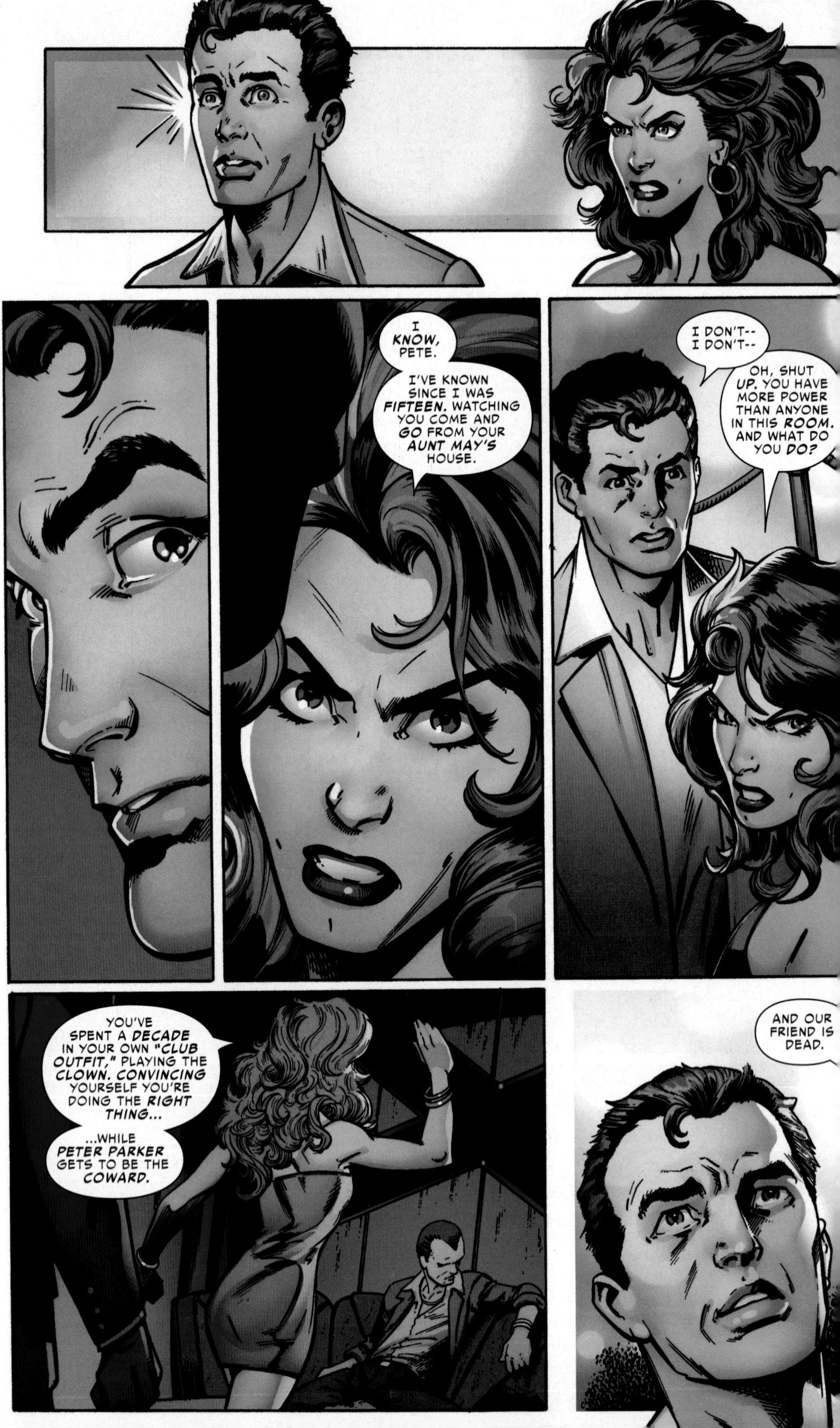

I KNOW, PETE.
I'VE KNOWN SINCE I WAS FIFTEEN. WATCHING YOU COME AND GO FROM YOUR AUNT MAY'S HOUSE.
I DON'T-- I DON'T--
OH, SHUT UP. YOU HAVE MORE POWER THAN ANYONE IN THIS ROOM. AND WHAT DO YOU DO?
YOU'VE SPENT A DECADE IN YOUR OWN "CLUB OUTFIT," PLAYING THE CLOWN. CONVINCING YOURSELF YOU'RE DOING THE RIGHT THING...
...WHILE PETER PARKER GETS TO BE THE COWARD.
AND OUR FRIEND IS DEAD.

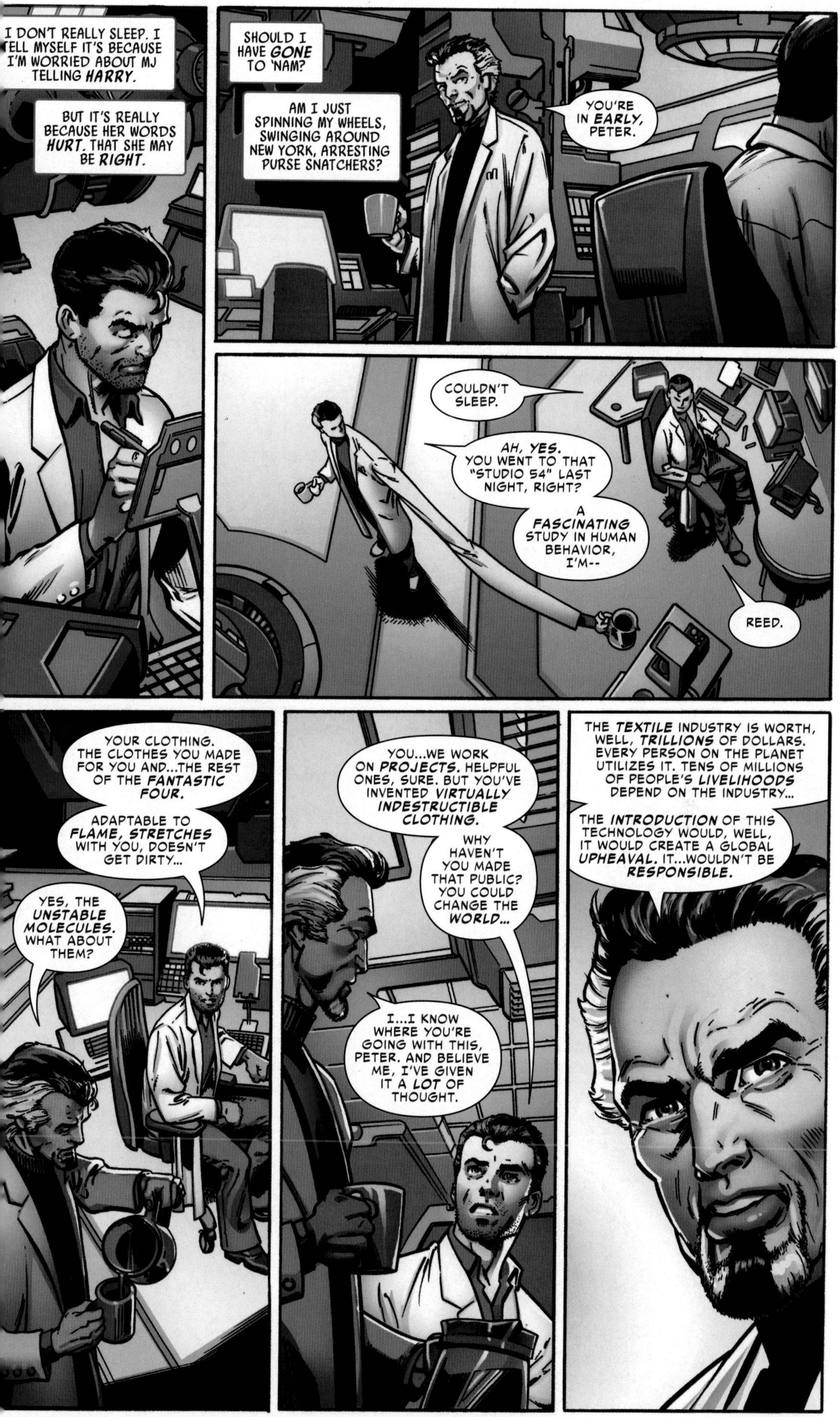
I DON'T REALLY SLEEP. I TELL MYSELF IT'S BECAUSE I'M WORRIED ABOUT MJ TELLING HARRY.
BUT IT'S REALLY BECAUSE HER WORDS HURT. THAT SHE MAY BE RIGHT.
SHOULD I HAVE GONE TO 'NAM?
AM I JUST SPINNING MY WHEELS, SWINGING AROUND NEW YORK, ARRESTING PURSE SNATCHERS?
YOU'RE IN EARLY, PETER.
COULDN'T SLEEP.
AH, YES. YOU WENT TO THAT "STUDIO 54" LAST NIGHT, RIGHT?
A FASCINATING STUDY IN HUMAN BEHAVIOR, I'M--
REED.
YOUR CLOTHING. THE CLOTHES YOU MADE FOR YOU AND...THE REST OF THE FANTASTIC FOUR.
ADAPTABLE TO FLAME, STRETCHES WITH YOU, DOESN'T GET DIRTY...
YES, THE UNSTABLE MOLECULES. WHAT ABOUT THEM?
YOU...WE WORK ON PROJECTS. HELPFUL ONES, SURE. BUT YOU'VE INVENTED VIRTUALLY INDESTRUCTIBLE CLOTHING.
WHY HAVEN'T YOU MADE THAT PUBLIC? YOU COULD CHANGE THE WORLD...
I...I KNOW WHERE YOU'RE GOING WITH THIS, PETER. AND BELIEVE ME, I'VE GIVEN IT A LOT OF THOUGHT.
THE TEXTILE INDUSTRY IS WORTH, WELL, TRILLIONS OF DOLLARS. EVERY PERSON ON THE PLANET UTILIZES IT. TENS OF MILLIONS OF PEOPLE'S LIVELIHOODS DEPEND ON THE INDUSTRY...
THE INTRODUCTION OF THIS TECHNOLOGY WOULD, WELL, IT WOULD CREATE A GLOBAL UPHEAVAL. IT...WOULDN'T BE RESPONSIBLE.

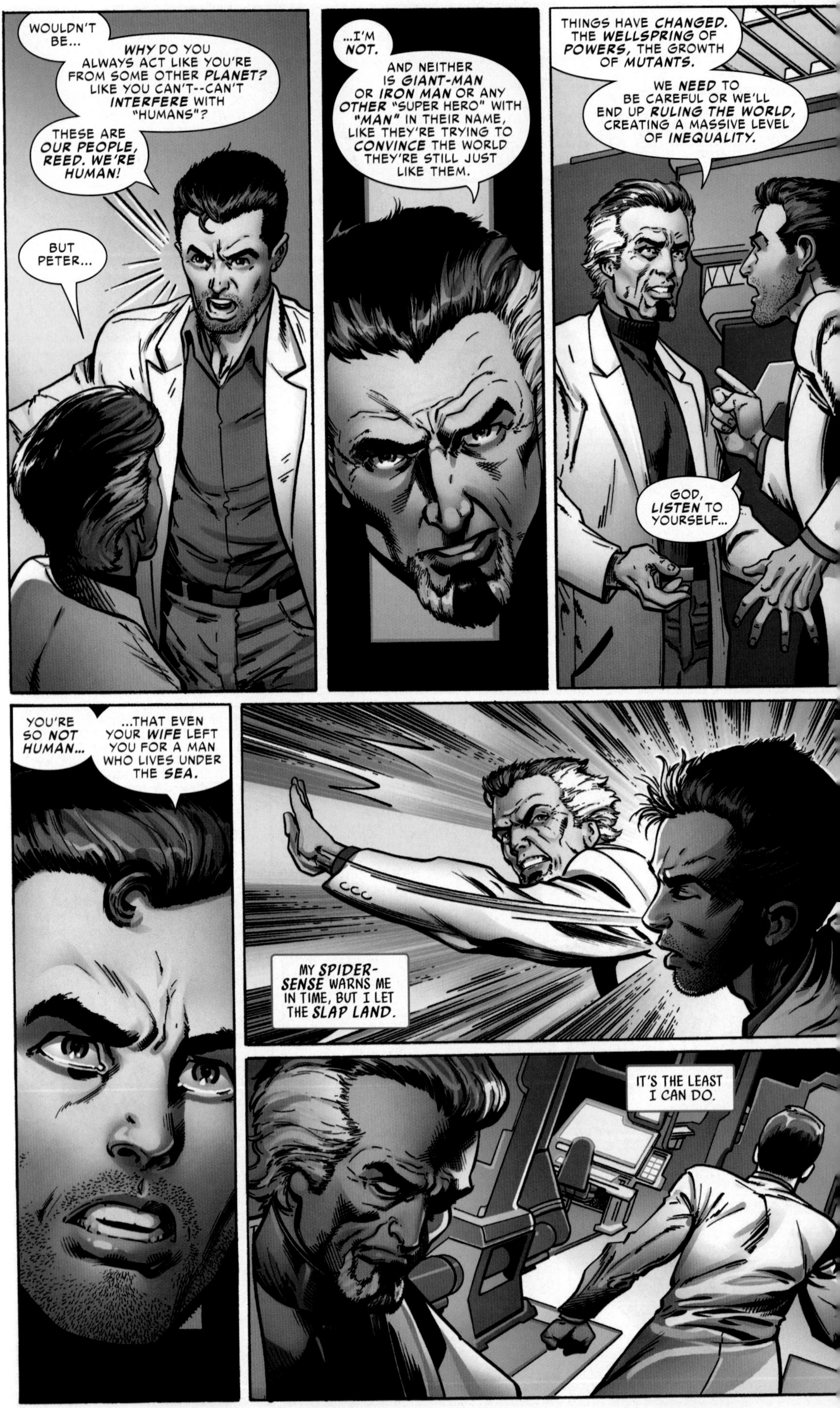
WOULDN'T BE...
WHY DO YOU ALWAYS ACT LIKE YOU'RE FROM SOME OTHER PLANET? LIKE YOU CAN'T--CAN'T INTERFERE WITH "HUMANS"?
THESE ARE OUR PEOPLE, REED. WE'RE HUMAN!
BUT PETER...
...I'M NOT.
AND NEITHER IS GIANT-MAN OR IRON MAN OR ANY OTHER "SUPER HERO" WITH "MAN" IN THEIR NAME, LIKE THEY'RE TRYING TO CONVINCE THE WORLD THEY'RE STILL JUST LIKE THEM.
THINGS HAVE CHANGED. THE WELLSPRING OF POWERS, THE GROWTH OF MUTANTS.
WE NEED TO BE CAREFUL OR WE'LL END UP RULING THE WORLD, CREATING A MASSIVE LEVEL OF INEQUALITY.
GOD, LISTEN TO YOURSELF...
YOU'RE SO NOT HUMAN...
...THAT EVEN YOUR WIFE LEFT YOU FOR A MAN WHO LIVES UNDER THE SEA.
MY SPIDER-SENSE WARNS ME IN TIME, BUT I LET THE SLAP LAND.
IT'S THE LEAST I CAN DO.

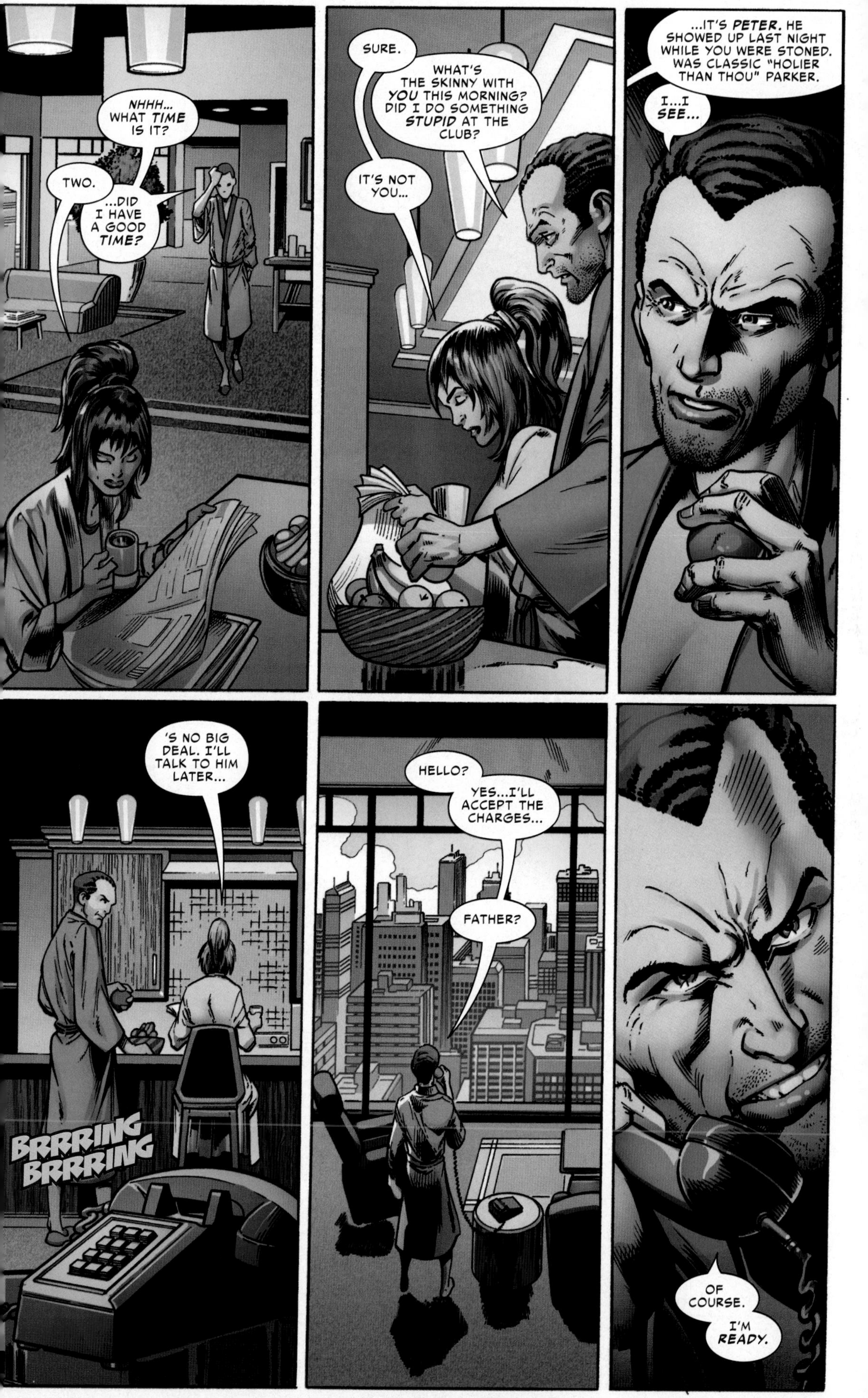
NHHH... WHAT TIME IS IT?
TWO.
...DID I HAVE A GOOD TIME?
SURE.
WHAT'S THE SKINNY WITH YOU THIS MORNING? DID I DO SOMETHING STUPID AT THE CLUB?
IT'S NOT YOU...
...IT'S PETER. HE SHOWED UP LAST NIGHT WHILE YOU WERE STONED. WAS CLASSIC "HOLIER THAN THOU" PARKER.
I...I SEE...
'S NO BIG DEAL. I'LL TALK TO HIM LATER...
BRRRING BRRRING
HELLO?
YES...I'LL ACCEPT THE CHARGES...
FATHER?
OF COURSE.
I'M READY.

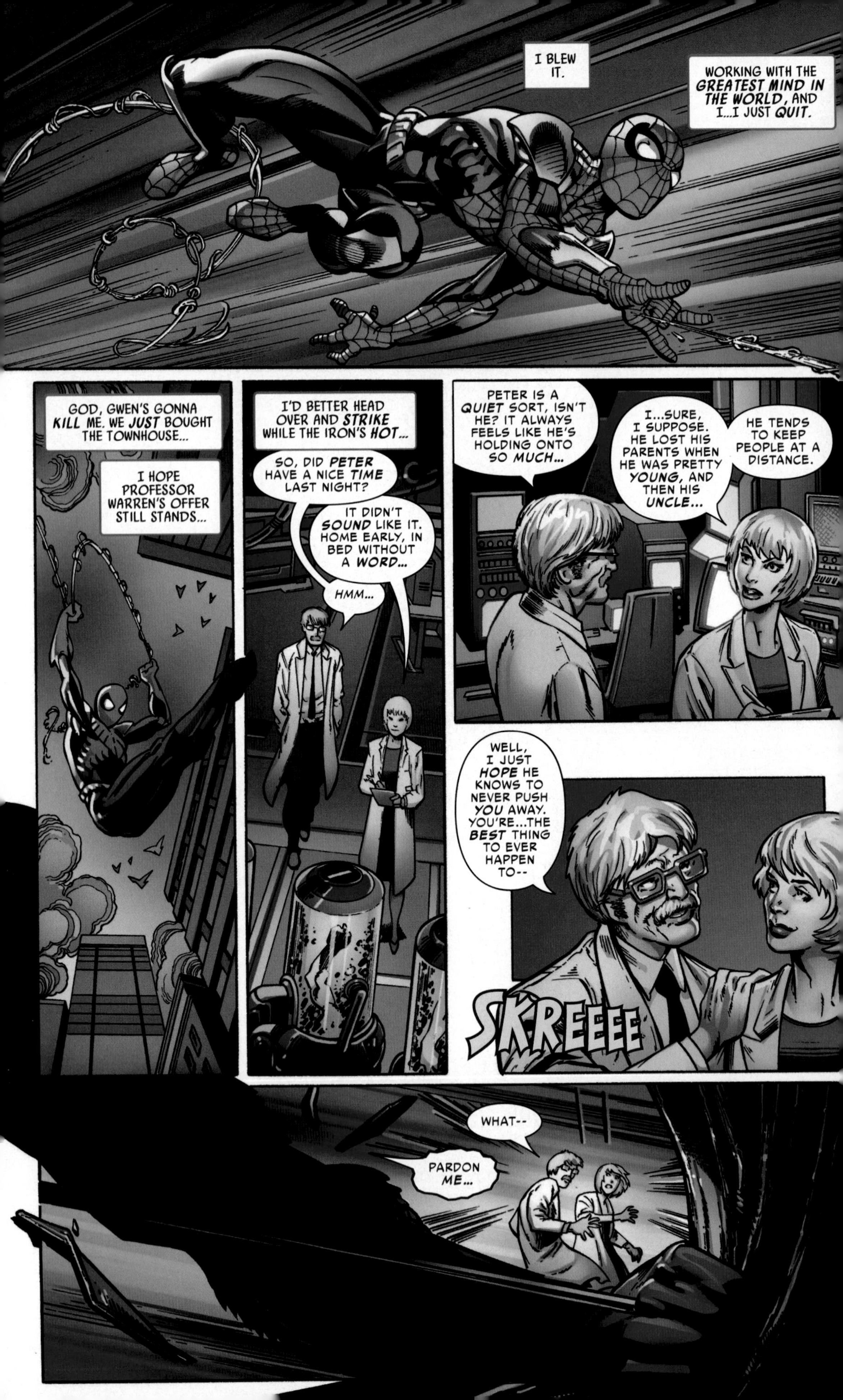
I BLEW IT.
WORKING WITH THE GREATEST MIND IN THE WORLD, AND I...I JUST QUIT.
GOD, GWEN'S GONNA KILL ME. WE JUST BOUGHT THE TOWNHOUSE...
I HOPE PROFESSOR WARREN'S OFFER STILL STANDS...
I'D BETTER HEAD OVER AND STRIKE WHILE THE IRON'S HOT...
SO, DID PETER HAVE A NICE TIME LAST NIGHT?
IT DIDN'T SOUND LIKE IT. HOME EARLY, IN BED WITHOUT A WORD...
HMM...
PETER IS A QUIET SORT, ISN'T HE? IT ALWAYS FEELS LIKE HE'S HOLDING ONTO SO MUCH...
I...SURE, I SUPPOSE. HE LOST HIS PARENTS WHEN HE WAS PRETTY YOUNG, AND THEN HIS UNCLE...
HE TENDS TO KEEP PEOPLE AT A DISTANCE.
WELL, I JUST HOPE HE KNOWS TO NEVER PUSH YOU AWAY. YOU'RE...THE BEST THING TO EVER HAPPEN TO--
SKREEEE
WHAT--
PARDON ME...

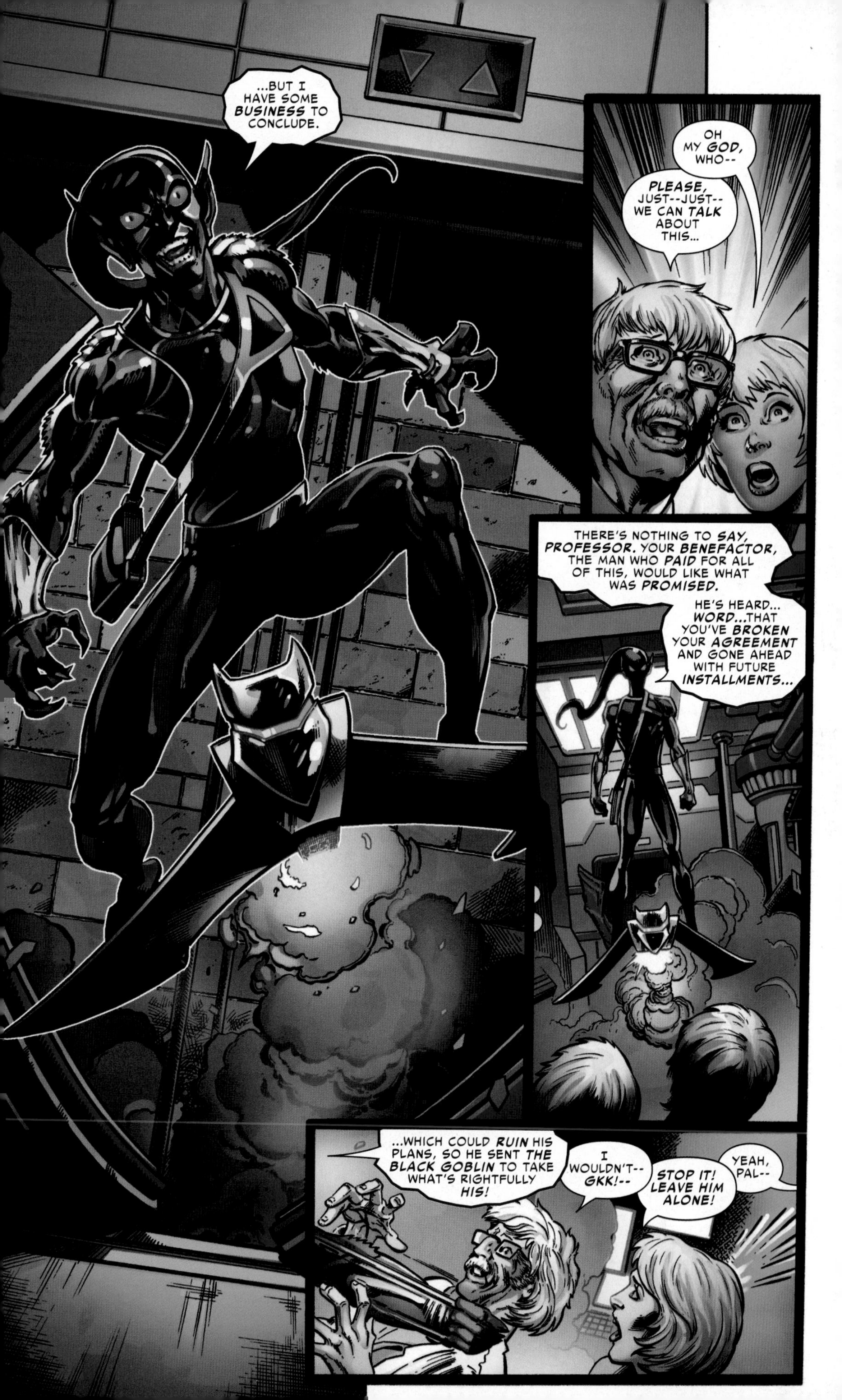
...BUT I HAVE SOME BUSINESS TO CONCLUDE.
OH MY GOD, WHO--
PLEASE, JUST--JUST-- WE CAN TALK ABOUT THIS...
THERE'S NOTHING TO SAY, PROFESSOR. YOUR BENEFACTOR, THE MAN WHO PAID FOR ALL OF THIS, WOULD LIKE WHAT WAS PROMISED.
HE'S HEARD... WORD...THAT YOU'VE BROKEN YOUR AGREEMENT AND GONE AHEAD WITH FUTURE INSTALLMENTS...
...WHICH COULD RUIN HIS PLANS, SO HE SENT THE BLACK GOBLIN TO TAKE WHAT'S RIGHTFULLY HIS!
I WOULDN'T--GKK!--
STOP IT! LEAVE HIM ALONE!
YEAH, PAL--

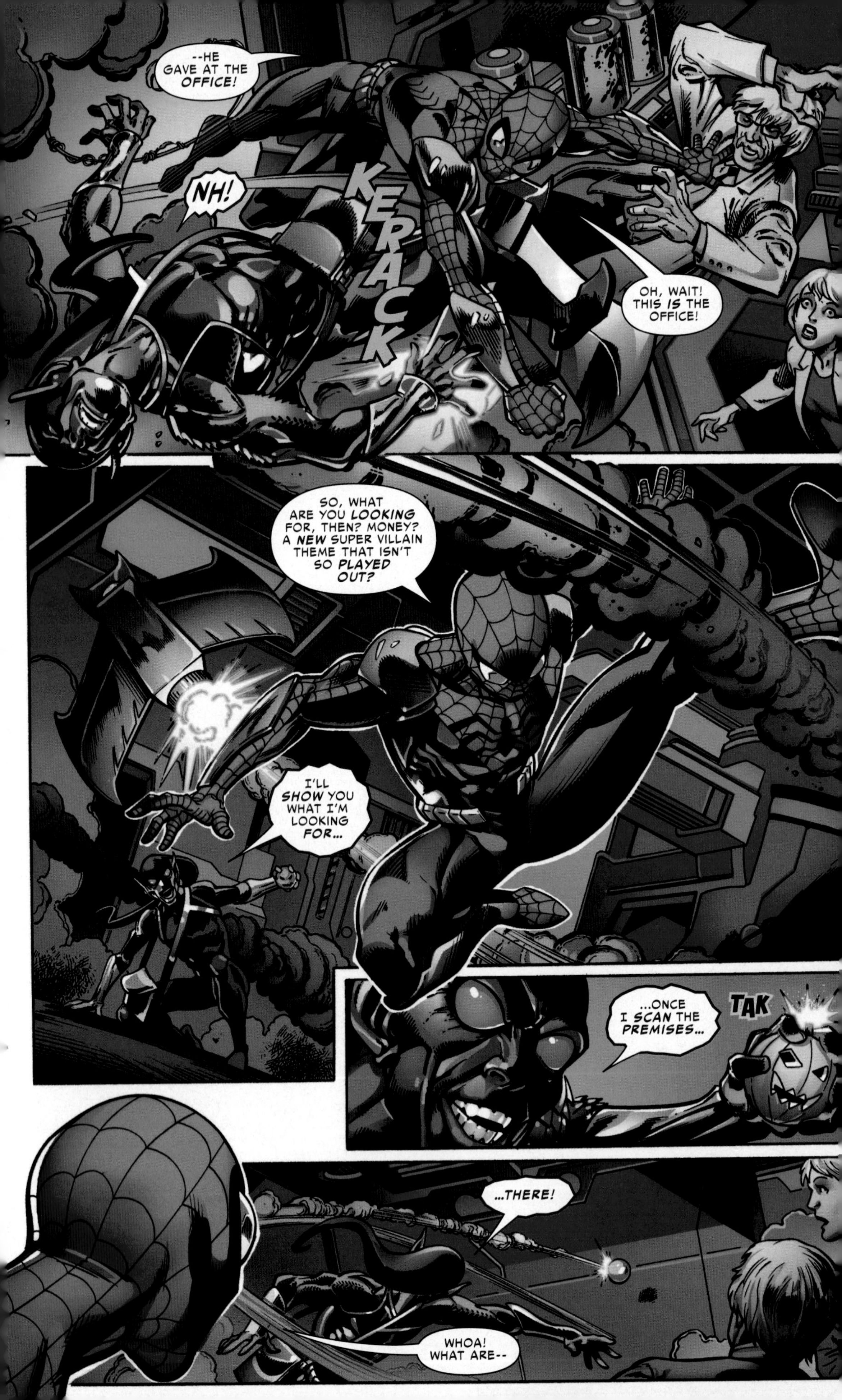
--HE GAVE AT THE OFFICE!
NH!
KERACK
OH, WAIT! THIS IS THE OFFICE!
SO, WHAT ARE YOU LOOKING FOR, THEN? MONEY? A NEW SUPER VILLAIN THEME THAT ISN'T SO PLAYED OUT?
I'LL SHOW YOU WHAT I'M LOOKING FOR...
...ONCE I SCAN THE PREMISES...
TAK
...THERE!
WHOA! WHAT ARE--

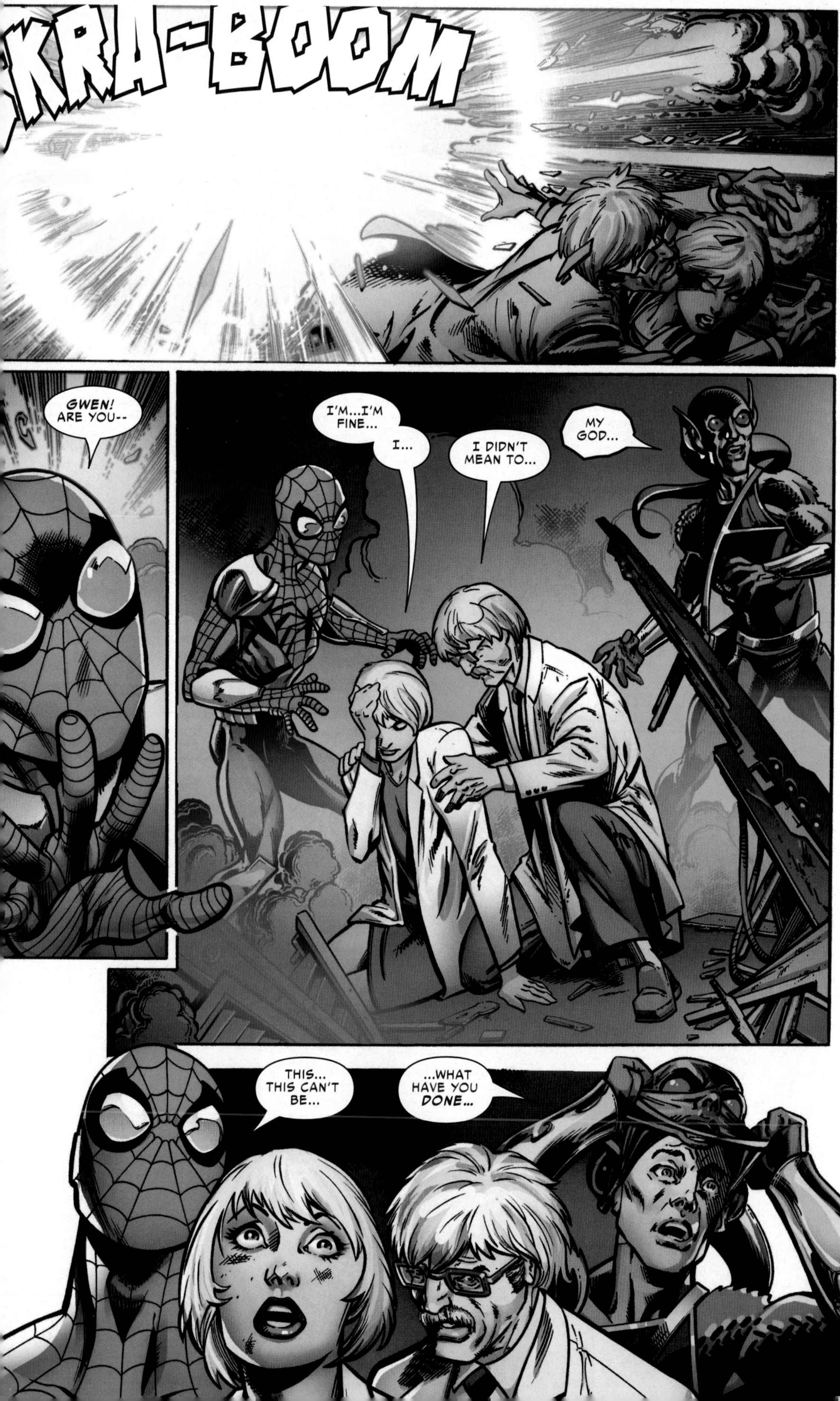
KRA-BOOM
GWEN! ARE YOU--
I'M...I'M FINE...
I...
I DIDN'T MEAN TO...
MY GOD...
THIS... THIS CAN'T BE...
...WHAT HAVE YOU DONE...

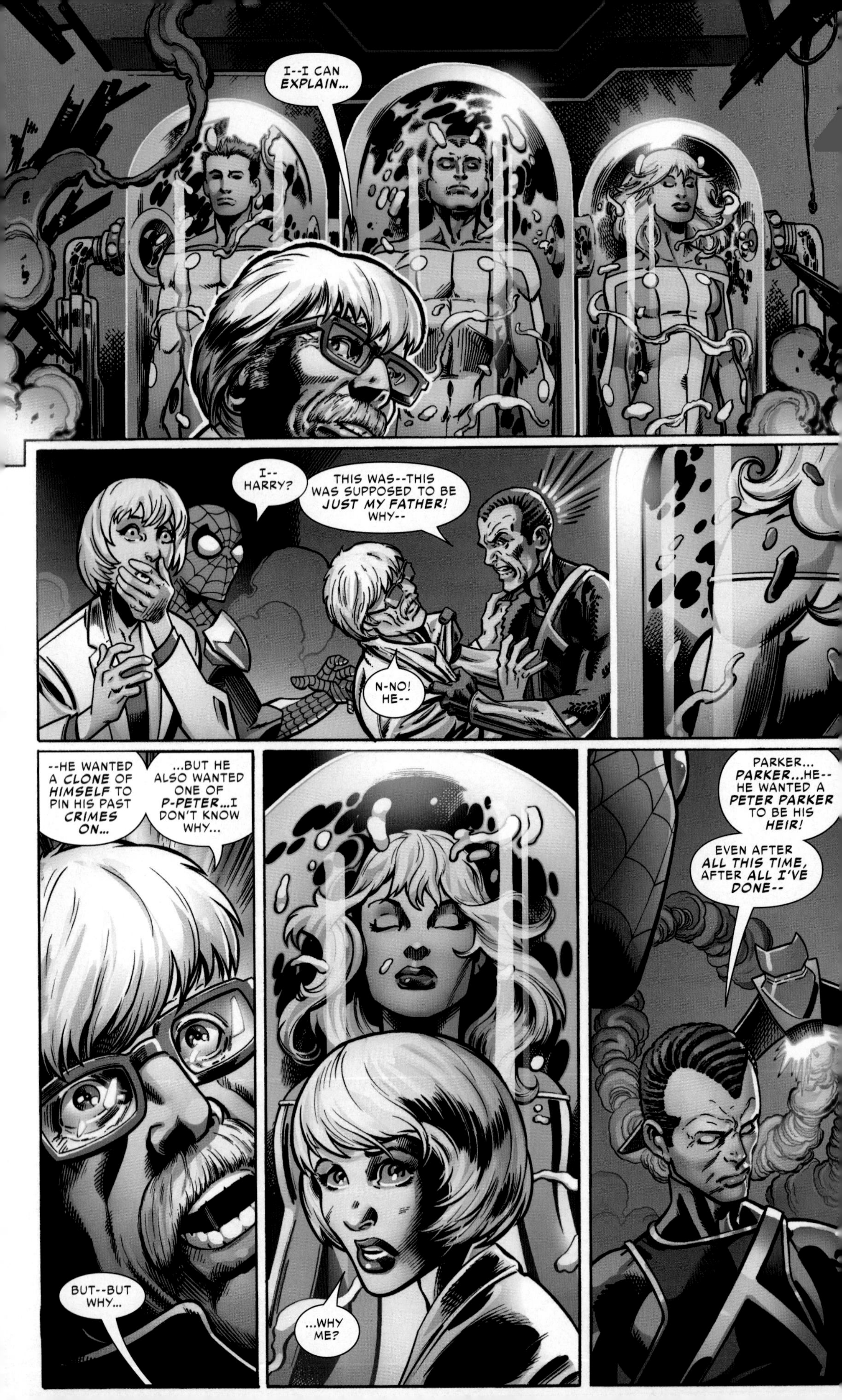
I--I CAN EXPLAIN...
I-- HARRY?
THIS WAS--THIS WAS SUPPOSED TO BE JUST MY FATHER! WHY--
N-NO! HE--
--HE WANTED A CLONE OF HIMSELF TO PIN HIS PAST CRIMES ON...
...BUT HE ALSO WANTED ONE OF P-PETER...I DON'T KNOW WHY...
BUT--BUT WHY...
...WHY ME?
PARKER... PARKER...HE-- HE WANTED A PETER PARKER TO BE HIS HEIR!
EVEN AFTER ALL THIS TIME, AFTER ALL I'VE DONE--

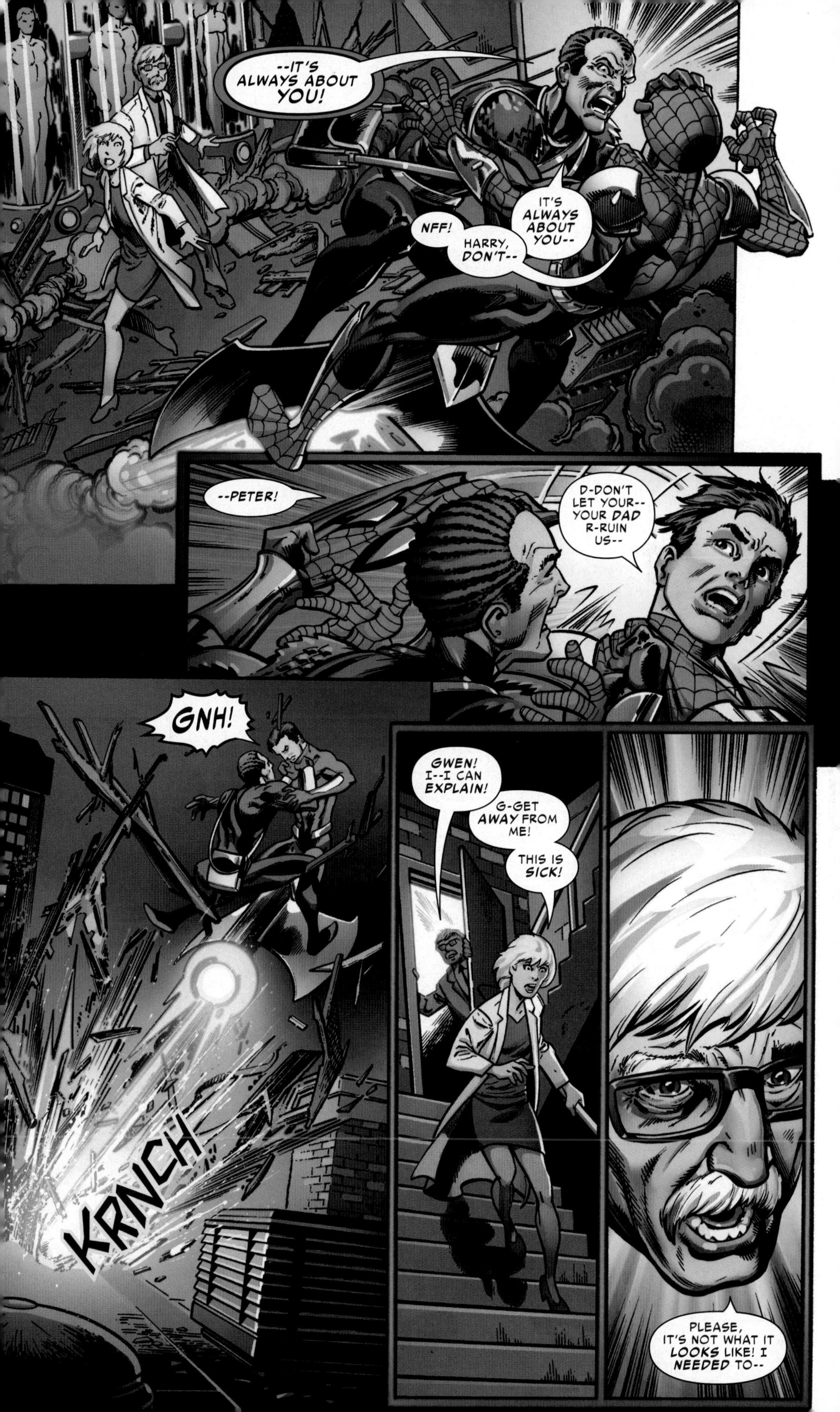

--IT'S ALWAYS ABOUT YOU!
IT'S ALWAYS ABOUT YOU--
NFF!
HARRY, DON'T--
--PETER!
D-DON'T LET YOUR-- YOUR DAD R-RUIN US--
GNH!
KRNCH
GWEN! I--I CAN EXPLAIN!
G-GET AWAY FROM ME!
THIS IS SICK!
PLEASE, IT'S NOT WHAT IT LOOKS LIKE! I NEEDED TO--

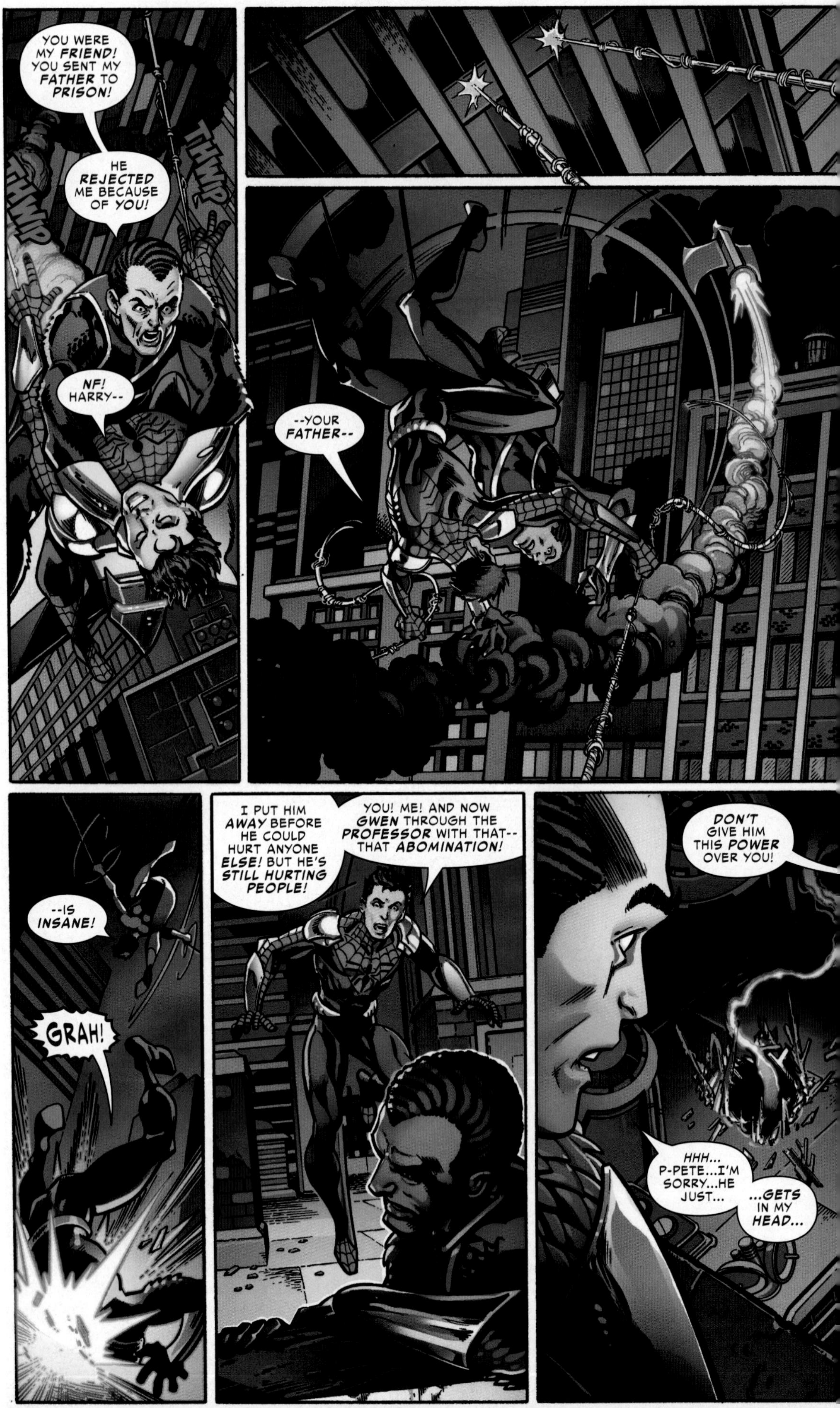
YOU WERE MY FRIEND! YOU SENT MY FATHER TO PRISON!
HE REJECTED ME BECAUSE OF YOU!
THWIP
THWIP
NF! HARRY--
--YOUR FATHER--
--IS INSANE!
GRAH!
I PUT HIM AWAY BEFORE HE COULD HURT ANYONE ELSE! BUT HE'S STILL HURTING PEOPLE!
YOU! ME! AND NOW GWEN THROUGH THE PROFESSOR WITH THAT--THAT ABOMINATION!
DON'T GIVE HIM THIS POWER OVER YOU!
HHH... P-PETE...I'M SORRY...HE JUST...
...GETS IN MY HEAD...

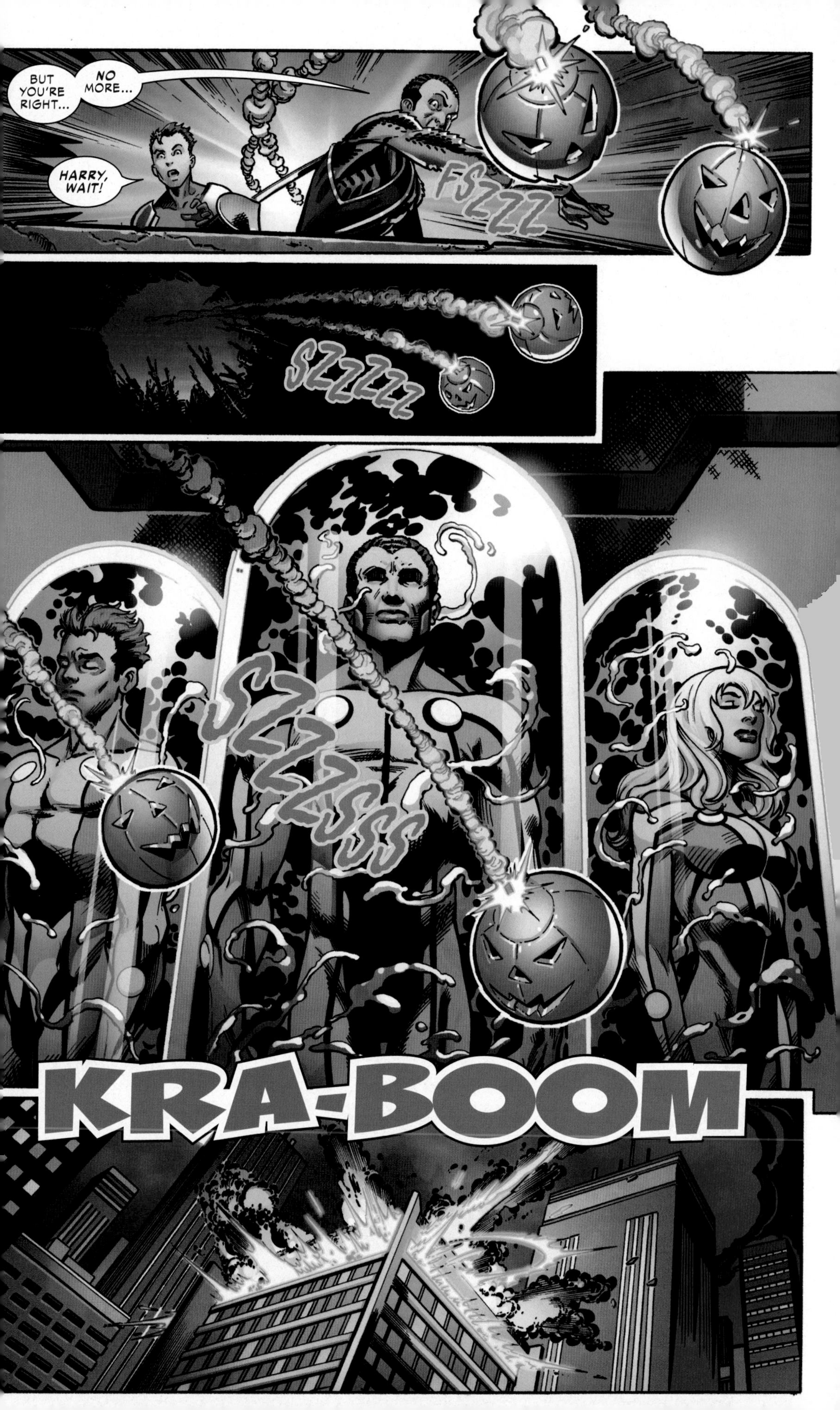

BUT YOU'RE RIGHT...
NO MORE...
HARRY, WAIT!
FSZZZ
SZZZZZZ
SZZZSSS
KRA-BOOM

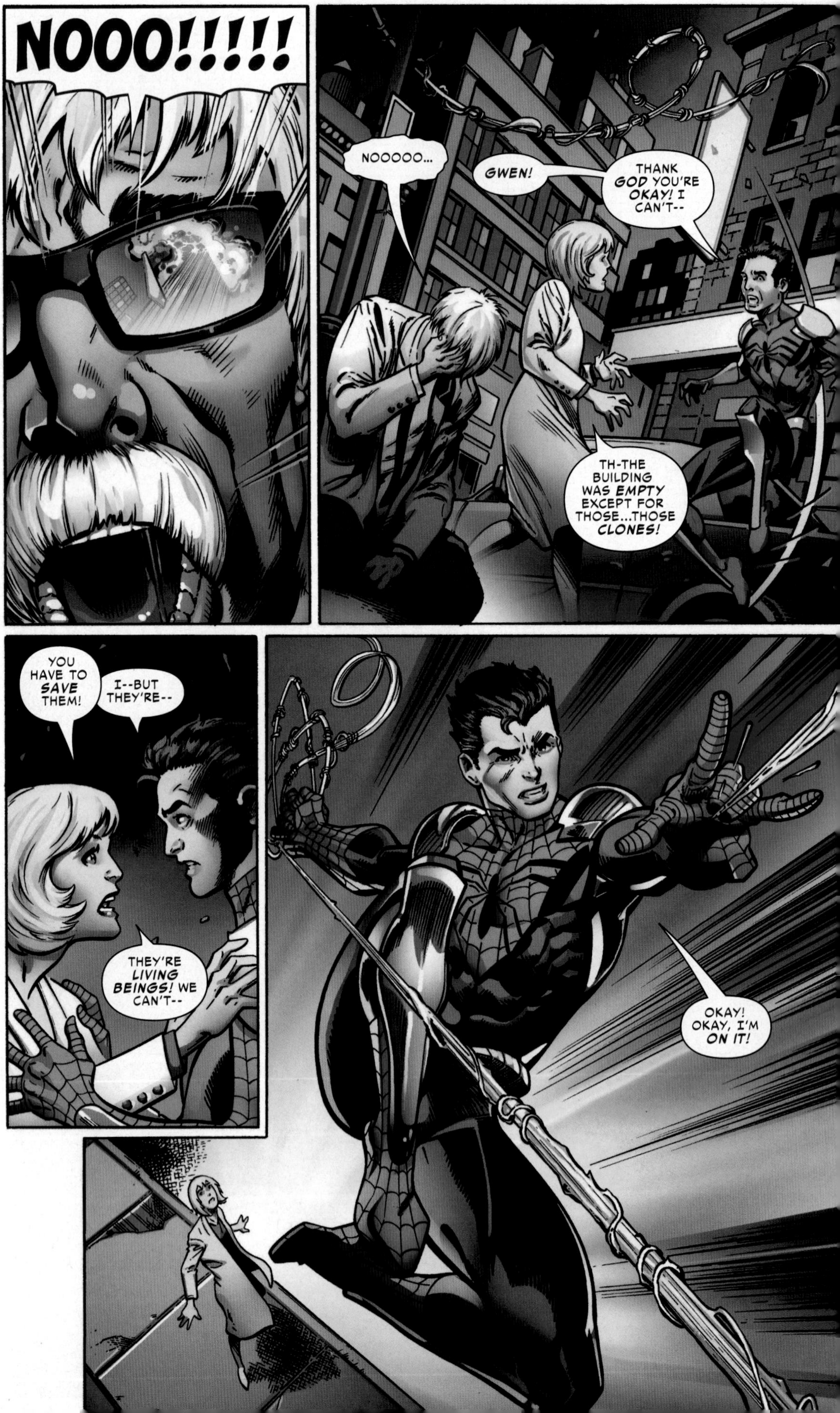
NOOO!!!!!
NOOOOO...
GWEN!
THANK GOD YOU'RE OKAY! I CAN'T--
TH-THE BUILDING WAS EMPTY EXCEPT FOR THOSE...THOSE CLONES!
YOU HAVE TO SAVE THEM!
I--BUT THEY'RE--
THEY'RE LIVING BEINGS! WE CAN'T--
OKAY! OKAY, I'M ON IT!

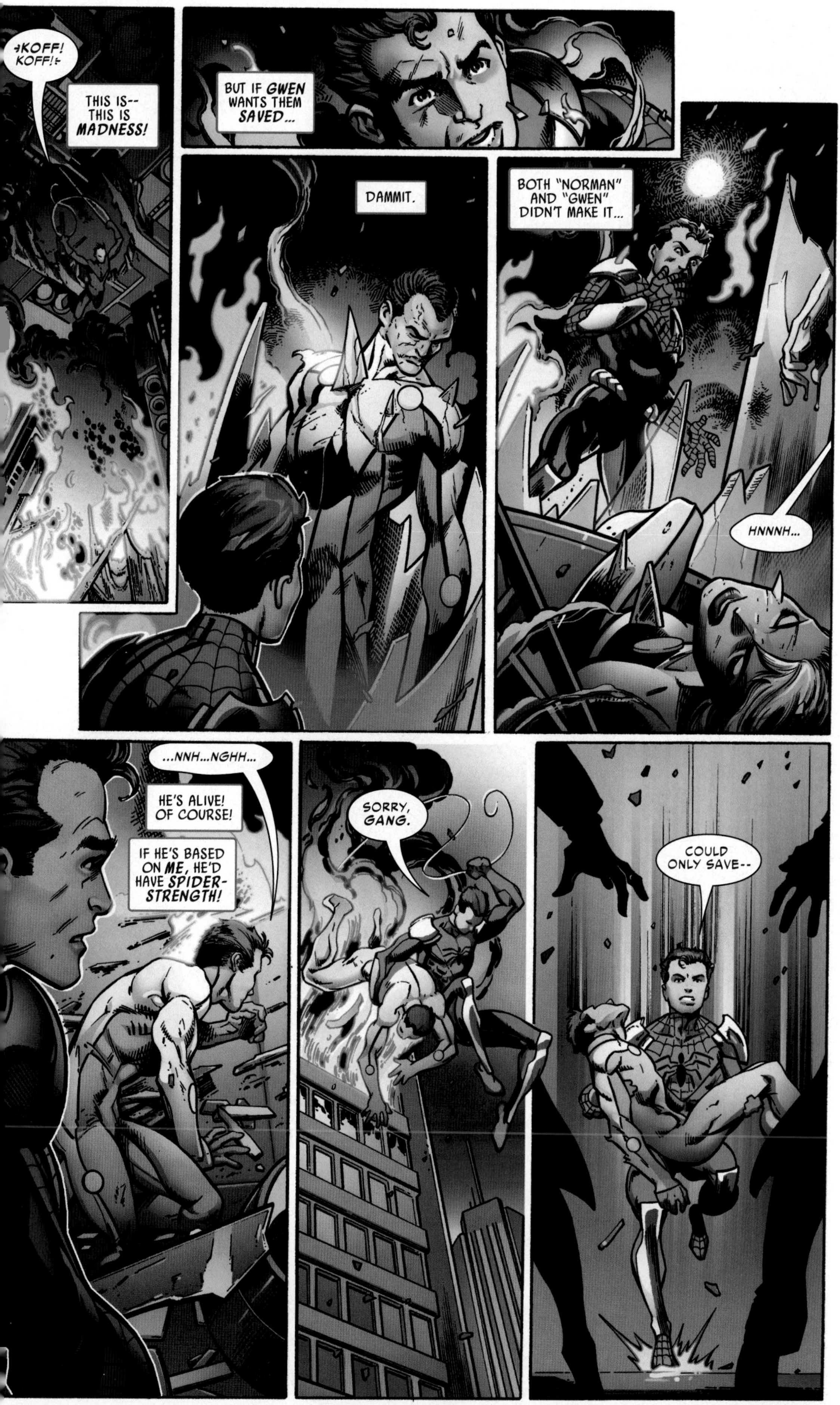

≁KOFF! KOFF!≁
THIS IS-- THIS IS MADNESS!
BUT IF GWEN WANTS THEM SAVED...
DAMMIT.
BOTH "NORMAN" AND "GWEN" DIDN'T MAKE IT...
HNNNH...
...NNH...NGHH...
HE'S ALIVE! OF COURSE!
IF HE'S BASED ON ME, HE'D HAVE SPIDER-STRENGTH!
SORRY, GANG.
COULD ONLY SAVE--

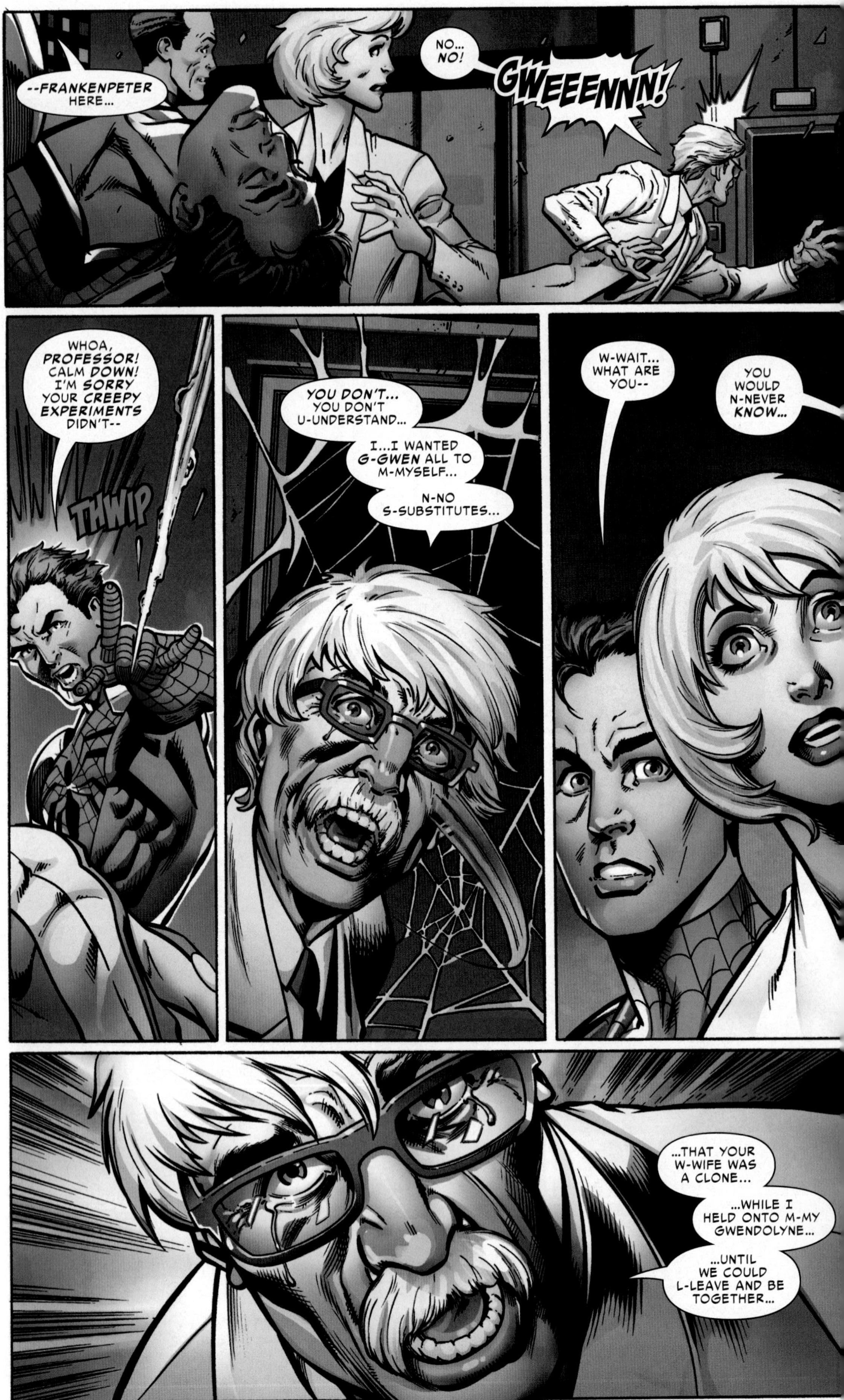
--FRANKENPETER HERE...
NO... NO!
GWEEENNN!
WHOA, PROFESSOR! CALM DOWN! I'M SORRY YOUR CREEPY EXPERIMENTS DIDN'T--
THWIP
YOU DON'T... YOU DON'T U-UNDERSTAND...
I...I WANTED G-GWEN ALL TO M-MYSELF...
N-NO S-SUBSTITUTES...
W-WAIT... WHAT ARE YOU--
YOU WOULD N-NEVER KNOW...
...THAT YOUR W-WIFE WAS A CLONE...
...WHILE I HELD ONTO M-MY GWENDOLYNE...
...UNTIL WE COULD L-LEAVE AND BE TOGETHER...

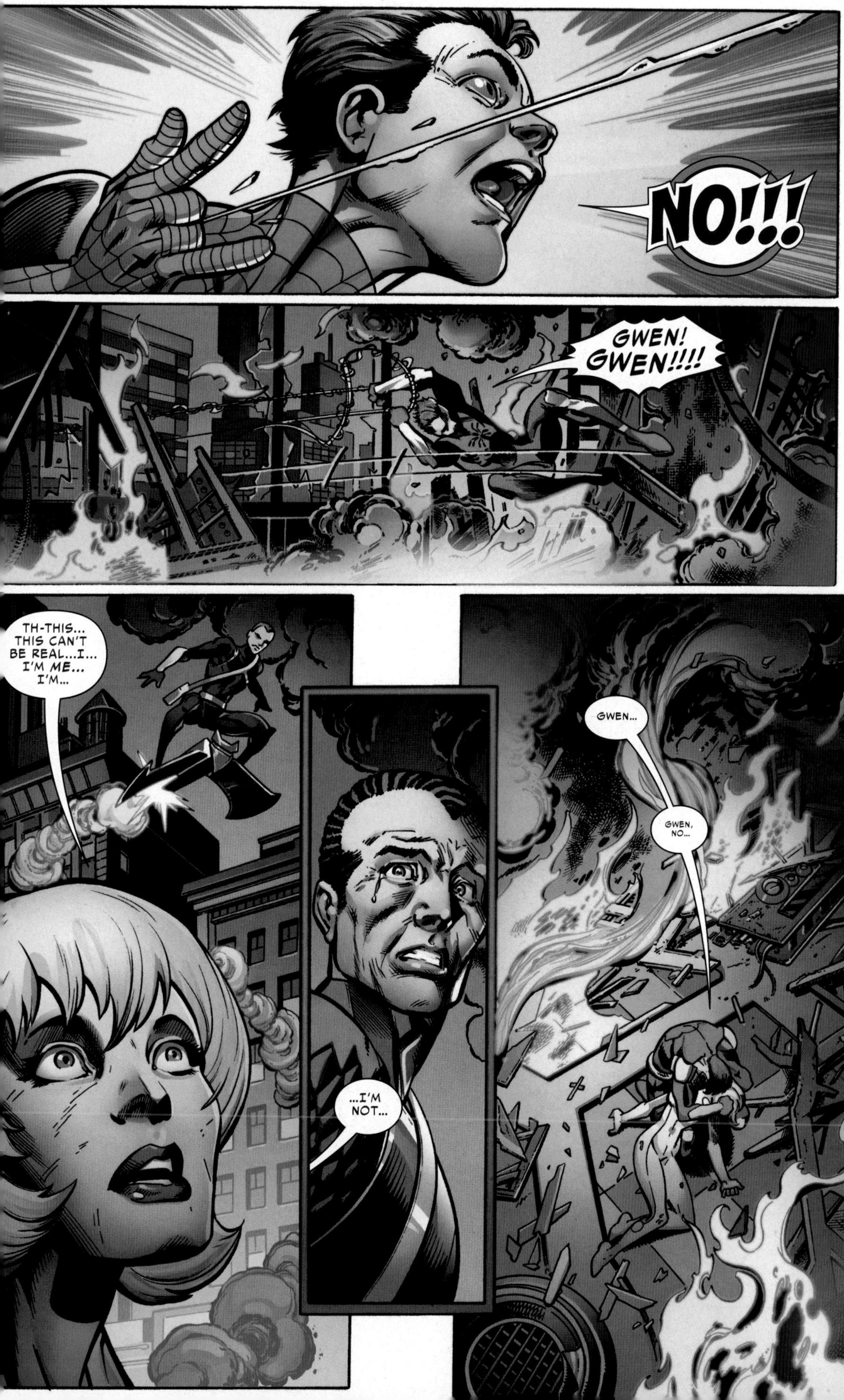
NO!!!
GWEN! GWEN!!!!
TH-THIS... THIS CAN'T BE REAL...I... I'M ME... I'M...
...I'M NOT...
GWEN...
GWEN, NO...

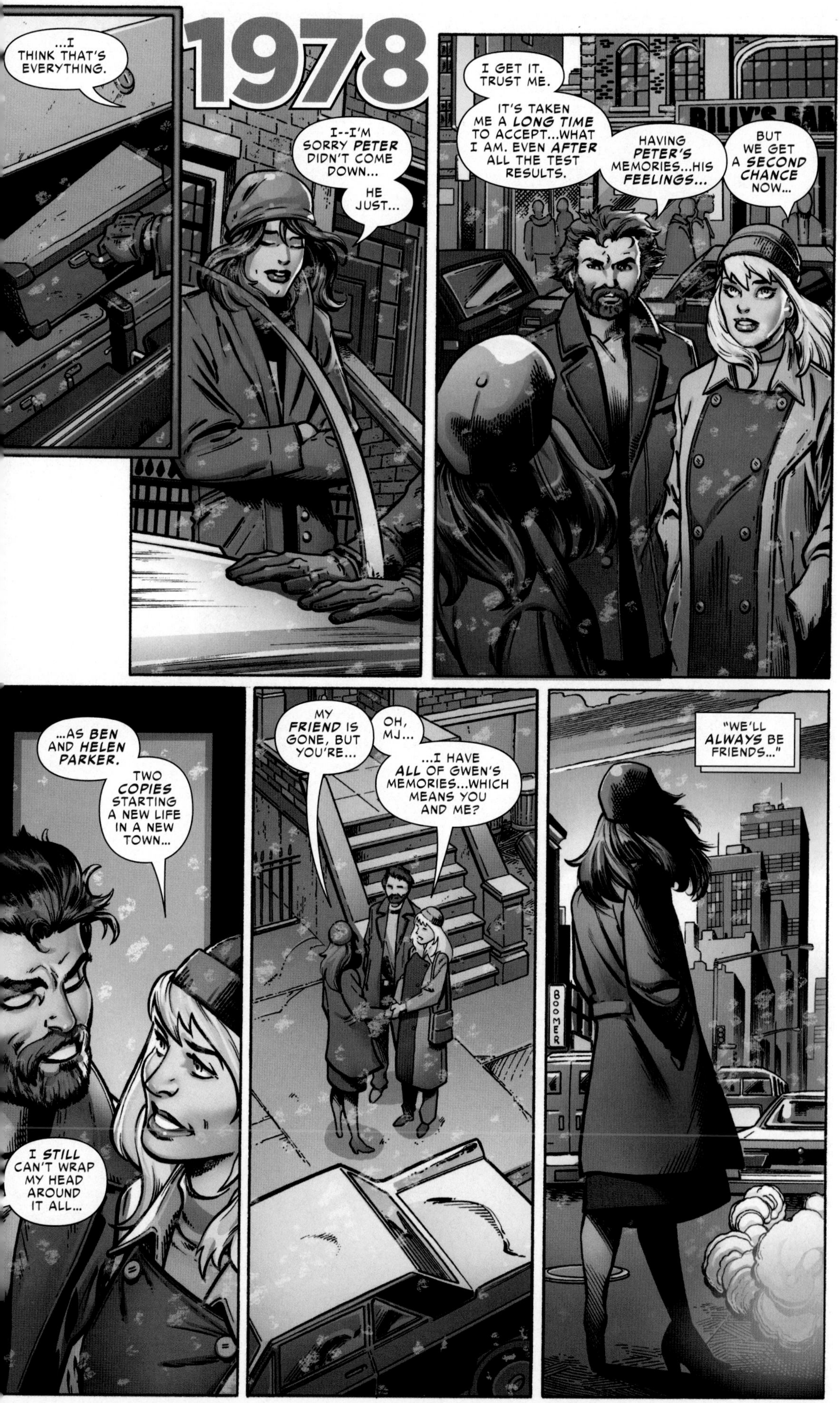
1978
...I THINK THAT'S EVERYTHING.
I--I'M SORRY PETER DIDN'T COME DOWN...
HE JUST...
I GET IT. TRUST ME.
IT'S TAKEN ME A LONG TIME TO ACCEPT...WHAT I AM. EVEN AFTER ALL THE TEST RESULTS.
HAVING PETER'S MEMORIES...HIS FEELINGS...
BUT WE GET A SECOND CHANCE NOW...
...AS BEN AND HELEN PARKER.
TWO COPIES STARTING A NEW LIFE IN A NEW TOWN...
I STILL CAN'T WRAP MY HEAD AROUND IT ALL...
MY FRIEND IS GONE, BUT YOU'RE...
OH, MJ...
...I HAVE ALL OF GWEN'S MEMORIES...WHICH MEANS YOU AND ME?
"WE'LL ALWAYS BE FRIENDS..."
BOOMER

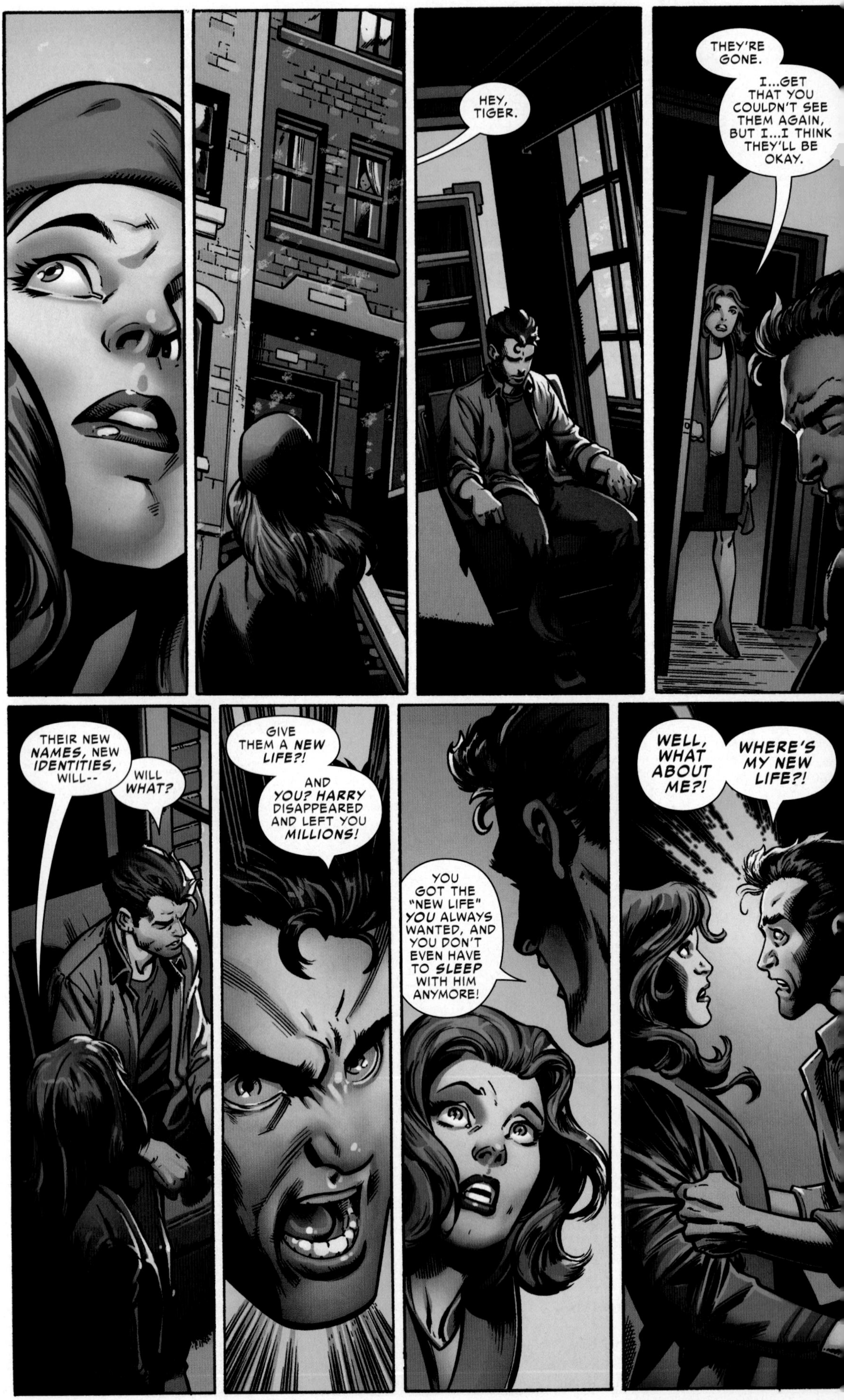
HEY, TIGER.
THEY'RE GONE.
I...GET THAT YOU COULDN'T SEE THEM AGAIN, BUT I...I THINK THEY'LL BE OKAY.
THEIR NEW NAMES, NEW IDENTITIES, WILL--
WILL WHAT?
GIVE THEM A NEW LIFE?!
AND YOU? HARRY DISAPPEARED AND LEFT YOU MILLIONS!
YOU GOT THE "NEW LIFE" YOU ALWAYS WANTED, AND YOU DON'T EVEN HAVE TO SLEEP WITH HIM ANYMORE!
WELL, WHAT ABOUT ME?!
WHERE'S MY NEW LIFE?!

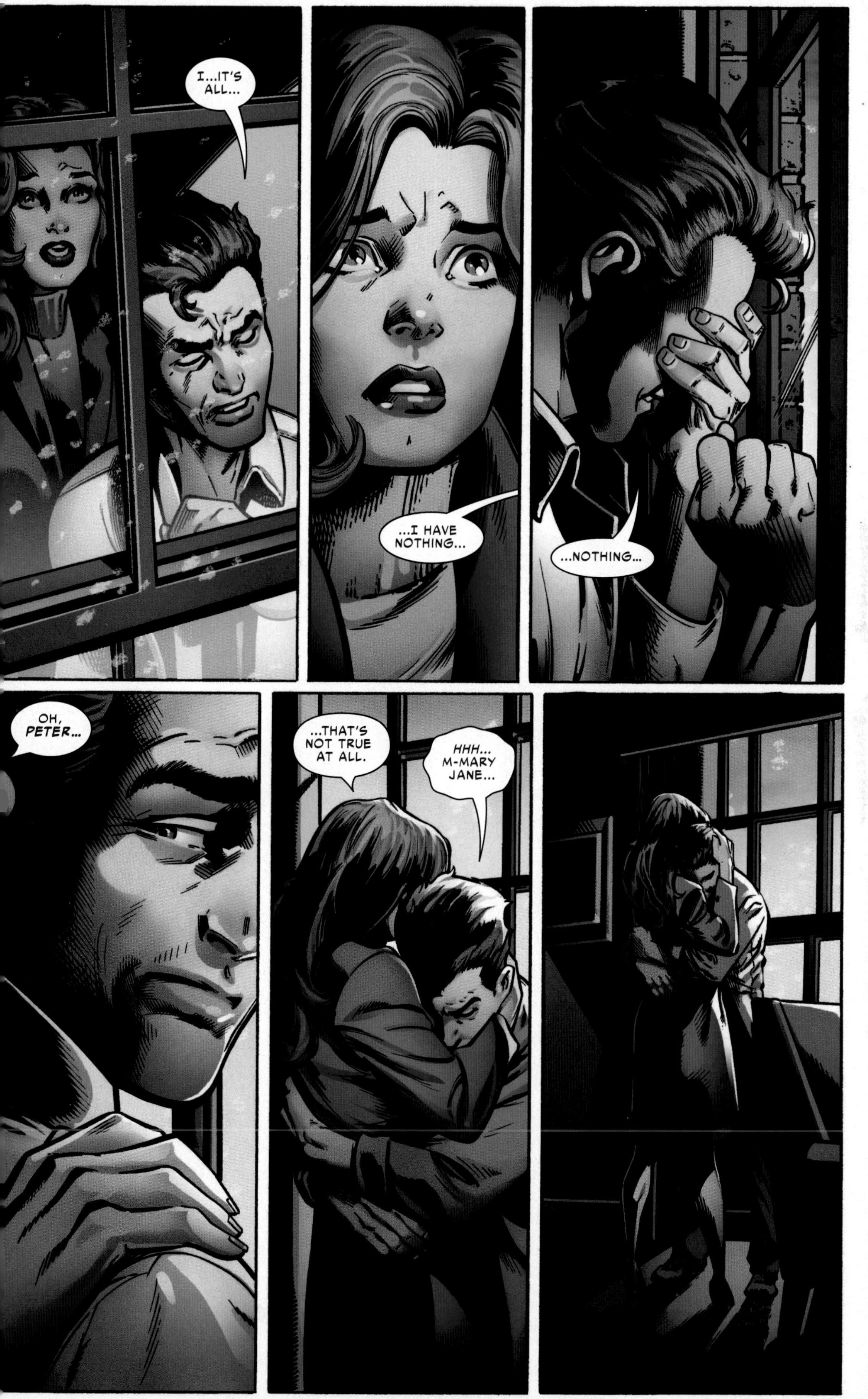
I...IT'S ALL...
...I HAVE NOTHING...
...NOTHING...
OH, PETER...
...THAT'S NOT TRUE AT ALL.
HHH... M-MARY JANE...

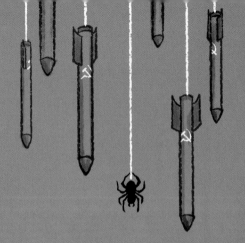

SPIDER-MAN
Life Story **3** The '80s

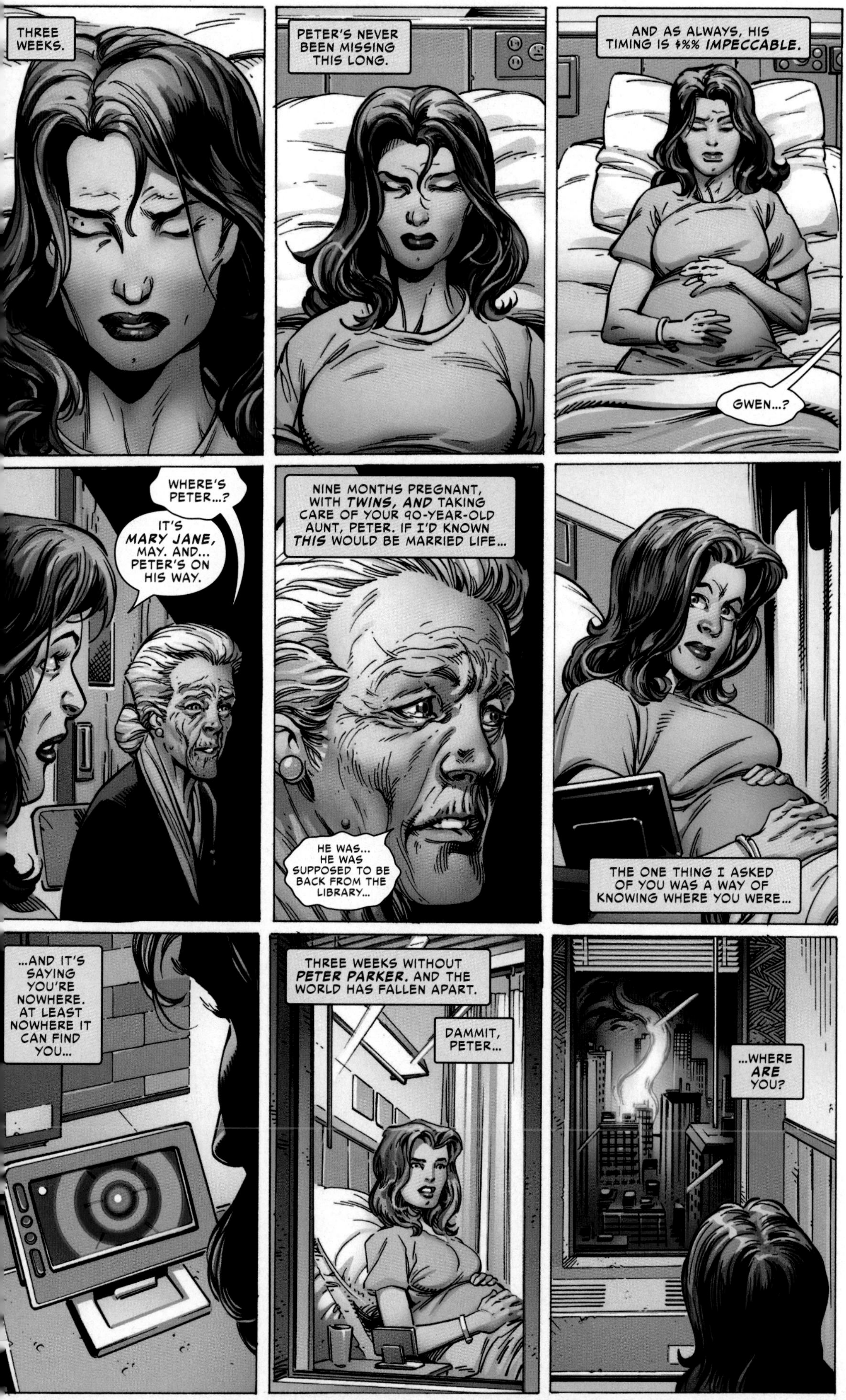
THREE WEEKS.
PETER'S NEVER BEEN MISSING THIS LONG.
AND AS ALWAYS, HIS TIMING IS $%% IMPECCABLE.
GWEN...?
WHERE'S PETER...?
IT'S MARY JANE, MAY. AND... PETER'S ON HIS WAY.
NINE MONTHS PREGNANT, WITH TWINS, AND TAKING CARE OF YOUR 90-YEAR-OLD AUNT, PETER. IF I'D KNOWN THIS WOULD BE MARRIED LIFE...
HE WAS... HE WAS SUPPOSED TO BE BACK FROM THE LIBRARY...
THE ONE THING I ASKED OF YOU WAS A WAY OF KNOWING WHERE YOU WERE...
...AND IT'S SAYING YOU'RE NOWHERE. AT LEAST NOWHERE IT CAN FIND YOU...
THREE WEEKS WITHOUT PETER PARKER. AND THE WORLD HAS FALLEN APART.
DAMMIT, PETER...
...WHERE ARE YOU?

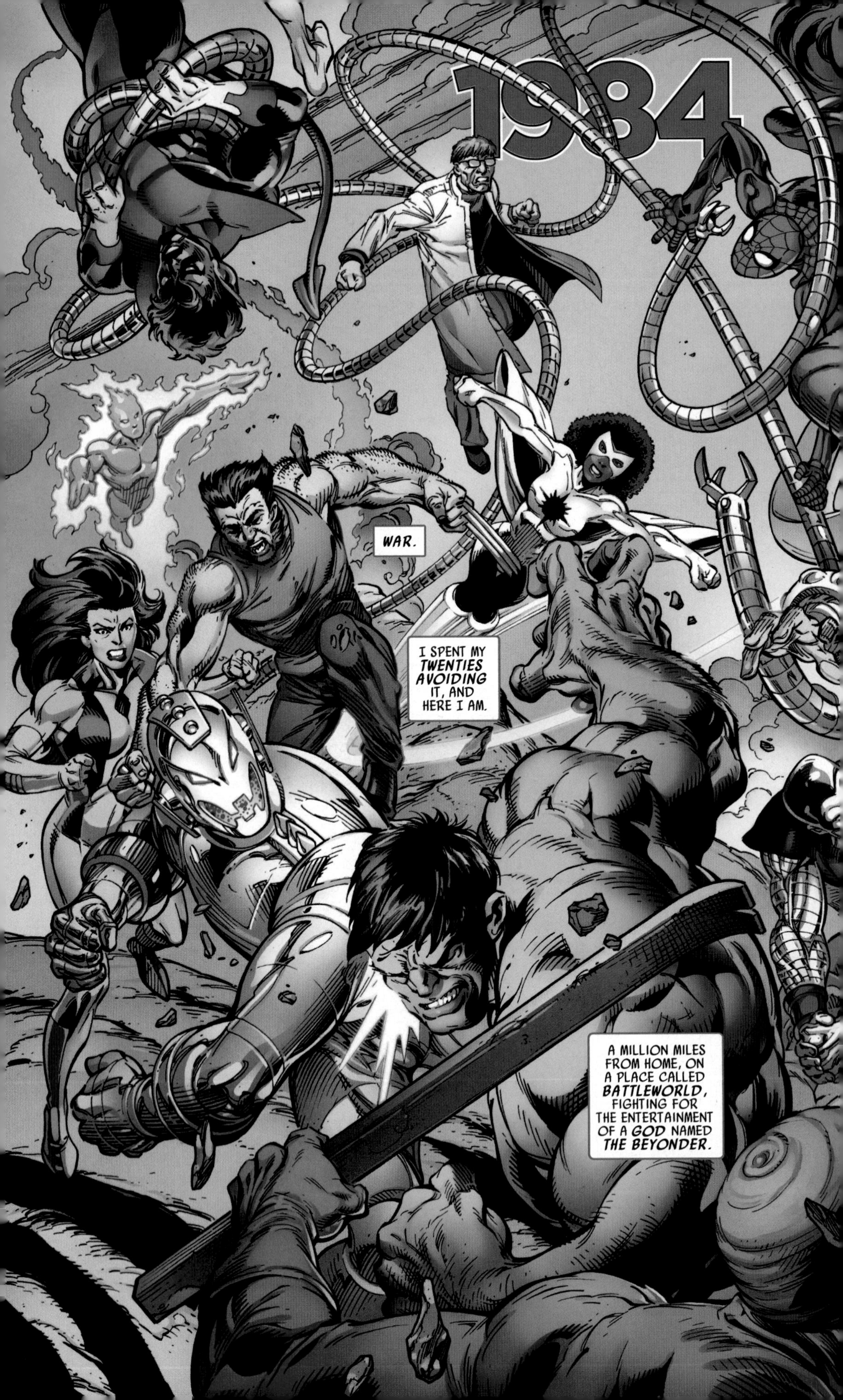
1984
WAR.
I SPENT MY TWENTIES AVOIDING IT, AND HERE I AM.
A MILLION MILES FROM HOME, ON A PLACE CALLED BATTLEWORLD, FIGHTING FOR THE ENTERTAINMENT OF A GOD NAMED THE BEYONDER.

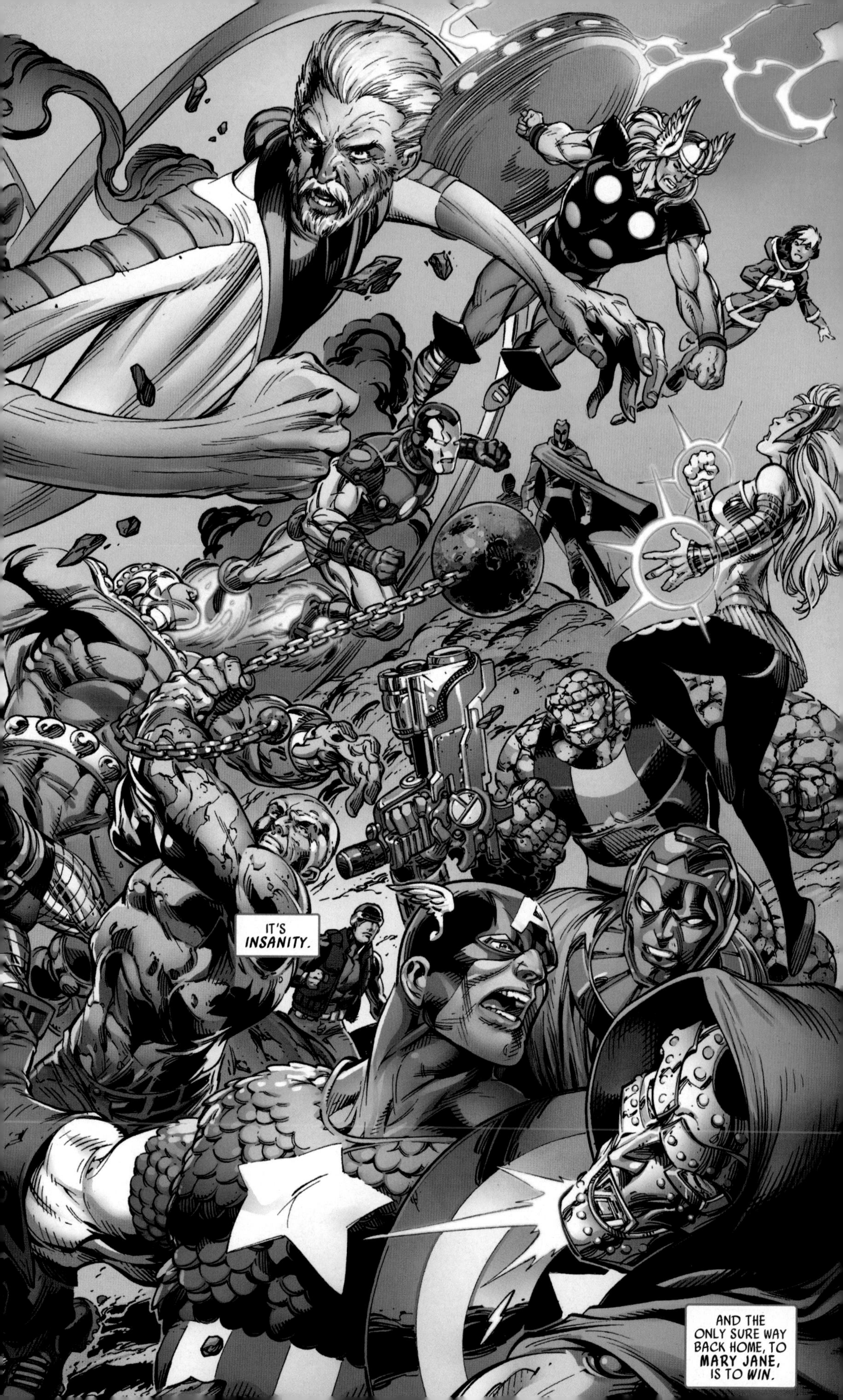
IT'S INSANITY.
AND THE ONLY SURE WAY BACK HOME, TO MARY JANE, IS TO WIN.

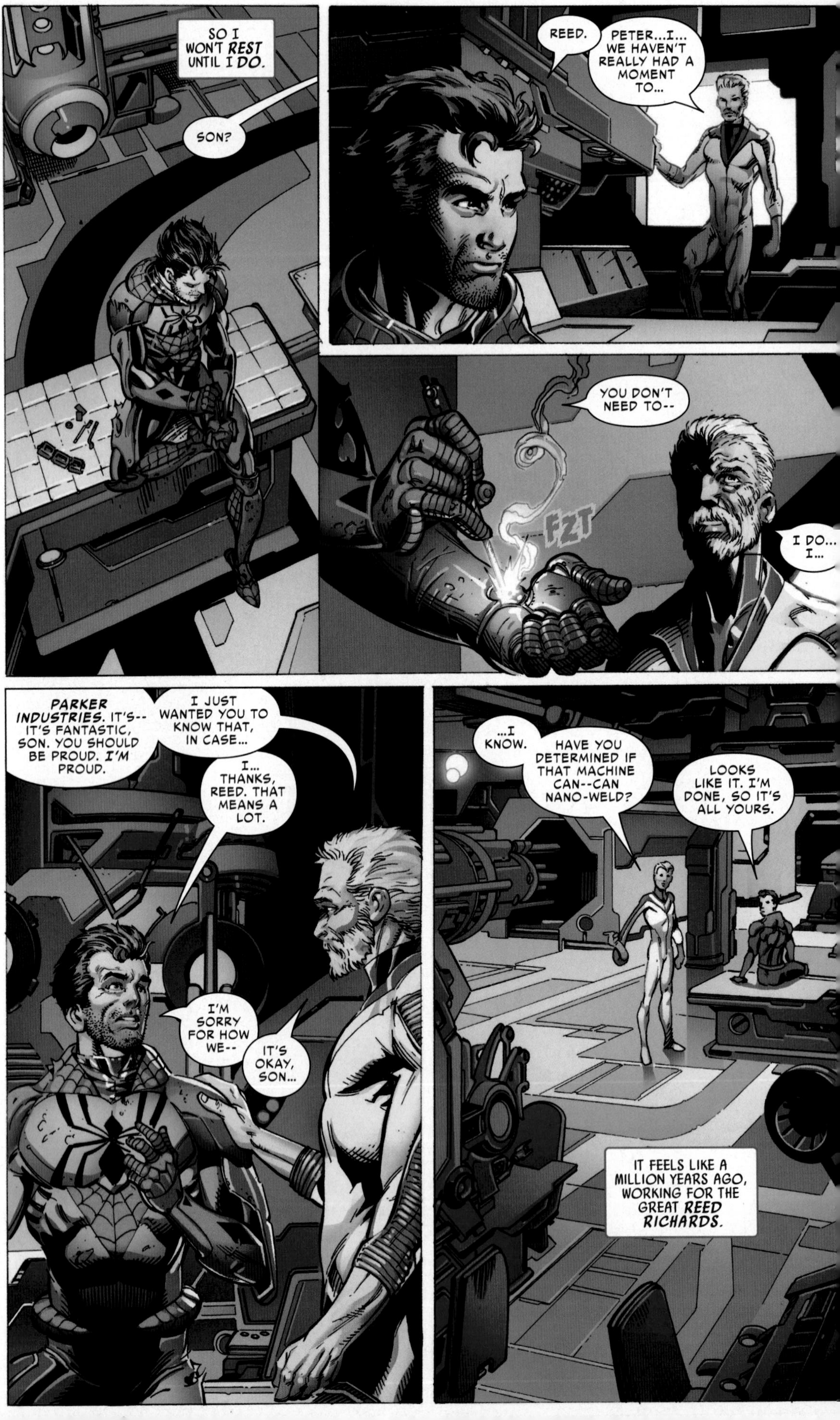

SO I WON'T REST UNTIL I DO.
SON?
REED.
PETER...I... WE HAVEN'T REALLY HAD A MOMENT TO...
YOU DON'T NEED TO--
FZT
I DO... I...
PARKER INDUSTRIES. IT'S--IT'S FANTASTIC, SON. YOU SHOULD BE PROUD. I'M PROUD.
I JUST WANTED YOU TO KNOW THAT, IN CASE...
I... THANKS, REED. THAT MEANS A LOT.
I'M SORRY FOR HOW WE--
IT'S OKAY, SON...
...I KNOW.
HAVE YOU DETERMINED IF THAT MACHINE CAN--CAN NANO-WELD?
LOOKS LIKE IT. I'M DONE, SO IT'S ALL YOURS.
IT FEELS LIKE A MILLION YEARS AGO, WORKING FOR THE GREAT REED RICHARDS.

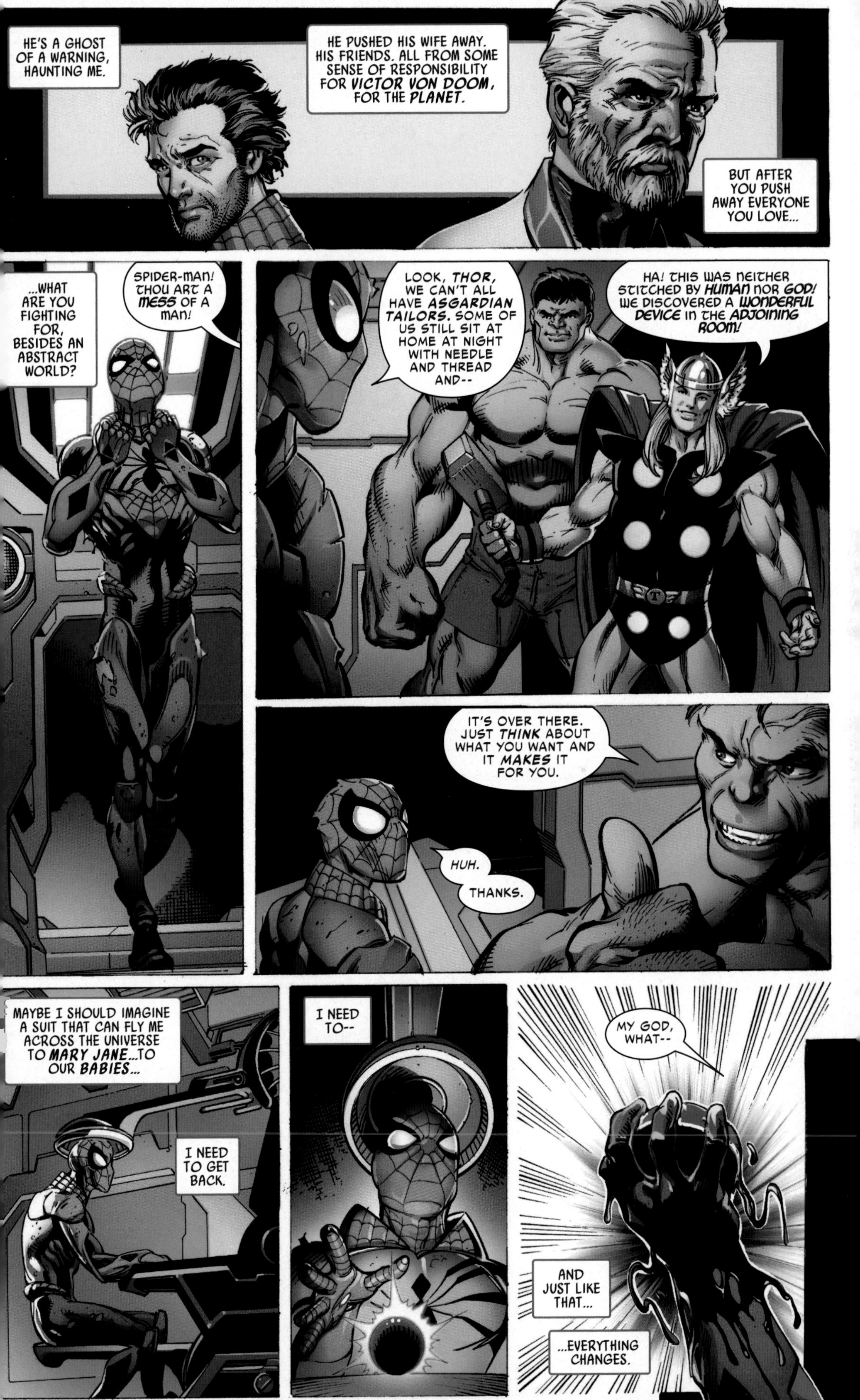
HE'S A GHOST OF A WARNING, HAUNTING ME.
HE PUSHED HIS WIFE AWAY. HIS FRIENDS. ALL FROM SOME SENSE OF RESPONSIBILITY FOR VICTOR VON DOOM, FOR THE PLANET.
BUT AFTER YOU PUSH AWAY EVERYONE YOU LOVE...
...WHAT ARE YOU FIGHTING FOR, BESIDES AN ABSTRACT WORLD?
SPIDER-MAN! THOU ART A MESS OF A MAN!
LOOK, THOR, WE CAN'T ALL HAVE ASGARDIAN TAILORS. SOME OF US STILL SIT AT HOME AT NIGHT WITH NEEDLE AND THREAD AND--
HA! THIS WAS NEITHER STITCHED BY HUMAN NOR GOD! WE DISCOVERED A WONDERFUL DEVICE IN THE ADJOINING ROOM!
IT'S OVER THERE. JUST THINK ABOUT WHAT YOU WANT AND IT MAKES IT FOR YOU.
HUH.
THANKS.
MAYBE I SHOULD IMAGINE A SUIT THAT CAN FLY ME ACROSS THE UNIVERSE TO MARY JANE...TO OUR BABIES...
I NEED TO GET BACK.
I NEED TO--
MY GOD, WHAT--
AND JUST LIKE THAT...
...EVERYTHING CHANGES.

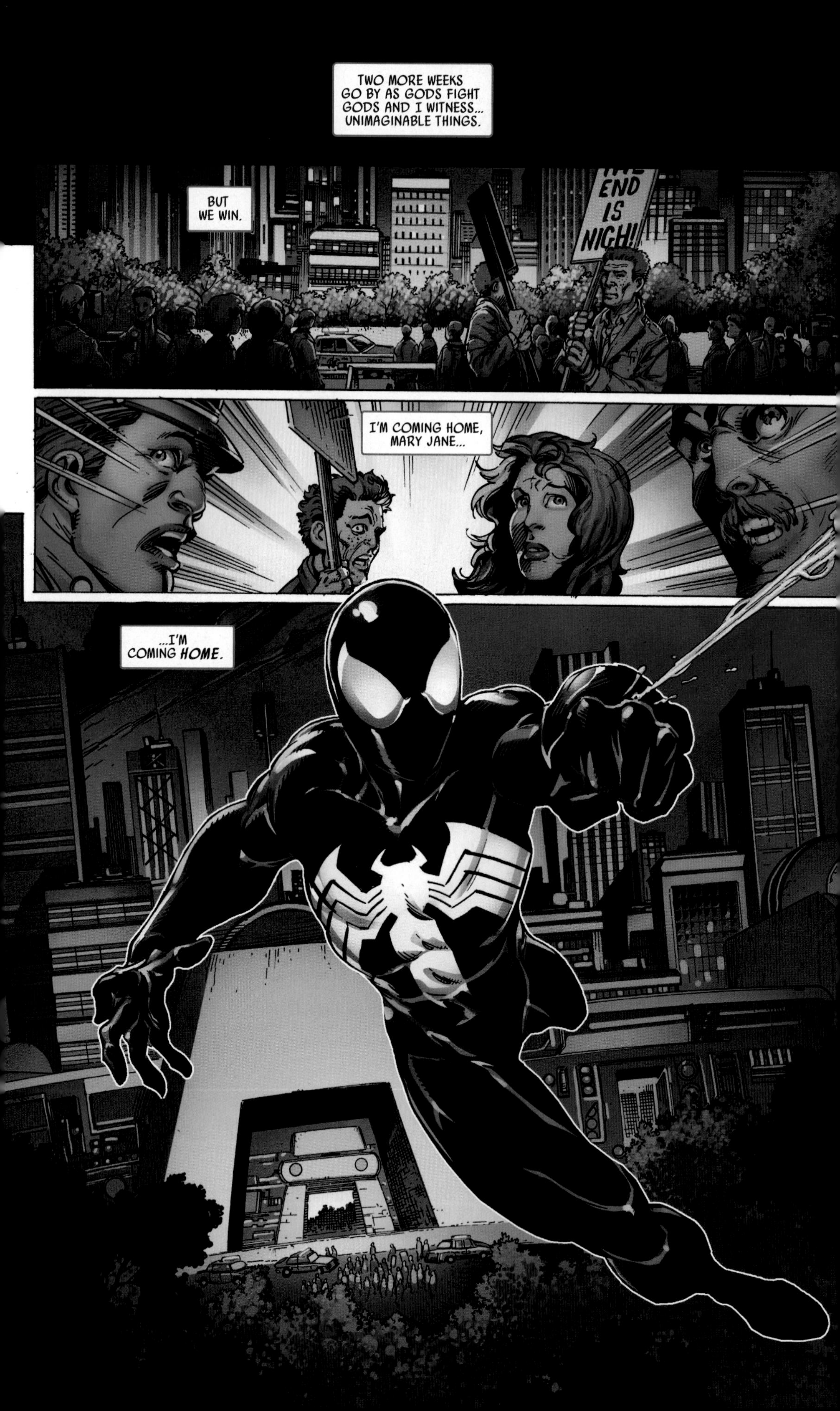
TWO MORE WEEKS GO BY AS GODS FIGHT GODS AND I WITNESS... UNIMAGINABLE THINGS.
BUT WE WIN.
THE END IS NIGH!!
I'M COMING HOME, MARY JANE...
...I'M COMING HOME.

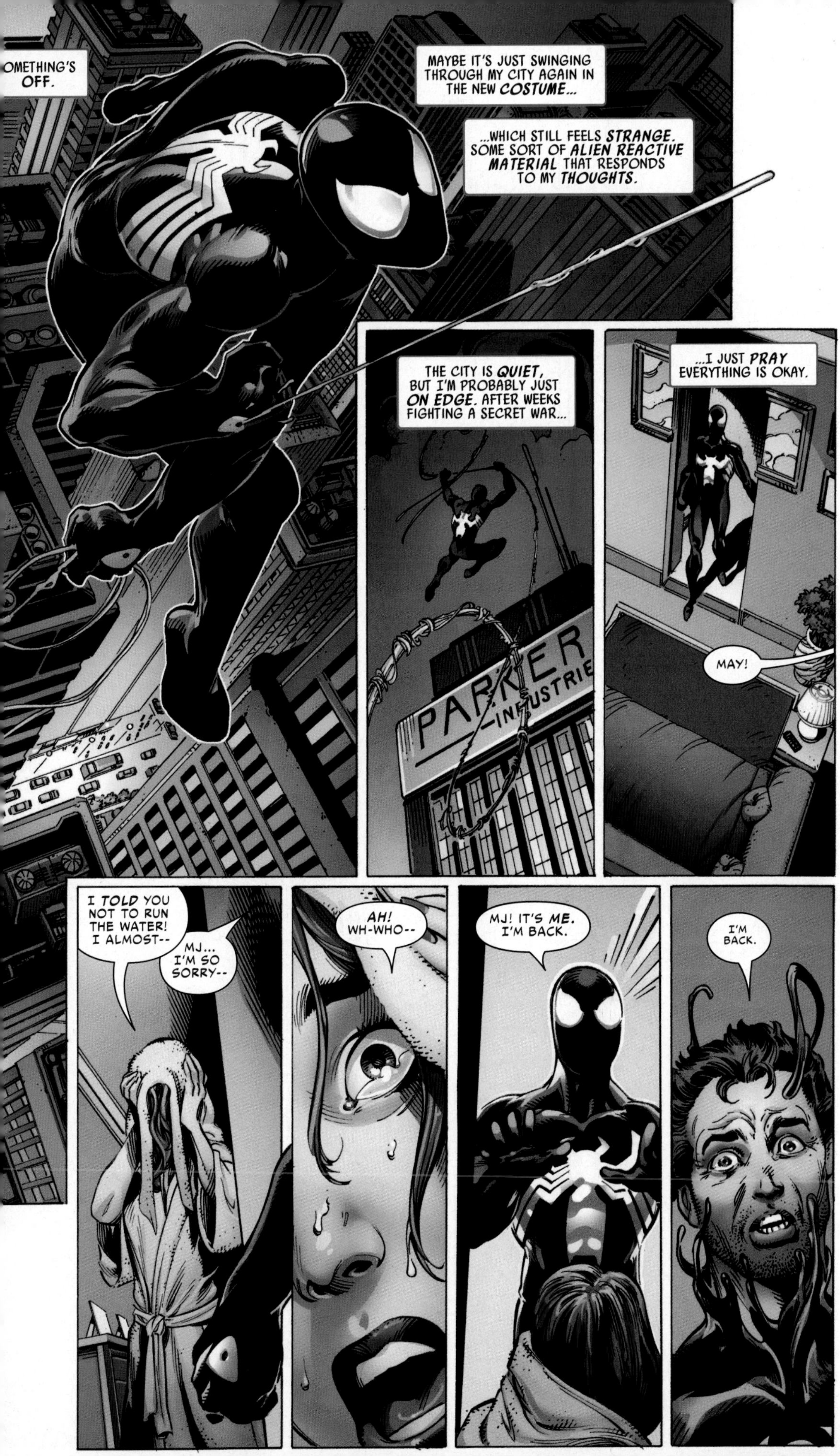
OMETHING'S OFF.
MAYBE IT'S JUST SWINGING THROUGH MY CITY AGAIN IN THE NEW COSTUME...
...WHICH STILL FEELS STRANGE. SOME SORT OF ALIEN REACTIVE MATERIAL THAT RESPONDS TO MY THOUGHTS.
THE CITY IS QUIET, BUT I'M PROBABLY JUST ON EDGE. AFTER WEEKS FIGHTING A SECRET WAR...
PARKER INDUSTRIE
...I JUST PRAY EVERYTHING IS OKAY.
MAY!
I TOLD YOU NOT TO RUN THE WATER! I ALMOST--
MJ... I'M SO SORRY--
AH! WH-WHO--
MJ! IT'S ME. I'M BACK.
I'M BACK.

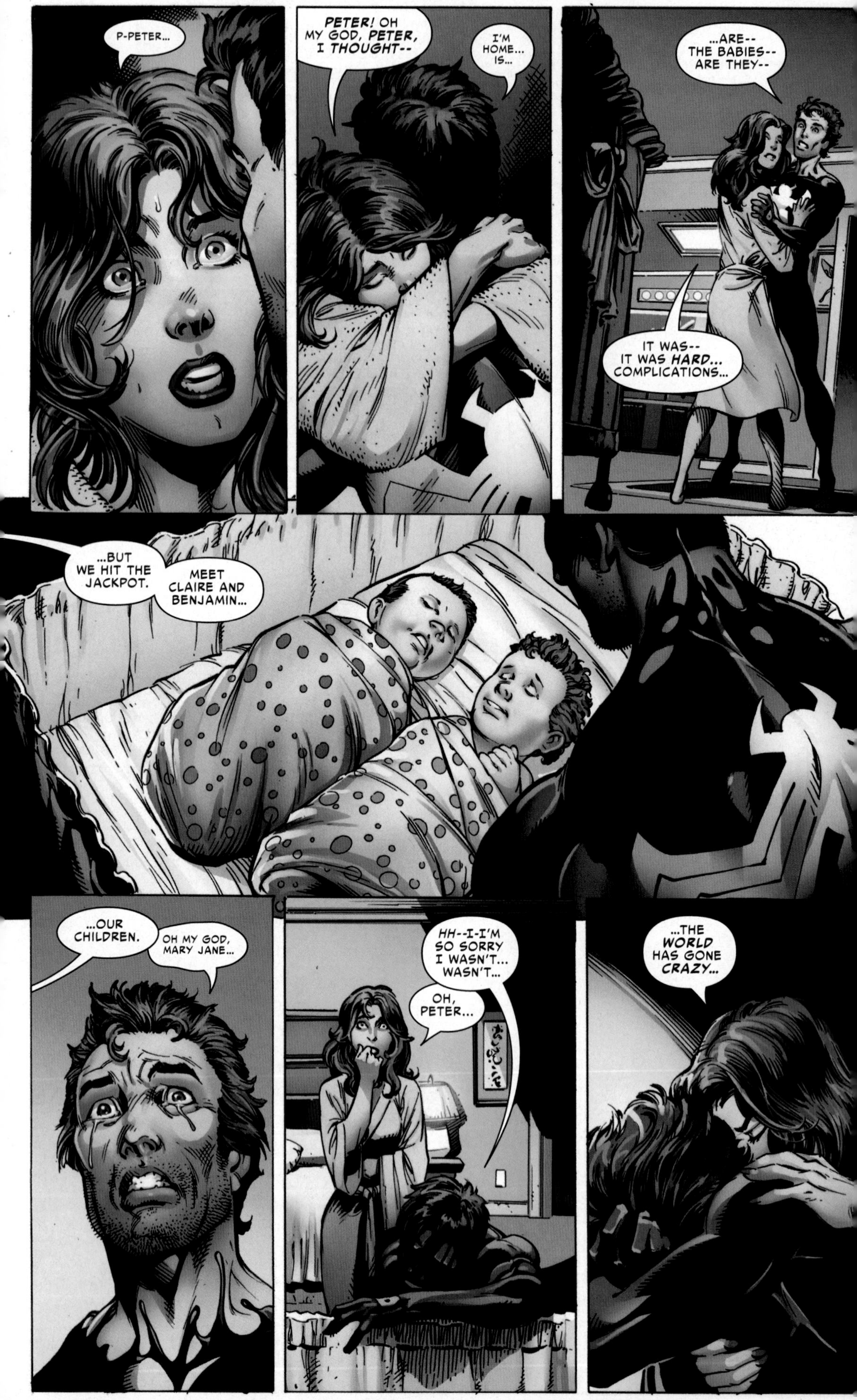
P-PETER...
PETER! OH MY GOD, PETER, I THOUGHT--
I'M HOME... IS...
...ARE-- THE BABIES-- ARE THEY--
IT WAS-- IT WAS HARD... COMPLICATIONS...
...BUT WE HIT THE JACKPOT.
MEET CLAIRE AND BENJAMIN...
...OUR CHILDREN.
OH MY GOD, MARY JANE...
HH--I-I'M SO SORRY I WASN'T... WASN'T...
OH, PETER...
...THE WORLD HAS GONE CRAZY...

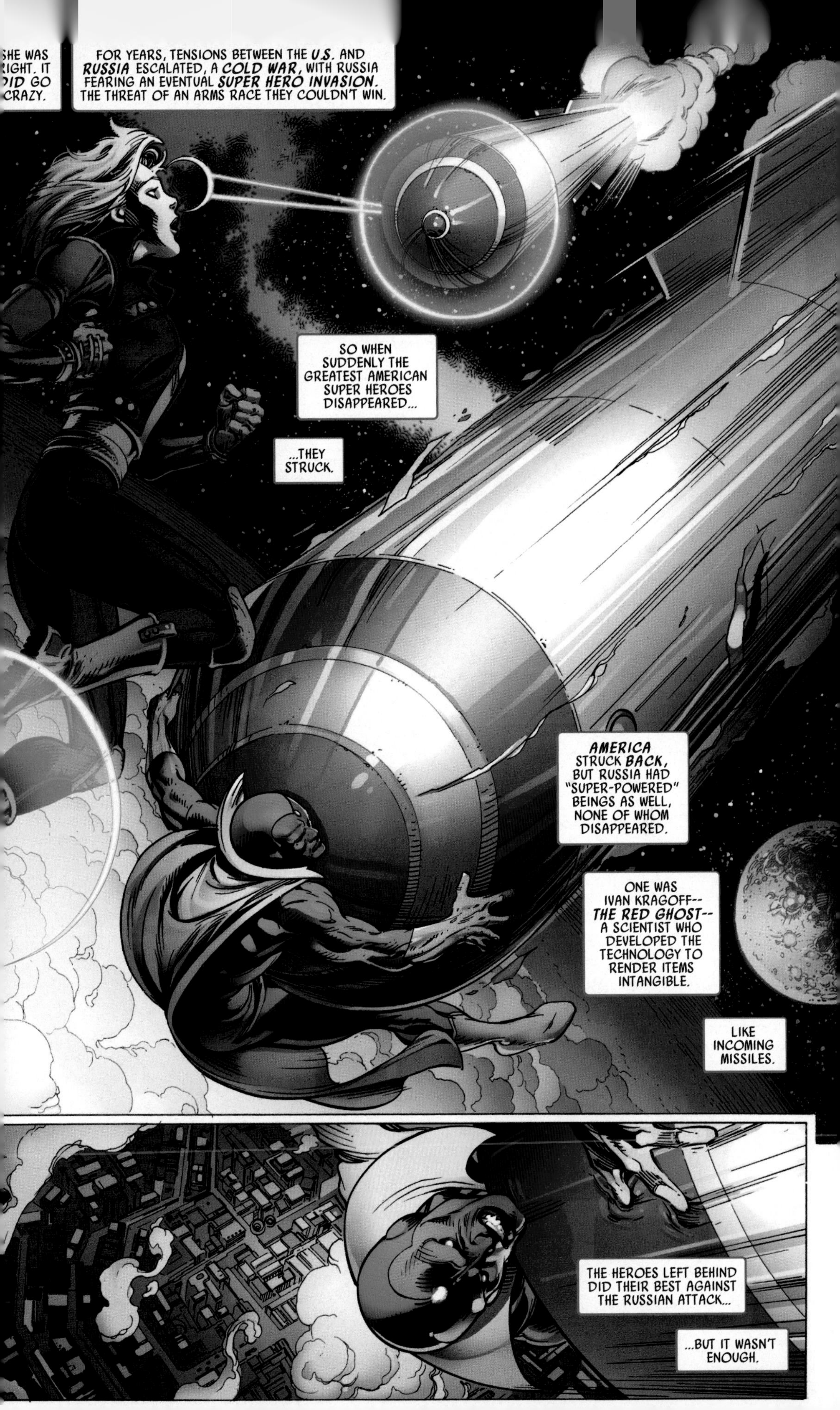
SHE WAS RIGHT. IT DID GO CRAZY.
FOR YEARS, TENSIONS BETWEEN THE U.S. AND RUSSIA ESCALATED, A COLD WAR, WITH RUSSIA FEARING AN EVENTUAL SUPER HERO INVASION. THE THREAT OF AN ARMS RACE THEY COULDN'T WIN.
SO WHEN SUDDENLY THE GREATEST AMERICAN SUPER HEROES DISAPPEARED...
...THEY STRUCK.
AMERICA STRUCK BACK, BUT RUSSIA HAD "SUPER-POWERED" BEINGS AS WELL, NONE OF WHOM DISAPPEARED.
ONE WAS IVAN KRAGOFF-- THE RED GHOST-- A SCIENTIST WHO DEVELOPED THE TECHNOLOGY TO RENDER ITEMS INTANGIBLE.
LIKE INCOMING MISSILES.
THE HEROES LEFT BEHIND DID THEIR BEST AGAINST THE RUSSIAN ATTACK...
...BUT IT WASN'T ENOUGH.

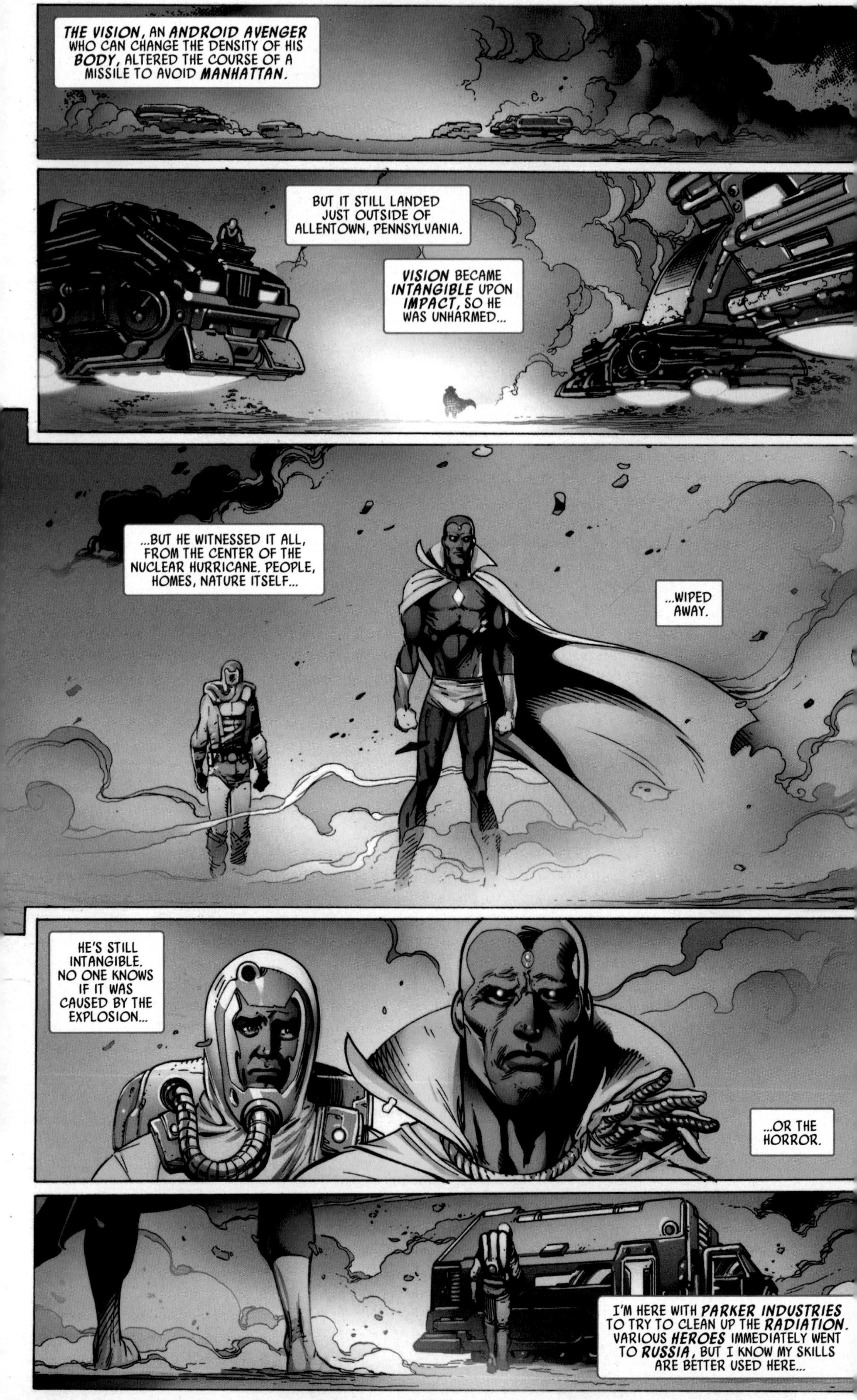
THE VISION, AN ANDROID AVENGER WHO CAN CHANGE THE DENSITY OF HIS BODY, ALTERED THE COURSE OF A MISSILE TO AVOID MANHATTAN.
BUT IT STILL LANDED JUST OUTSIDE OF ALLENTOWN, PENNSYLVANIA.
VISION BECAME INTANGIBLE UPON IMPACT, SO HE WAS UNHARMED...
...BUT HE WITNESSED IT ALL, FROM THE CENTER OF THE NUCLEAR HURRICANE. PEOPLE, HOMES, NATURE ITSELF...
...WIPED AWAY.
HE'S STILL INTANGIBLE. NO ONE KNOWS IF IT WAS CAUSED BY THE EXPLOSION...
...OR THE HORROR.
I'M HERE WITH PARKER INDUSTRIES TO TRY TO CLEAN UP THE RADIATION. VARIOUS HEROES IMMEDIATELY WENT TO RUSSIA, BUT I KNOW MY SKILLS ARE BETTER USED HERE...

...WITH REED.

ANY LUCK OUT THERE?

HE'S STILL NON-RESPONSIVE.

BUT THE RADIO-SPONGES ARE ALMOST ALL SET UP. HOPEFULLY WE CAN ABSORB ENOUGH RADIATION TO SAVE THE AREA...

LOOKS LIKE YOU HAVE SOME PROBLEMS AT HOME...

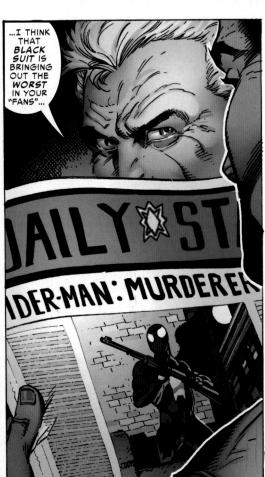

...I THINK THAT BLACK SUIT IS BRINGING OUT THE WORST IN YOUR "FANS"...

DAILY ST...
...DER-MAN: MURDERER

UNBELIEVABLE. I NEVER USED TO HAVE CRAZY COPYCATS...

...MAYBE I SHOULD JUST HAVE THE SUIT MIMIC MY OLD COSTUME...

SON... THERE'S SOMETHING I SHOULD TELL YOU...

...SINCE WE'VE BEEN...WORKING TOGETHER AGAIN...I'VE BEEN STUDYING YOUR NEW COSTUME... SCANNING IT...

IT WOULD APPEAR...

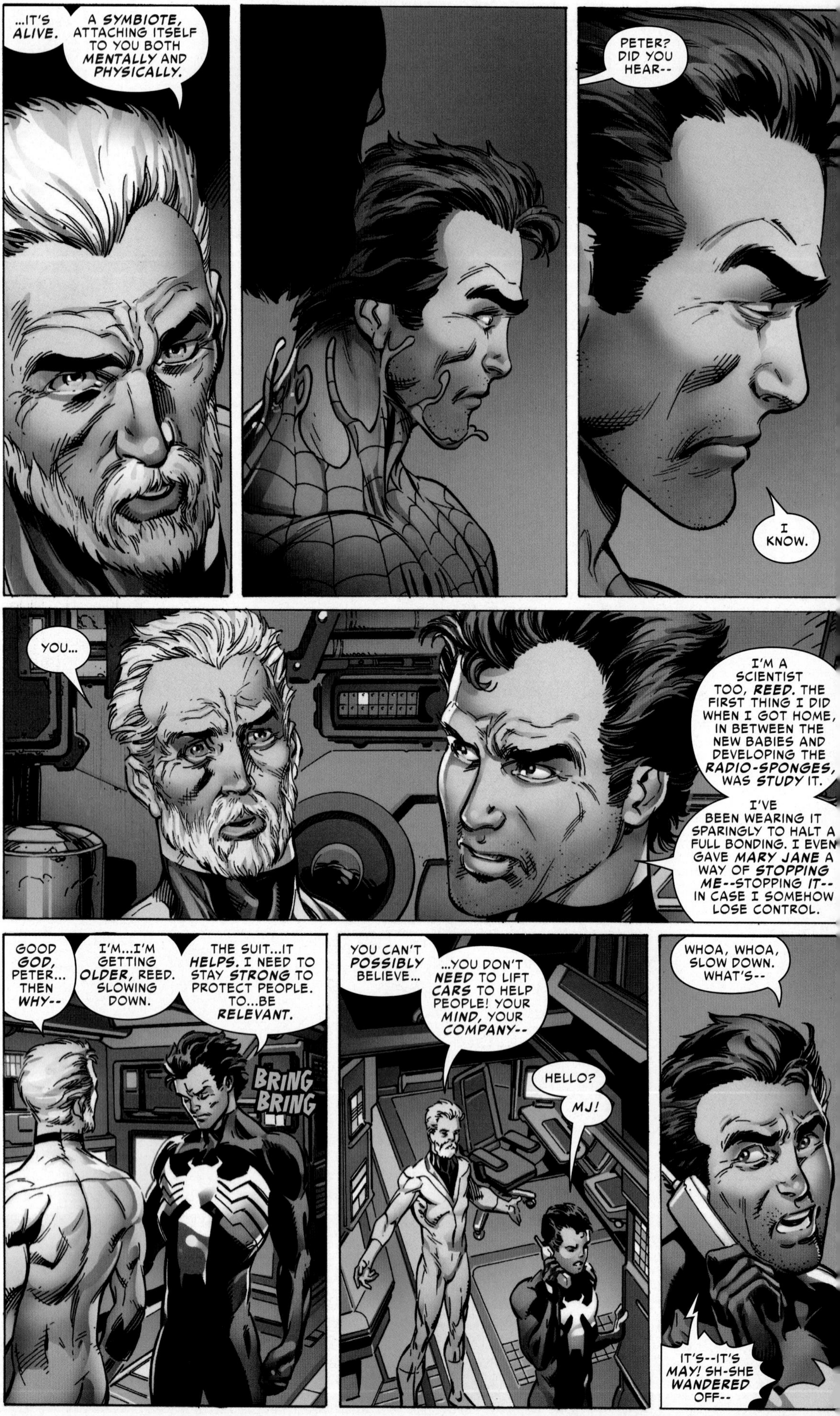
...IT'S ALIVE.
A SYMBIOTE, ATTACHING ITSELF TO YOU BOTH MENTALLY AND PHYSICALLY.
PETER? DID YOU HEAR--
I KNOW.
YOU...
I'M A SCIENTIST TOO, REED. THE FIRST THING I DID WHEN I GOT HOME, IN BETWEEN THE NEW BABIES AND DEVELOPING THE RADIO-SPONGES, WAS STUDY IT.
I'VE BEEN WEARING IT SPARINGLY TO HALT A FULL BONDING. I EVEN GAVE MARY JANE A WAY OF STOPPING ME--STOPPING IT--IN CASE I SOMEHOW LOSE CONTROL.
GOOD GOD, PETER... THEN WHY--
I'M...I'M GETTING OLDER, REED. SLOWING DOWN.
THE SUIT...IT HELPS. I NEED TO STAY STRONG TO PROTECT PEOPLE. TO...BE RELEVANT.
BRING BRING
YOU CAN'T POSSIBLY BELIEVE...
...YOU DON'T NEED TO LIFT CARS TO HELP PEOPLE! YOUR MIND, YOUR COMPANY--
HELLO?
MJ!
WHOA, WHOA, SLOW DOWN. WHAT'S--
IT'S--IT'S MAY! SH-SHE WANDERED OFF--

"--WITH THE BABIES!"

MARY JANE!

WHOA THERE, MISTER! WHO--

GET YOUR HANDS--

IT'S OKAY--

--HE'S MY HUSBAND.

OH THANK GOD, THEY'RE ALL RIGHT! WHERE'S--

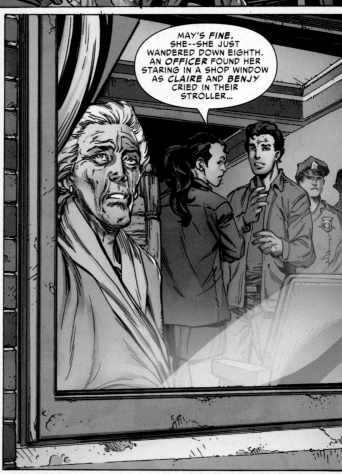

MAY'S FINE. SHE--SHE JUST WANDERED DOWN EIGHTH. AN OFFICER FOUND HER STARING IN A SHOP WINDOW AS CLAIRE AND BENJY CRIED IN THEIR STROLLER...

GLAD EVERYTHING TURNED OUT OKAY. IF YOU NEED ANY MORE SUGGESTIONS, DON'T HESITATE TO CALL...

WHAT DID HE MEAN, "SUGGESTIONS"?

I... SPECIALISTS FOR MAY...

A SENIOR'S HOME--

NO! ABSOLUTELY NOT!

WWAHH! WAHHHH--

SHE *RAISED* ME WHEN MY *PARENTS* DIED! SHE *TOOK CARE* OF ME WHEN *NO ONE ELSE* WOULD! SHE--

THEN TAKE CARE OF HER!

WAAAAAHHH!

SPIDER-MAN! PARKER INDUSTRIES!

I COULD TOLERATE YOU IGNORING ME, YOUR *WIFE*! I GO IT! I'M *USED* TO FEELING LIKE THE *RUNNER-UP* TO TH' PERFECT *GHOST* OF GWEN STACY!

DON'T-

WAAAAAHHH!

WAAAAAAAAAHHHHH!

BUT YOU'RE A *FATHER* NOW! AND A *CARETAKER*! YOU NEED TO BE *HERE* WITH US!

EVEN THAT STUPID *SUIT* IS INTERFERING!

IT'S LIKE YOU'RE *ADDICTED* TO--

I DON'T *NEED* IT!

EVERYONE THINKS THEY KNOW WHAT'S *RIGHT* FOR ME! I DON'T NEED THE SUIT--

THEN WHAT *DO* YOU NEED, PETER?

DO YOU EVEN *KNOW*?

YEAH, I DO.

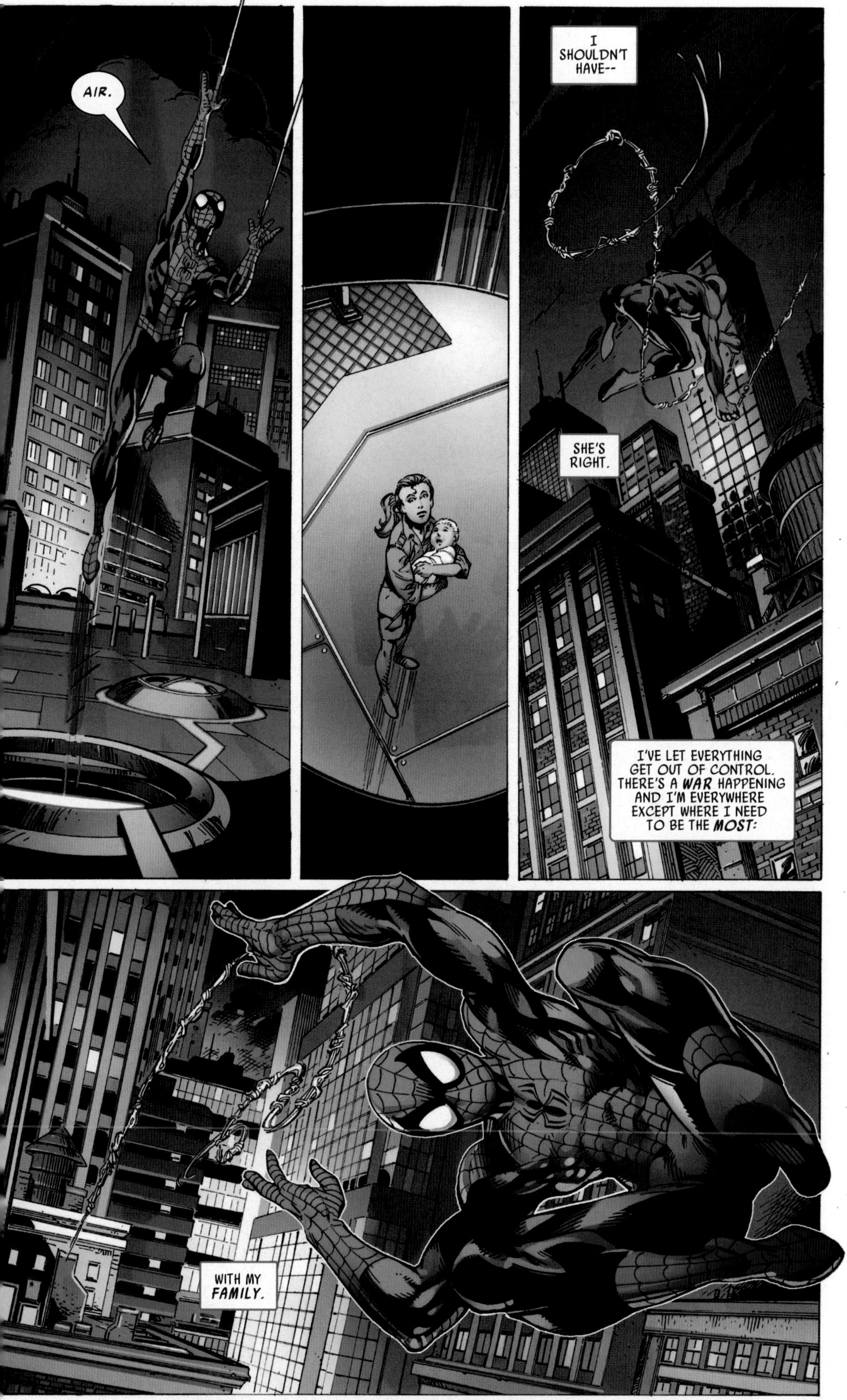
AIR.
I SHOULDN'T HAVE--
SHE'S RIGHT.
I'VE LET EVERYTHING GET OUT OF CONTROL. THERE'S A WAR HAPPENING AND I'M EVERYWHERE EXCEPT WHERE I NEED TO BE THE MOST:
WITH MY FAMILY.

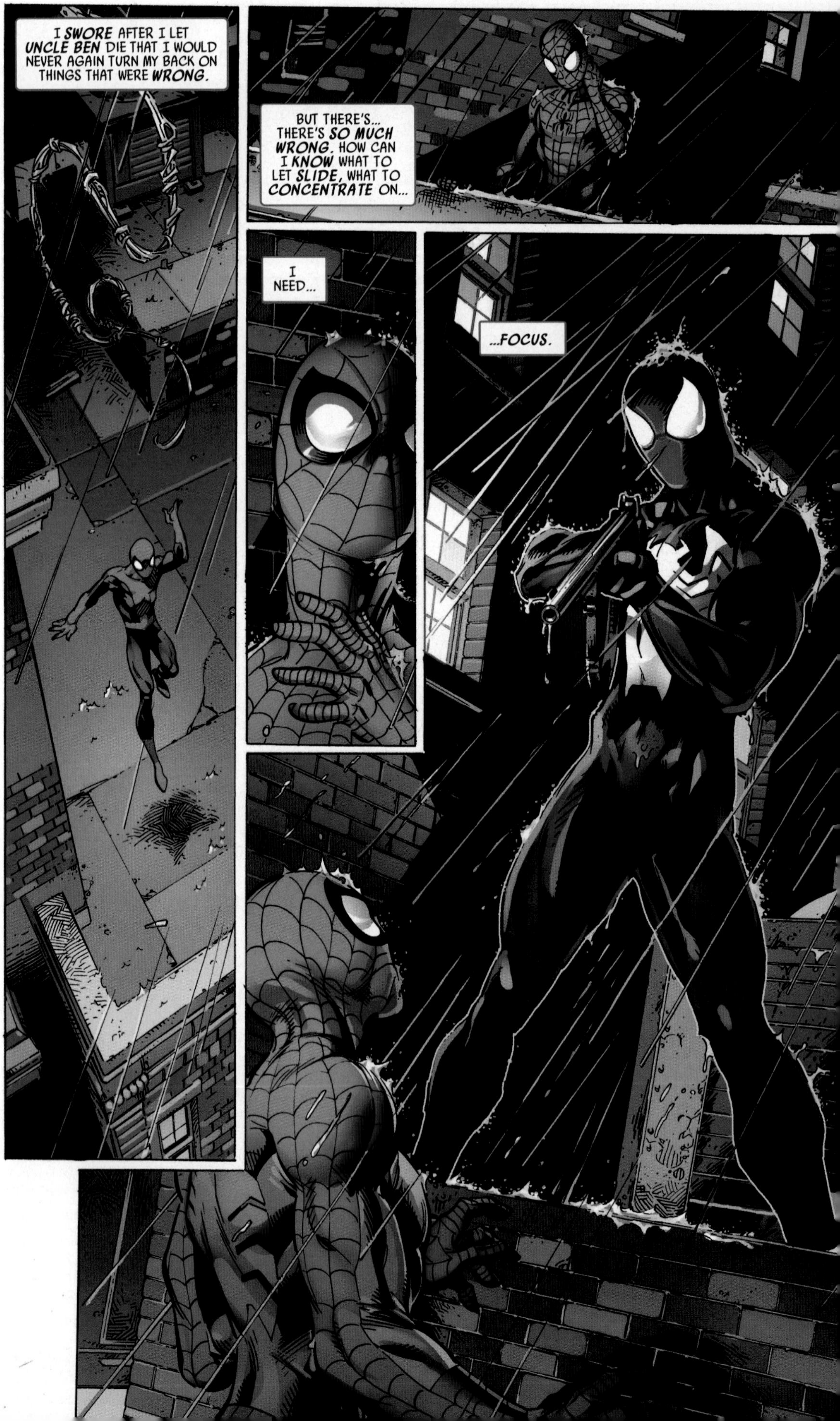

I SWORE AFTER I LET UNCLE BEN DIE THAT I WOULD NEVER AGAIN TURN MY BACK ON THINGS THAT WERE WRONG.
BUT THERE'S... THERE'S SO MUCH WRONG. HOW CAN I KNOW WHAT TO LET SLIDE, WHAT TO CONCENTRATE ON...
I NEED...
...FOCUS.

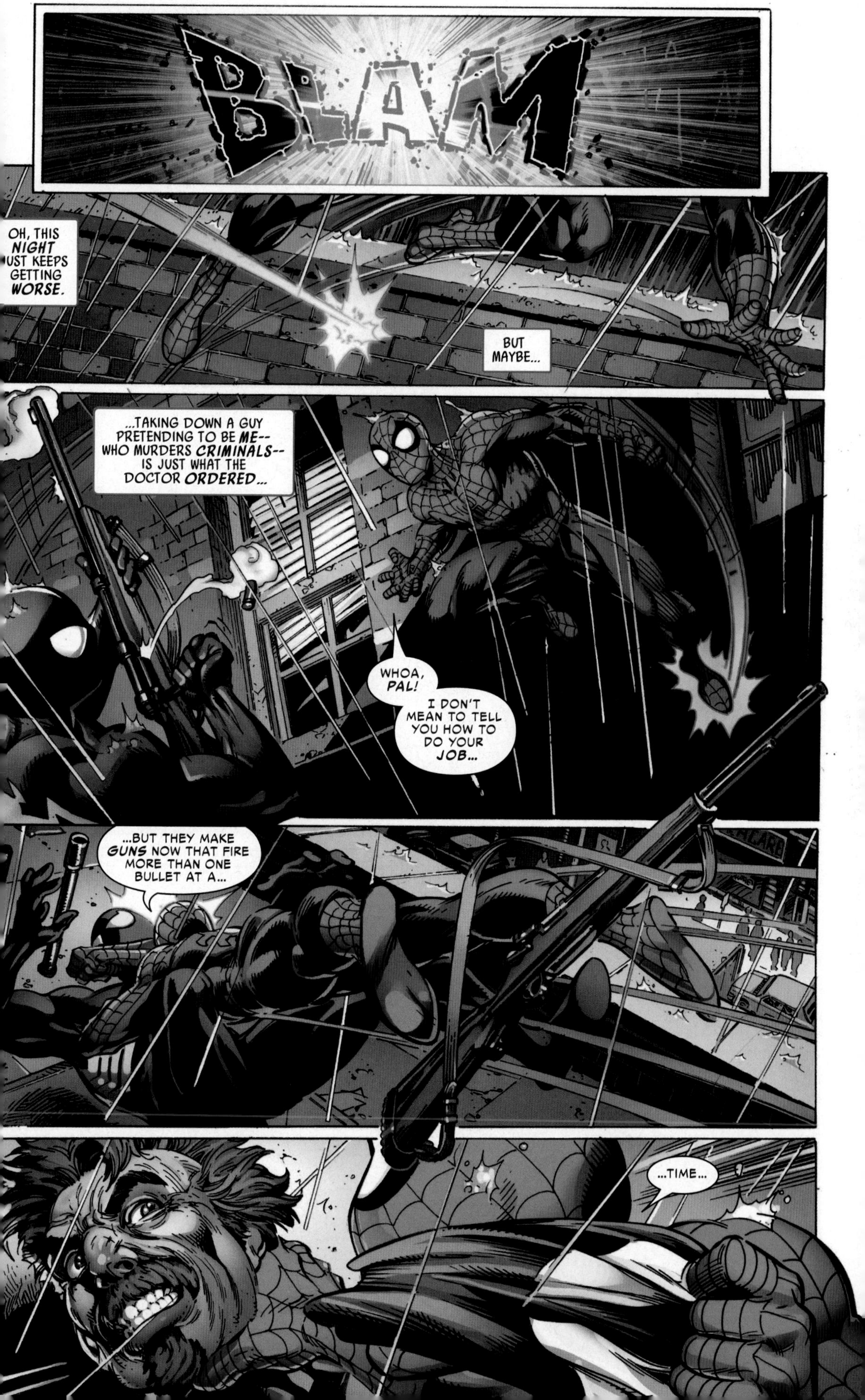
BLAM
OH, THIS NIGHT JUST KEEPS GETTING WORSE.
BUT MAYBE...
...TAKING DOWN A GUY PRETENDING TO BE ME-- WHO MURDERS CRIMINALS-- IS JUST WHAT THE DOCTOR ORDERED...
WHOA, PAL!
I DON'T MEAN TO TELL YOU HOW TO DO YOUR JOB...
...BUT THEY MAKE GUNS NOW THAT FIRE MORE THAN ONE BULLET AT A...
...TIME...

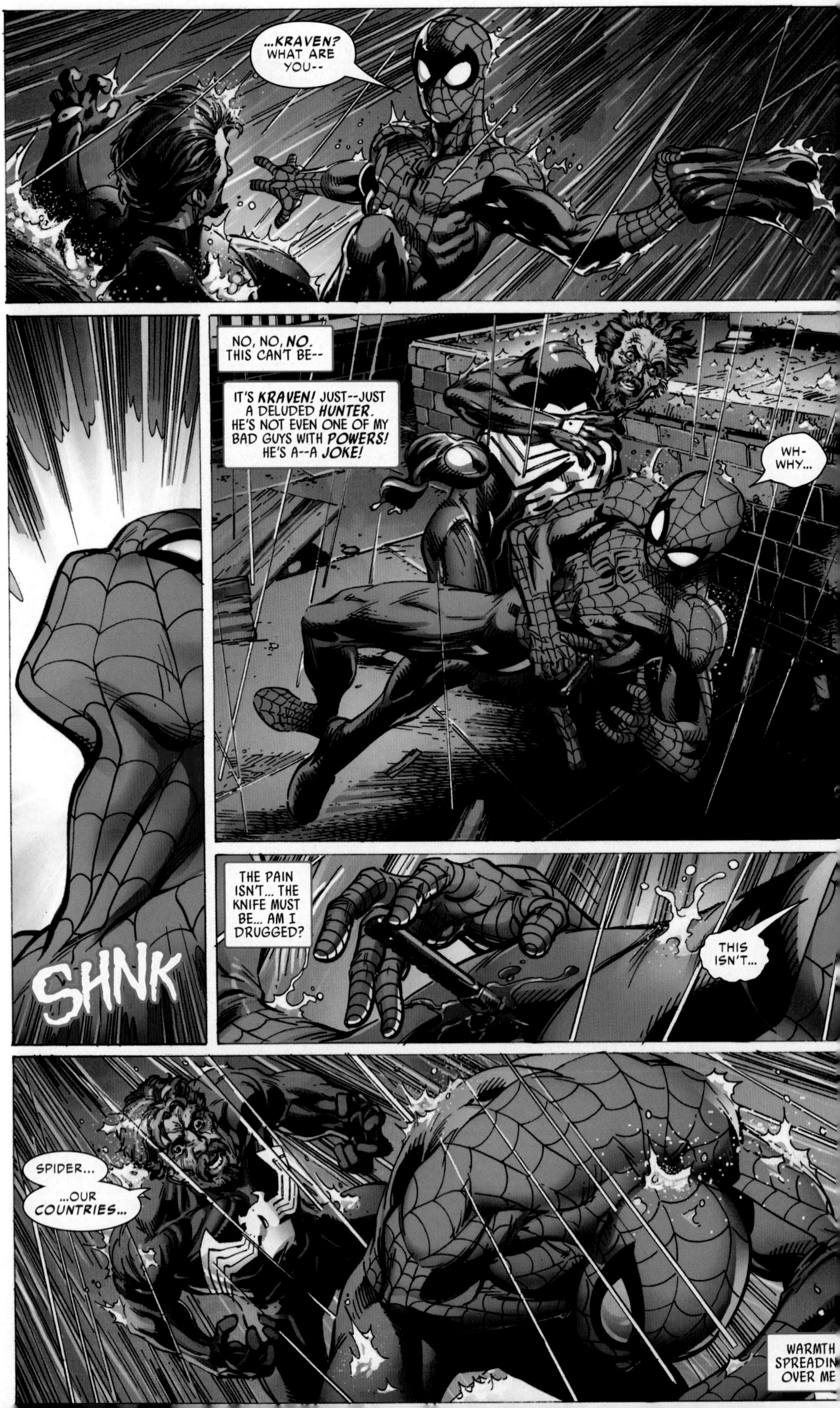

...KRAVEN? WHAT ARE YOU--
NO, NO, NO. THIS CAN'T BE--
IT'S KRAVEN! JUST--JUST A DELUDED HUNTER. HE'S NOT EVEN ONE OF MY BAD GUYS WITH POWERS! HE'S A--A JOKE!
WH- WHY...
SHNK
THE PAIN ISN'T... THE KNIFE MUST BE... AM I DRUGGED?
THIS ISN'T...
SPIDER...
...OUR COUNTRIES...
WARMTH SPREADIN OVER ME

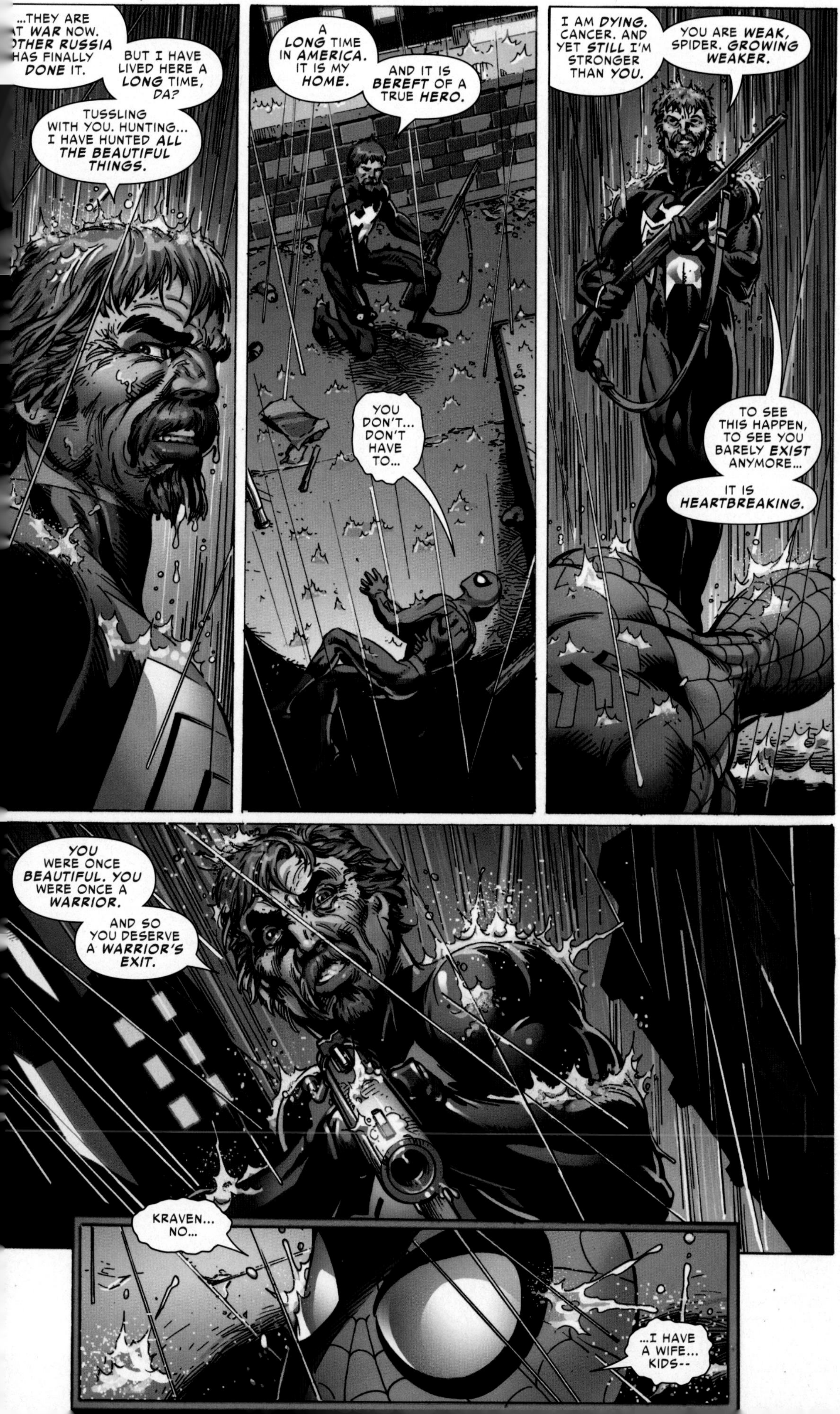

...THEY ARE AT WAR NOW. MOTHER RUSSIA HAS FINALLY DONE IT.
BUT I HAVE LIVED HERE A LONG TIME, DA?
TUSSLING WITH YOU. HUNTING... I HAVE HUNTED ALL THE BEAUTIFUL THINGS.
A LONG TIME IN AMERICA. IT IS MY HOME.
AND IT IS BEREFT OF A TRUE HERO.
YOU DON'T... DON'T HAVE TO...
I AM DYING. CANCER. AND YET STILL I'M STRONGER THAN YOU.
YOU ARE WEAK, SPIDER. GROWING WEAKER.
TO SEE THIS HAPPEN, TO SEE YOU BARELY EXIST ANYMORE...
IT IS HEARTBREAKING.
YOU WERE ONCE BEAUTIFUL. YOU WERE ONCE A WARRIOR.
AND SO YOU DESERVE A WARRIOR'S EXIT.
KRAVEN... NO...
...I HAVE A WIFE... KIDS--

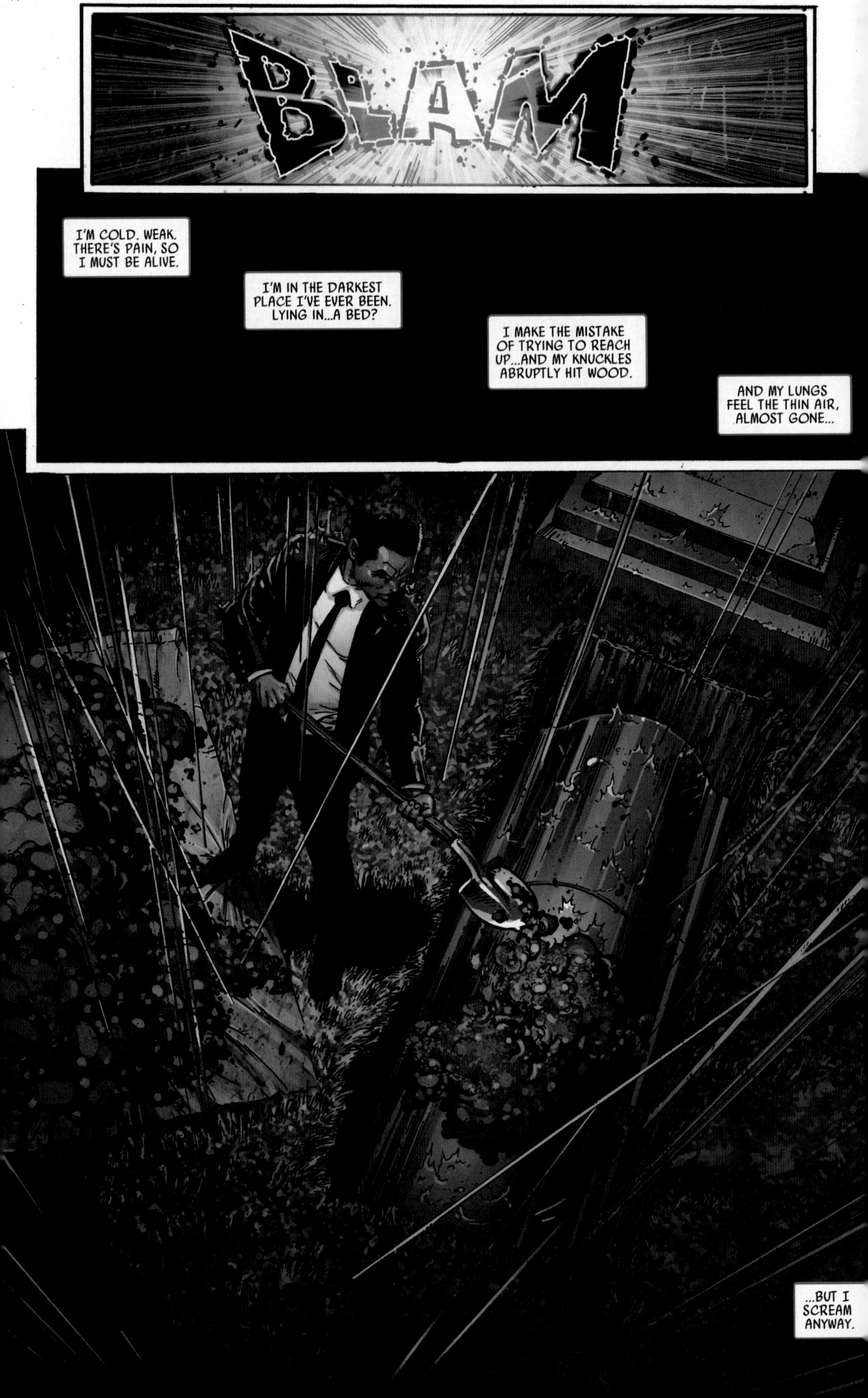
BLAM
I'M COLD. WEAK. THERE'S PAIN, SO I MUST BE ALIVE.
I'M IN THE DARKEST PLACE I'VE EVER BEEN. LYING IN...A BED?
I MAKE THE MISTAKE OF TRYING TO REACH UP...AND MY KNUCKLES ABRUPTLY HIT WOOD.
AND MY LUNGS FEEL THE THIN AIR, ALMOST GONE...
...BUT I SCREAM ANYWAY.

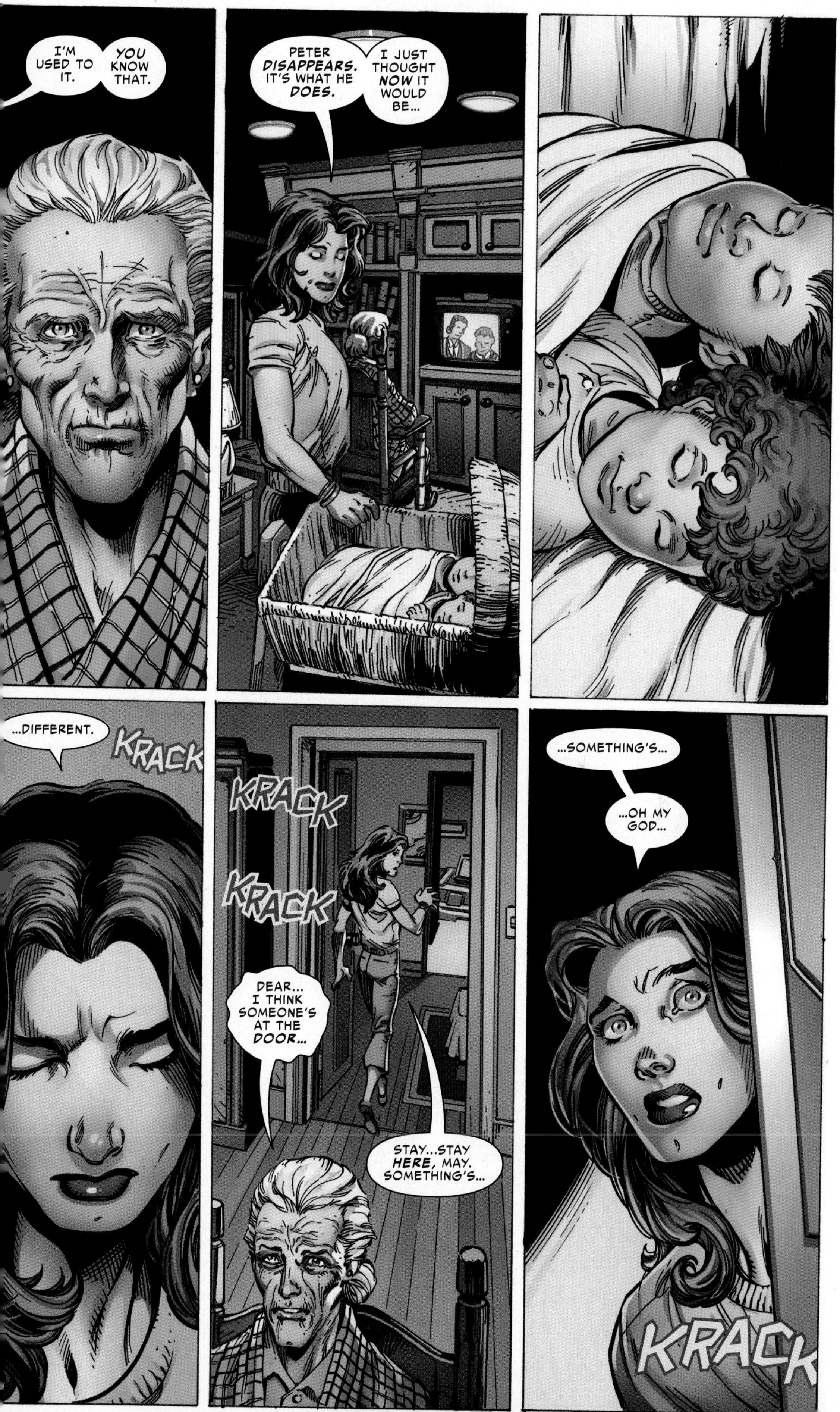
I'M USED TO IT.
YOU KNOW THAT.
PETER DISAPPEARS. IT'S WHAT HE DOES.
I JUST THOUGHT NOW IT WOULD BE...
...DIFFERENT.
KRACK
KRACK
KRACK
DEAR... I THINK SOMEONE'S AT THE DOOR...
STAY...STAY HERE, MAY. SOMETHING'S...
...SOMETHING'S...
...OH MY GOD...
KRACK

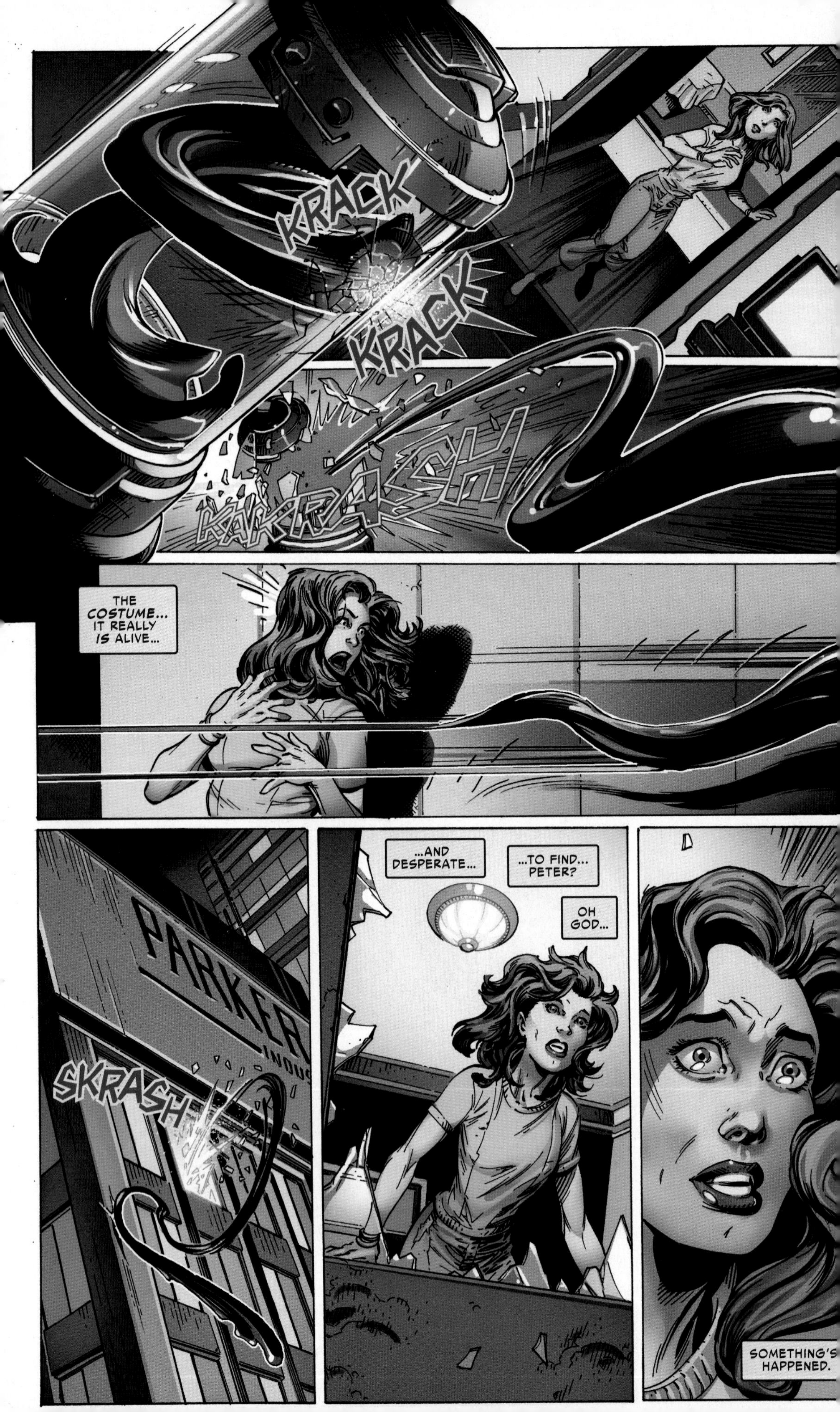
KRACK
KRACK
KAKRASH
THE COSTUME... IT REALLY IS ALIVE...
PARKER INDUS
SKRASH
...AND DESPERATE...
...TO FIND... PETER?
OH GOD...
SOMETHING'S HAPPENED.

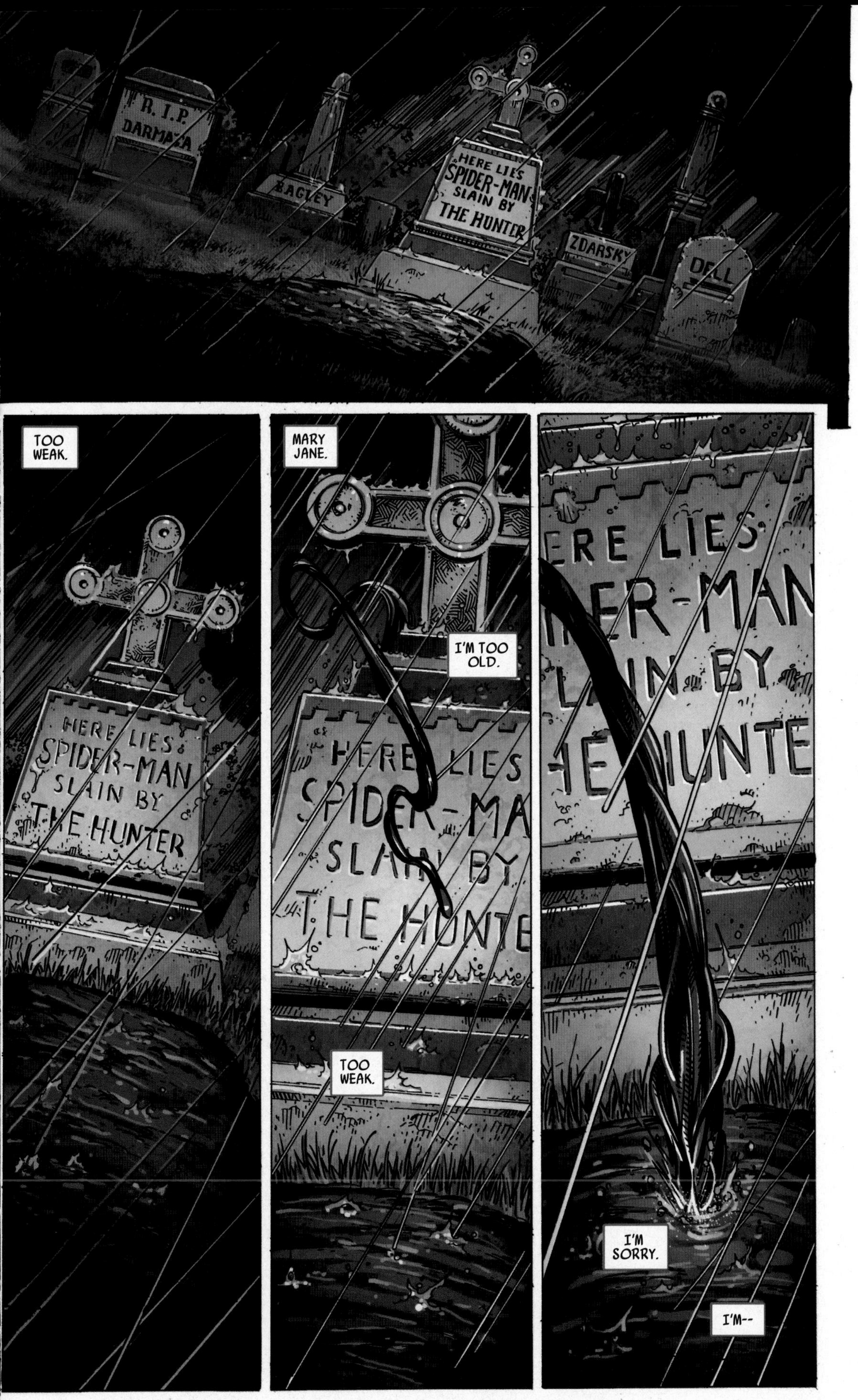
R.I.P.
BAGLEY
HERE LIES SPIDER-MAN SLAIN BY THE HUNTER
ZDARSKY
DELL
TOO WEAK.
HERE LIES SPIDER-MAN SLAIN BY THE HUNTER
MARY JANE.
I'M TOO OLD.
TOO WEAK.
I'M SORRY.
I'M--

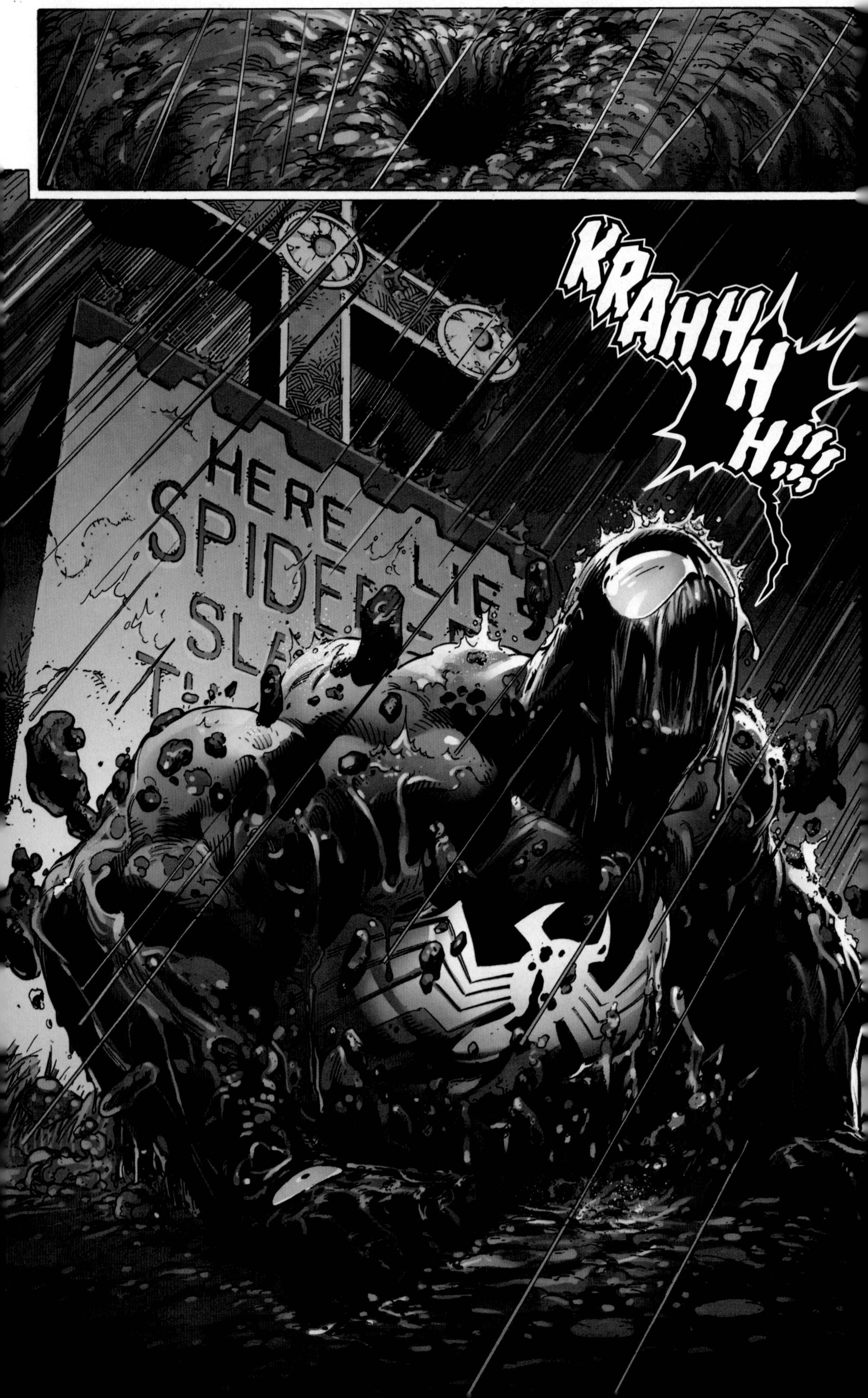
KRAHHHH!!!
HERE

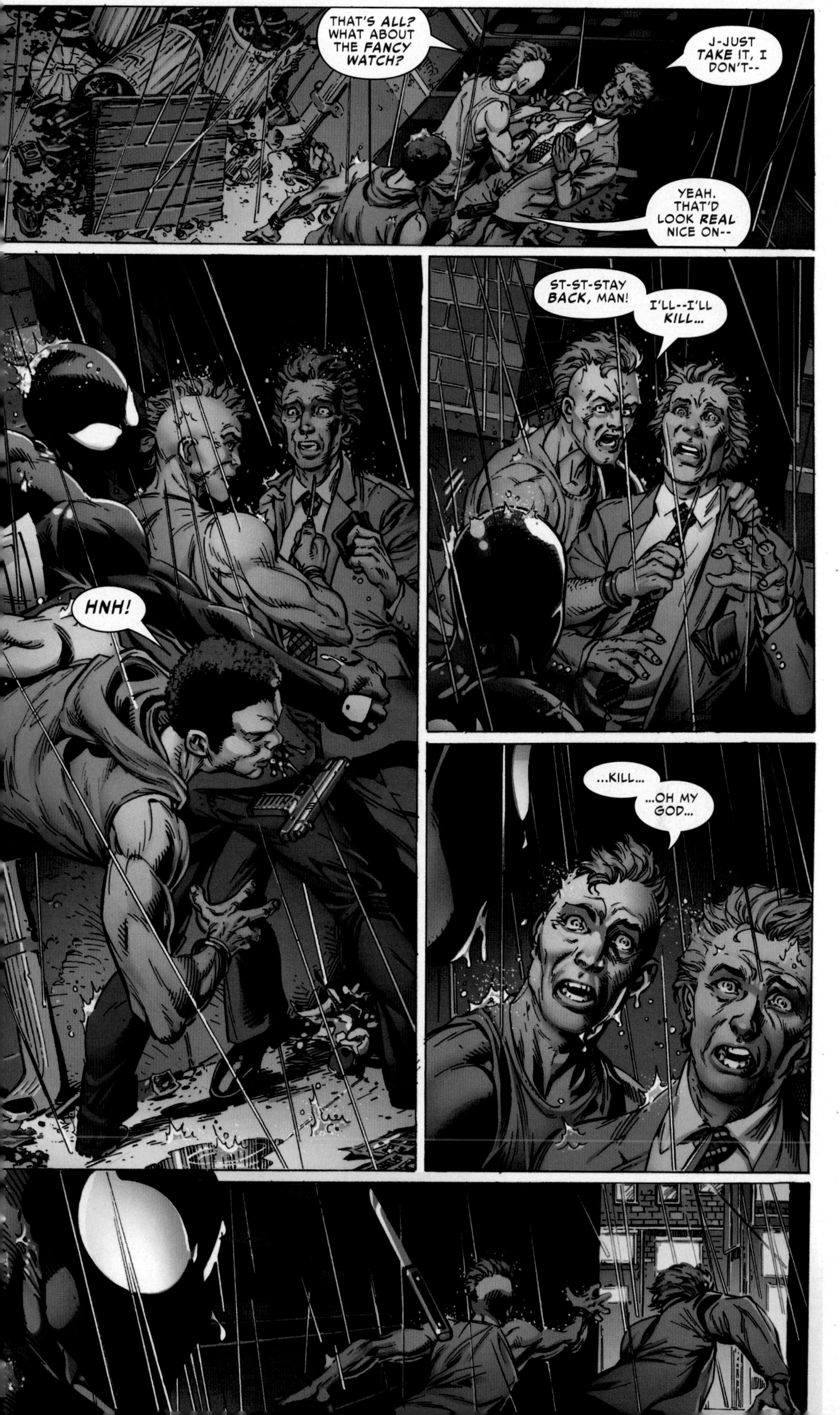
THAT'S ALL? WHAT ABOUT THE FANCY WATCH?
J-JUST TAKE IT, I DON'T--
YEAH. THAT'D LOOK REAL NICE ON--
HNH!
ST-ST-STAY BACK, MAN!
I'LL--I'LL KILL...
...KILL...
...OH MY GOD...

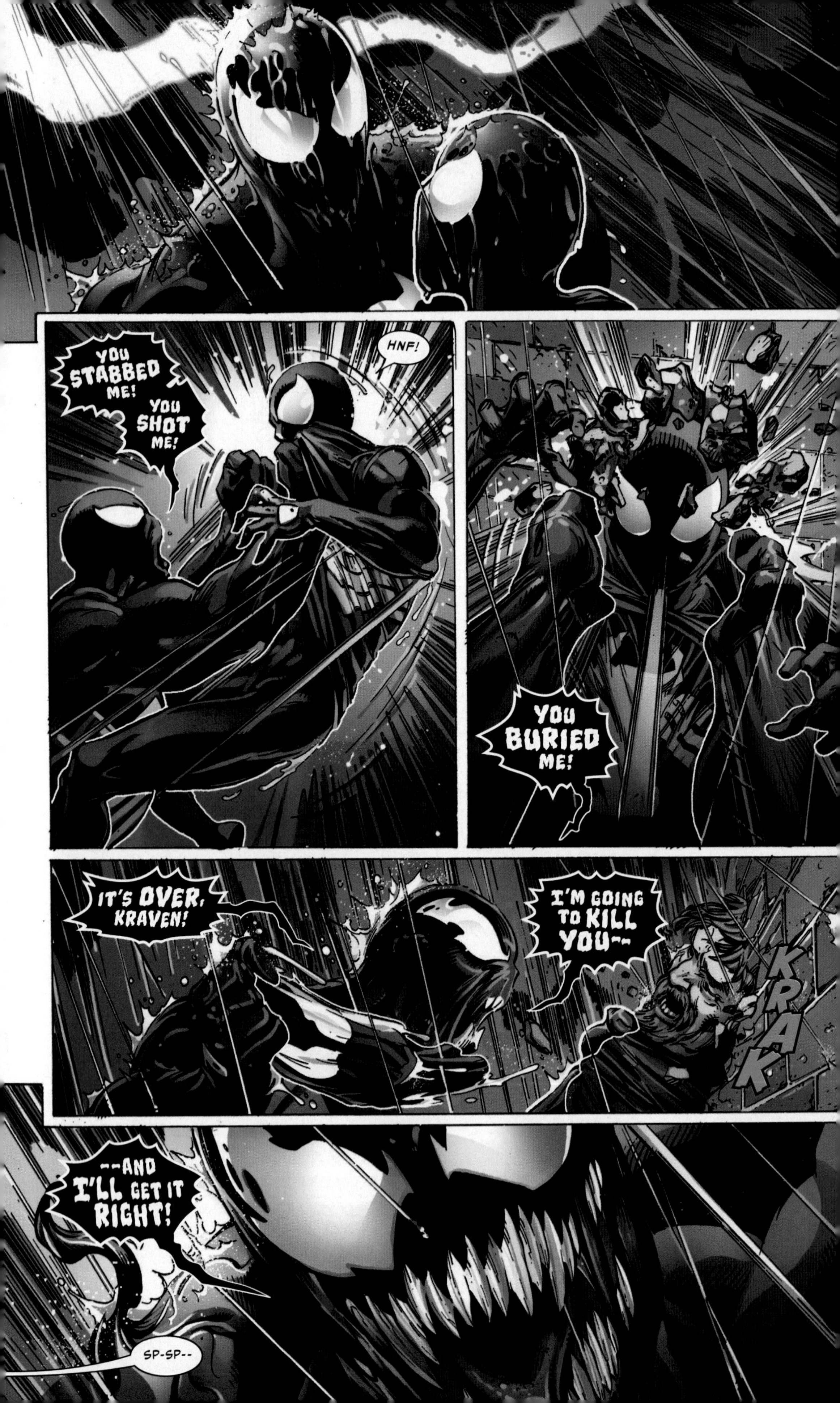

YOU STABBED ME!
YOU SHOT ME!
HNF!
YOU BURIED ME!
IT'S OVER, KRAVEN!
I'M GOING TO KILL YOU--
KRAK
--AND I'LL GET IT RIGHT!
SP-SP--

SPIDER-MAN...?

L-LOOK AT YOU...

...YOU'VE DONE IT... BECOME WHAT YOU *NEEDED* TO...

YOU'RE... YOU'RE SO...

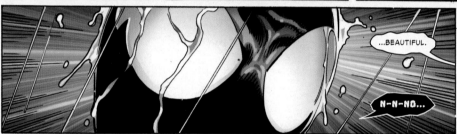

...BEAUTIFUL.

N-N-NO...

M-M-MARY J-JANE...

...IT -HAPPENED. YOU NEED TO...

...YOU KN-KNOW WH-WHAT TO DO...

I-I-I *CAN'T!* PL-PLEASE DON'T M-MAKE ME--

MJ...

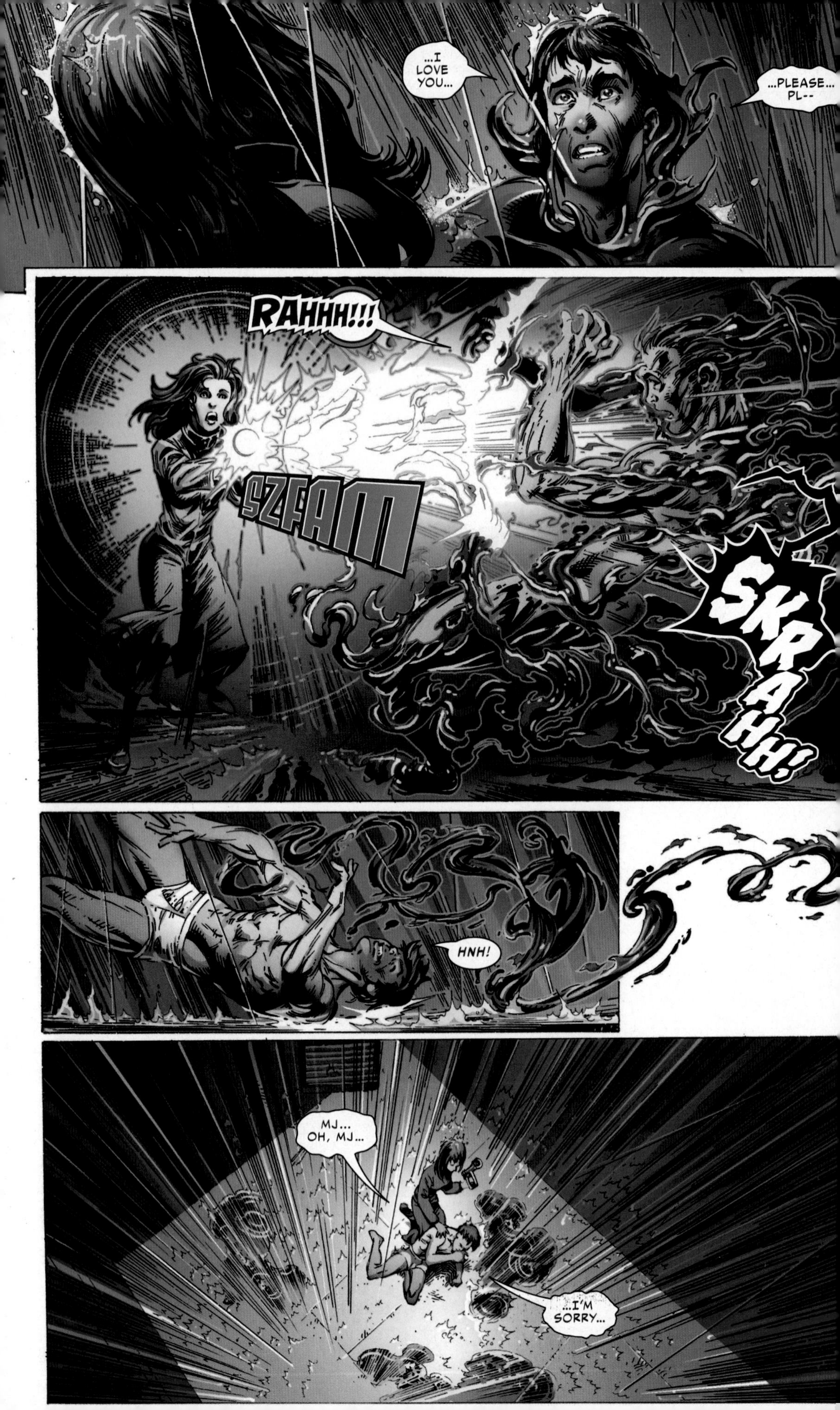
...I LOVE YOU...
...PLEASE... PL--
RAHHH!!!
SZFAM
SKRAHH!
HNH!
MJ... OH, MJ...
...I'M SORRY...

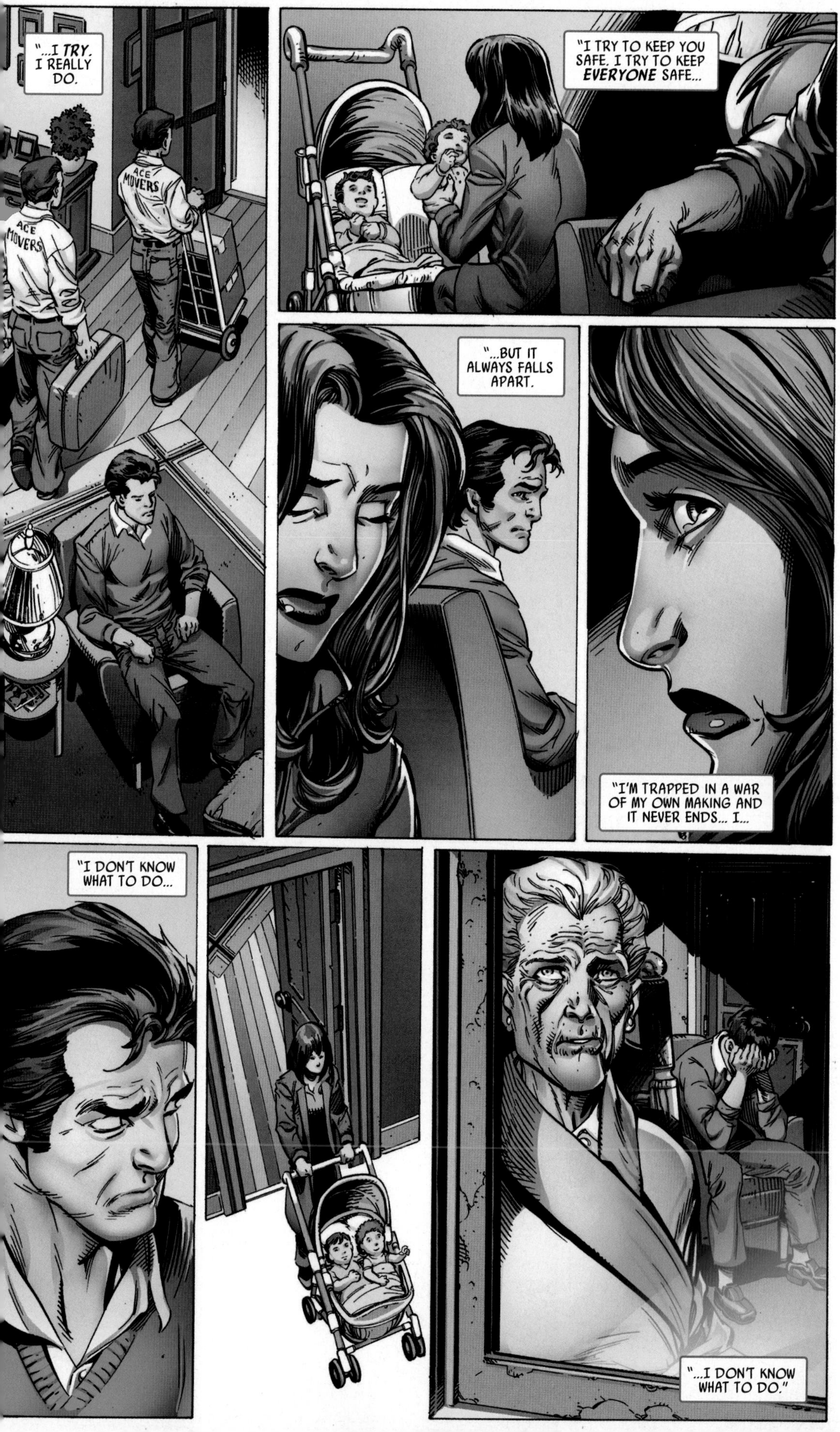
"...I TRY. I REALLY DO.
ACE MOVERS
ACE MOVERS
"I TRY TO KEEP YOU SAFE. I TRY TO KEEP EVERYONE SAFE...
"...BUT IT ALWAYS FALLS APART.
"I'M TRAPPED IN A WAR OF MY OWN MAKING AND IT NEVER ENDS... I...
"I DON'T KNOW WHAT TO DO...
"...I DON'T KNOW WHAT TO DO."

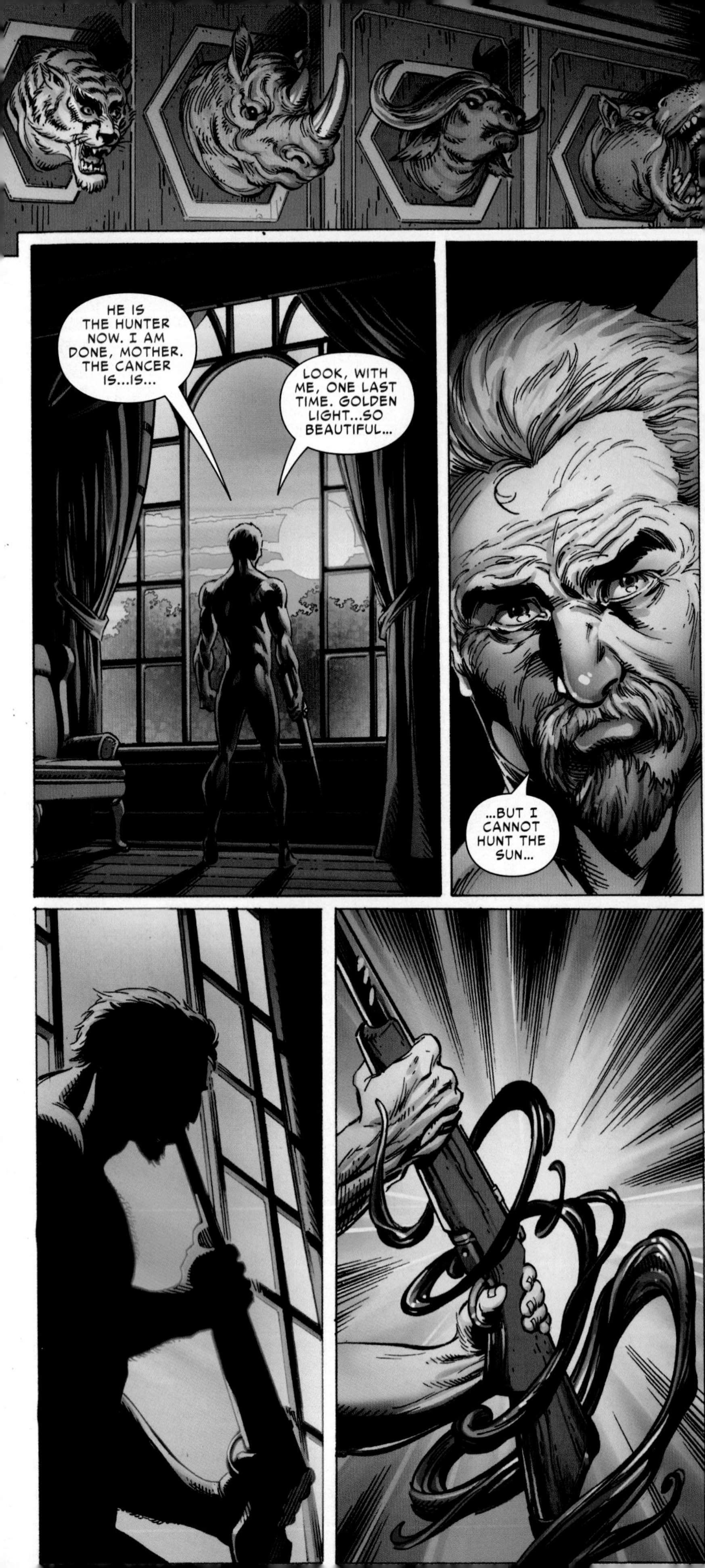
HE IS THE HUNTER NOW. I AM DONE, MOTHER. THE CANCER IS...IS...
LOOK, WITH ME, ONE LAST TIME. GOLDEN LIGHT...SO BEAUTIFUL...
...BUT I CANNOT HUNT THE SUN...

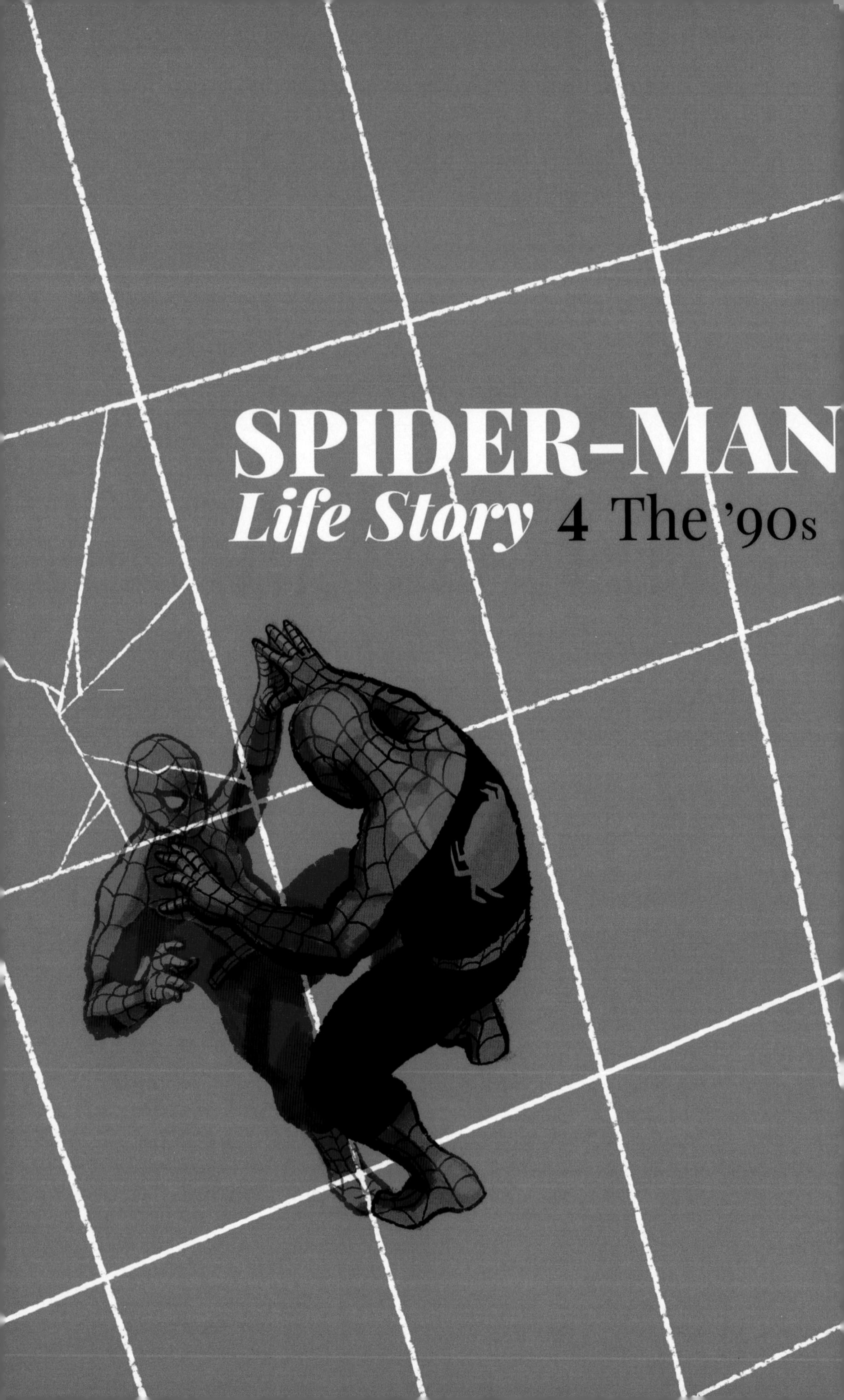
SPIDER-MAN
Life Story 4 The '90s

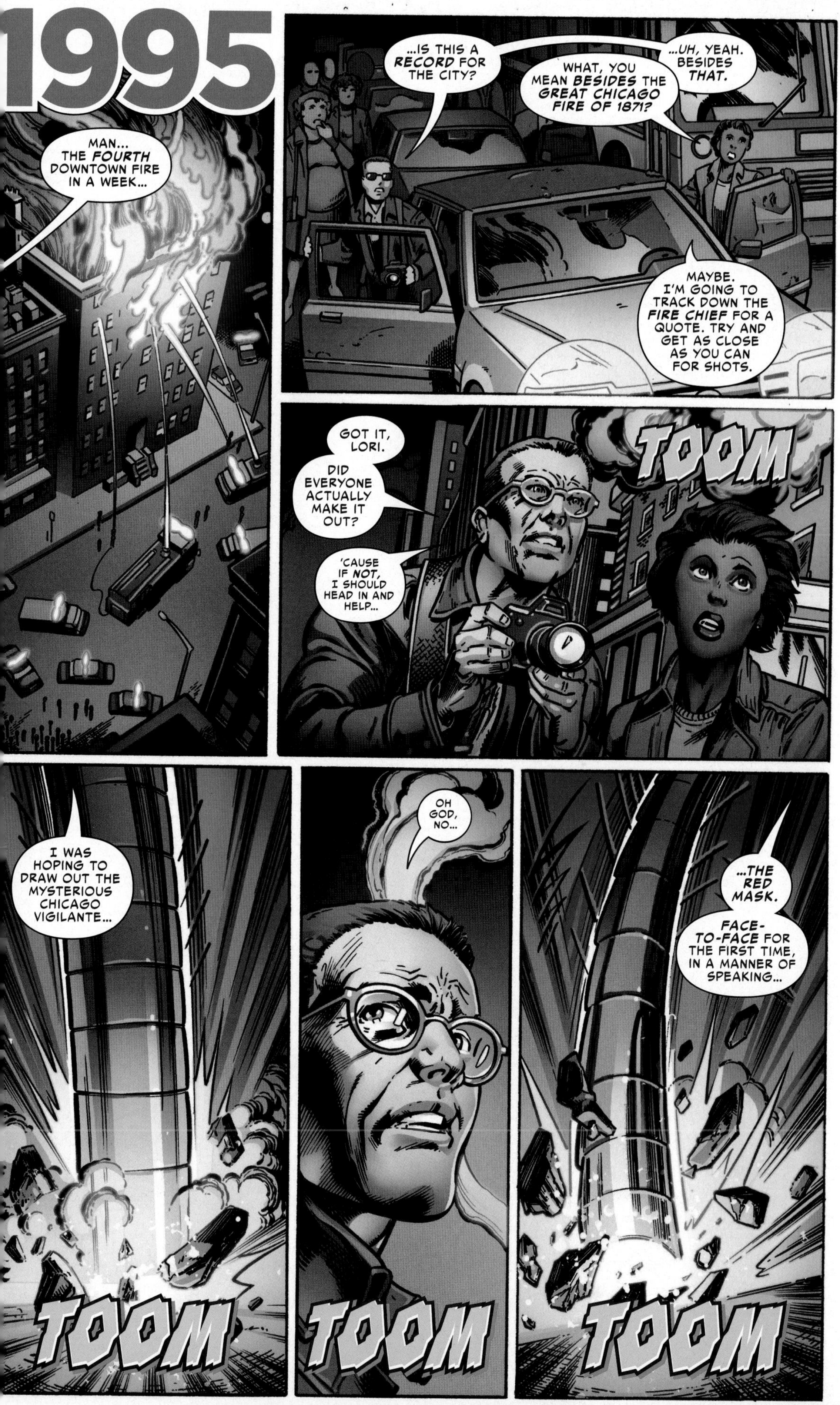

1995
MAN... THE FOURTH DOWNTOWN FIRE IN A WEEK...
...IS THIS A RECORD FOR THE CITY?
WHAT, YOU MEAN BESIDES THE GREAT CHICAGO FIRE OF 1871?
...UH, YEAH. BESIDES THAT.
MAYBE. I'M GOING TO TRACK DOWN THE FIRE CHIEF FOR A QUOTE. TRY AND GET AS CLOSE AS YOU CAN FOR SHOTS.
GOT IT, LORI.
DID EVERYONE ACTUALLY MAKE IT OUT?
'CAUSE IF NOT, I SHOULD HEAD IN AND HELP...
TOOM
I WAS HOPING TO DRAW OUT THE MYSTERIOUS CHICAGO VIGILANTE...
TOOM
OH GOD, NO...
TOOM
...THE RED MASK.
FACE-TO-FACE FOR THE FIRST TIME, IN A MANNER OF SPEAKING...
TOOM

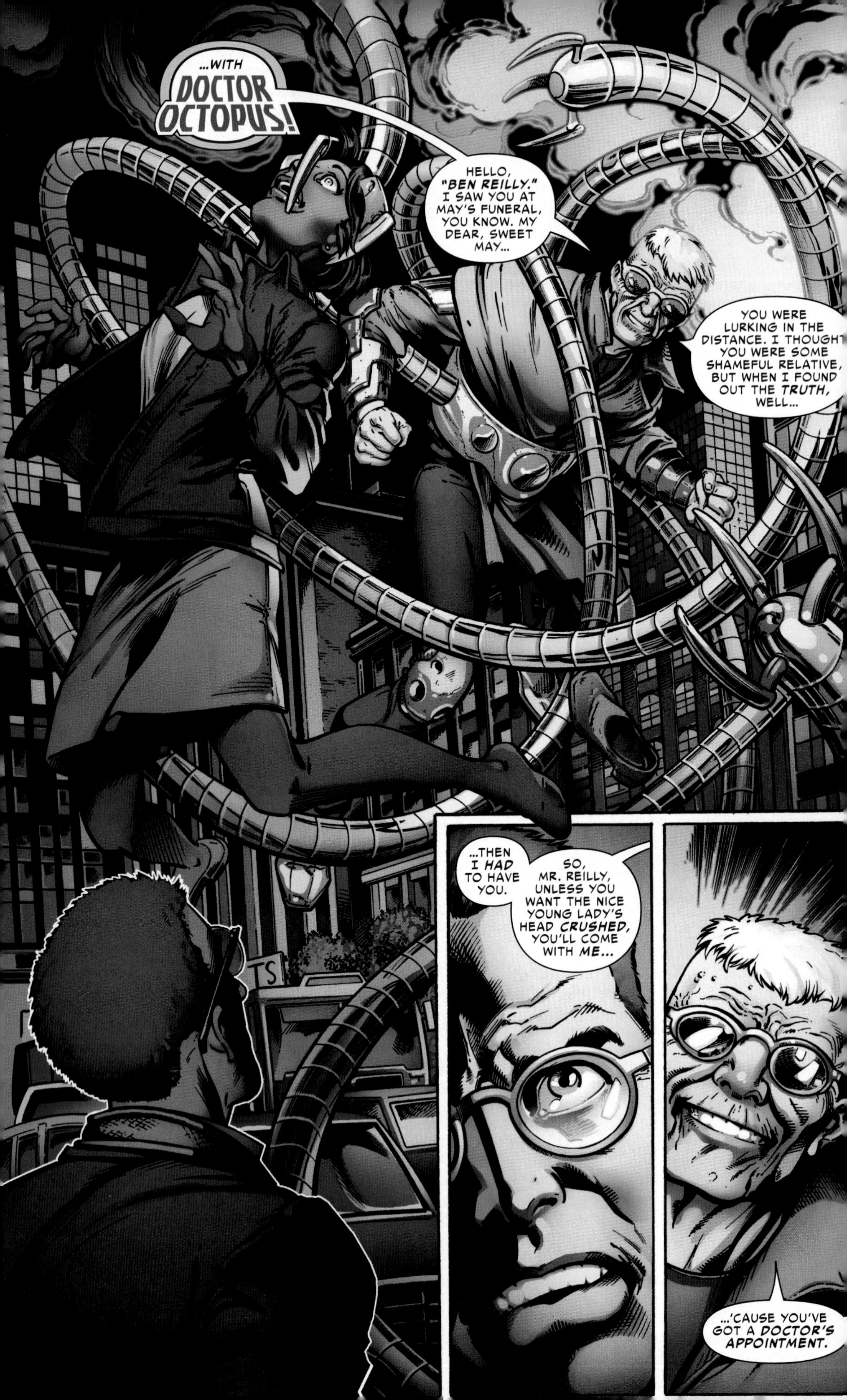
...WITH DOCTOR OCTOPUS!
HELLO, "BEN REILLY." I SAW YOU AT MAY'S FUNERAL, YOU KNOW. MY DEAR, SWEET MAY...
YOU WERE LURKING IN THE DISTANCE. I THOUGHT YOU WERE SOME SHAMEFUL RELATIVE, BUT WHEN I FOUND OUT THE TRUTH, WELL...
...THEN I HAD TO HAVE YOU.
SO, MR. REILLY, UNLESS YOU WANT THE NICE YOUNG LADY'S HEAD CRUSHED, YOU'LL COME WITH ME...
...'CAUSE YOU'VE GOT A DOCTOR'S APPOINTMENT.

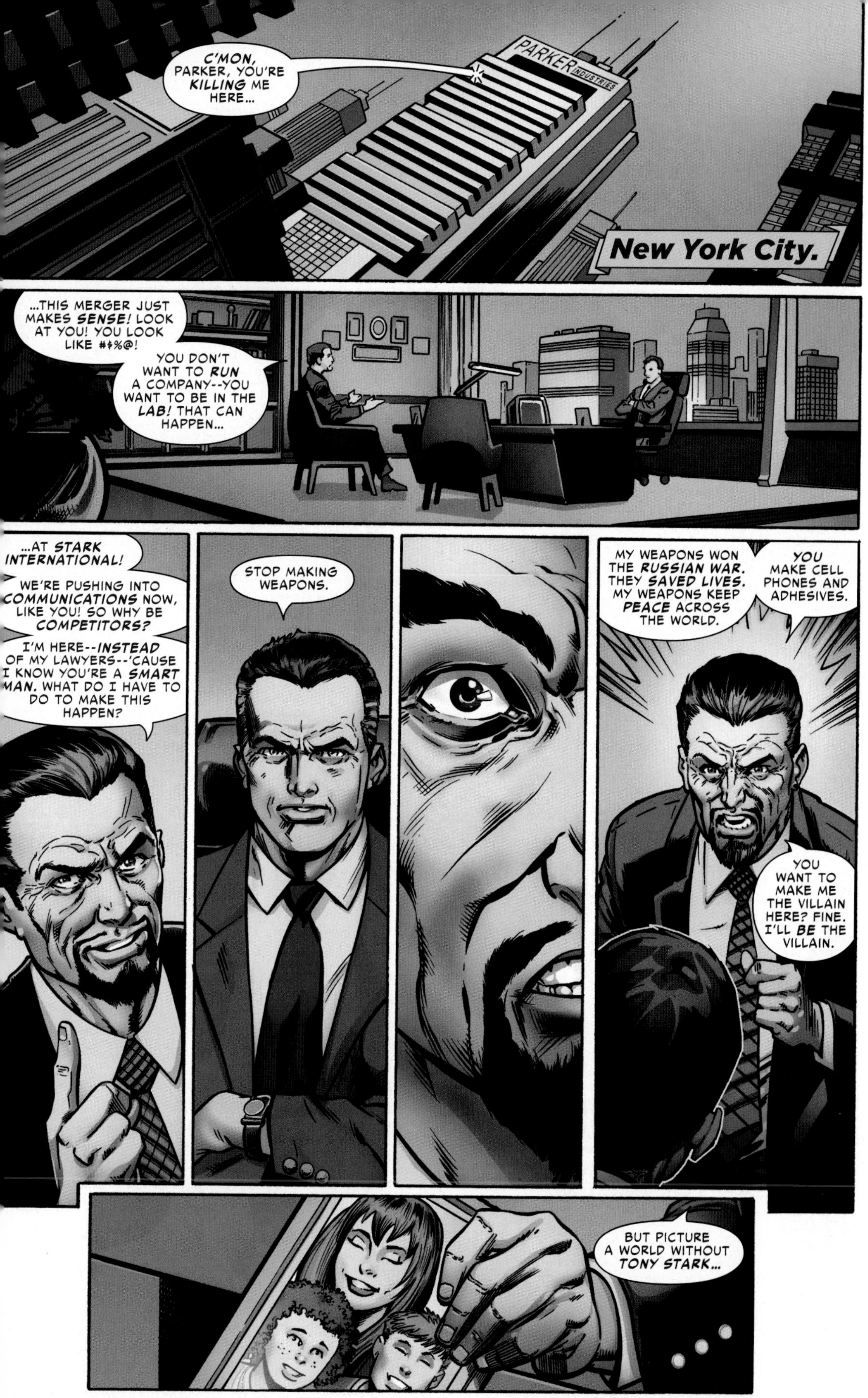
C'MON, PARKER, YOU'RE KILLING ME HERE...
PARKER INDUSTRIES
New York City.
...THIS MERGER JUST MAKES SENSE! LOOK AT YOU! YOU LOOK LIKE #$%@!
YOU DON'T WANT TO RUN A COMPANY--YOU WANT TO BE IN THE LAB! THAT CAN HAPPEN...
...AT STARK INTERNATIONAL!
WE'RE PUSHING INTO COMMUNICATIONS NOW, LIKE YOU! SO WHY BE COMPETITORS?
I'M HERE--INSTEAD OF MY LAWYERS--'CAUSE I KNOW YOU'RE A SMART MAN. WHAT DO I HAVE TO DO TO MAKE THIS HAPPEN?
STOP MAKING WEAPONS.
MY WEAPONS WON THE RUSSIAN WAR. THEY SAVED LIVES. MY WEAPONS KEEP PEACE ACROSS THE WORLD.
YOU MAKE CELL PHONES AND ADHESIVES.
YOU WANT TO MAKE ME THE VILLAIN HERE? FINE. I'LL BE THE VILLAIN.
BUT PICTURE A WORLD WITHOUT TONY STARK...

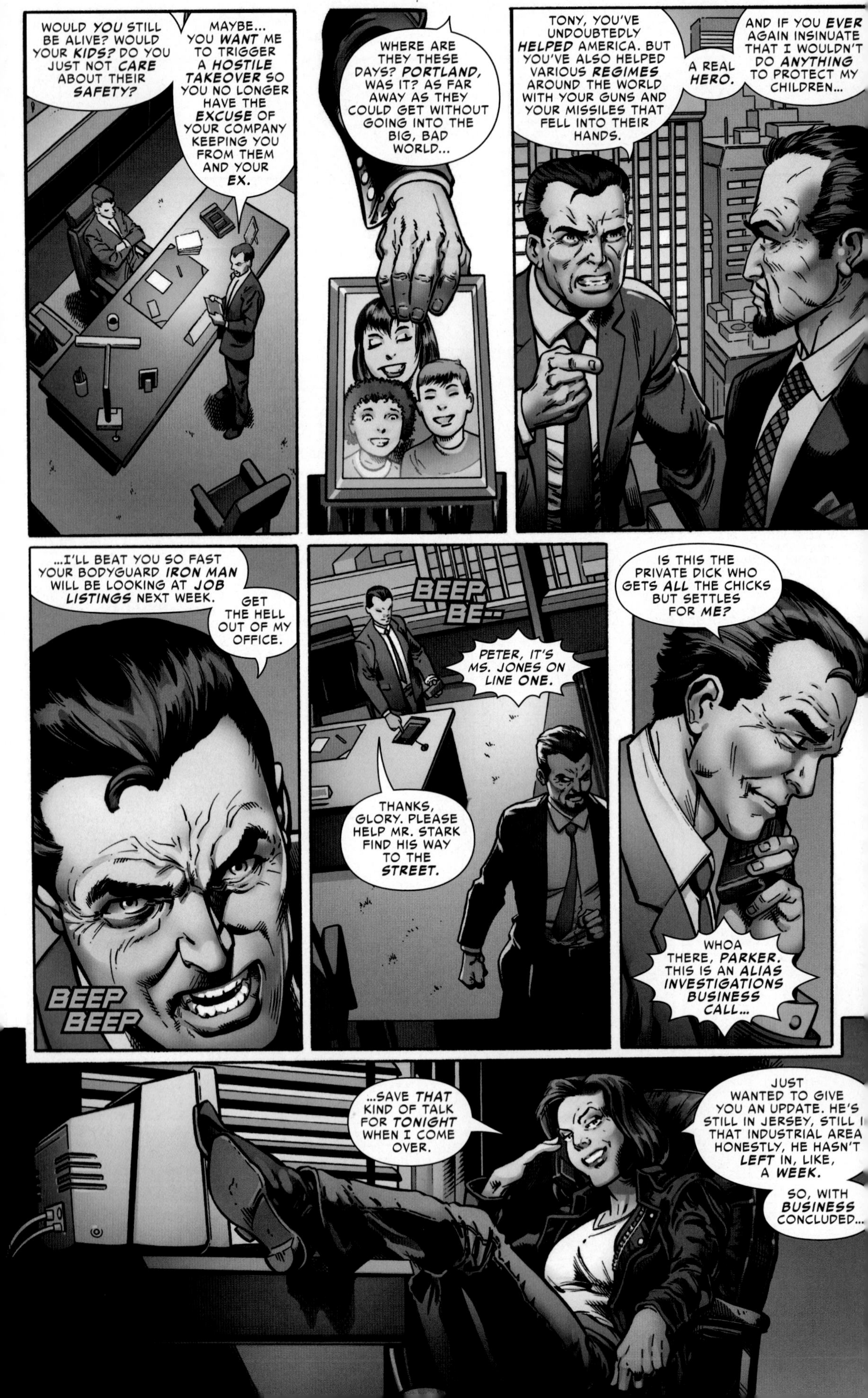
WOULD YOU STILL BE ALIVE? WOULD YOUR KIDS? DO YOU JUST NOT CARE ABOUT THEIR SAFETY?
MAYBE... YOU WANT ME TO TRIGGER A HOSTILE TAKEOVER SO YOU NO LONGER HAVE THE EXCUSE OF YOUR COMPANY KEEPING YOU FROM THEM AND YOUR EX.
WHERE ARE THEY THESE DAYS? PORTLAND, WAS IT? AS FAR AWAY AS THEY COULD GET WITHOUT GOING INTO THE BIG, BAD WORLD...
TONY, YOU'VE UNDOUBTEDLY HELPED AMERICA. BUT YOU'VE ALSO HELPED VARIOUS REGIMES AROUND THE WORLD WITH YOUR GUNS AND YOUR MISSILES THAT FELL INTO THEIR HANDS.
A REAL HERO.
AND IF YOU EVER AGAIN INSINUATE THAT I WOULDN'T DO ANYTHING TO PROTECT MY CHILDREN...
...I'LL BEAT YOU SO FAST YOUR BODYGUARD IRON MAN WILL BE LOOKING AT JOB LISTINGS NEXT WEEK.
GET THE HELL OUT OF MY OFFICE.
BEEP BEEP
BEEP BE--
PETER, IT'S MS. JONES ON LINE ONE.
THANKS, GLORY. PLEASE HELP MR. STARK FIND HIS WAY TO THE STREET.
IS THIS THE PRIVATE DICK WHO GETS ALL THE CHICKS BUT SETTLES FOR ME?
WHOA THERE, PARKER. THIS IS AN ALIAS INVESTIGATIONS BUSINESS CALL...
JUST WANTED TO GIVE YOU AN UPDATE. HE'S STILL IN JERSEY, STILL I THAT INDUSTRIAL AREA HONESTLY, HE HASN'T LEFT IN, LIKE, A WEEK.
SO, WITH BUSINESS CONCLUDED...
...SAVE THAT KIND OF TALK FOR TONIGHT WHEN I COME OVER.

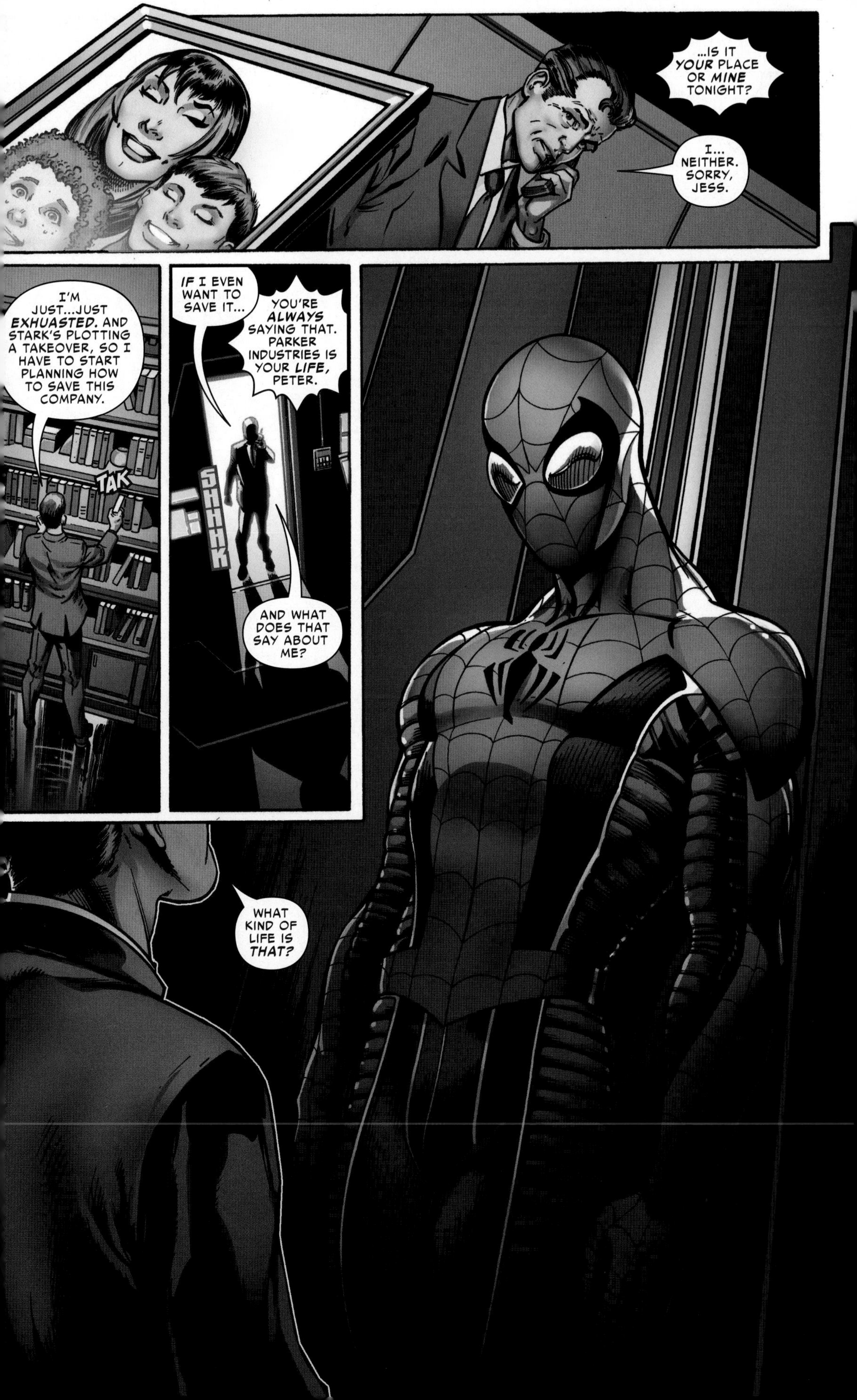
...IS IT YOUR PLACE OR MINE TONIGHT?
I... NEITHER. SORRY, JESS.
I'M JUST...JUST EXHAUSTED. AND STARK'S PLOTTING A TAKEOVER, SO I HAVE TO START PLANNING HOW TO SAVE THIS COMPANY.
TAK
IF I EVEN WANT TO SAVE IT...
YOU'RE ALWAYS SAYING THAT. PARKER INDUSTRIES IS YOUR LIFE, PETER.
SHHHK
AND WHAT DOES THAT SAY ABOUT ME?
WHAT KIND OF LIFE IS THAT?

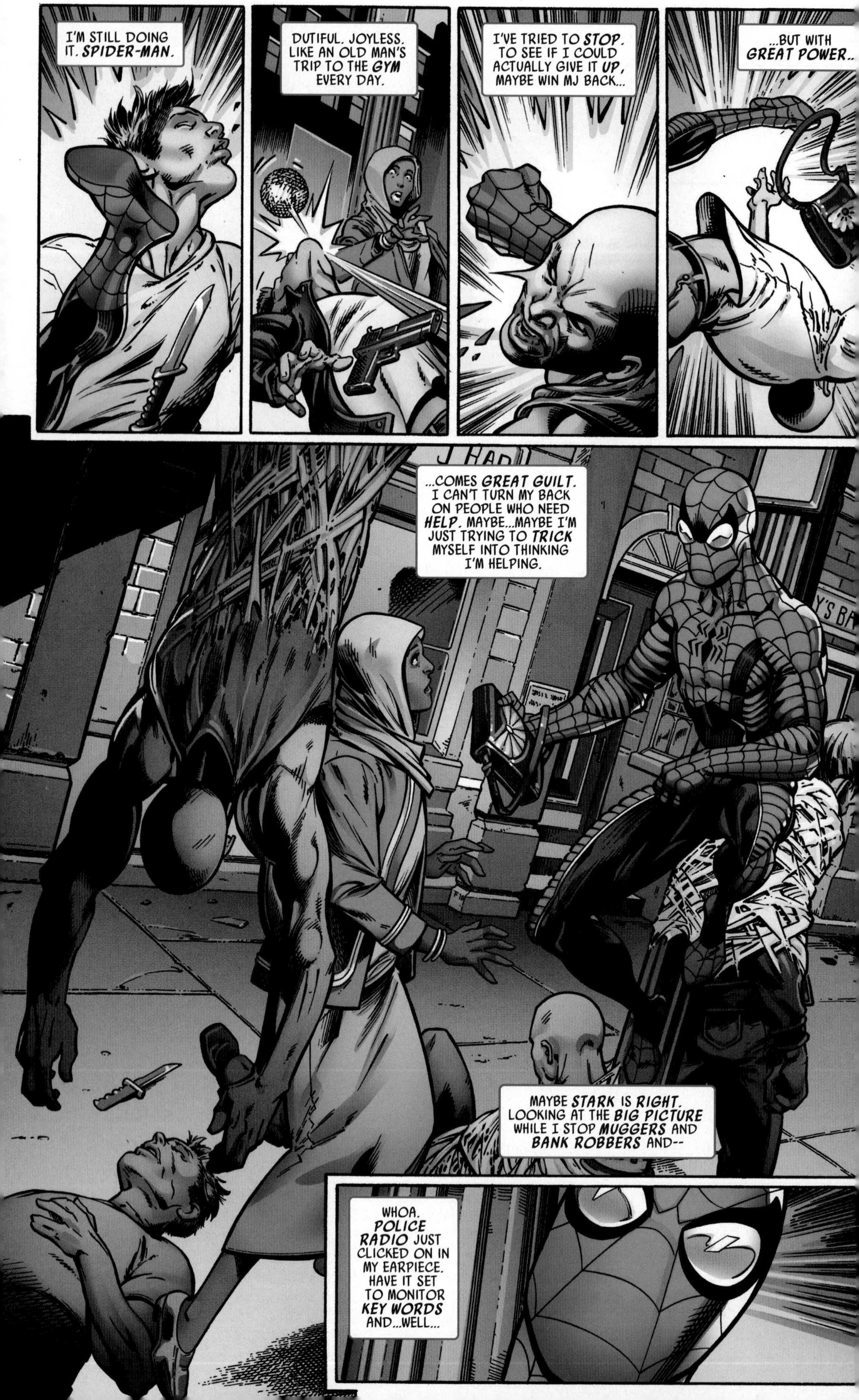
I'M STILL DOING IT. SPIDER-MAN.
DUTIFUL. JOYLESS. LIKE AN OLD MAN'S TRIP TO THE GYM EVERY DAY.
I'VE TRIED TO STOP. TO SEE IF I COULD ACTUALLY GIVE IT UP, MAYBE WIN MJ BACK...
...BUT WITH GREAT POWER...
...COMES GREAT GUILT. I CAN'T TURN MY BACK ON PEOPLE WHO NEED HELP. MAYBE...MAYBE I'M JUST TRYING TO TRICK MYSELF INTO THINKING I'M HELPING.
MAYBE STARK IS RIGHT. LOOKING AT THE BIG PICTURE WHILE I STOP MUGGERS AND BANK ROBBERS AND--
WHOA. POLICE RADIO JUST CLICKED ON IN MY EARPIECE. HAVE IT SET TO MONITOR KEY WORDS AND...WELL...

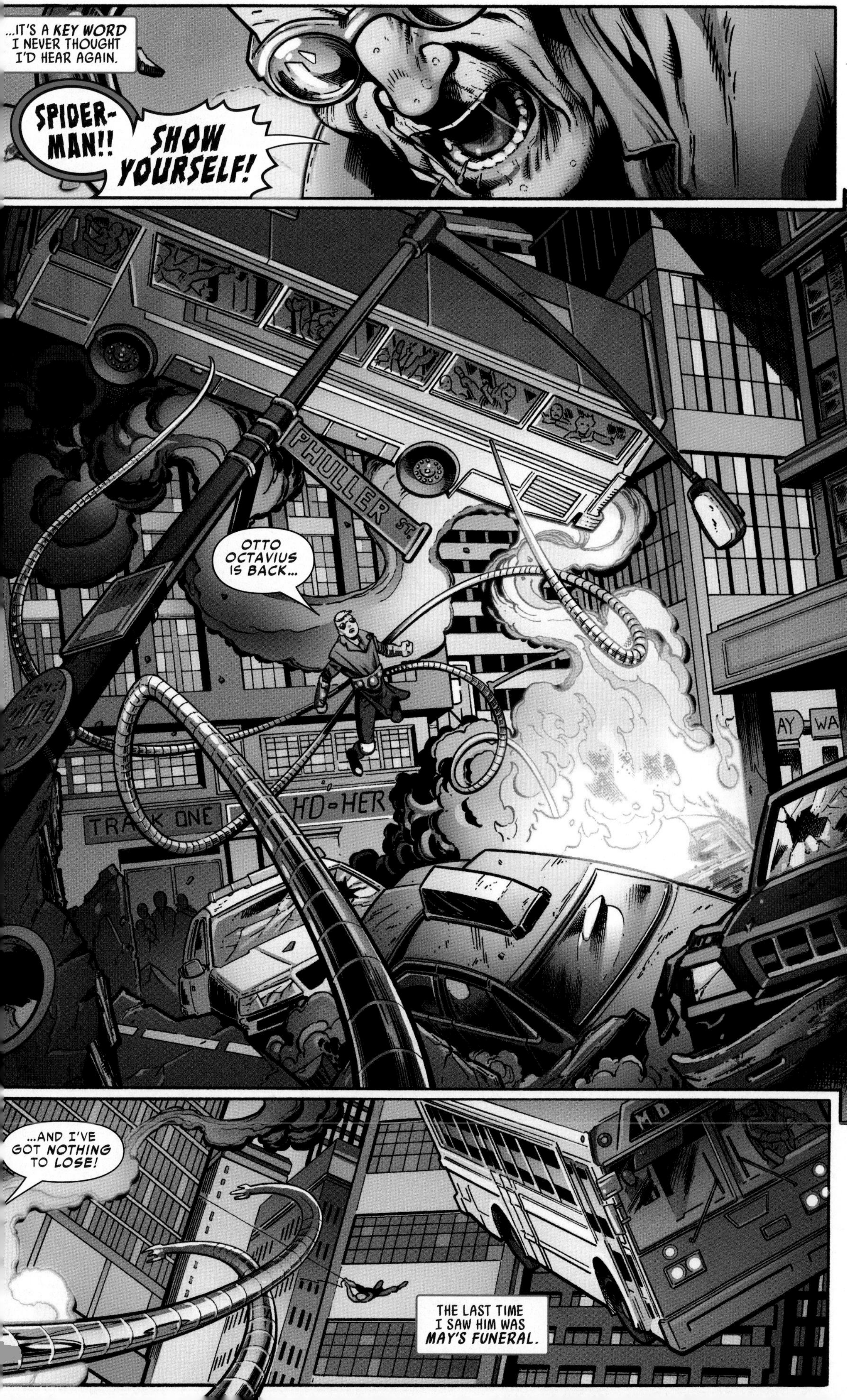
...IT'S A KEY WORD I NEVER THOUGHT I'D HEAR AGAIN.
SPIDER-MAN!!
SHOW YOURSELF!
PHULLER ST.
OTTO OCTAVIUS IS BACK...
...AND I'VE GOT NOTHING TO LOSE!
THE LAST TIME I SAW HIM WAS MAY'S FUNERAL.

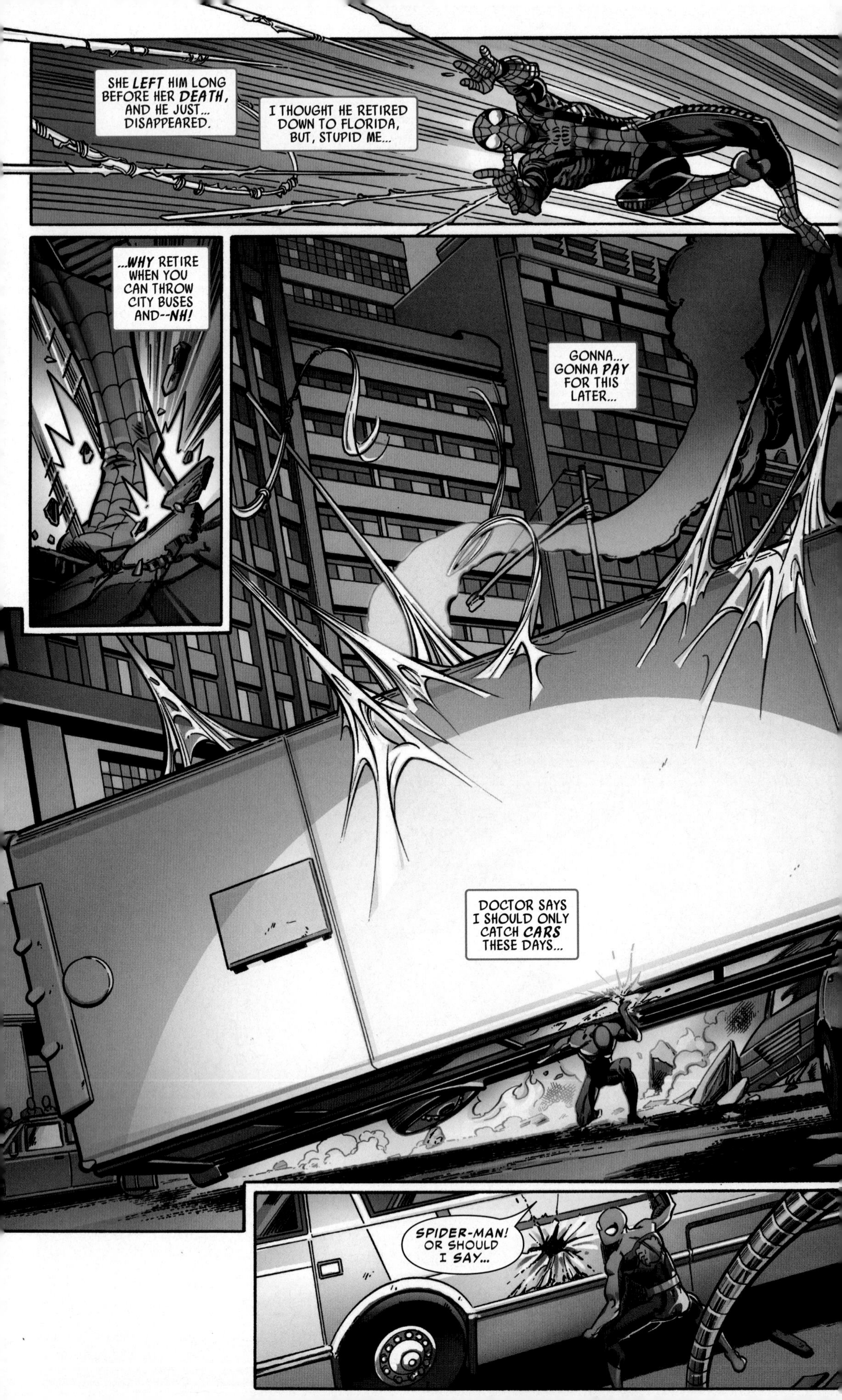
SHE LEFT HIM LONG BEFORE HER DEATH, AND HE JUST... DISAPPEARED.
I THOUGHT HE RETIRED DOWN TO FLORIDA, BUT, STUPID ME...
...WHY RETIRE WHEN YOU CAN THROW CITY BUSES AND--NH!
GONNA... GONNA PAY FOR THIS LATER...
DOCTOR SAYS I SHOULD ONLY CATCH CARS THESE DAYS...
SPIDER-MAN! OR SHOULD I SAY...

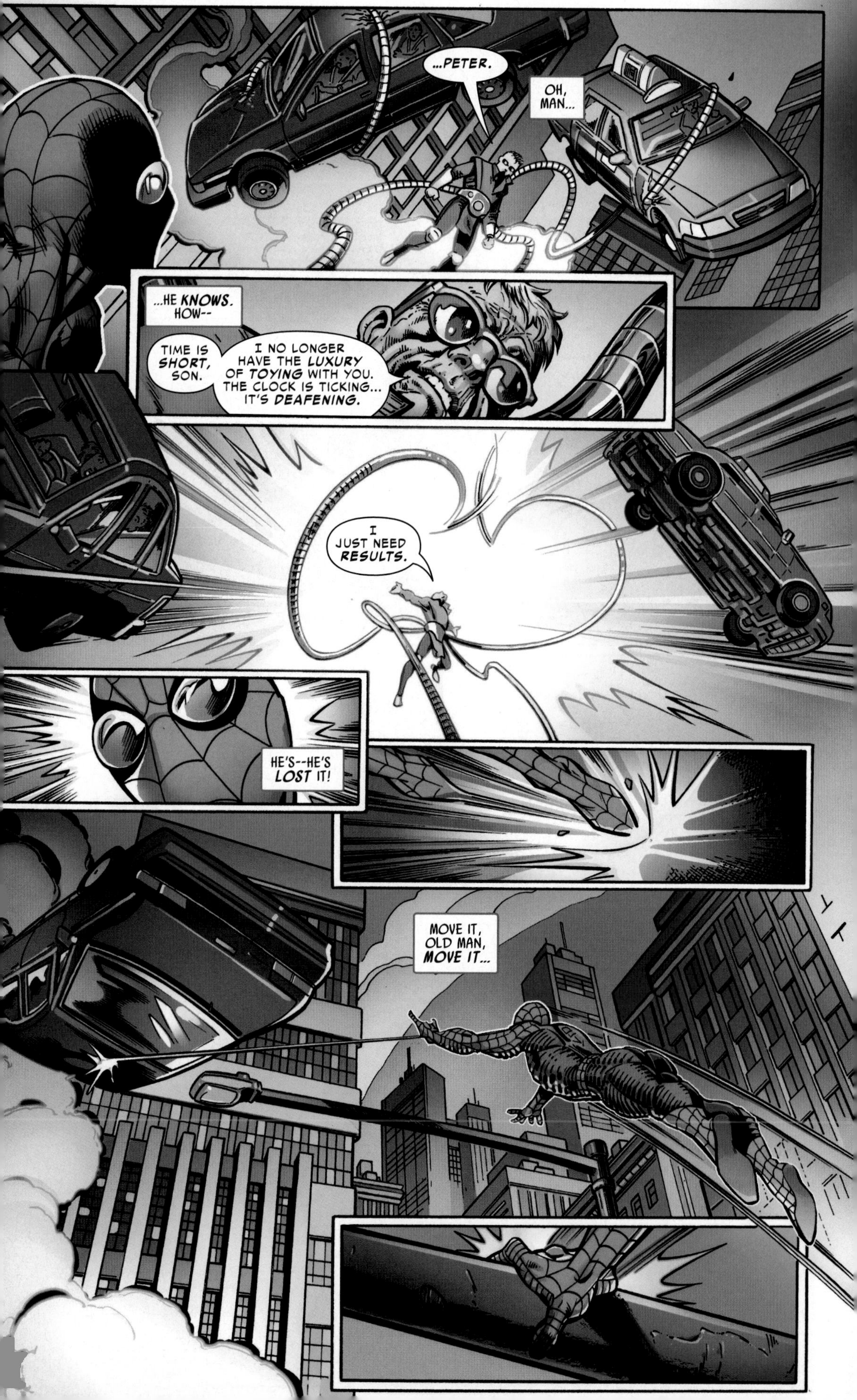

...PETER.
OH, MAN...
...HE KNOWS. HOW--
TIME IS SHORT, SON.
I NO LONGER HAVE THE LUXURY OF TOYING WITH YOU. THE CLOCK IS TICKING... IT'S DEAFENING.
I JUST NEED RESULTS.
HE'S--HE'S LOST IT!
MOVE IT, OLD MAN, MOVE IT...

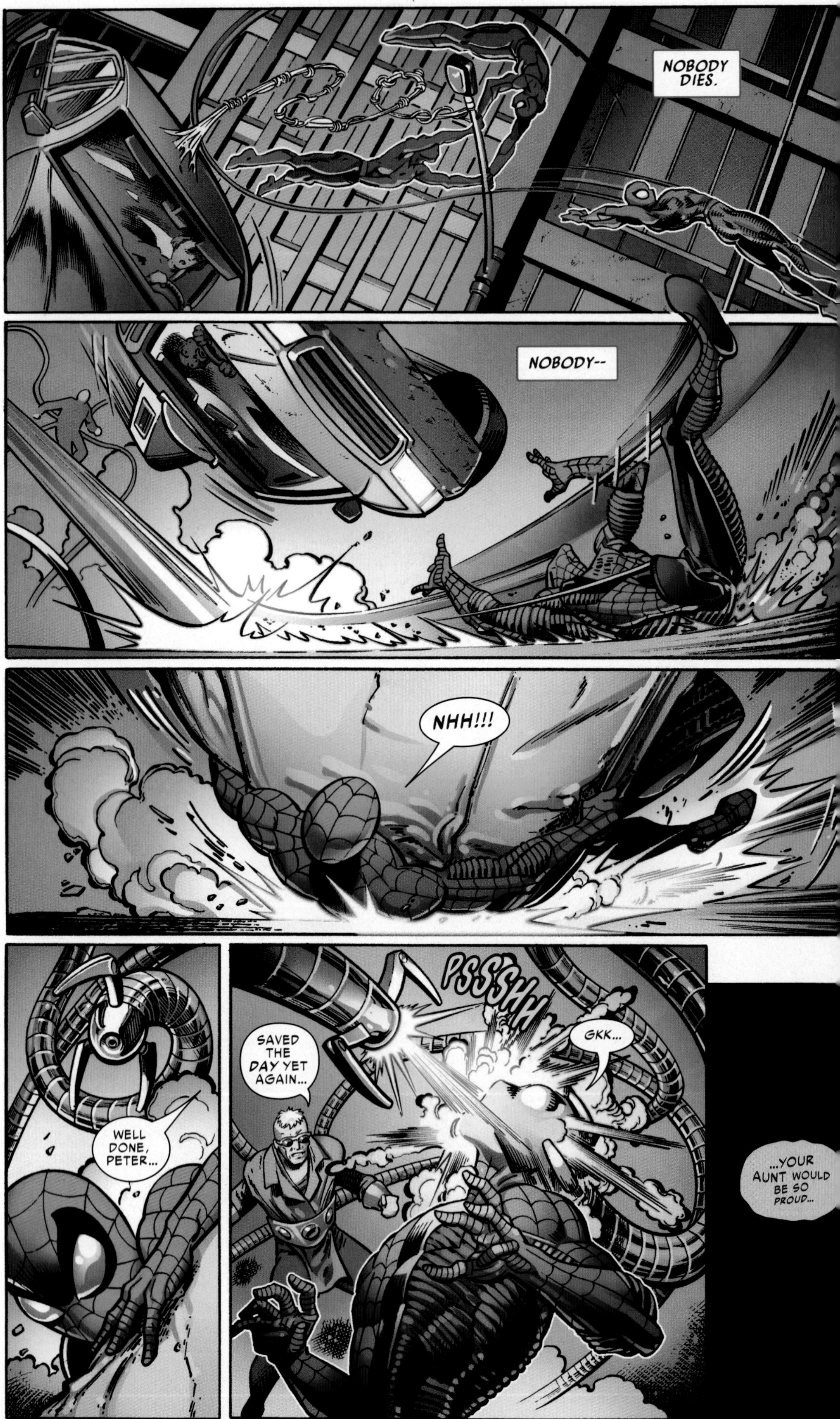
NOBODY DIES.
NOBODY--
NHH!!!
WELL DONE, PETER...
PSSSHH
SAVED THE DAY YET AGAIN...
GKK...
...YOUR AUNT WOULD BE SO PROUD...

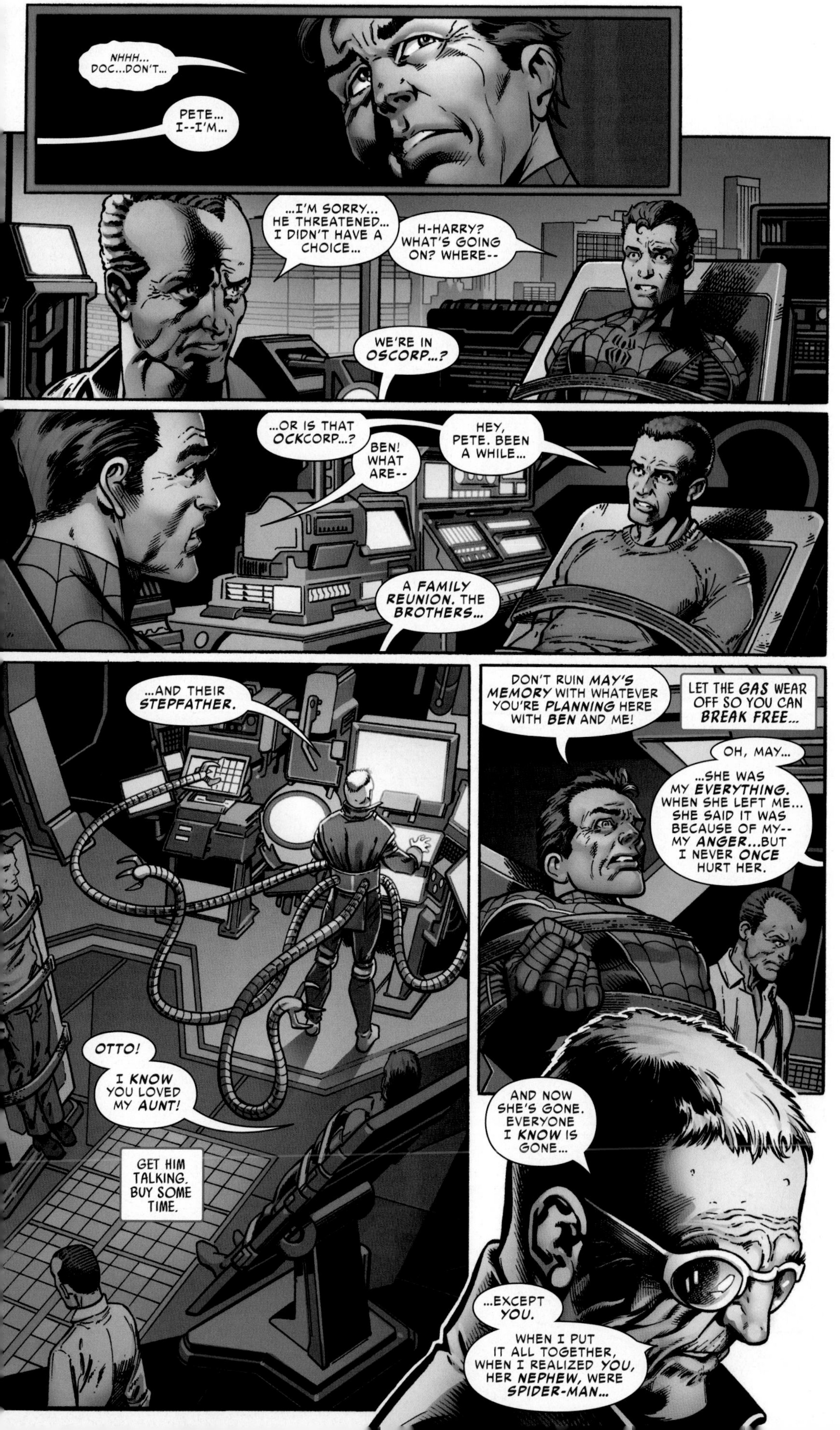
NHHH... DOC...DON'T...
PETE... I--I'M...
...I'M SORRY... HE THREATENED... I DIDN'T HAVE A CHOICE...
H-HARRY? WHAT'S GOING ON? WHERE--
WE'RE IN OSCORP...?
...OR IS THAT OCKCORP...?
BEN! WHAT ARE--
HEY, PETE. BEEN A WHILE...
A FAMILY REUNION. THE BROTHERS...
...AND THEIR STEPFATHER.
OTTO!
I KNOW YOU LOVED MY AUNT!
GET HIM TALKING. BUY SOME TIME.
DON'T RUIN MAY'S MEMORY WITH WHATEVER YOU'RE PLANNING HERE WITH BEN AND ME!
LET THE GAS WEAR OFF SO YOU CAN BREAK FREE...
OH, MAY...
...SHE WAS MY EVERYTHING. WHEN SHE LEFT ME... SHE SAID IT WAS BECAUSE OF MY-- MY ANGER...BUT I NEVER ONCE HURT HER.
AND NOW SHE'S GONE. EVERYONE I KNOW IS GONE...
...EXCEPT YOU.
WHEN I PUT IT ALL TOGETHER, WHEN I REALIZED YOU, HER NEPHEW, WERE SPIDER-MAN...

...IT ALL *MADE SENSE.* YOU MADE HER *LEAVE ME!* MY OLDEST *ENEMY* COULDN'T *STAND* US BEING *HAPPY!*

AND NOW *SHE'S DEAD!*

AND *SOON* I'LL JOIN HER...

BUT I *CAN'T...*I JUST...JUST *CAN'T.* I HAVE TOO MUCH TO DO. YOU DON'T UNDERSTAND YET, WHAT IT'S *LIKE* TO BE STARING INTO THE *VOID* WITHOUT-- WITHOUT ACCOMPLISHING ANYTHING.

I COULD FEEL DEATH *STALKING* ME, BUT THEN I FOUND OUT ABOUT *YOU...*

...AND *PROFESSOR WARREN'S CLONE.*

I HAVE A NAM YOU KNOW

CLONING! A CHANCE AT A *NEW LIFE!* BUT THE *PROFESSOR'S* WORK WAS DESTROYED. THE ONLY BITS OF IT THAT REMAINED WERE IN *FILES* HERE AT *OSCORP.* AND...

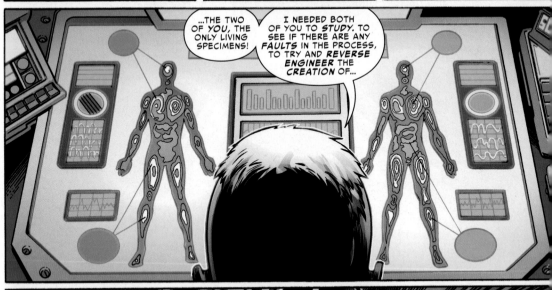

...THE TWO OF *YOU,* THE ONLY LIVING *SPECIMENS!*

I NEEDED BOTH OF YOU TO *STUDY.* TO SEE IF THERE ARE ANY *FAULTS* IN THE PROCESS, TO TRY AND *REVERSE ENGINEER* THE *CREATION* OF...

...OF...

...THIS *CAN'T* BE RIGHT...

PETER... PETER PARKER...

...IS THE *CLONE!*

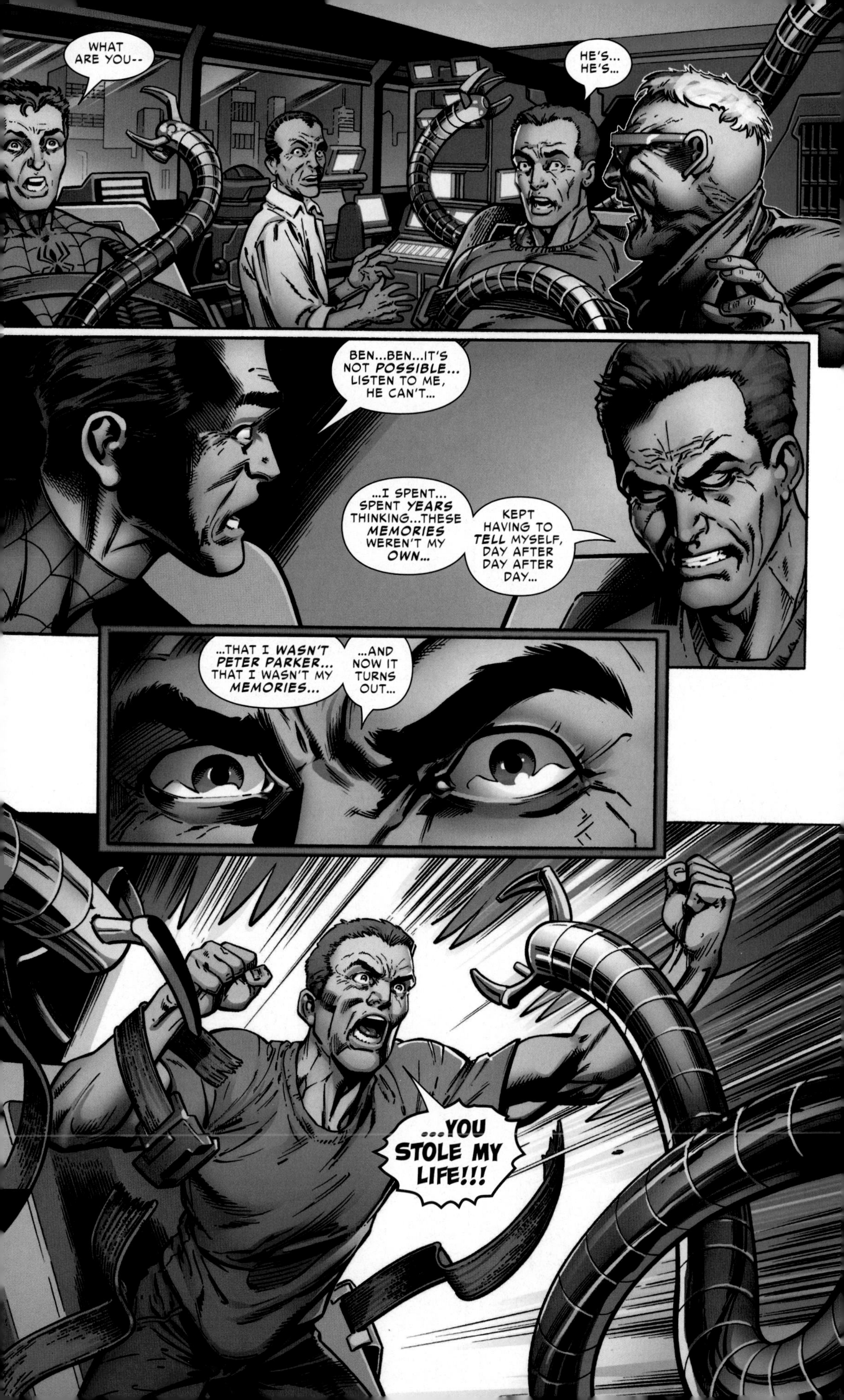
WHAT ARE YOU--
HE'S... HE'S...
BEN...BEN...IT'S NOT POSSIBLE... LISTEN TO ME, HE CAN'T...
...I SPENT... SPENT YEARS THINKING...THESE MEMORIES WEREN'T MY OWN...
KEPT HAVING TO TELL MYSELF, DAY AFTER DAY AFTER DAY...
...THAT I WASN'T PETER PARKER... THAT I WASN'T MY MEMORIES...
...AND NOW IT TURNS OUT...
...YOU STOLE MY LIFE!!!

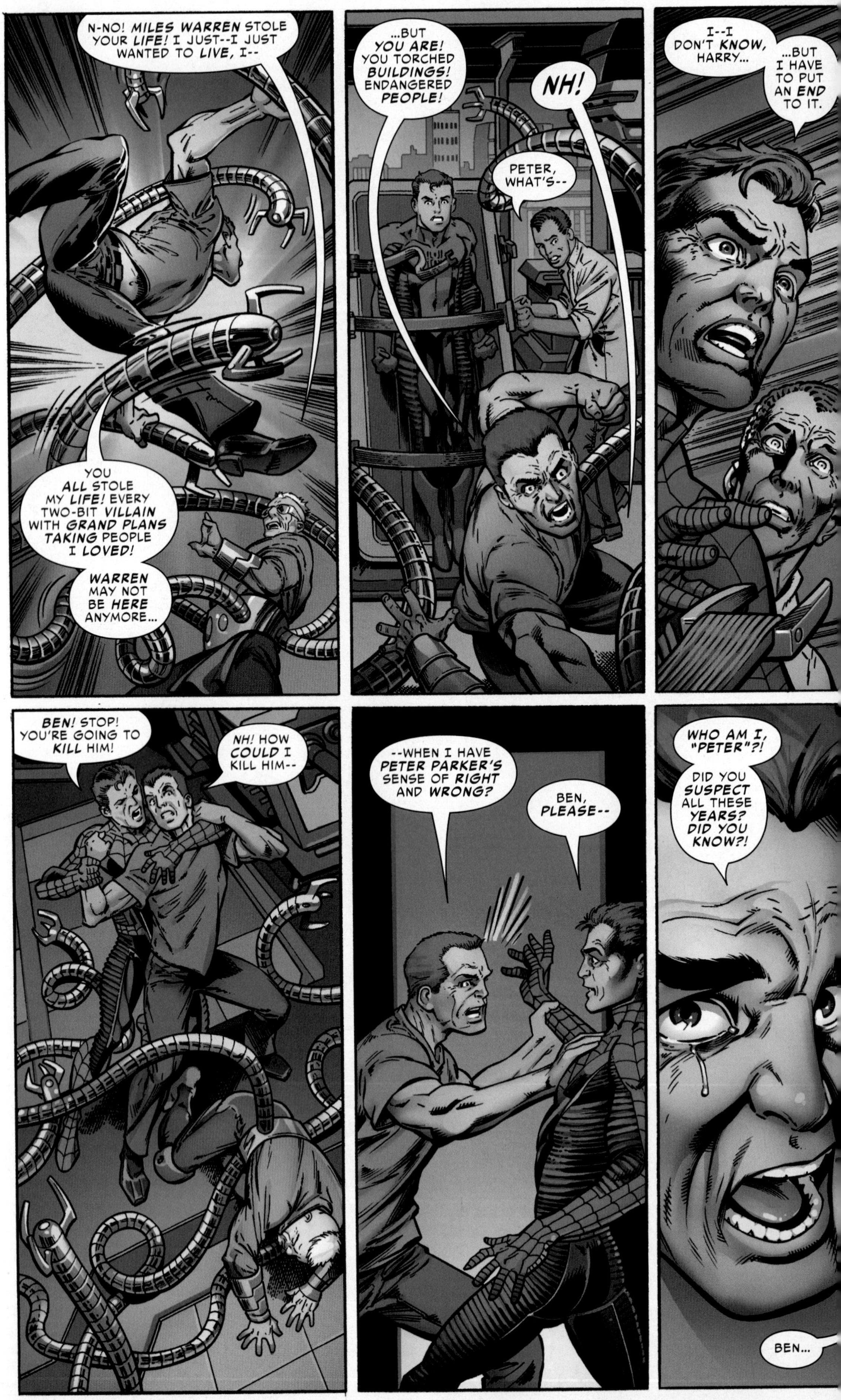

N-NO! MILES WARREN STOLE YOUR LIFE! I JUST--I JUST WANTED TO LIVE, I--
YOU ALL STOLE MY LIFE! EVERY TWO-BIT VILLAIN WITH GRAND PLANS TAKING PEOPLE I LOVED!
WARREN MAY NOT BE HERE ANYMORE...
...BUT YOU ARE! YOU TORCHED BUILDINGS! ENDANGERED PEOPLE!
NH!
PETER, WHAT'S--
I--I DON'T KNOW, HARRY...
...BUT I HAVE TO PUT AN END TO IT.
BEN! STOP! YOU'RE GOING TO KILL HIM!
NH! HOW COULD I KILL HIM--
--WHEN I HAVE PETER PARKER'S SENSE OF RIGHT AND WRONG?
BEN, PLEASE--
WHO AM I, "PETER"?!
DID YOU SUSPECT ALL THESE YEARS? DID YOU KNOW?!
BEN...

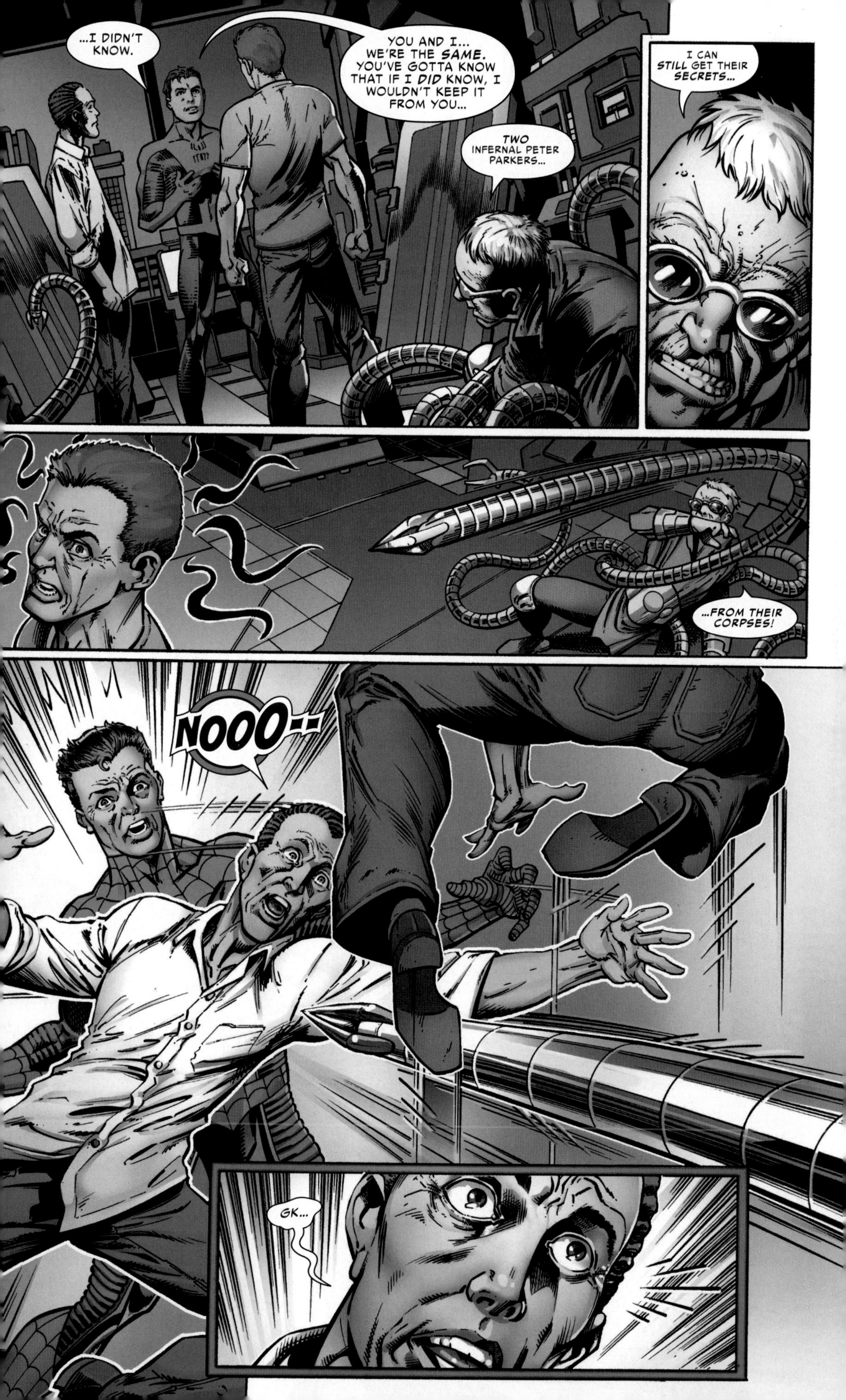
...I DIDN'T KNOW.
YOU AND I... WE'RE THE SAME. YOU'VE GOTTA KNOW THAT IF I DID KNOW, I WOULDN'T KEEP IT FROM YOU...
TWO INFERNAL PETER PARKERS...
I CAN STILL GET THEIR SECRETS...
...FROM THEIR CORPSES!
NOOO--!
GK...

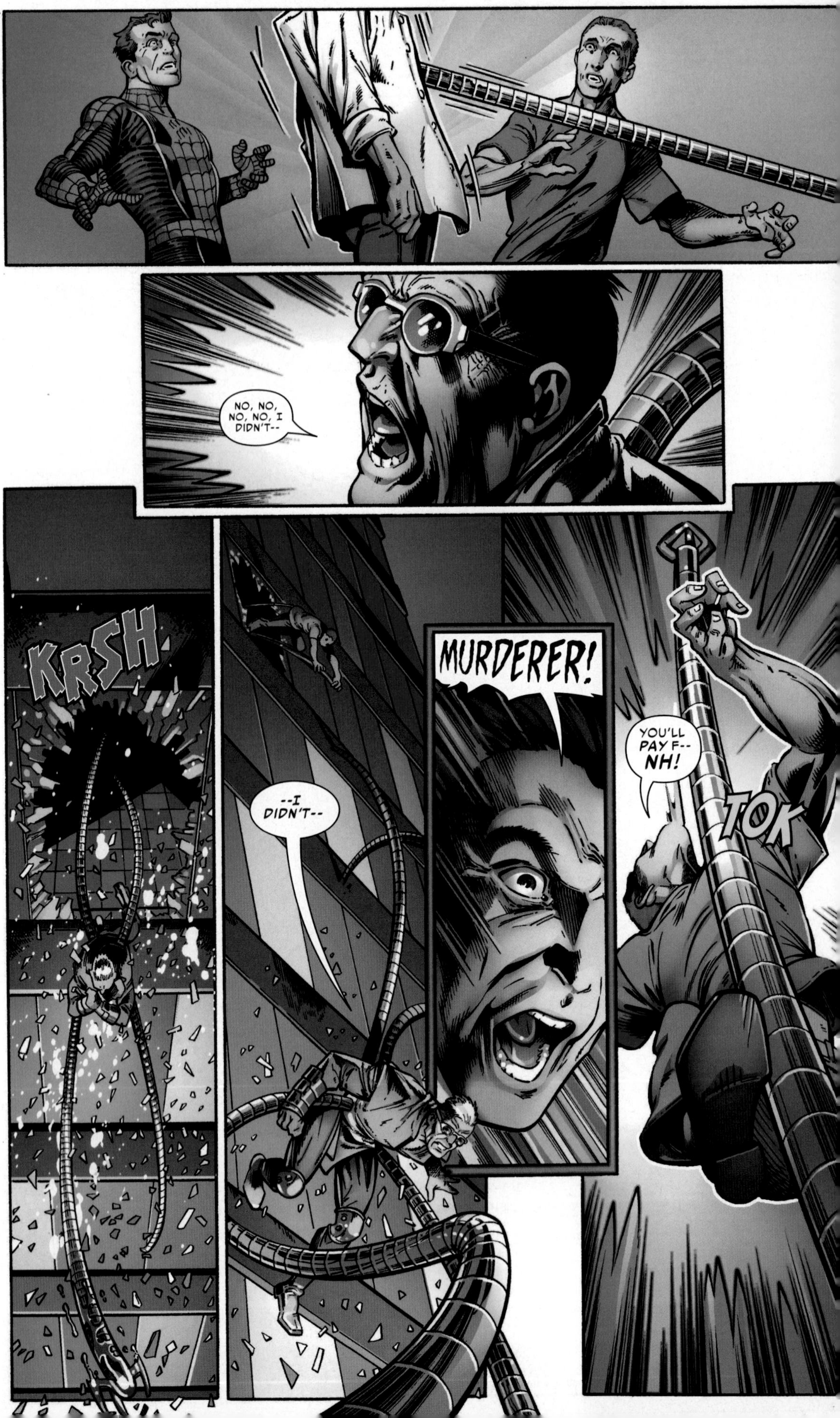
NO, NO, NO, NO, I DIDN'T--
KRSH
--I DIDN'T--
MURDERER!
YOU'LL PAY F-- NH!
TOK

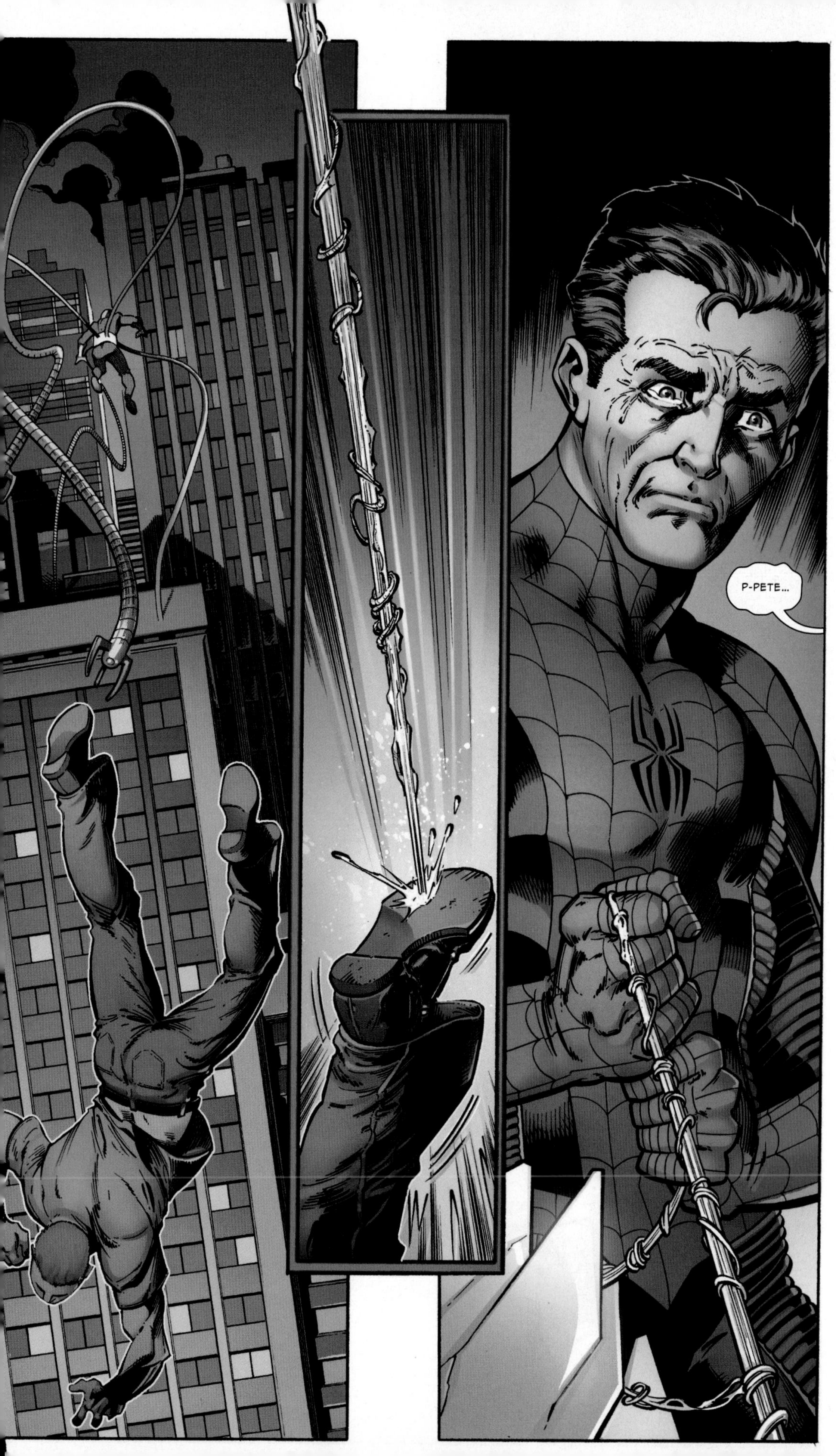
P-PETE...

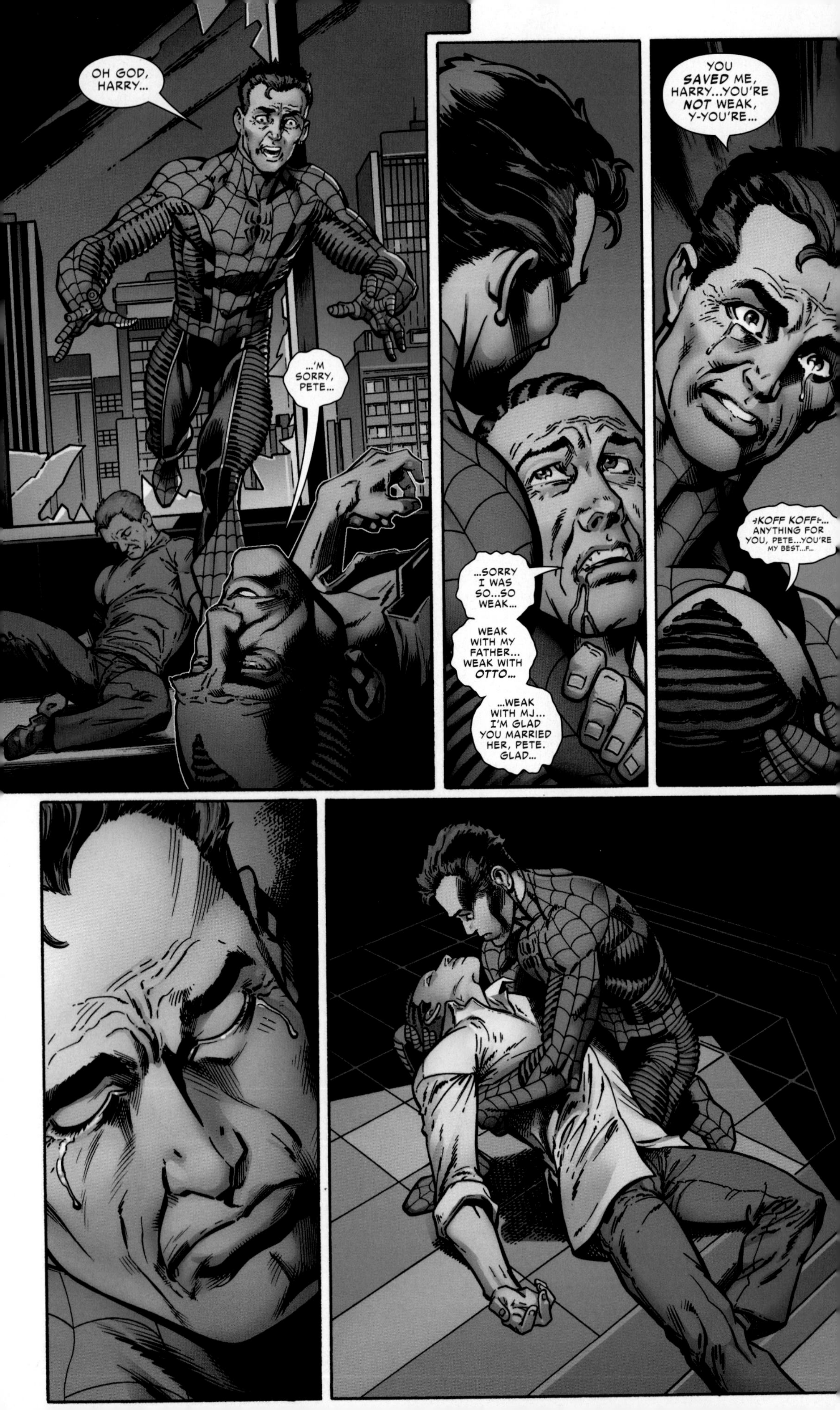

OH GOD, HARRY...
...'M SORRY, PETE...
...SORRY I WAS SO...SO WEAK...
WEAK WITH MY FATHER... WEAK WITH OTTO...
...WEAK WITH MJ... I'M GLAD YOU MARRIED HER, PETE. GLAD...
YOU SAVED ME, HARRY...YOU'RE NOT WEAK, Y-YOU'RE...
⸗KOFF KOFF⸗... ANYTHING FOR YOU, PETE...YOU'RE MY BEST...F...

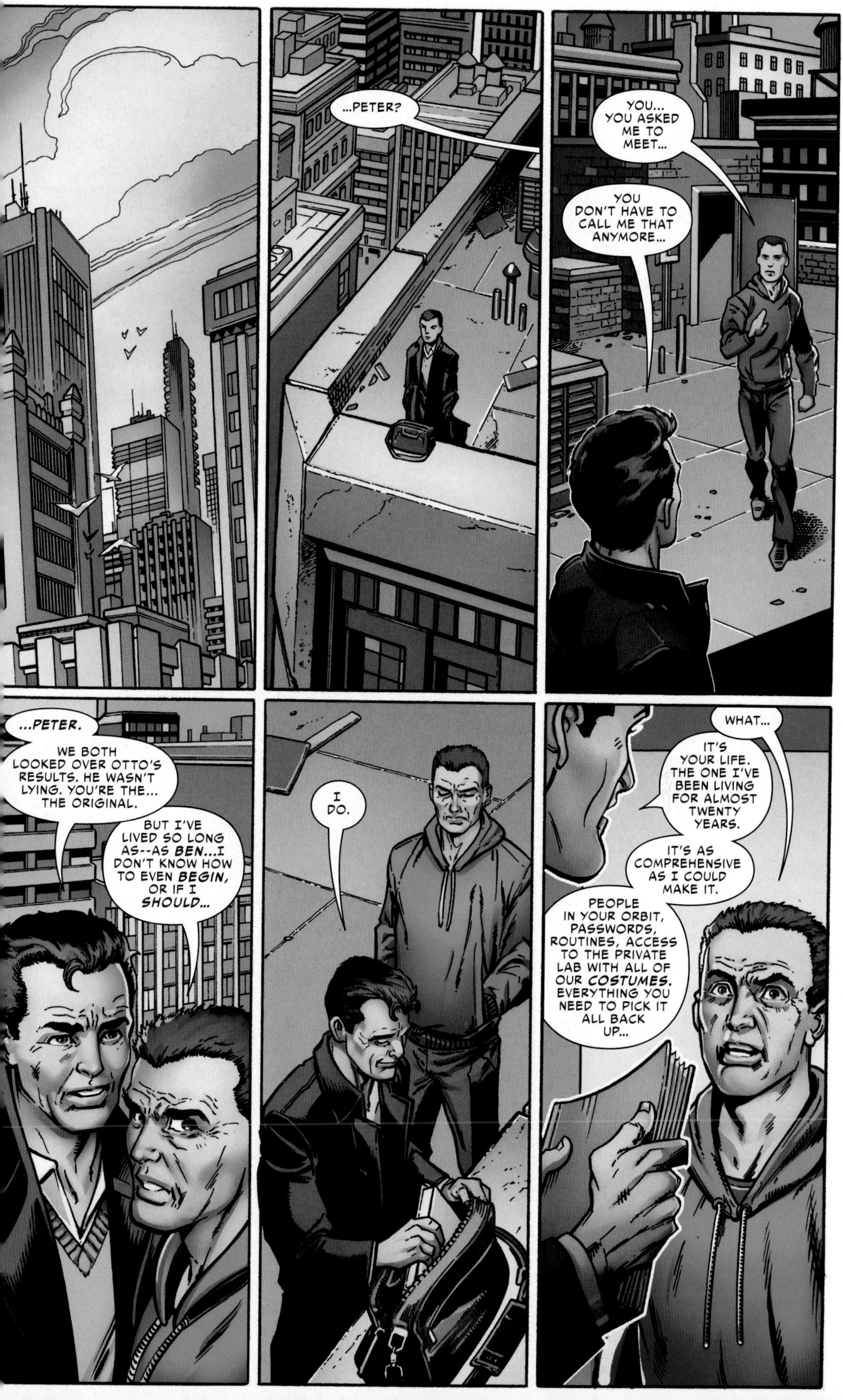

...PETER?
YOU... YOU ASKED ME TO MEET...
YOU DON'T HAVE TO CALL ME THAT ANYMORE...
...PETER.
WE BOTH LOOKED OVER OTTO'S RESULTS. HE WASN'T LYING. YOU'RE THE... THE ORIGINAL.
BUT I'VE LIVED SO LONG AS--AS *BEN*...I DON'T KNOW HOW TO EVEN *BEGIN,* OR IF I *SHOULD*...
I DO.
WHAT...
IT'S YOUR LIFE. THE ONE I'VE BEEN LIVING FOR ALMOST TWENTY YEARS.
IT'S AS COMPREHENSIVE AS I COULD MAKE IT.
PEOPLE IN YOUR ORBIT, PASSWORDS, ROUTINES, ACCESS TO THE PRIVATE LAB WITH ALL OF OUR *COSTUMES.* EVERYTHING YOU NEED TO PICK IT ALL BACK UP...

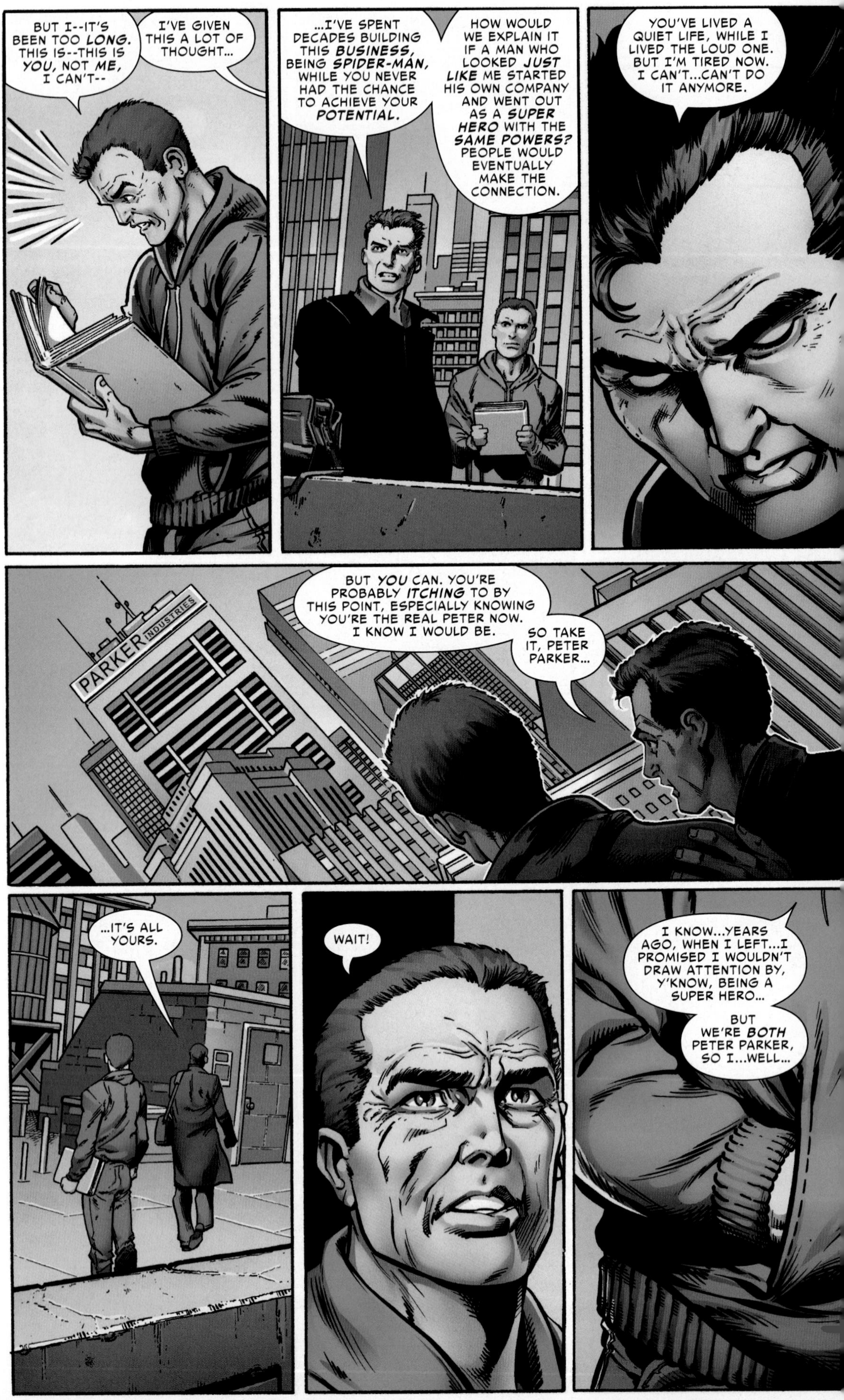
BUT I--IT'S BEEN TOO LONG. THIS IS--THIS IS YOU, NOT ME, I CAN'T--
I'VE GIVEN THIS A LOT OF THOUGHT...
...I'VE SPENT DECADES BUILDING THIS BUSINESS, BEING SPIDER-MAN, WHILE YOU NEVER HAD THE CHANCE TO ACHIEVE YOUR POTENTIAL.
HOW WOULD WE EXPLAIN IT IF A MAN WHO LOOKED JUST LIKE ME STARTED HIS OWN COMPANY AND WENT OUT AS A SUPER HERO WITH THE SAME POWERS? PEOPLE WOULD EVENTUALLY MAKE THE CONNECTION.
YOU'VE LIVED A QUIET LIFE, WHILE I LIVED THE LOUD ONE. BUT I'M TIRED NOW. I CAN'T...CAN'T DO IT ANYMORE.
PARKER INDUSTRIES
BUT YOU CAN. YOU'RE PROBABLY ITCHING TO BY THIS POINT, ESPECIALLY KNOWING YOU'RE THE REAL PETER NOW. I KNOW I WOULD BE.
SO TAKE IT, PETER PARKER...
...IT'S ALL YOURS.
WAIT!
I KNOW...YEARS AGO, WHEN I LEFT...I PROMISED I WOULDN'T DRAW ATTENTION BY, Y'KNOW, BEING A SUPER HERO...
BUT WE'RE BOTH PETER PARKER, SO I...WELL...

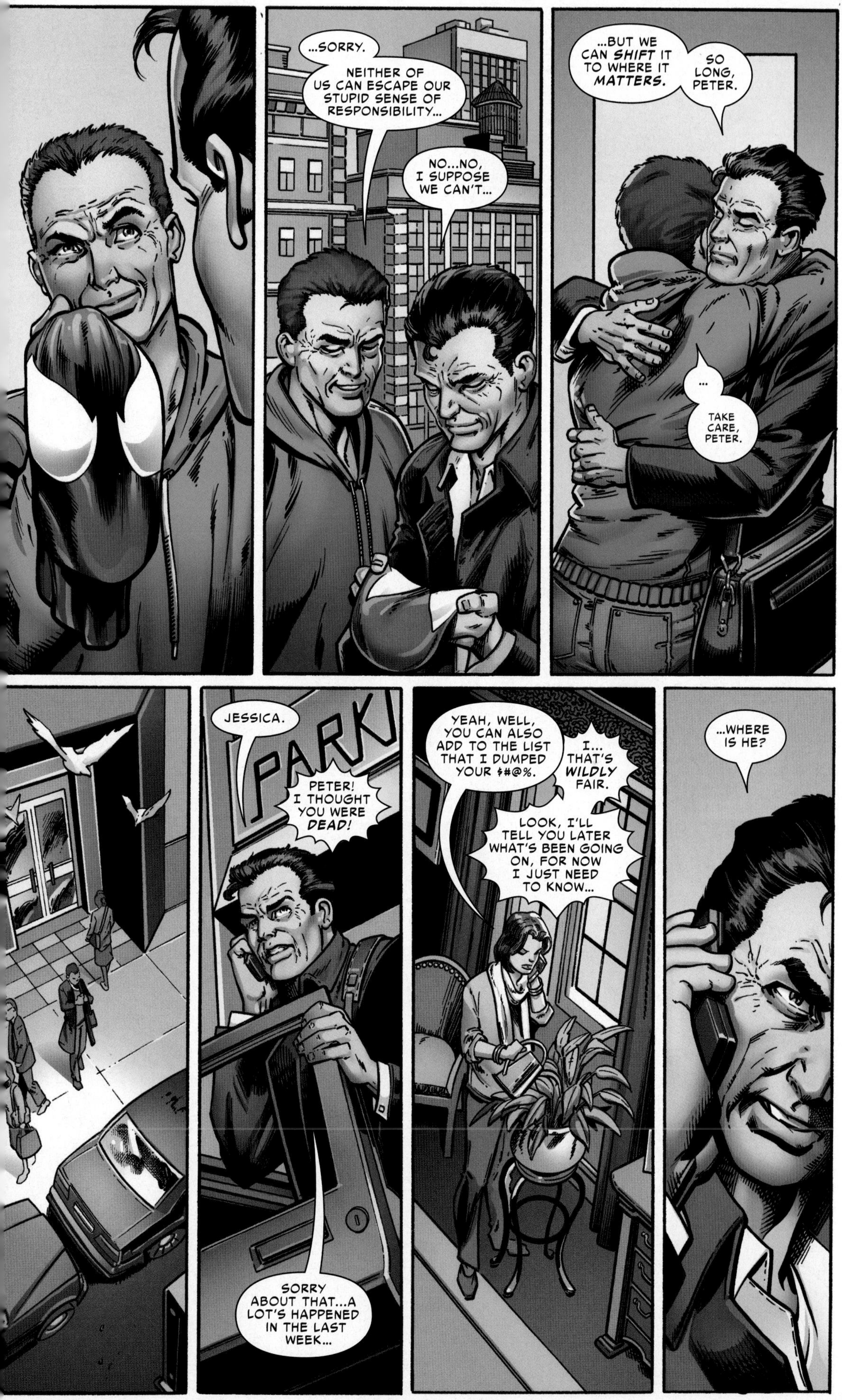
...SORRY.
NEITHER OF US CAN ESCAPE OUR STUPID SENSE OF RESPONSIBILITY...
NO...NO, I SUPPOSE WE CAN'T...
...BUT WE CAN SHIFT IT TO WHERE IT MATTERS.
SO LONG, PETER.
...
TAKE CARE, PETER.
JESSICA.
PETER! I THOUGHT YOU WERE DEAD!
SORRY ABOUT THAT...A LOT'S HAPPENED IN THE LAST WEEK...
PARK
YEAH, WELL, YOU CAN ALSO ADD TO THE LIST THAT I DUMPED YOUR $#@%.
I... THAT'S WILDLY FAIR.
LOOK, I'LL TELL YOU LATER WHAT'S BEEN GOING ON, FOR NOW I JUST NEED TO KNOW...
...WHERE IS HE?

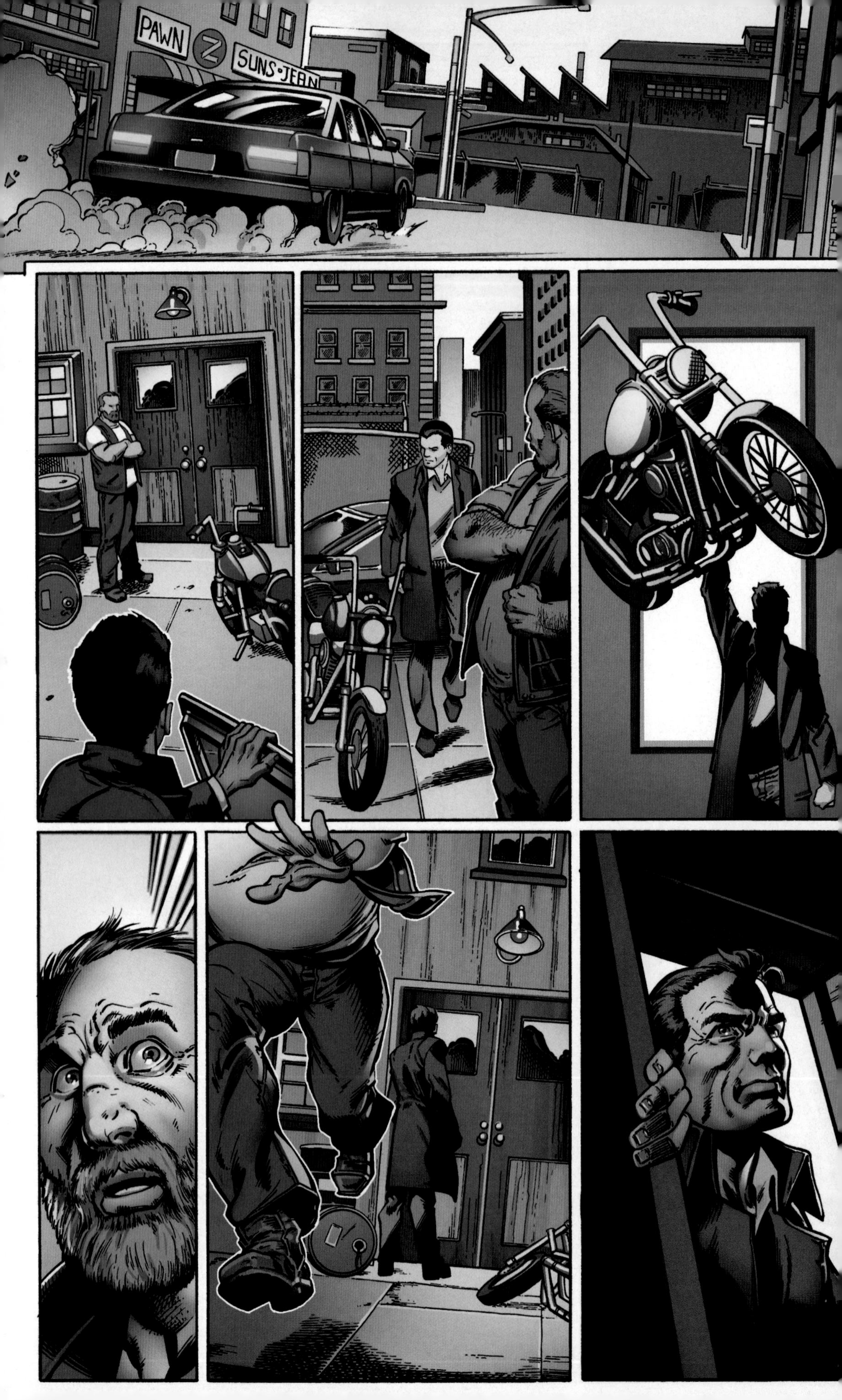
PAWN
Z
SUNS•JEAN

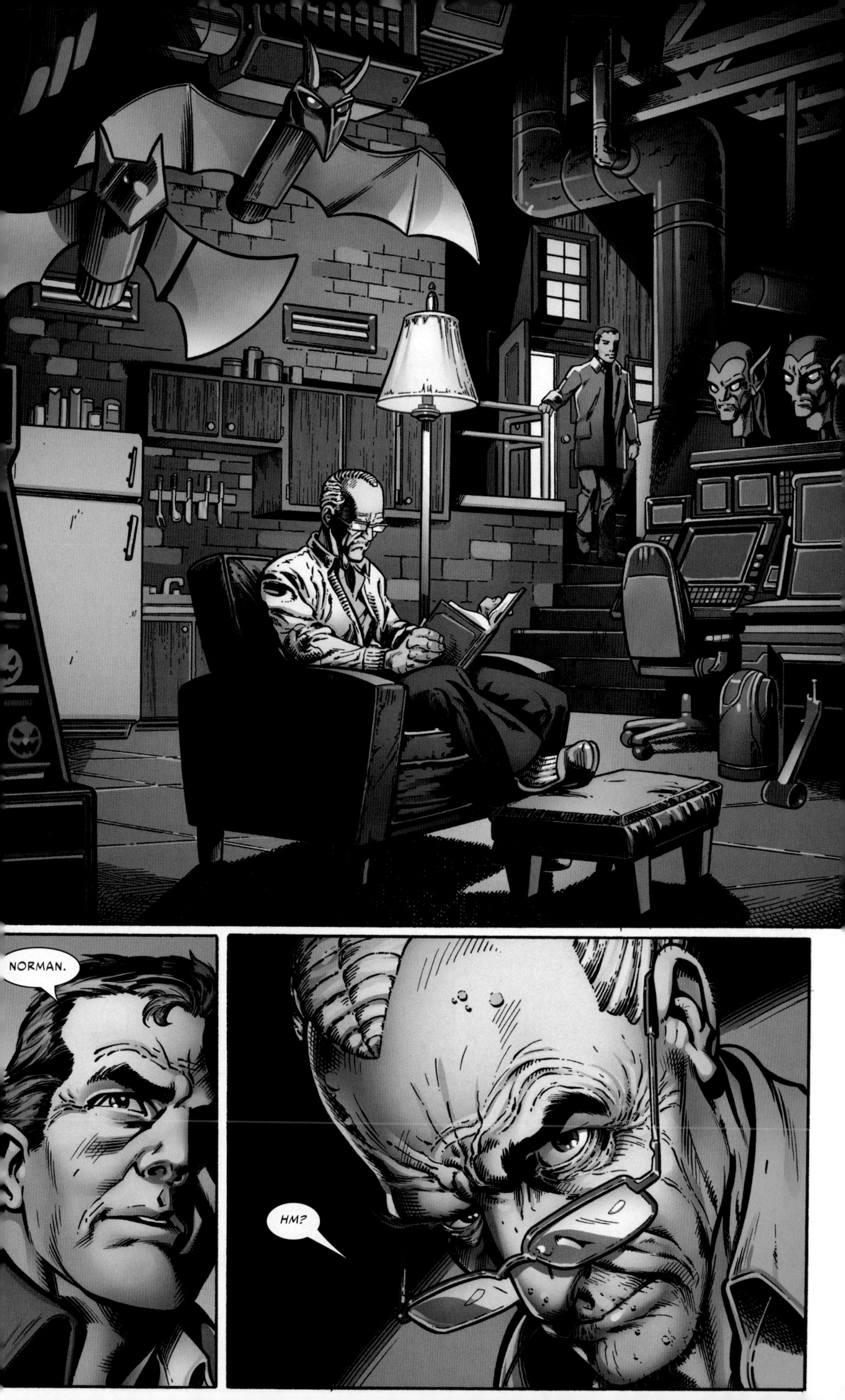
NORMAN.
HM?

AH! PETER PARKER, ESTEEMED HEAD OF *PARKER INDUSTRIES!*

I'M AFRAID IF YOU'RE HERE ON *OSCORP* BUSINESS I NO LONGER--

I KNOW, NORMAN.

EXCUSE ME?

DROP THE CRAZY OLD MAN SCHTICK. EVER SINCE YOU WERE RELEASED FROM PRISON YOU'VE PRETENDED TO BE *BROKEN,* A GREAT MIND OUT TO PASTURE.

AND THEN YOU WENT *MISSING.* BUT I KEPT TABS, NORMAN. HOW COULD I NOT?

YOU TOLD *OTTO* WHO I WAS. YOU TOLD HIM ABOUT THE *CLONING.*

AND, MOST *IMPORTANTLY,* YOU GAVE HIM ACCESS TO YOUR OLD EQUIPMENT AT *OSCORP,* WHERE THE RESULTS WERE *BAKED IN,* PREDETERMINED BY *YOU.*

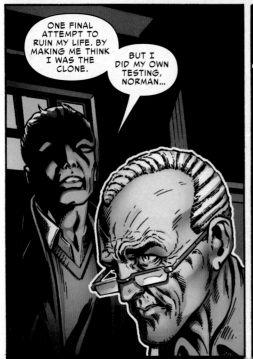

ONE FINAL ATTEMPT TO RUIN MY LIFE. BY MAKING ME THINK I WAS THE CLONE.

BUT I DID MY OWN TESTING, NORMAN...

...I'M STILL THE ORIGINAL. I'M *PETER PARKER.*

CLEVERRRR BOYYYY...

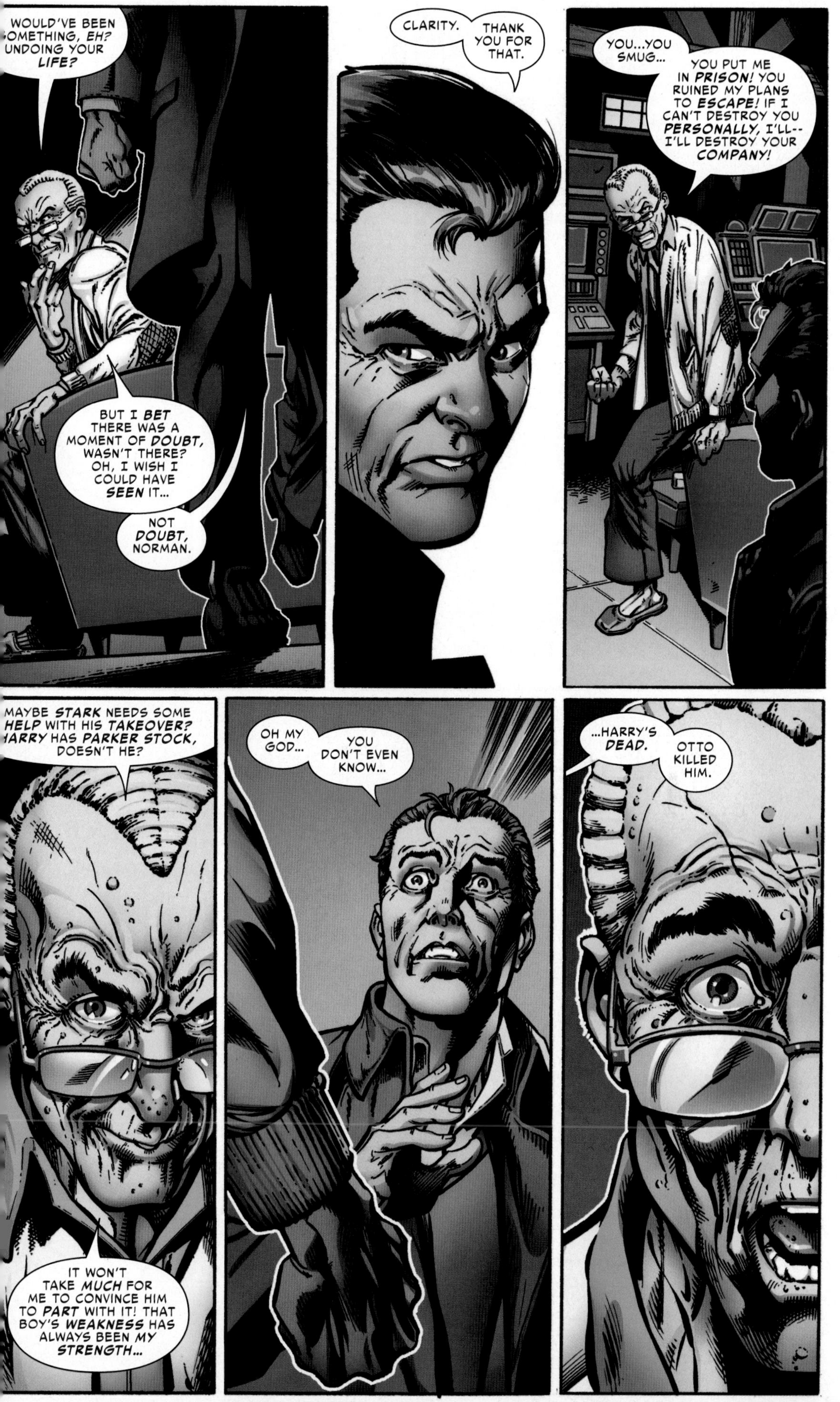
WOULD'VE BEEN SOMETHING, EH? UNDOING YOUR LIFE?
BUT I BET THERE WAS A MOMENT OF DOUBT, WASN'T THERE? OH, I WISH I COULD HAVE SEEN IT...
NOT DOUBT, NORMAN.
CLARITY.
THANK YOU FOR THAT.
YOU...YOU SMUG...
YOU PUT ME IN PRISON! YOU RUINED MY PLANS TO ESCAPE! IF I CAN'T DESTROY YOU PERSONALLY, I'LL-- I'LL DESTROY YOUR COMPANY!
MAYBE STARK NEEDS SOME HELP WITH HIS TAKEOVER? HARRY HAS PARKER STOCK, DOESN'T HE?
IT WON'T TAKE MUCH FOR ME TO CONVINCE HIM TO PART WITH IT! THAT BOY'S WEAKNESS HAS ALWAYS BEEN MY STRENGTH...
OH MY GOD...
YOU DON'T EVEN KNOW...
...HARRY'S DEAD.
OTTO KILLED HIM.

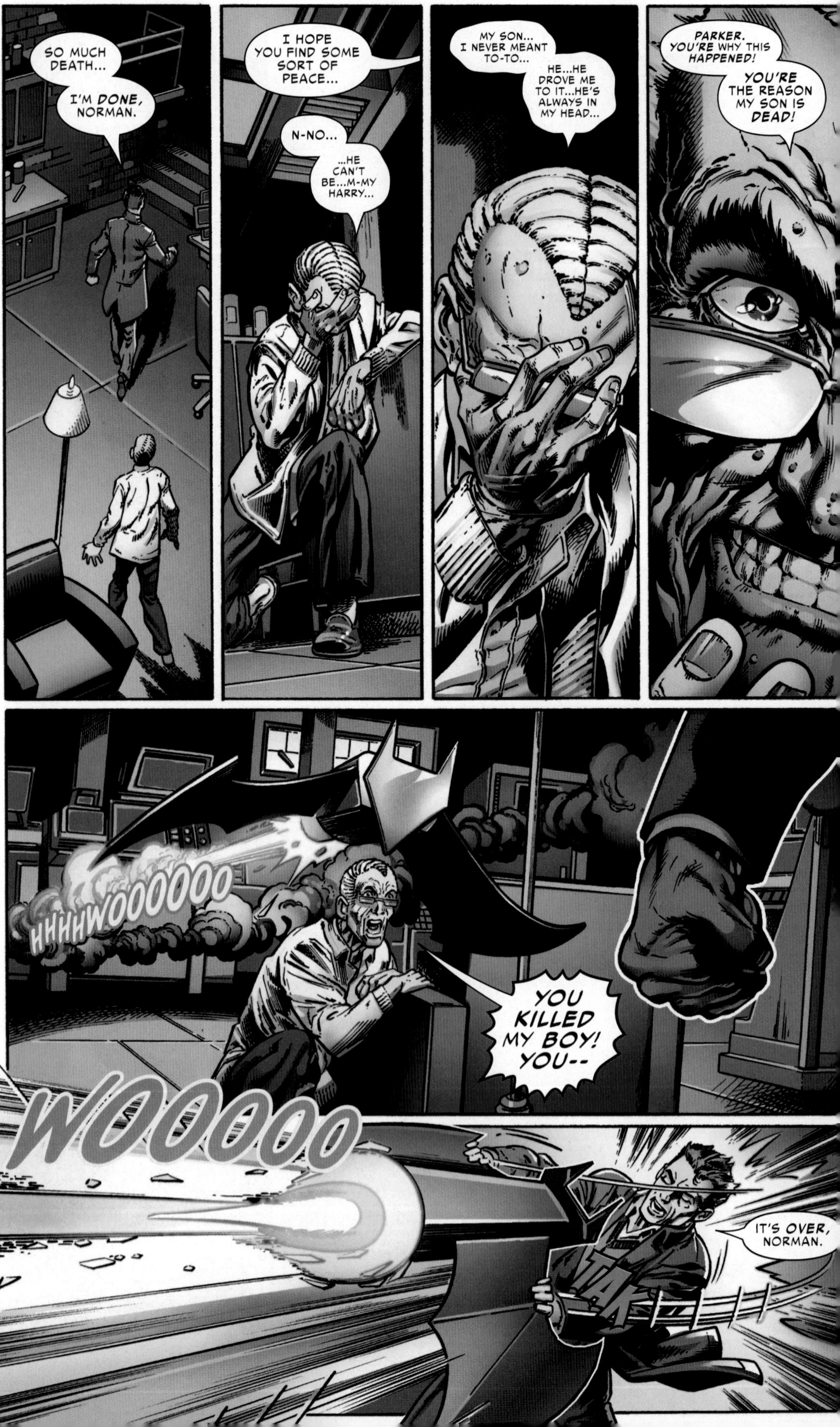

SO MUCH DEATH...
I'M DONE, NORMAN.
I HOPE YOU FIND SOME SORT OF PEACE...
N-NO...
...HE CAN'T BE...M-MY HARRY...
MY SON... I NEVER MEANT TO-TO...
HE...HE DROVE ME TO IT...HE'S ALWAYS IN MY HEAD...
PARKER. YOU'RE WHY THIS HAPPENED!
YOU'RE THE REASON MY SON IS DEAD!
HHHHWOOOOOO
YOU KILLED MY BOY! YOU--
WOOOOO
TAK
IT'S OVER, NORMAN.

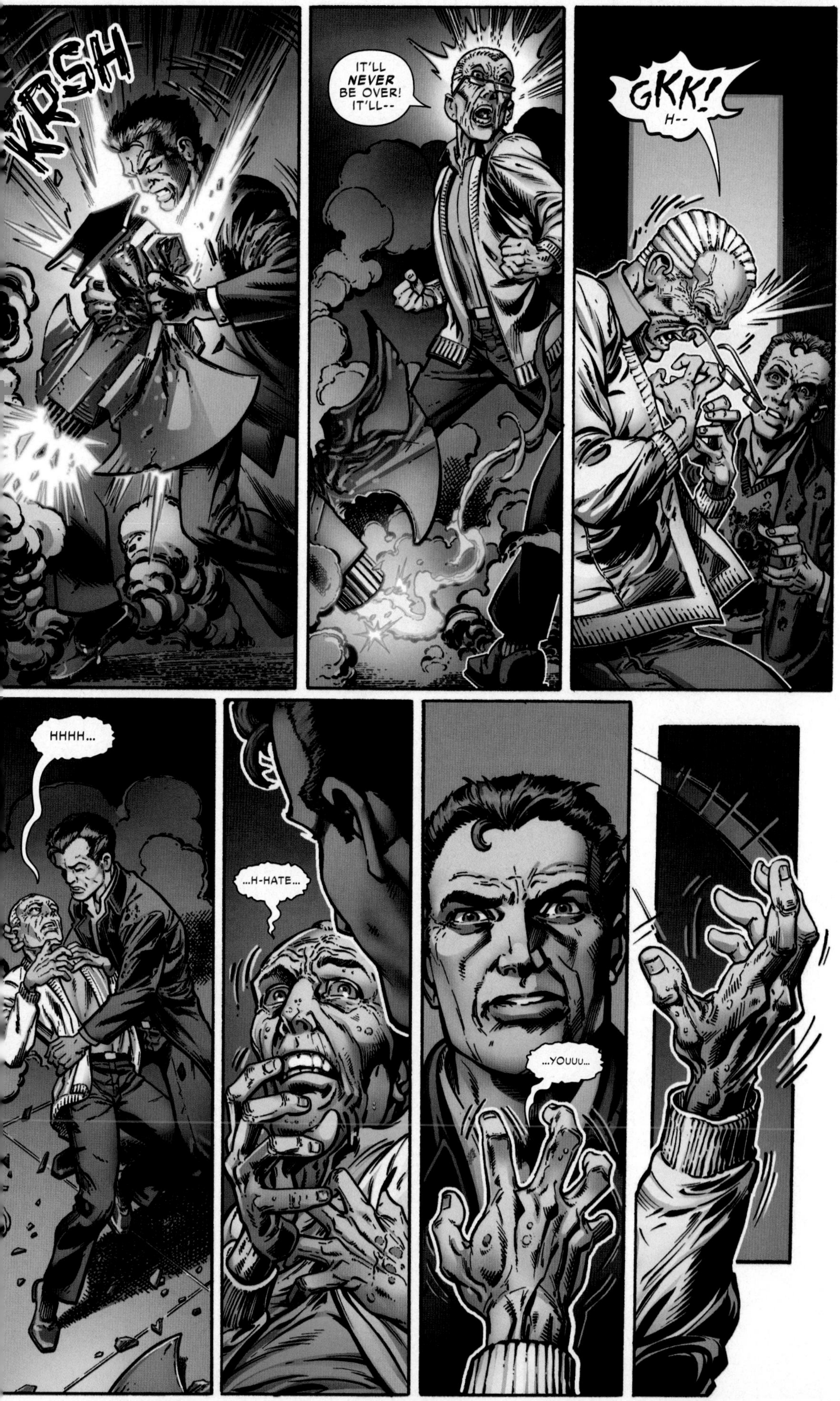
KRSH
IT'LL NEVER BE OVER! IT'LL--
GKK! H--
HHHH...
...H-HATE...
...YOUUU...

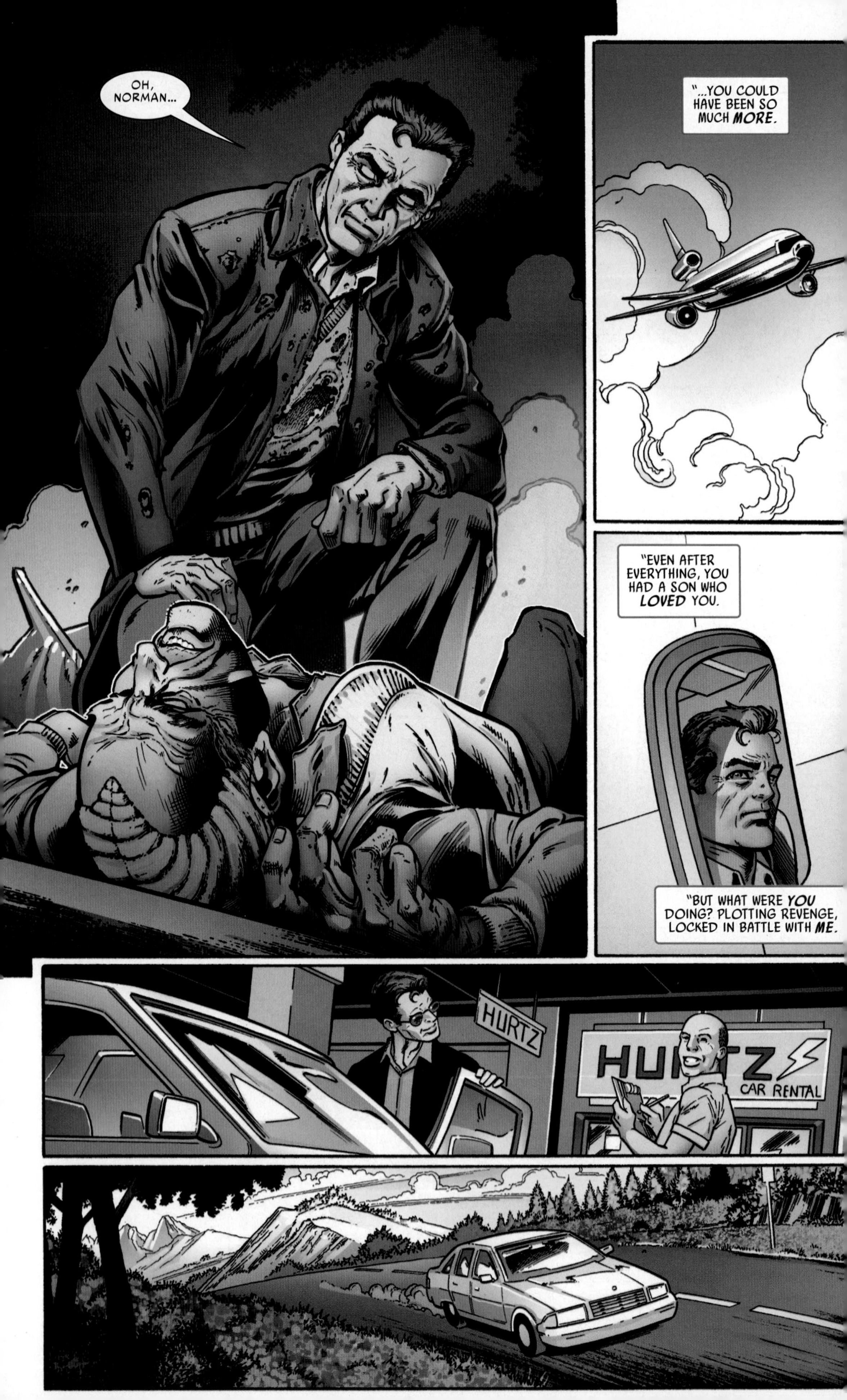
OH, NORMAN...
"...YOU COULD HAVE BEEN SO MUCH MORE.
"EVEN AFTER EVERYTHING, YOU HAD A SON WHO LOVED YOU.
"BUT WHAT WERE YOU DOING? PLOTTING REVENGE, LOCKED IN BATTLE WITH ME.
HURTZ
CAR RENTAL

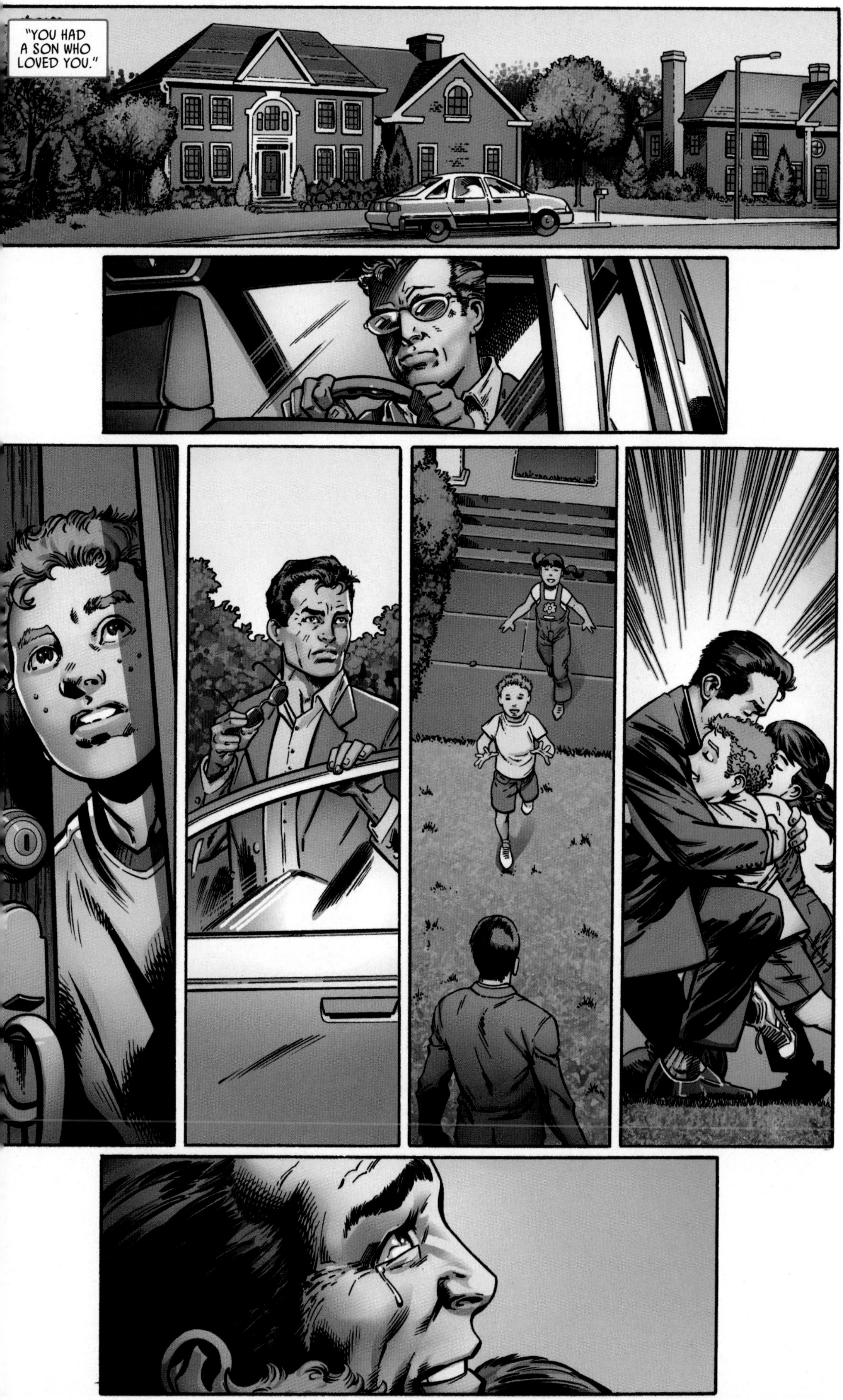
"YOU HAD A SON WHO LOVED YOU."

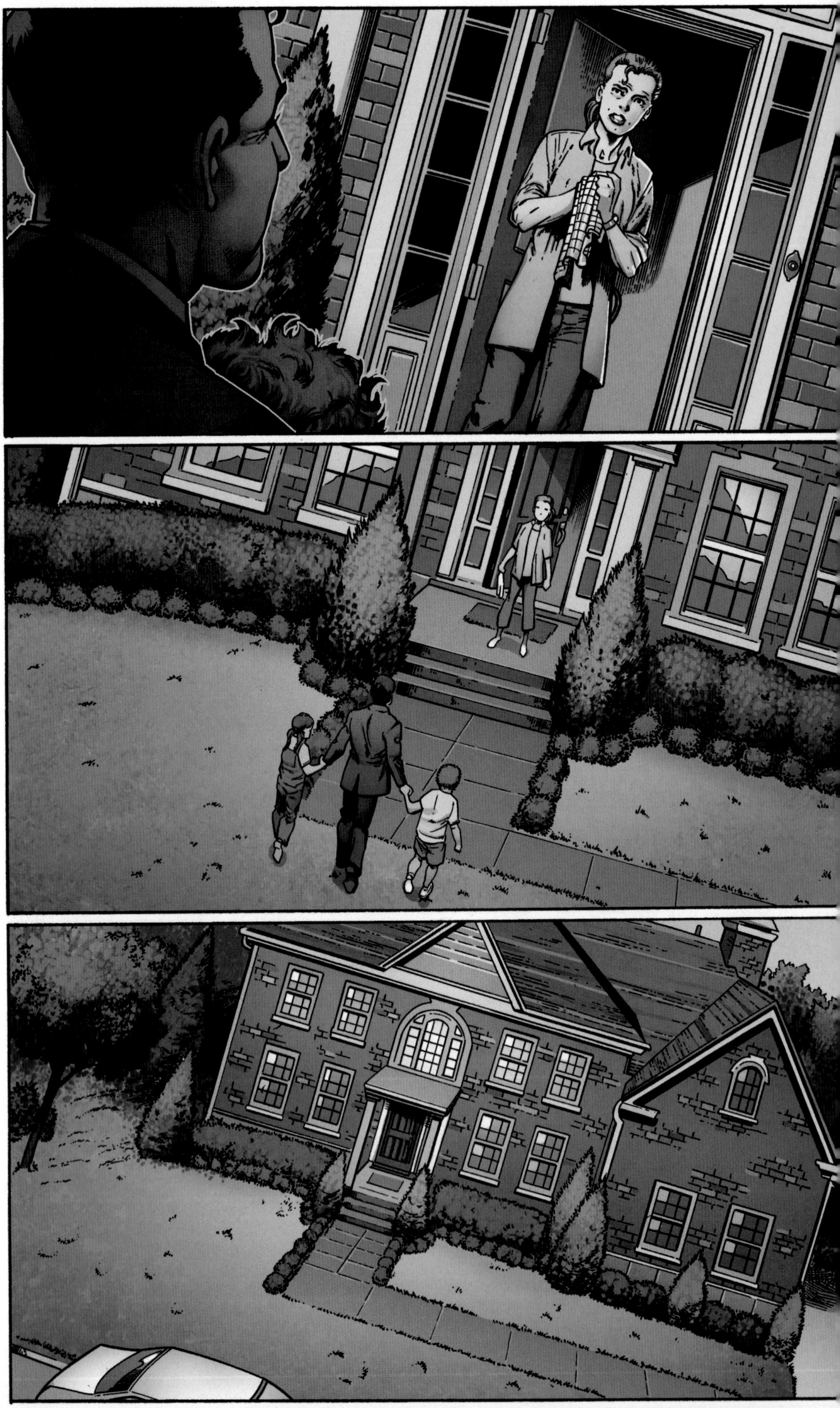

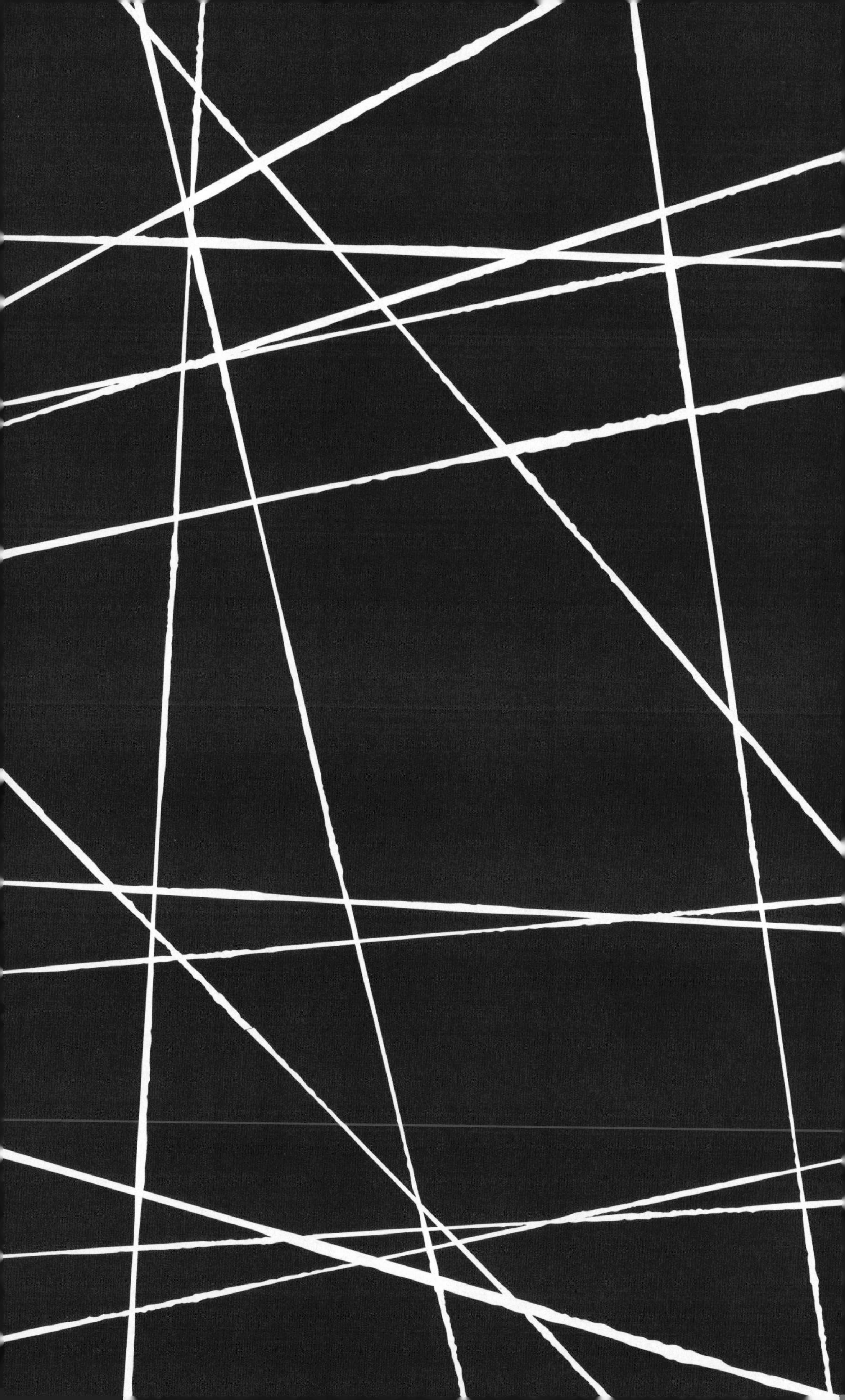

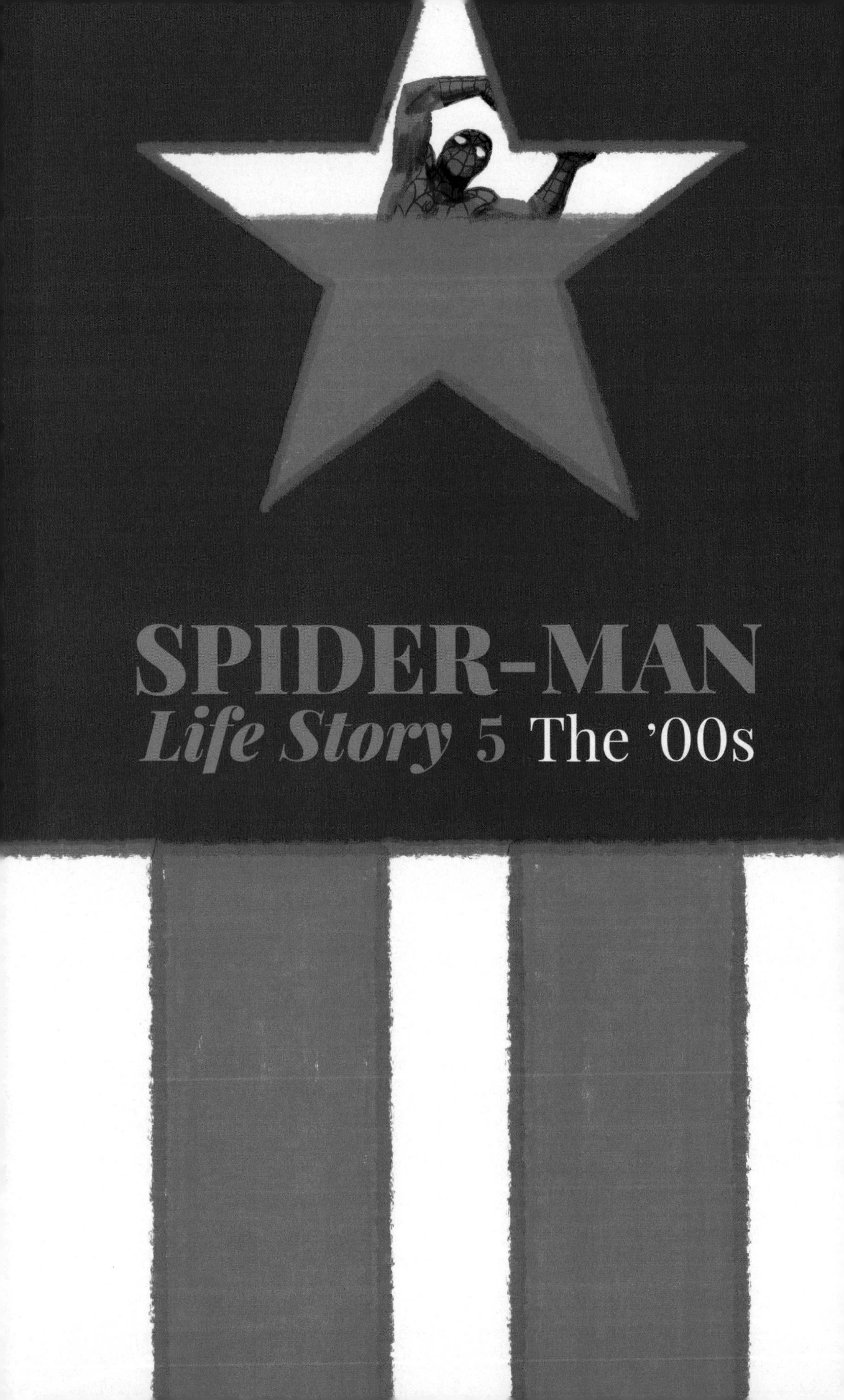
SPIDER-MAN
Life Story 5 The '00s

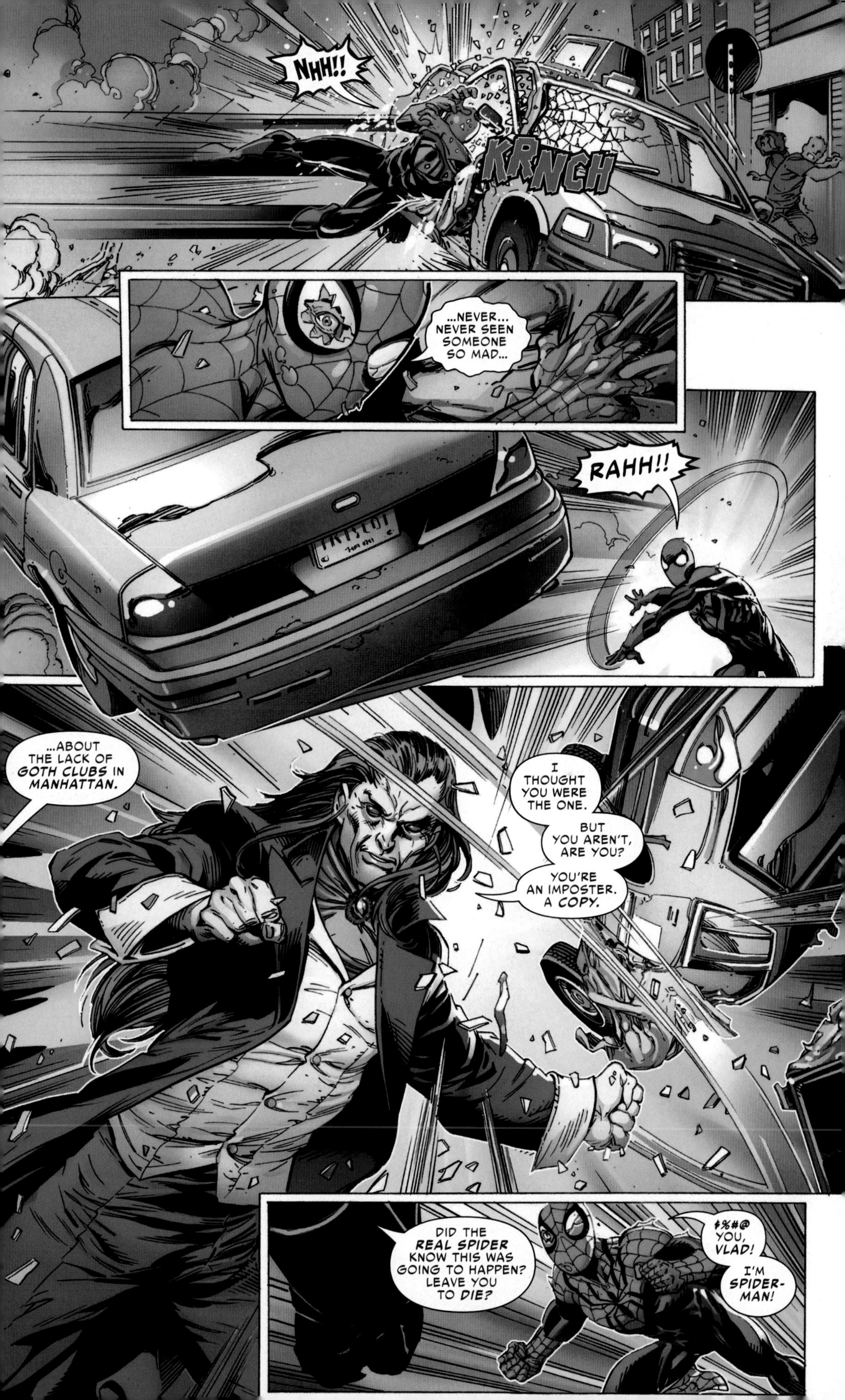
NHH!!
KRNCH
...NEVER... NEVER SEEN SOMEONE SO MAD...
RAHH!!
...ABOUT THE LACK OF GOTH CLUBS IN MANHATTAN.
I THOUGHT YOU WERE THE ONE.
BUT YOU AREN'T, ARE YOU?
YOU'RE AN IMPOSTER. A COPY.
DID THE REAL SPIDER KNOW THIS WAS GOING TO HAPPEN? LEAVE YOU TO DIE?
$%#@ YOU, VLAD!
I'M SPIDER-MAN!

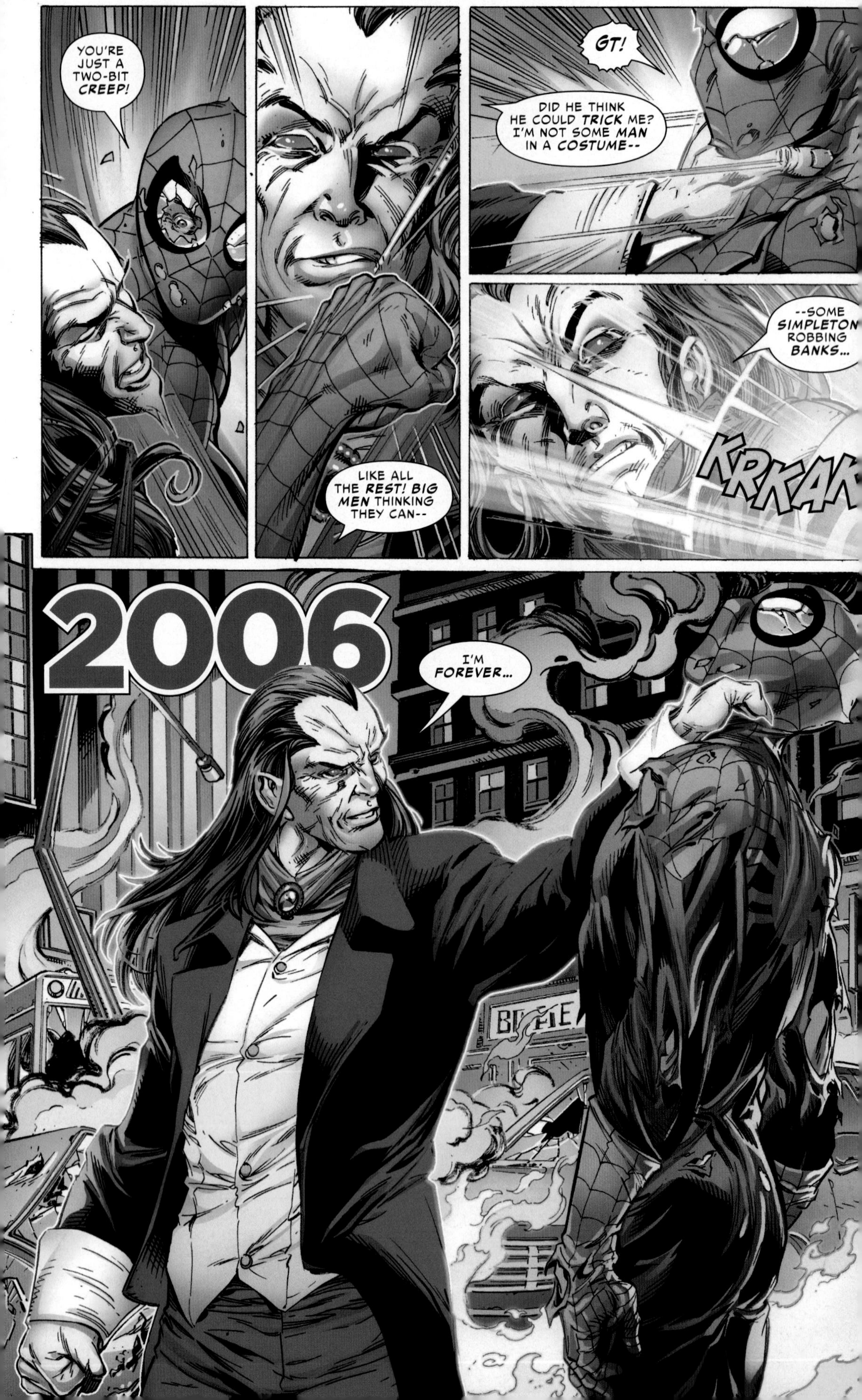

YOU'RE JUST A TWO-BIT CREEP!
LIKE ALL THE REST! BIG MEN THINKING THEY CAN--
GT!
DID HE THINK HE COULD TRICK ME? I'M NOT SOME MAN IN A COSTUME--
--SOME SIMPLETON ROBBING BANKS...
KRKAK
2006
I'M FOREVER...

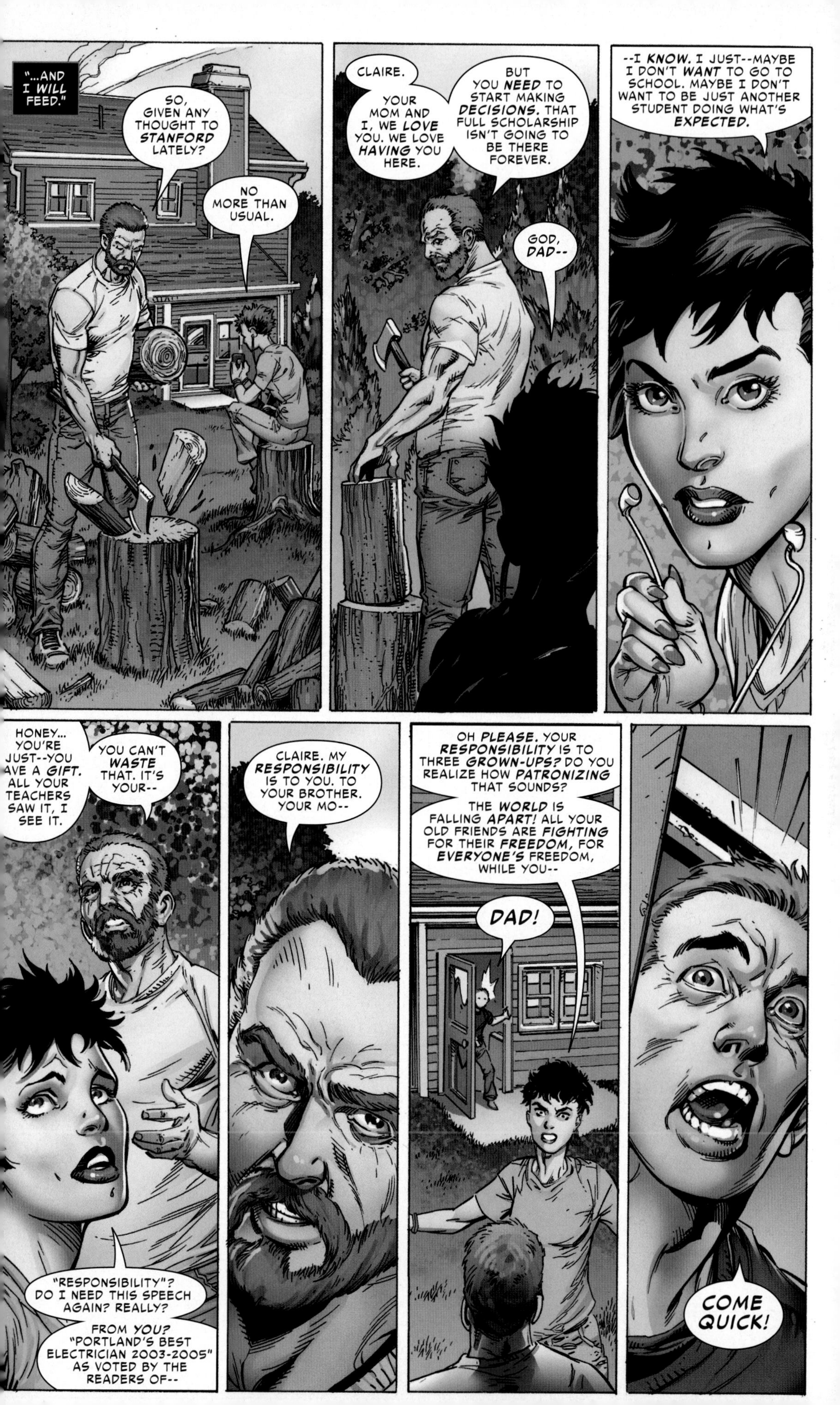
"...AND I WILL FEED."
SO, GIVEN ANY THOUGHT TO STANFORD LATELY?
NO MORE THAN USUAL.
CLAIRE.
YOUR MOM AND I, WE LOVE YOU. WE LOVE HAVING YOU HERE.
BUT YOU NEED TO START MAKING DECISIONS. THAT FULL SCHOLARSHIP ISN'T GOING TO BE THERE FOREVER.
GOD, DAD--
--I KNOW. I JUST--MAYBE I DON'T WANT TO GO TO SCHOOL. MAYBE I DON'T WANT TO BE JUST ANOTHER STUDENT DOING WHAT'S EXPECTED.
HONEY... YOU'RE JUST--YOU AVE A GIFT. ALL YOUR TEACHERS SAW IT, I SEE IT.
YOU CAN'T WASTE THAT. IT'S YOUR--
"RESPONSIBILITY"? DO I NEED THIS SPEECH AGAIN? REALLY?
FROM YOU? "PORTLAND'S BEST ELECTRICIAN 2003-2005" AS VOTED BY THE READERS OF--
CLAIRE. MY RESPONSIBILITY IS TO YOU. TO YOUR BROTHER. YOUR MO--
OH PLEASE. YOUR RESPONSIBILITY IS TO THREE GROWN-UPS? DO YOU REALIZE HOW PATRONIZING THAT SOUNDS?
THE WORLD IS FALLING APART! ALL YOUR OLD FRIENDS ARE FIGHTING FOR THEIR FREEDOM, FOR EVERYONE'S FREEDOM, WHILE YOU--
DAD!
COME QUICK!

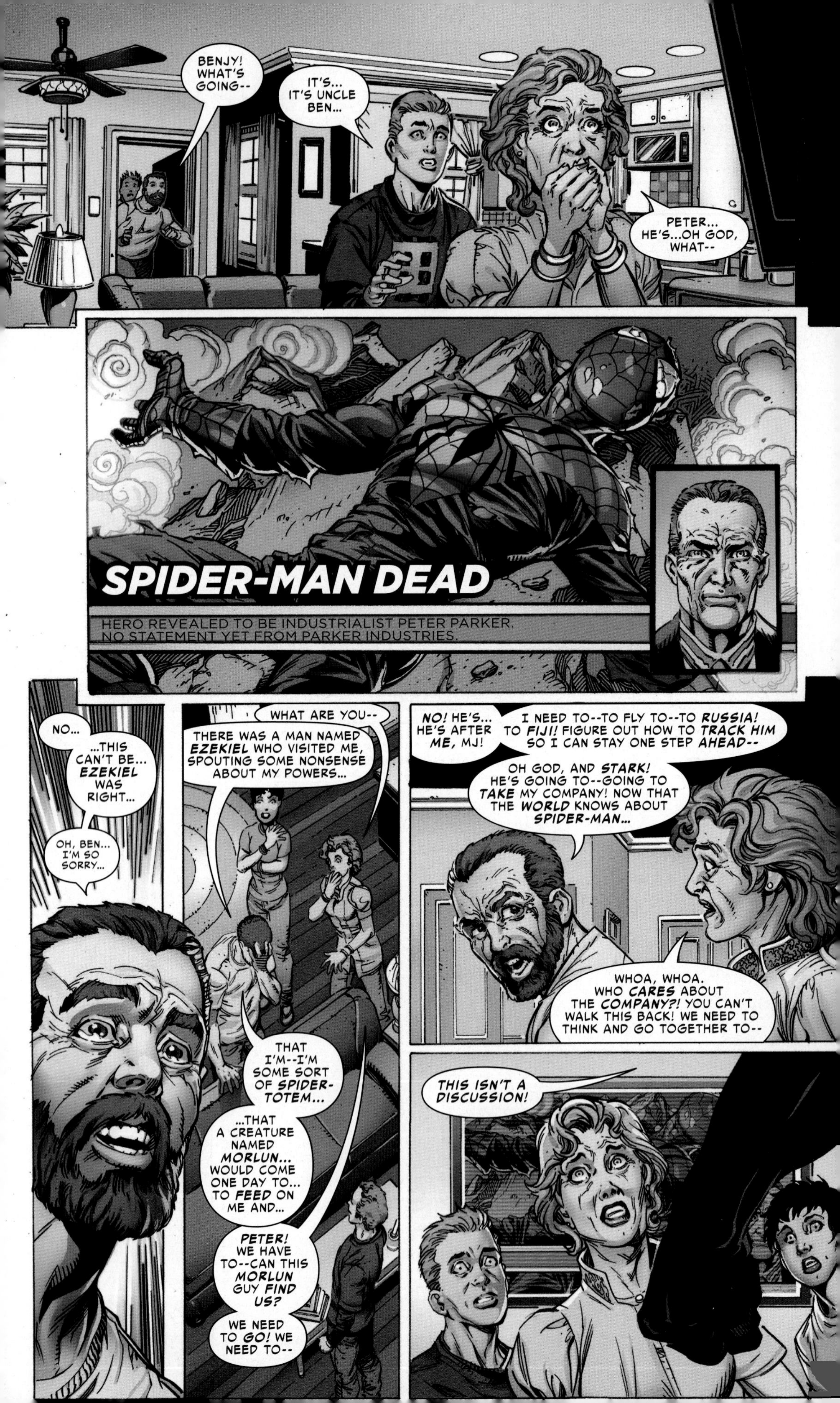
BENJY! WHAT'S GOING--
IT'S... IT'S UNCLE BEN...
PETER... HE'S...OH GOD, WHAT--
SPIDER-MAN DEAD
HERO REVEALED TO BE INDUSTRIALIST PETER PARKER.
NO STATEMENT YET FROM PARKER INDUSTRIES.
NO...
...THIS CAN'T BE... EZEKIEL WAS RIGHT...
OH, BEN... I'M SO SORRY...
WHAT ARE YOU--
THERE WAS A MAN NAMED EZEKIEL WHO VISITED ME, SPOUTING SOME NONSENSE ABOUT MY POWERS...
THAT I'M--I'M SOME SORT OF SPIDER-TOTEM...
...THAT A CREATURE NAMED MORLUN... WOULD COME ONE DAY TO... TO FEED ON ME AND...
PETER! WE HAVE TO--CAN THIS MORLUN GUY FIND US?
WE NEED TO GO! WE NEED TO--
NO! HE'S... HE'S AFTER ME, MJ!
I NEED TO--TO FLY TO--TO RUSSIA! TO FIJI! FIGURE OUT HOW TO TRACK HIM SO I CAN STAY ONE STEP AHEAD--
OH GOD, AND STARK! HE'S GOING TO--GOING TO TAKE MY COMPANY! NOW THAT THE WORLD KNOWS ABOUT SPIDER-MAN...
WHOA, WHOA. WHO CARES ABOUT THE COMPANY?! YOU CAN'T WALK THIS BACK! WE NEED TO THINK AND GO TOGETHER TO--
THIS ISN'T A DISCUSSION!

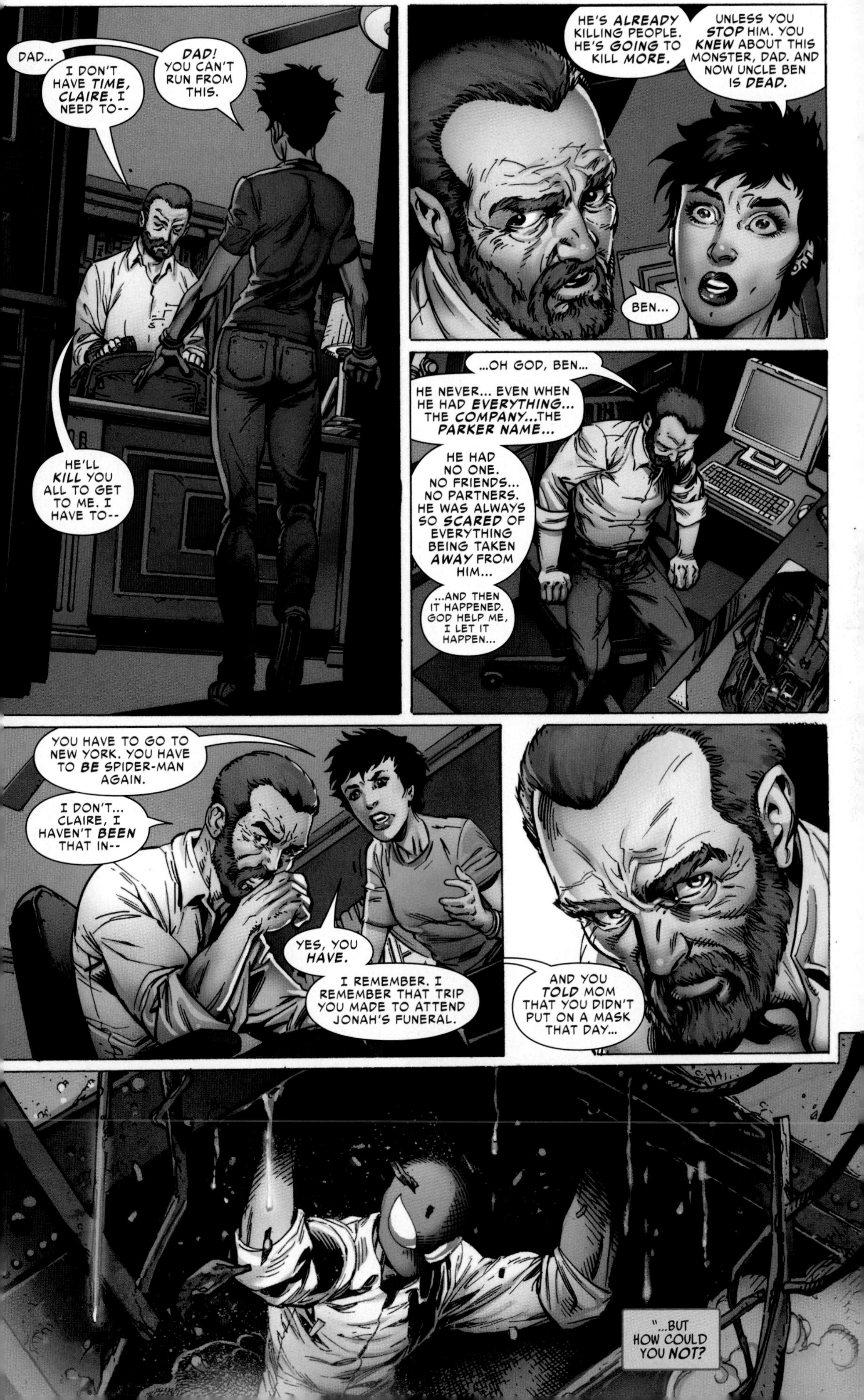
DAD...
I DON'T HAVE TIME, CLAIRE. I NEED TO--
DAD! YOU CAN'T RUN FROM THIS.
HE'LL KILL YOU ALL TO GET TO ME. I HAVE TO--
HE'S ALREADY KILLING PEOPLE. HE'S GOING TO KILL MORE.
UNLESS YOU STOP HIM. YOU KNEW ABOUT THIS MONSTER, DAD. AND NOW UNCLE BEN IS DEAD.
BEN...
...OH GOD, BEN...
HE NEVER... EVEN WHEN HE HAD EVERYTHING... THE COMPANY...THE PARKER NAME...
HE HAD NO ONE. NO FRIENDS... NO PARTNERS. HE WAS ALWAYS SO SCARED OF EVERYTHING BEING TAKEN AWAY FROM HIM...
...AND THEN IT HAPPENED. GOD HELP ME, I LET IT HAPPEN...
YOU HAVE TO GO TO NEW YORK. YOU HAVE TO BE SPIDER-MAN AGAIN.
I DON'T... CLAIRE, I HAVEN'T BEEN THAT IN--
YES, YOU HAVE.
I REMEMBER. I REMEMBER THAT TRIP YOU MADE TO ATTEND JONAH'S FUNERAL.
AND YOU TOLD MOM THAT YOU DIDN'T PUT ON A MASK THAT DAY...
"...BUT HOW COULD YOU NOT?

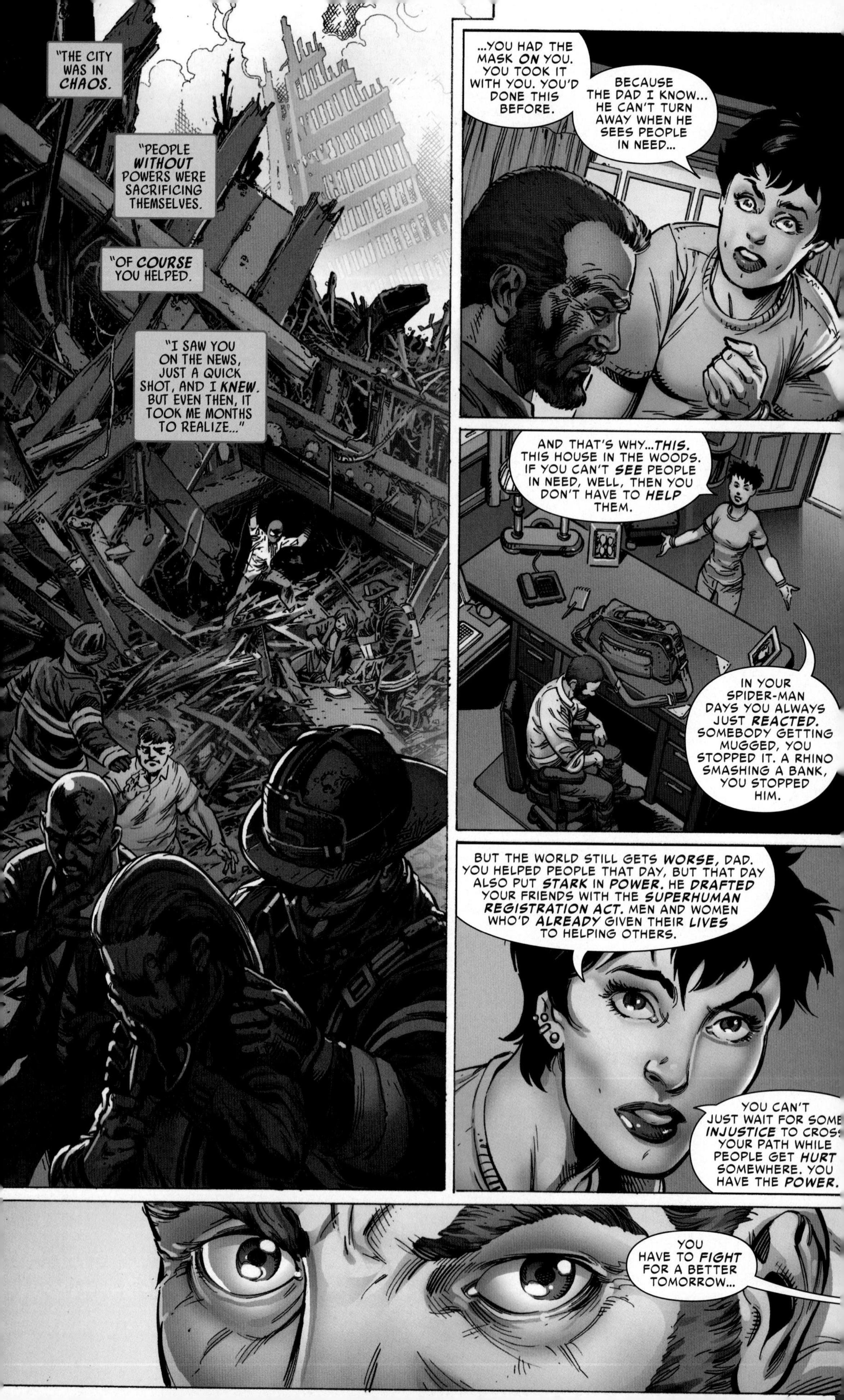
"THE CITY WAS IN CHAOS.
"PEOPLE WITHOUT POWERS WERE SACRIFICING THEMSELVES.
"OF COURSE YOU HELPED.
"I SAW YOU ON THE NEWS, JUST A QUICK SHOT, AND I KNEW. BUT EVEN THEN, IT TOOK ME MONTHS TO REALIZE..."
...YOU HAD THE MASK ON YOU. YOU TOOK IT WITH YOU. YOU'D DONE THIS BEFORE.
BECAUSE THE DAD I KNOW... HE CAN'T TURN AWAY WHEN HE SEES PEOPLE IN NEED...
AND THAT'S WHY...THIS. THIS HOUSE IN THE WOODS. IF YOU CAN'T SEE PEOPLE IN NEED, WELL, THEN YOU DON'T HAVE TO HELP THEM.
IN YOUR SPIDER-MAN DAYS YOU ALWAYS JUST REACTED. SOMEBODY GETTING MUGGED, YOU STOPPED IT. A RHINO SMASHING A BANK, YOU STOPPED HIM.
BUT THE WORLD STILL GETS WORSE, DAD. YOU HELPED PEOPLE THAT DAY, BUT THAT DAY ALSO PUT STARK IN POWER. HE DRAFTED YOUR FRIENDS WITH THE SUPERHUMAN REGISTRATION ACT. MEN AND WOMEN WHO'D ALREADY GIVEN THEIR LIVES TO HELPING OTHERS.
YOU CAN'T JUST WAIT FOR SOME INJUSTICE TO CROSS YOUR PATH WHILE PEOPLE GET HURT SOMEWHERE. YOU HAVE THE POWER.
YOU HAVE TO FIGHT FOR A BETTER TOMORROW...

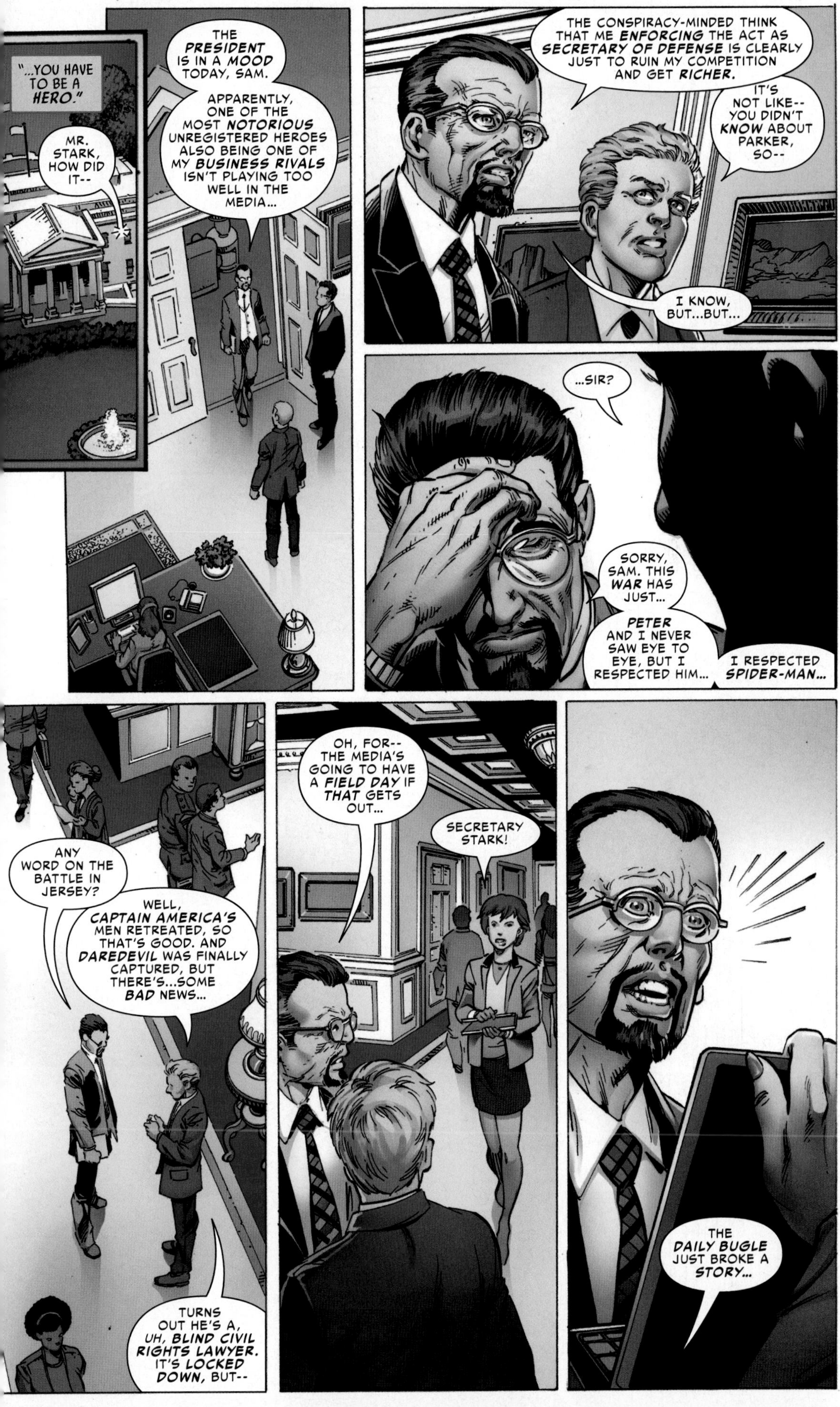
"...YOU HAVE TO BE A HERO."
MR. STARK, HOW DID IT--
THE PRESIDENT IS IN A MOOD TODAY, SAM.
APPARENTLY, ONE OF THE MOST NOTORIOUS UNREGISTERED HEROES ALSO BEING ONE OF MY BUSINESS RIVALS ISN'T PLAYING TOO WELL IN THE MEDIA...
THE CONSPIRACY-MINDED THINK THAT ME ENFORCING THE ACT AS SECRETARY OF DEFENSE IS CLEARLY JUST TO RUIN MY COMPETITION AND GET RICHER.
IT'S NOT LIKE-- YOU DIDN'T KNOW ABOUT PARKER, SO--
I KNOW, BUT...BUT...
...SIR?
SORRY, SAM. THIS WAR HAS JUST...
PETER AND I NEVER SAW EYE TO EYE, BUT I RESPECTED HIM...
I RESPECTED SPIDER-MAN...
ANY WORD ON THE BATTLE IN JERSEY?
WELL, CAPTAIN AMERICA'S MEN RETREATED, SO THAT'S GOOD. AND DAREDEVIL WAS FINALLY CAPTURED, BUT THERE'S...SOME BAD NEWS...
TURNS OUT HE'S A, UH, BLIND CIVIL RIGHTS LAWYER. IT'S LOCKED DOWN, BUT--
OH, FOR-- THE MEDIA'S GOING TO HAVE A FIELD DAY IF THAT GETS OUT...
SECRETARY STARK!
THE DAILY BUGLE JUST BROKE A STORY...

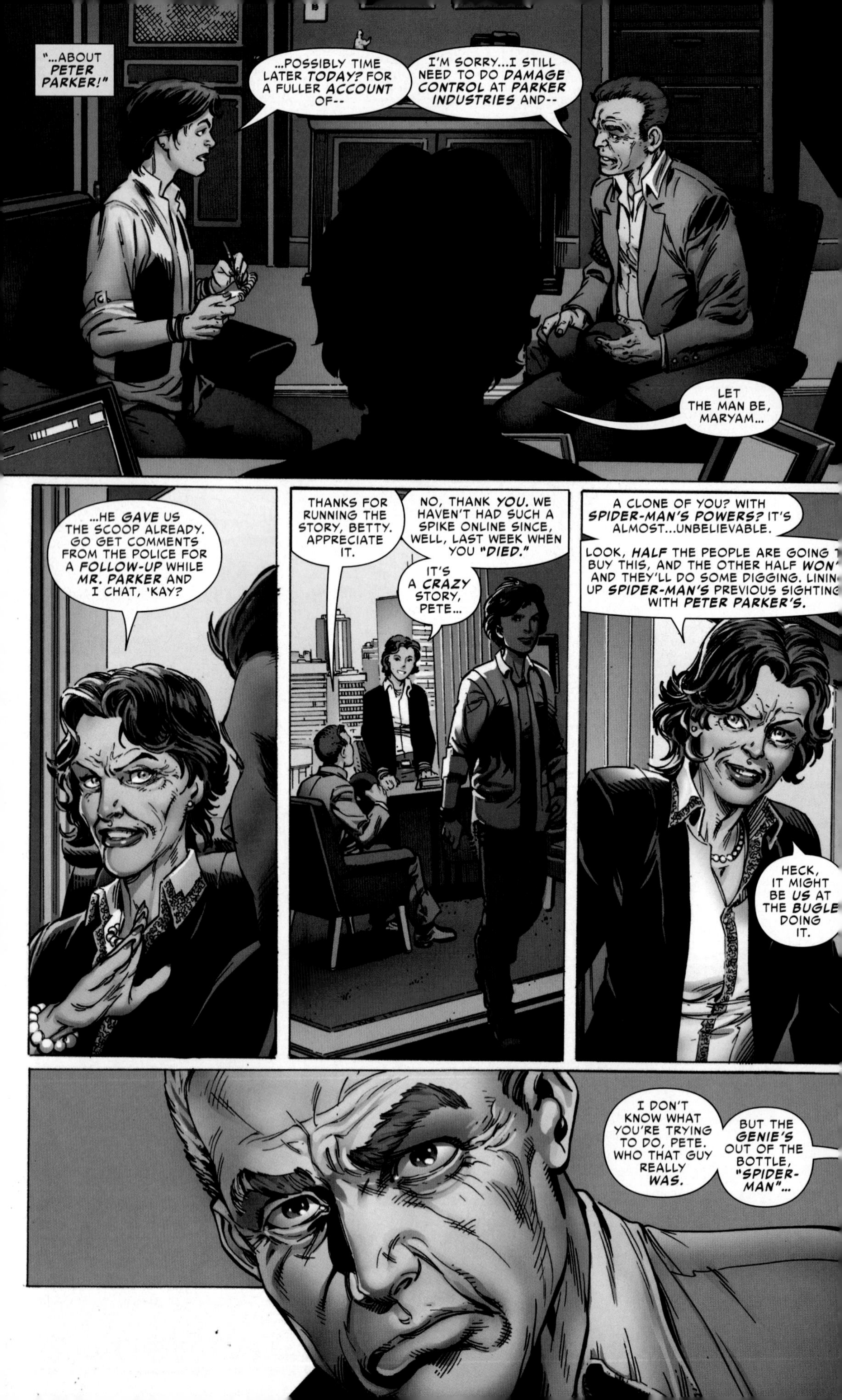

"...ABOUT PETER PARKER!"
...POSSIBLY TIME LATER TODAY? FOR A FULLER ACCOUNT OF--
I'M SORRY...I STILL NEED TO DO DAMAGE CONTROL AT PARKER INDUSTRIES AND--
LET THE MAN BE, MARYAM...
...HE GAVE US THE SCOOP ALREADY. GO GET COMMENTS FROM THE POLICE FOR A FOLLOW-UP WHILE MR. PARKER AND I CHAT, 'KAY?
THANKS FOR RUNNING THE STORY, BETTY. APPRECIATE IT.
NO, THANK YOU. WE HAVEN'T HAD SUCH A SPIKE ONLINE SINCE, WELL, LAST WEEK WHEN YOU "DIED."
IT'S A CRAZY STORY, PETE...
A CLONE OF YOU? WITH SPIDER-MAN'S POWERS? IT'S ALMOST...UNBELIEVABLE.
LOOK, HALF THE PEOPLE ARE GOING T BUY THIS, AND THE OTHER HALF WON' AND THEY'LL DO SOME DIGGING. LININ UP SPIDER-MAN'S PREVIOUS SIGHTING WITH PETER PARKER'S.
HECK, IT MIGHT BE US AT THE BUGLE DOING IT.
I DON'T KNOW WHAT YOU'RE TRYING TO DO, PETE. WHO THAT GUY REALLY WAS.
BUT THE GENIE'S OUT OF THE BOTTLE, "SPIDER-MAN"...

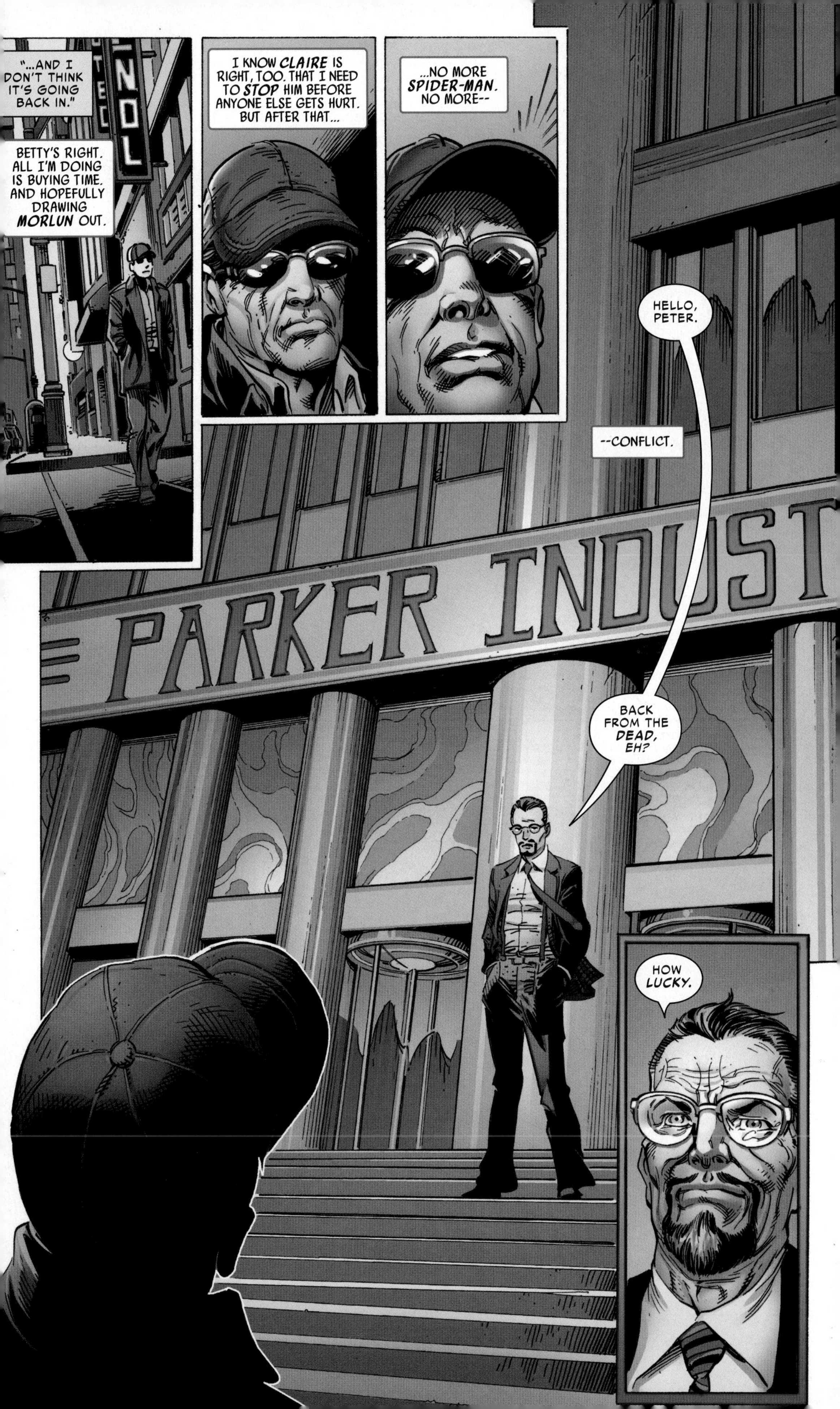
"...AND I DON'T THINK IT'S GOING BACK IN."
BETTY'S RIGHT. ALL I'M DOING IS BUYING TIME. AND HOPEFULLY DRAWING MORLUN OUT.
I KNOW CLAIRE IS RIGHT, TOO. THAT I NEED TO STOP HIM BEFORE ANYONE ELSE GETS HURT. BUT AFTER THAT...
...NO MORE SPIDER-MAN. NO MORE--
--CONFLICT.
HELLO, PETER.
BACK FROM THE DEAD, EH?
PARKER INDUST
HOW LUCKY.

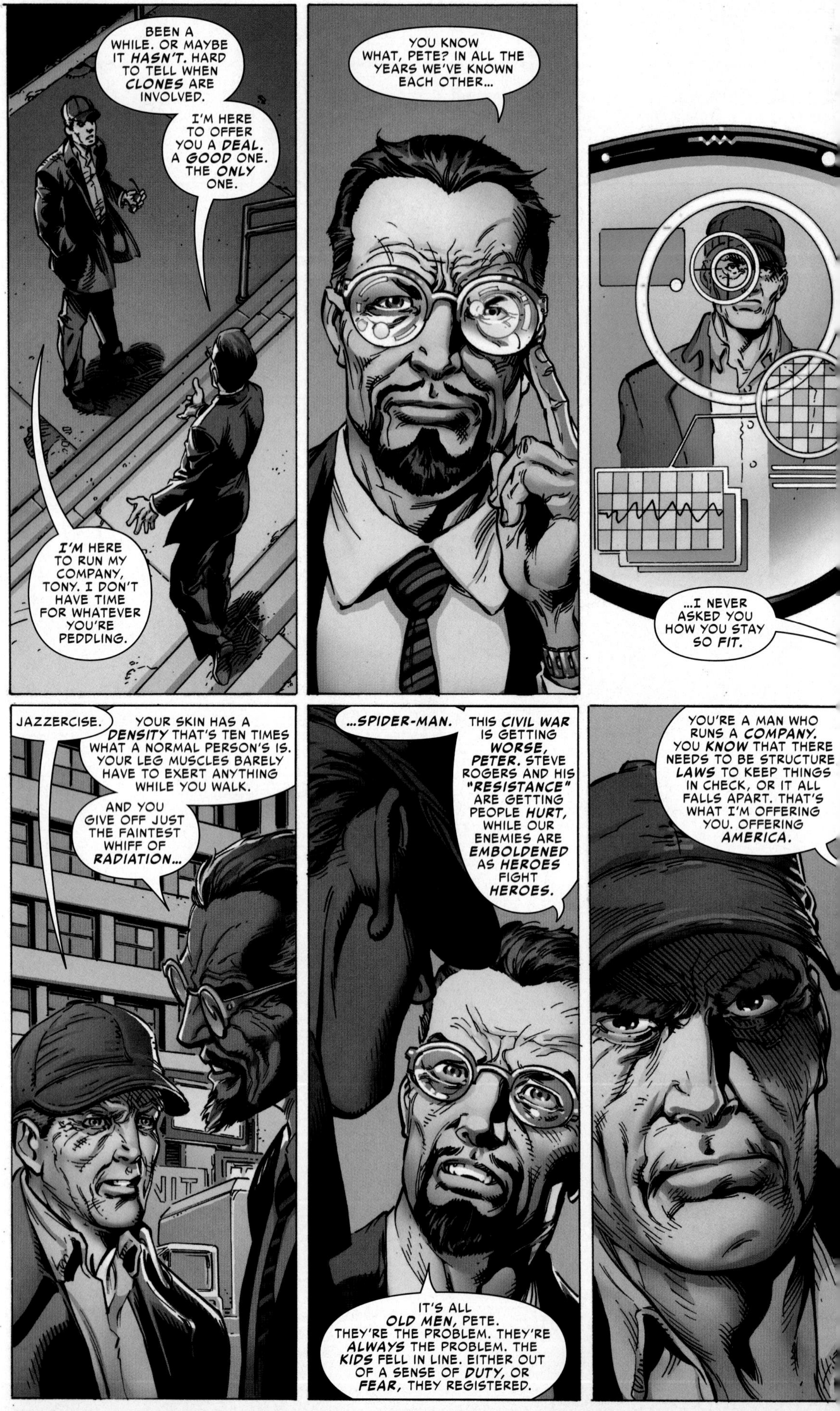

BEEN A WHILE. OR MAYBE IT HASN'T. HARD TO TELL WHEN CLONES ARE INVOLVED.
I'M HERE TO OFFER YOU A DEAL. A GOOD ONE. THE ONLY ONE.
I'M HERE TO RUN MY COMPANY, TONY. I DON'T HAVE TIME FOR WHATEVER YOU'RE PEDDLING.
YOU KNOW WHAT, PETE? IN ALL THE YEARS WE'VE KNOWN EACH OTHER...
...I NEVER ASKED YOU HOW YOU STAY SO FIT.
JAZZERCISE.
YOUR SKIN HAS A DENSITY THAT'S TEN TIMES WHAT A NORMAL PERSON'S IS. YOUR LEG MUSCLES BARELY HAVE TO EXERT ANYTHING WHILE YOU WALK.
AND YOU GIVE OFF JUST THE FAINTEST WHIFF OF RADIATION...
...SPIDER-MAN.
THIS CIVIL WAR IS GETTING WORSE, PETER. STEVE ROGERS AND HIS "RESISTANCE" ARE GETTING PEOPLE HURT, WHILE OUR ENEMIES ARE EMBOLDENED AS HEROES FIGHT HEROES.
IT'S ALL OLD MEN, PETE. THEY'RE THE PROBLEM. THEY'RE ALWAYS THE PROBLEM. THE KIDS FELL IN LINE. EITHER OUT OF A SENSE OF DUTY, OR FEAR, THEY REGISTERED.
YOU'RE A MAN WHO RUNS A COMPANY. YOU KNOW THAT THERE NEEDS TO BE STRUCTURE LAWS TO KEEP THINGS IN CHECK, OR IT ALL FALLS APART. THAT'S WHAT I'M OFFERING YOU. OFFERING AMERICA.

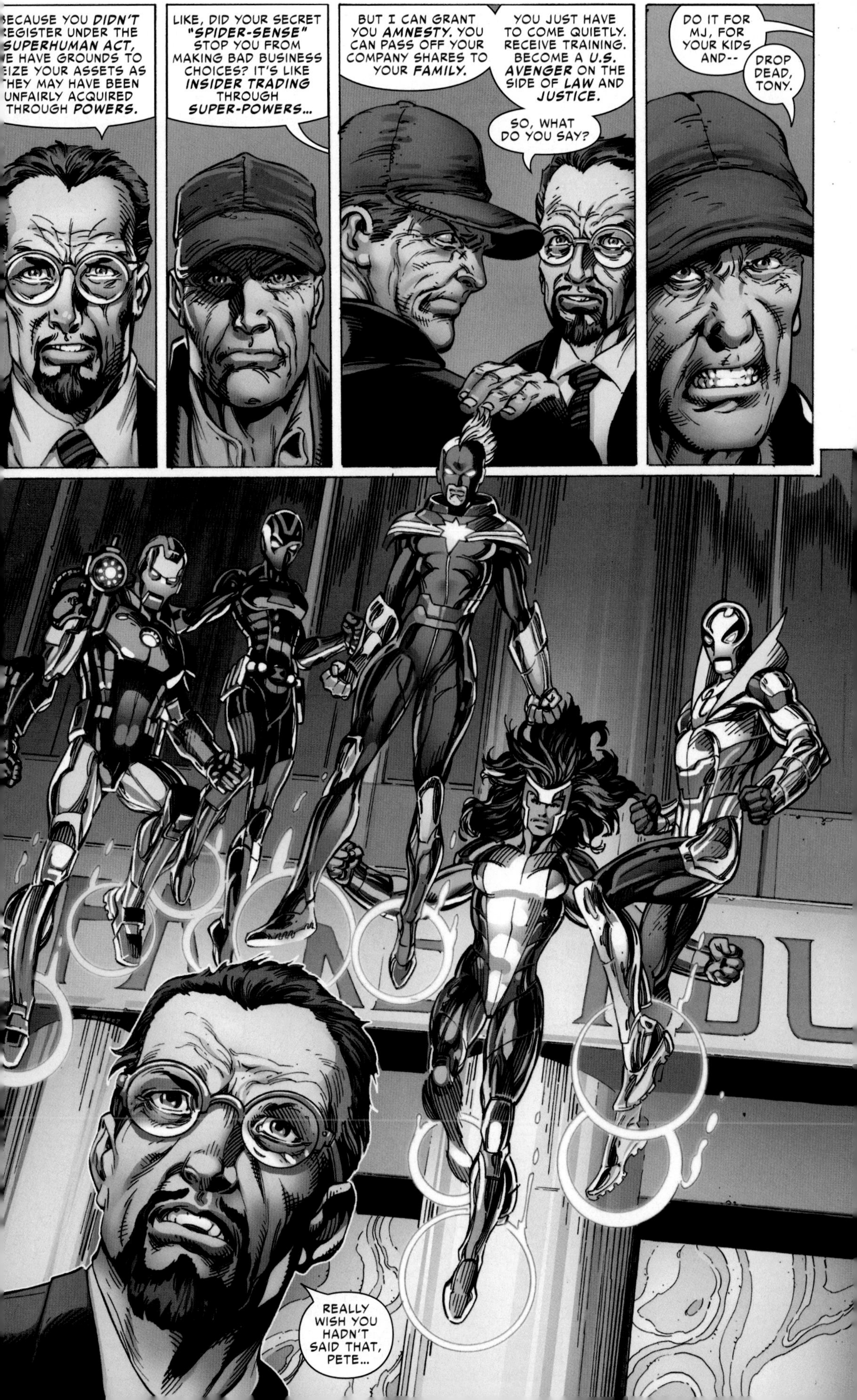

BECAUSE YOU DIDN'T REGISTER UNDER THE SUPERHUMAN ACT, WE HAVE GROUNDS TO SEIZE YOUR ASSETS AS THEY MAY HAVE BEEN UNFAIRLY ACQUIRED THROUGH POWERS.
LIKE, DID YOUR SECRET "SPIDER-SENSE" STOP YOU FROM MAKING BAD BUSINESS CHOICES? IT'S LIKE INSIDER TRADING THROUGH SUPER-POWERS...
BUT I CAN GRANT YOU AMNESTY. YOU CAN PASS OFF YOUR COMPANY SHARES TO YOUR FAMILY.
YOU JUST HAVE TO COME QUIETLY. RECEIVE TRAINING. BECOME A U.S. AVENGER ON THE SIDE OF LAW AND JUSTICE.
SO, WHAT DO YOU SAY?
DO IT FOR MJ, FOR YOUR KIDS AND--
DROP DEAD, TONY.
REALLY WISH YOU HADN'T SAID THAT, PETE...

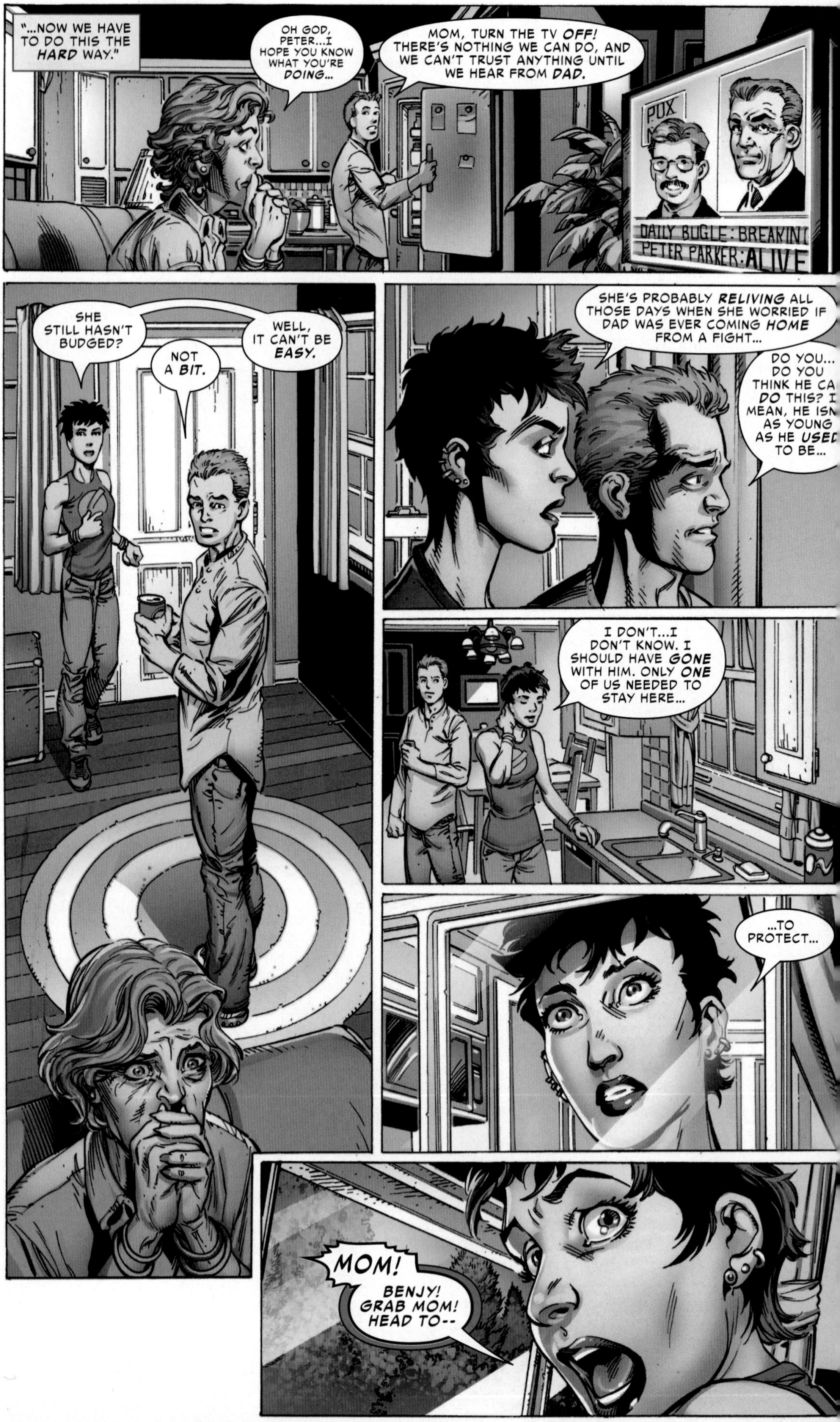
"...NOW WE HAVE TO DO THIS THE HARD WAY."
OH GOD, PETER...I HOPE YOU KNOW WHAT YOU'RE DOING...
MOM, TURN THE TV OFF! THERE'S NOTHING WE CAN DO, AND WE CAN'T TRUST ANYTHING UNTIL WE HEAR FROM DAD.
DAILY BUGLE: BREAKIN
PETER PARKER: ALIVE
SHE STILL HASN'T BUDGED?
NOT A BIT.
WELL, IT CAN'T BE EASY.
SHE'S PROBABLY RELIVING ALL THOSE DAYS WHEN SHE WORRIED IF DAD WAS EVER COMING HOME FROM A FIGHT...
DO YOU... DO YOU THINK HE CA DO THIS? I MEAN, HE ISN AS YOUNG AS HE USED TO BE...
I DON'T...I DON'T KNOW. I SHOULD HAVE GONE WITH HIM. ONLY ONE OF US NEEDED TO STAY HERE...
...TO PROTECT...
MOM!
BENJY! GRAB MOM! HEAD TO--

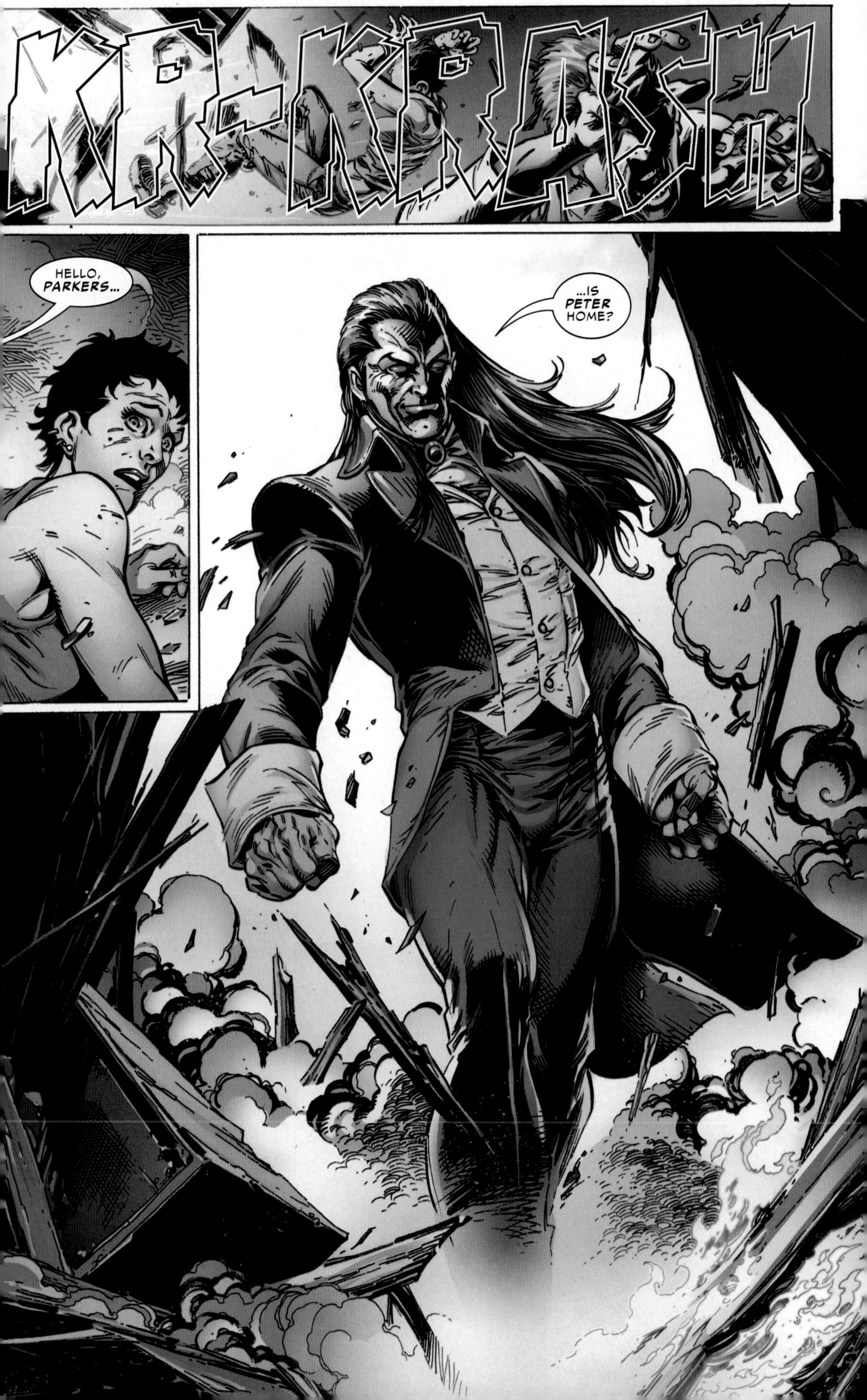

KA-KRASH
HELLO, PARKERS...
...IS PETER HOME?

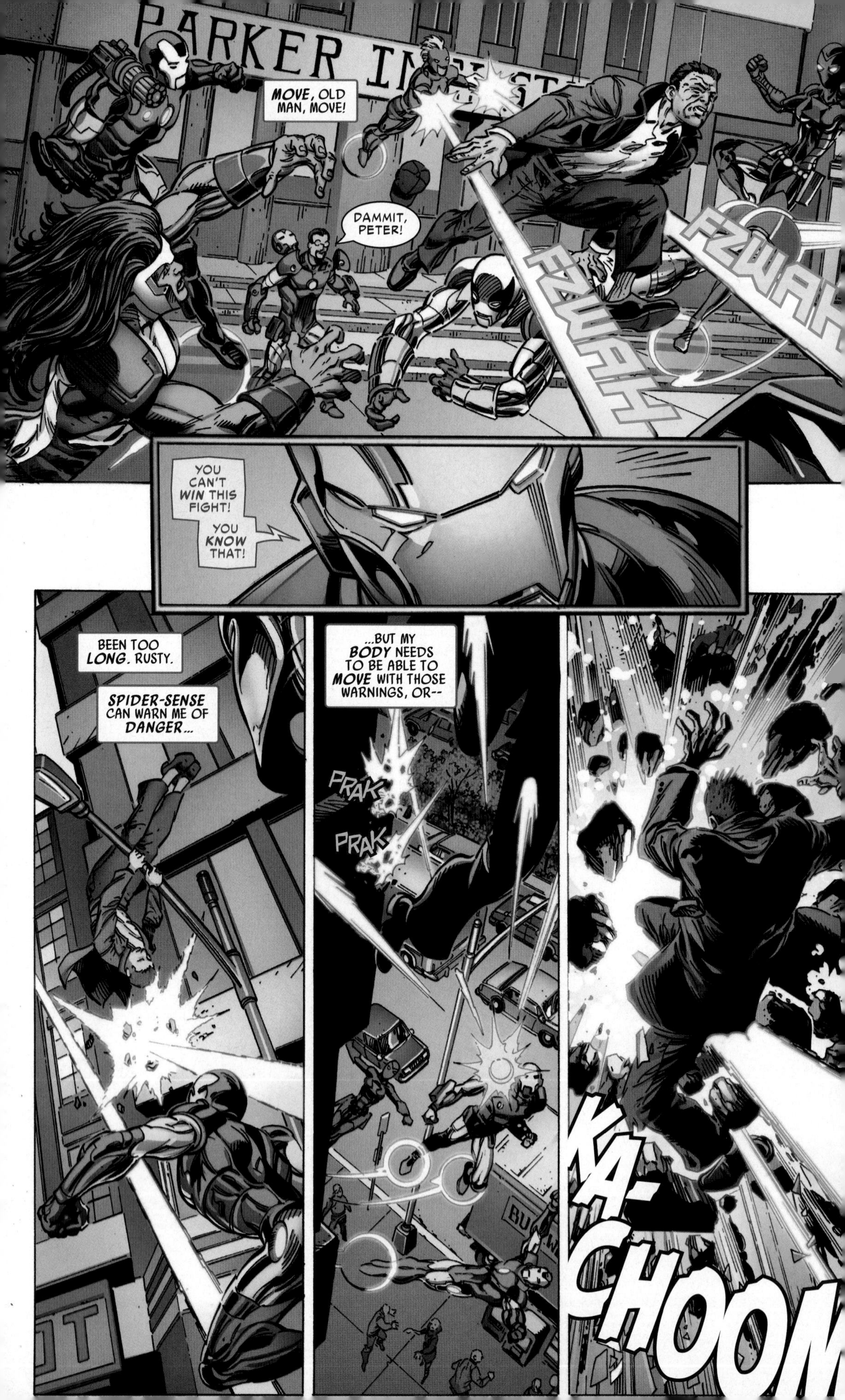
PARKER IN
MOVE, OLD MAN, MOVE!
DAMMIT, PETER!
FZWAH
FZWAH
YOU CAN'T WIN THIS FIGHT!
YOU KNOW THAT!
BEEN TOO LONG. RUSTY.
SPIDER-SENSE CAN WARN ME OF DANGER...
...BUT MY BODY NEEDS TO BE ABLE TO MOVE WITH THOSE WARNINGS, OR--
PRAK
PRAK
KA-CHOOM

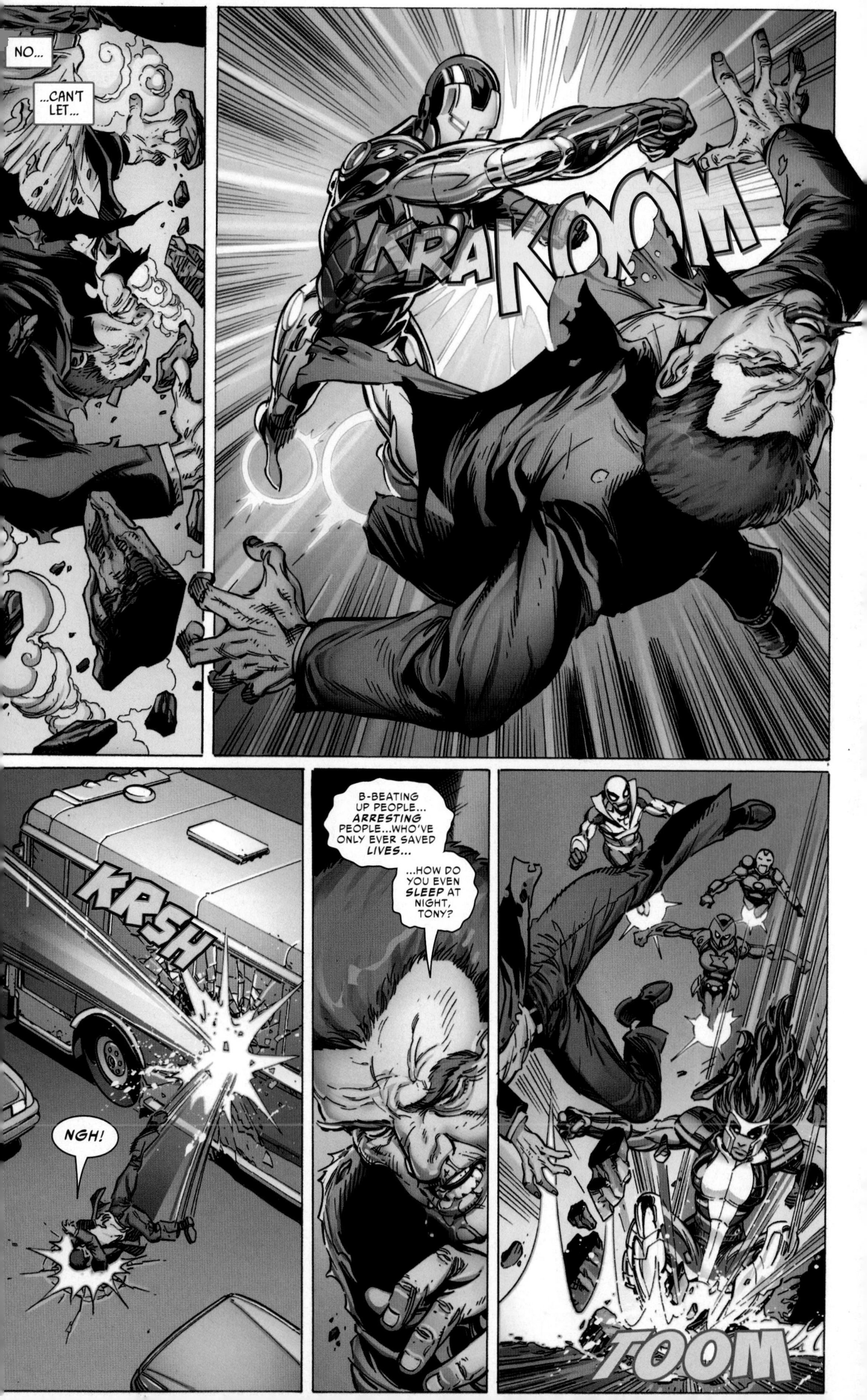
NO...
...CAN'T LET...
KRAKOOM
KRSH
NGH!
B-BEATING UP PEOPLE... ARRESTING PEOPLE...WHO'VE ONLY EVER SAVED LIVES...
...HOW DO YOU EVEN SLEEP AT NIGHT, TONY?
TOOM

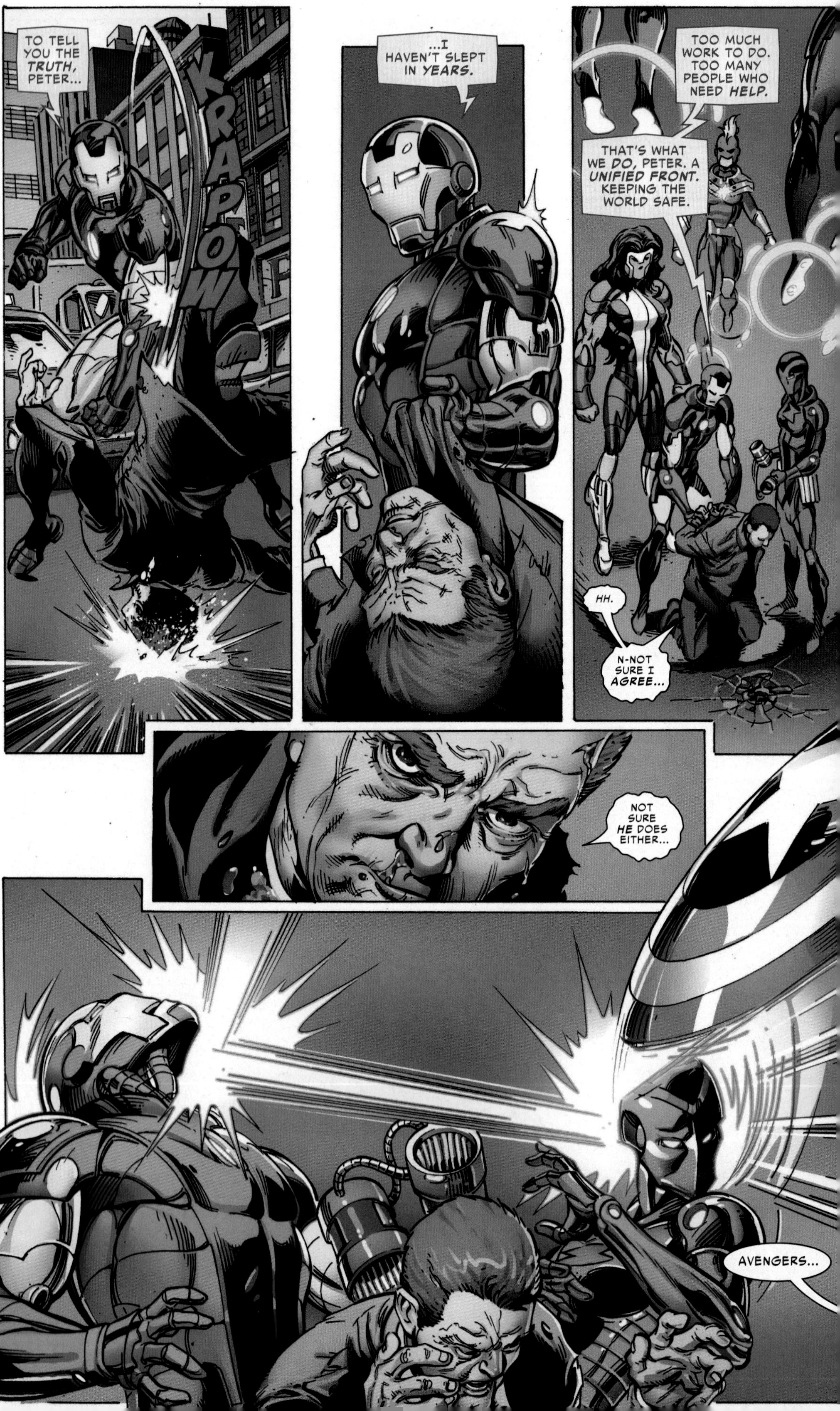
TO TELL YOU THE TRUTH, PETER...
KRAPOW
...I HAVEN'T SLEPT IN YEARS.
TOO MUCH WORK TO DO. TOO MANY PEOPLE WHO NEED HELP.
THAT'S WHAT WE DO, PETER. A UNIFIED FRONT. KEEPING THE WORLD SAFE.
HH.
N-NOT SURE I AGREE...
NOT SURE HE DOES EITHER...
AVENGERS...

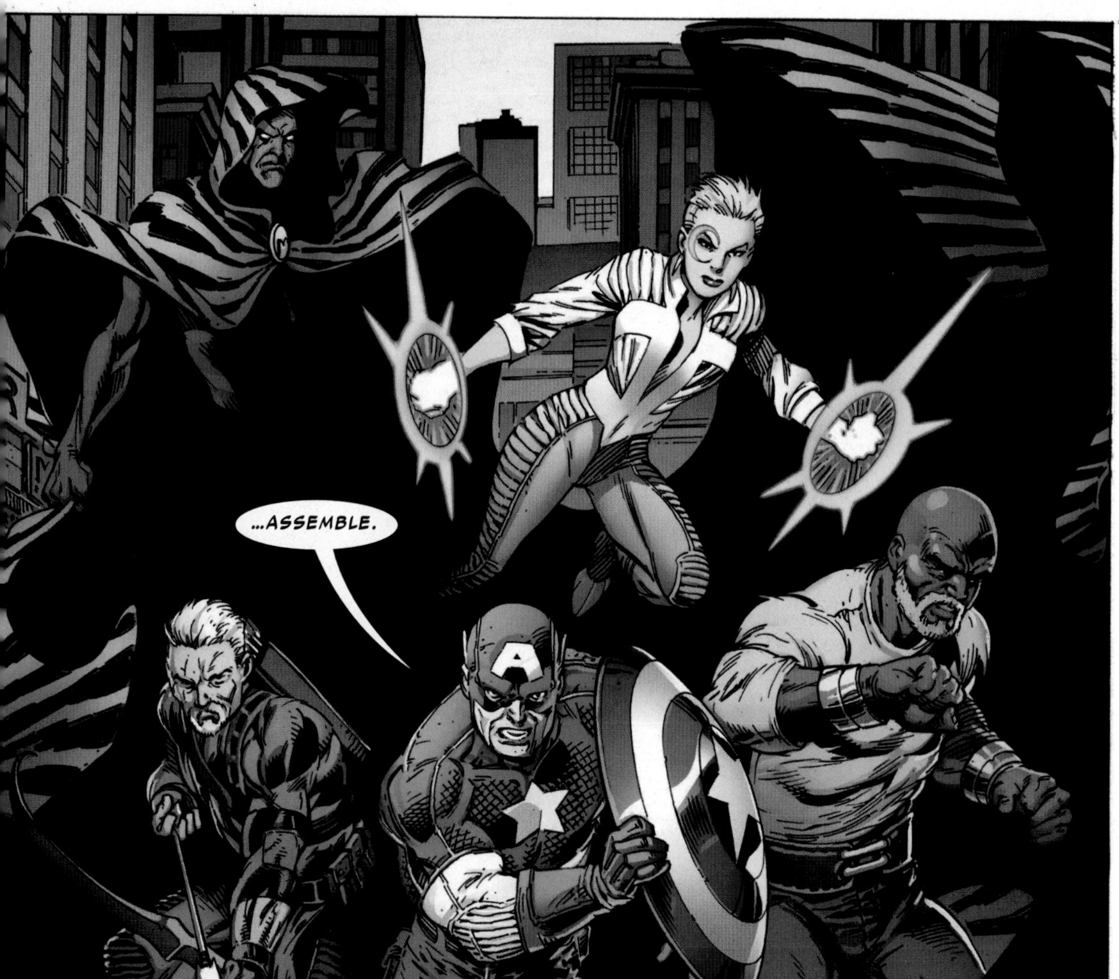
...ASSEMBLE.
BANKER BAR

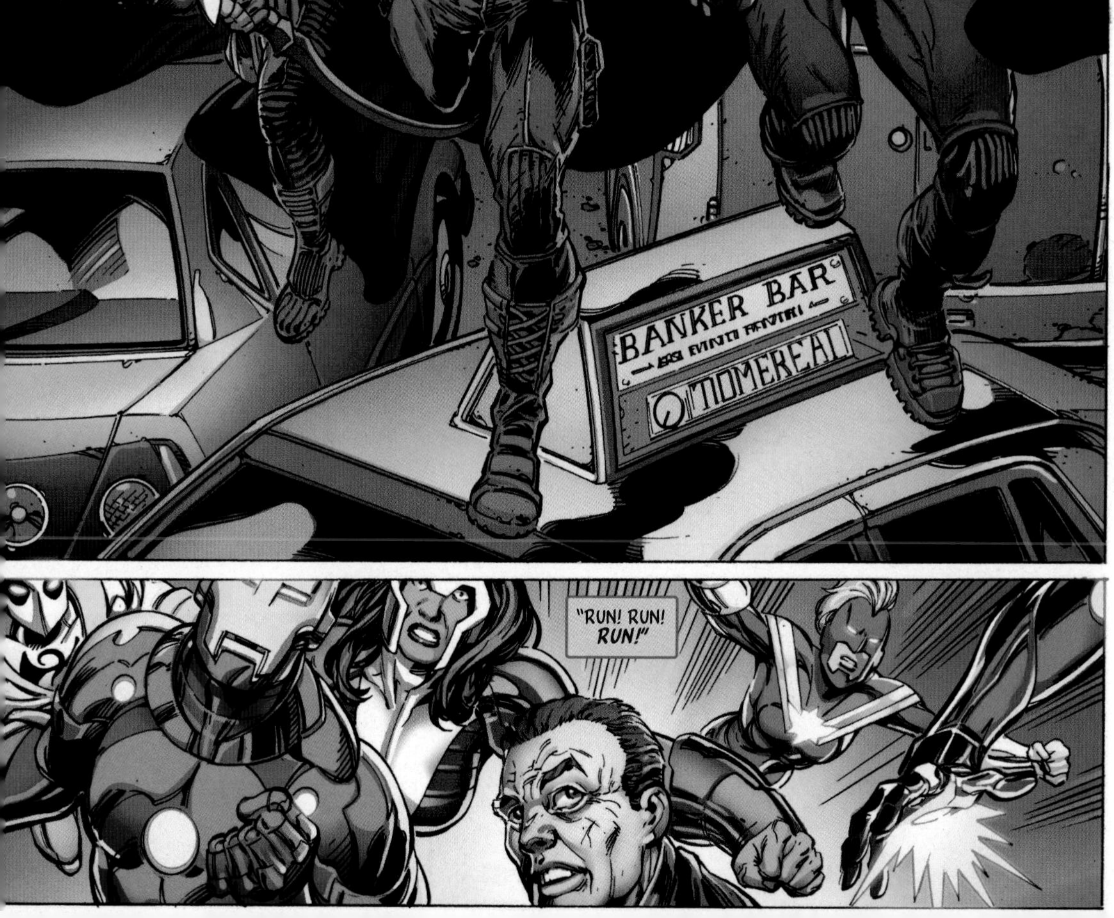
"RUN! RUN! RUN!"

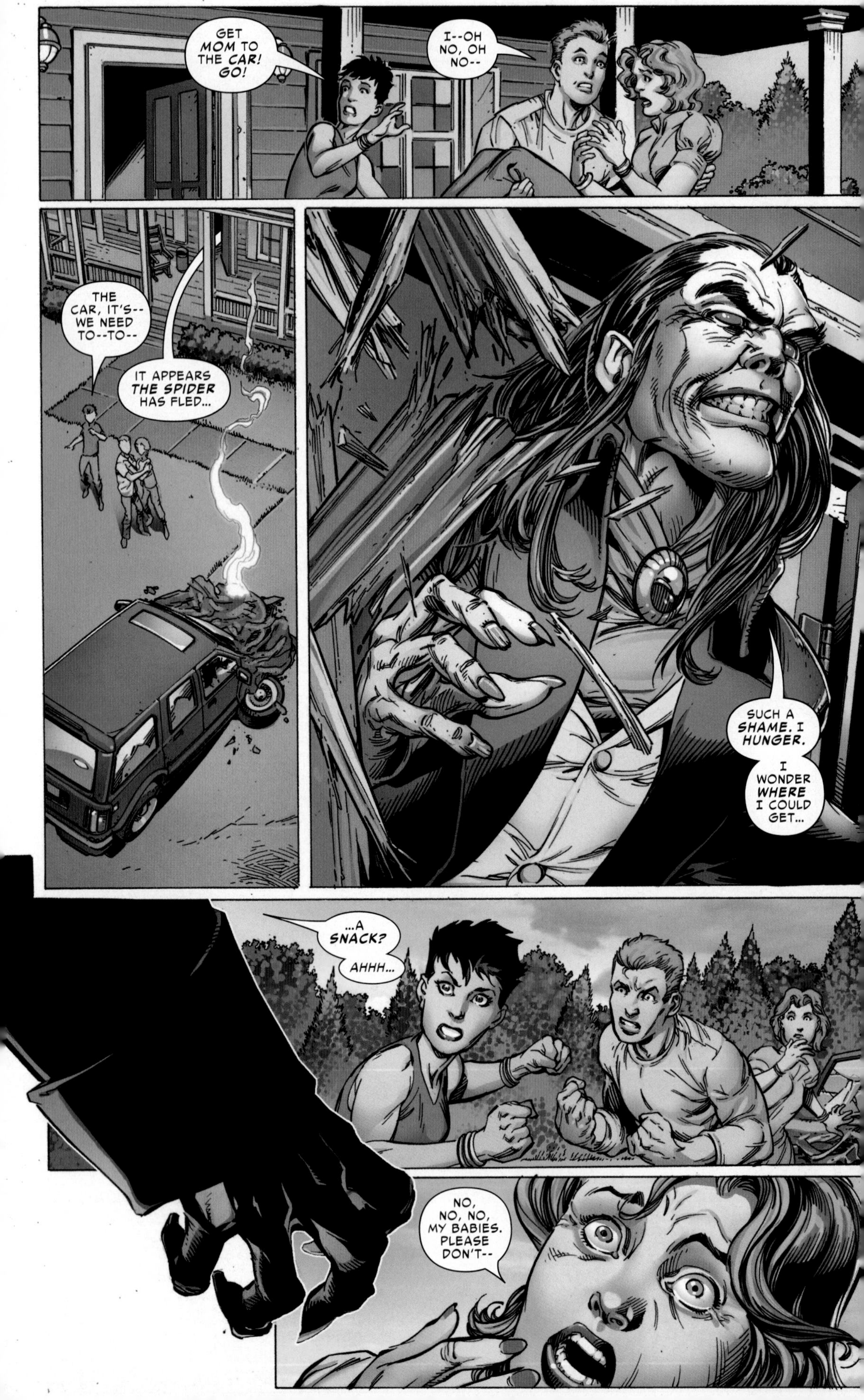
GET MOM TO THE CAR! GO!
I--OH NO, OH NO--
THE CAR, IT'S-- WE NEED TO--TO--
IT APPEARS THE SPIDER HAS FLED...
SUCH A SHAME. I HUNGER.
I WONDER WHERE I COULD GET...
...A SNACK?
AHHH...
NO, NO, NO, MY BABIES. PLEASE DON'T--

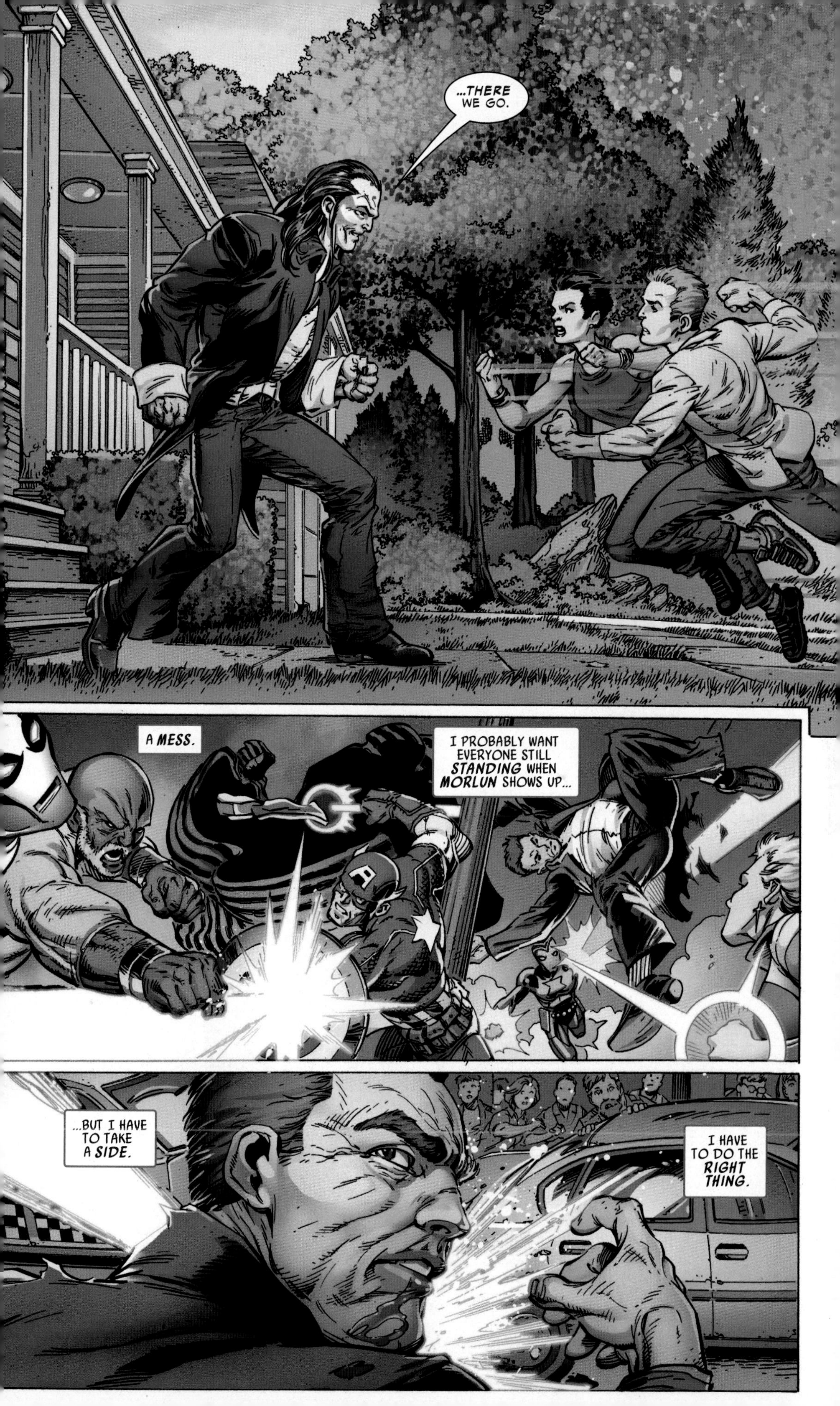

...THERE WE GO.
A MESS.
I PROBABLY WANT EVERYONE STILL STANDING WHEN MORLUN SHOWS UP...
...BUT I HAVE TO TAKE A SIDE.
I HAVE TO DO THE RIGHT THING.

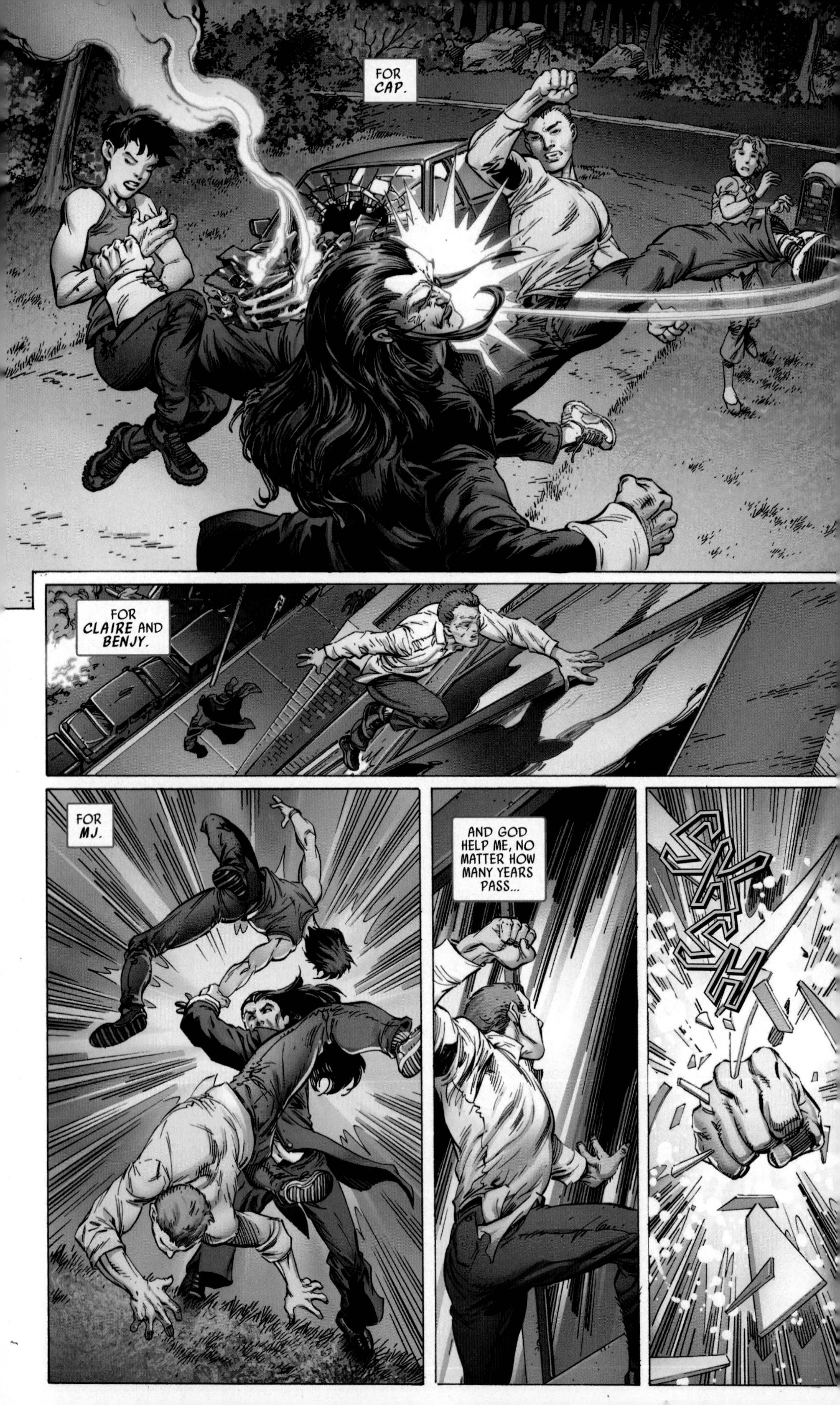

FOR CAP.
FOR CLAIRE AND BENJY.
FOR MJ.
AND GOD HELP ME, NO MATTER HOW MANY YEARS PASS...
SKASH!

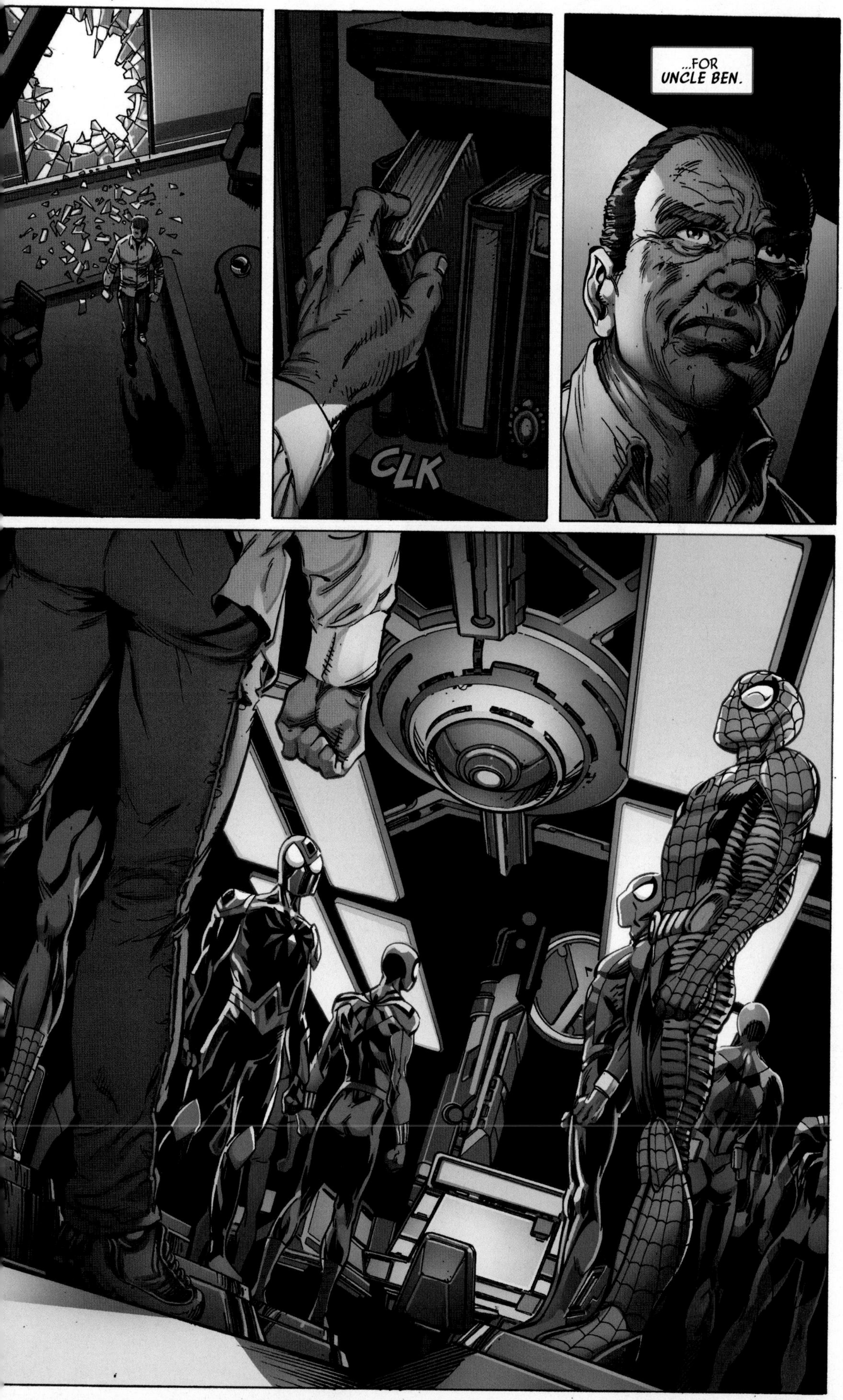
...FOR
UNCLE BEN.
CLK

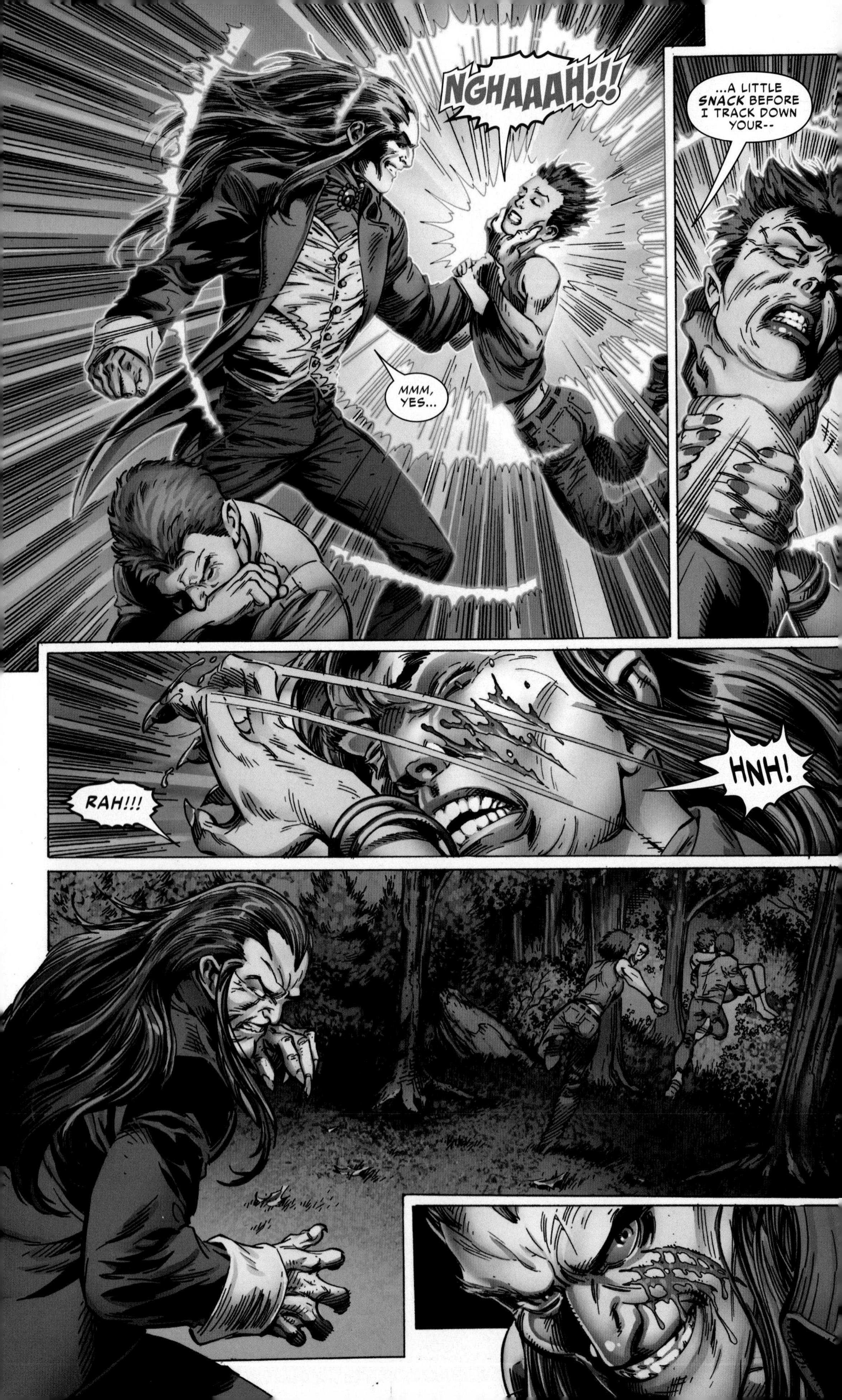
NGHAAAH!!!
MMM, YES...
...A LITTLE SNACK BEFORE I TRACK DOWN YOUR--
RAH!!!
HNH!

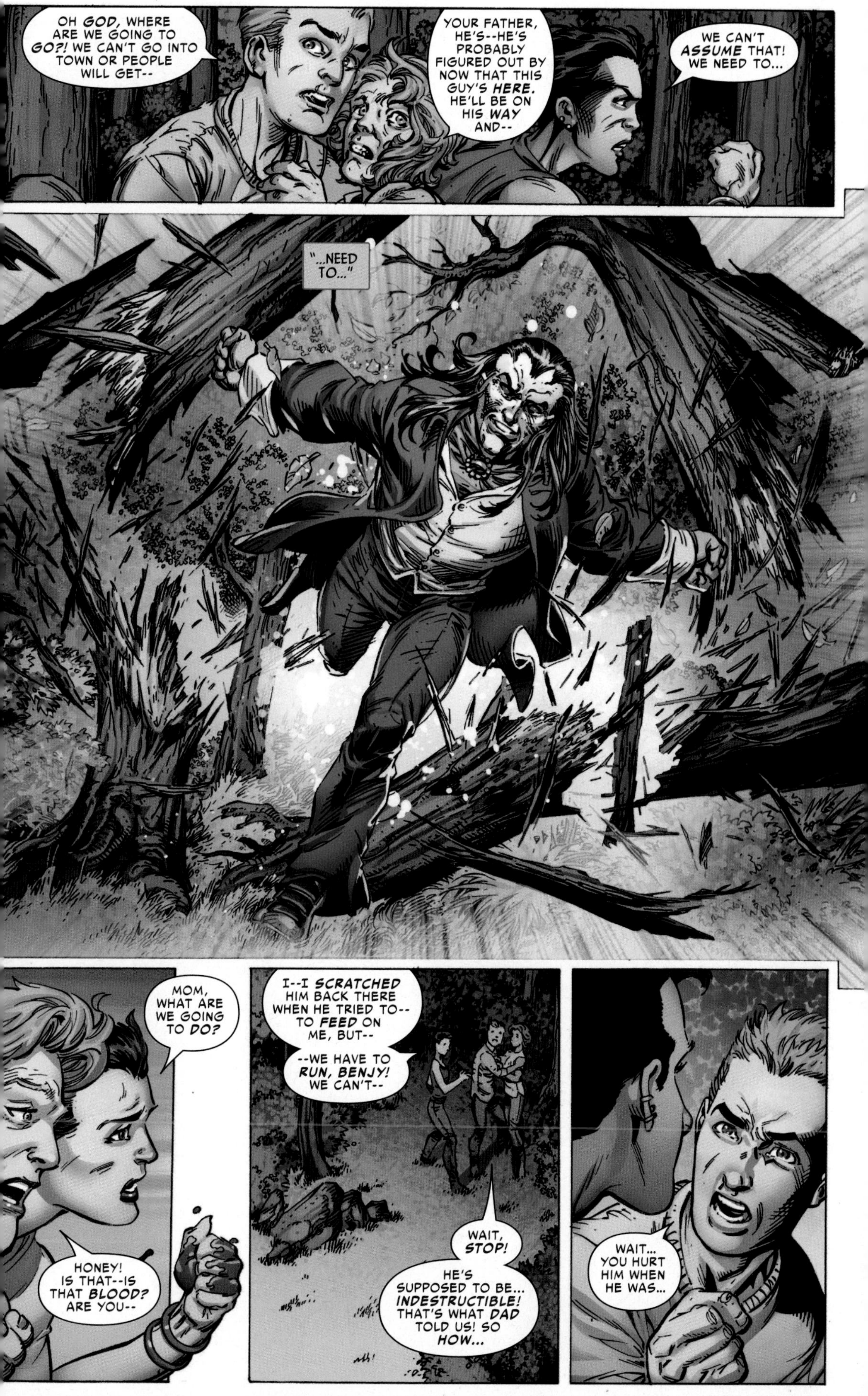
OH GOD, WHERE ARE WE GOING TO GO?! WE CAN'T GO INTO TOWN OR PEOPLE WILL GET--
YOUR FATHER, HE'S--HE'S PROBABLY FIGURED OUT BY NOW THAT THIS GUY'S HERE. HE'LL BE ON HIS WAY AND--
WE CAN'T ASSUME THAT! WE NEED TO...
"...NEED TO..."
MOM, WHAT ARE WE GOING TO DO?
HONEY! IS THAT--IS THAT BLOOD? ARE YOU--
I--I SCRATCHED HIM BACK THERE WHEN HE TRIED TO-- TO FEED ON ME, BUT--
--WE HAVE TO RUN, BENJY! WE CAN'T--
WAIT, STOP!
HE'S SUPPOSED TO BE... INDESTRUCTIBLE! THAT'S WHAT DAD TOLD US! SO HOW...
WAIT... YOU HURT HIM WHEN HE WAS...

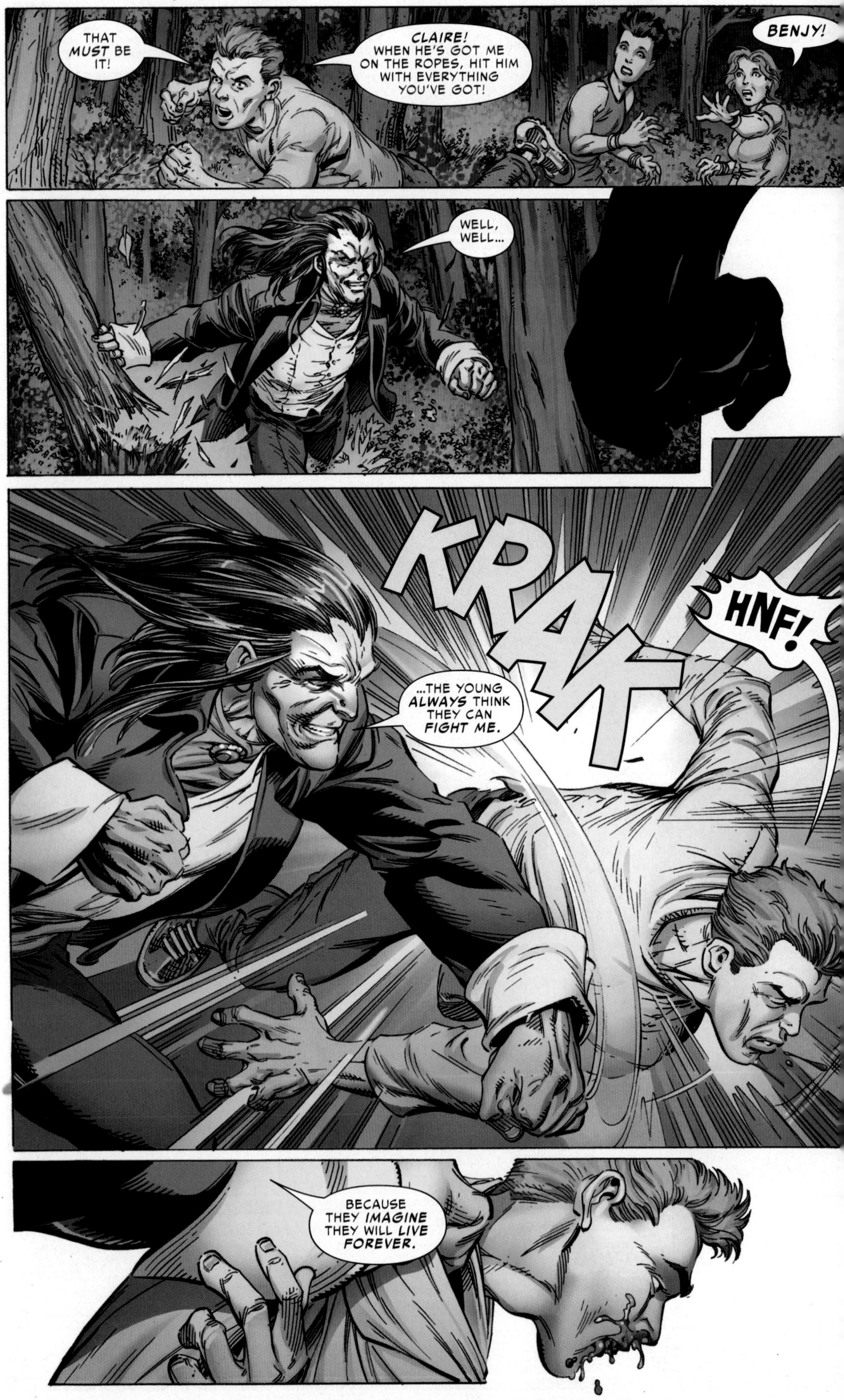
THAT MUST BE IT!
CLAIRE! WHEN HE'S GOT ME ON THE ROPES, HIT HIM WITH EVERYTHING YOU'VE GOT!
BENJY!
WELL, WELL...
KRAK
HNF!
...THE YOUNG ALWAYS THINK THEY CAN FIGHT ME.
BECAUSE THEY IMAGINE THEY WILL LIVE FOREVER.

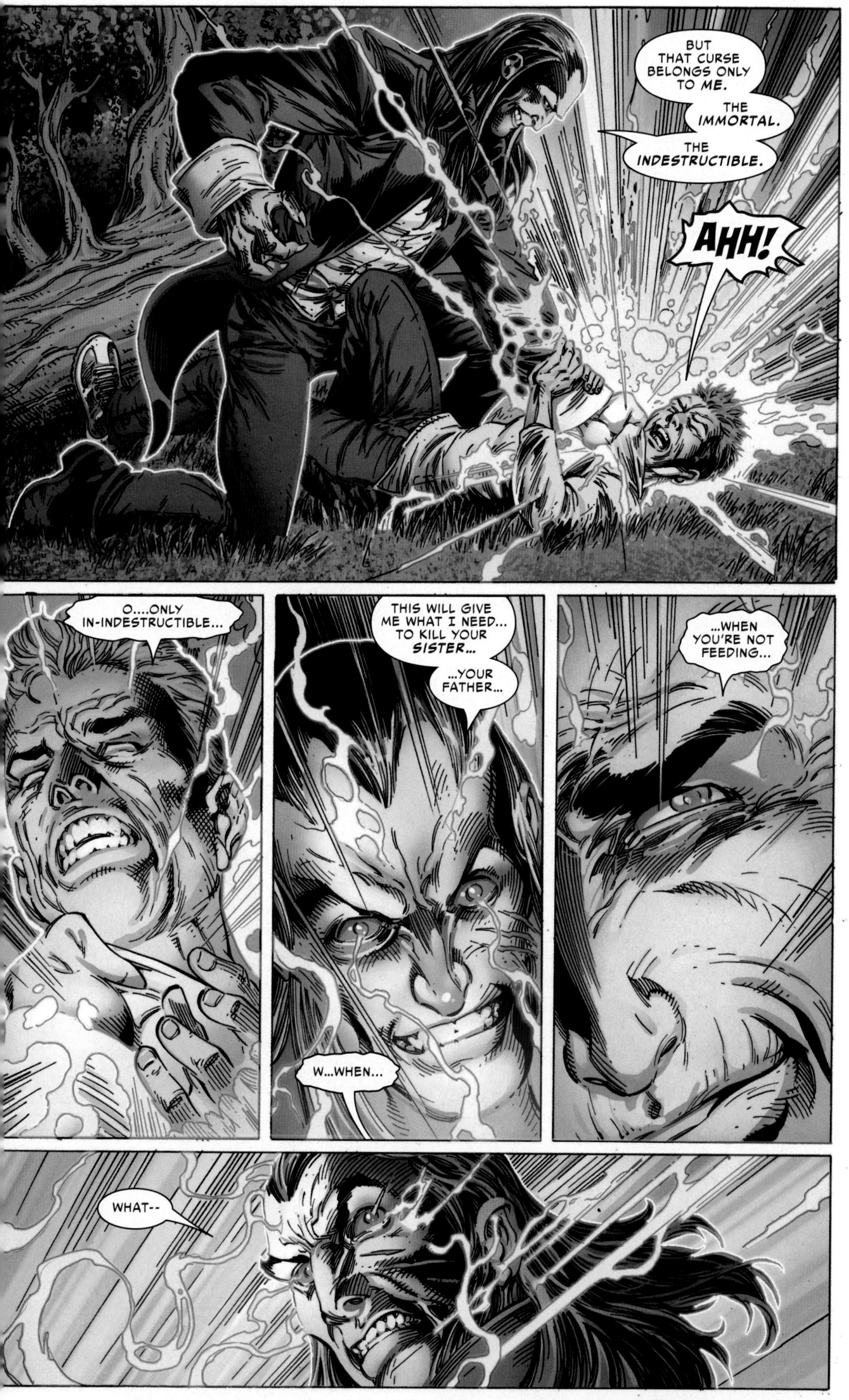
BUT THAT CURSE BELONGS ONLY TO ME.
THE IMMORTAL.
THE INDESTRUCTIBLE.
AHH!
O....ONLY IN-INDESTRUCTIBLE...
THIS WILL GIVE ME WHAT I NEED... TO KILL YOUR SISTER...
...YOUR FATHER...
W...WHEN...
...WHEN YOU'RE NOT FEEDING...
WHAT--

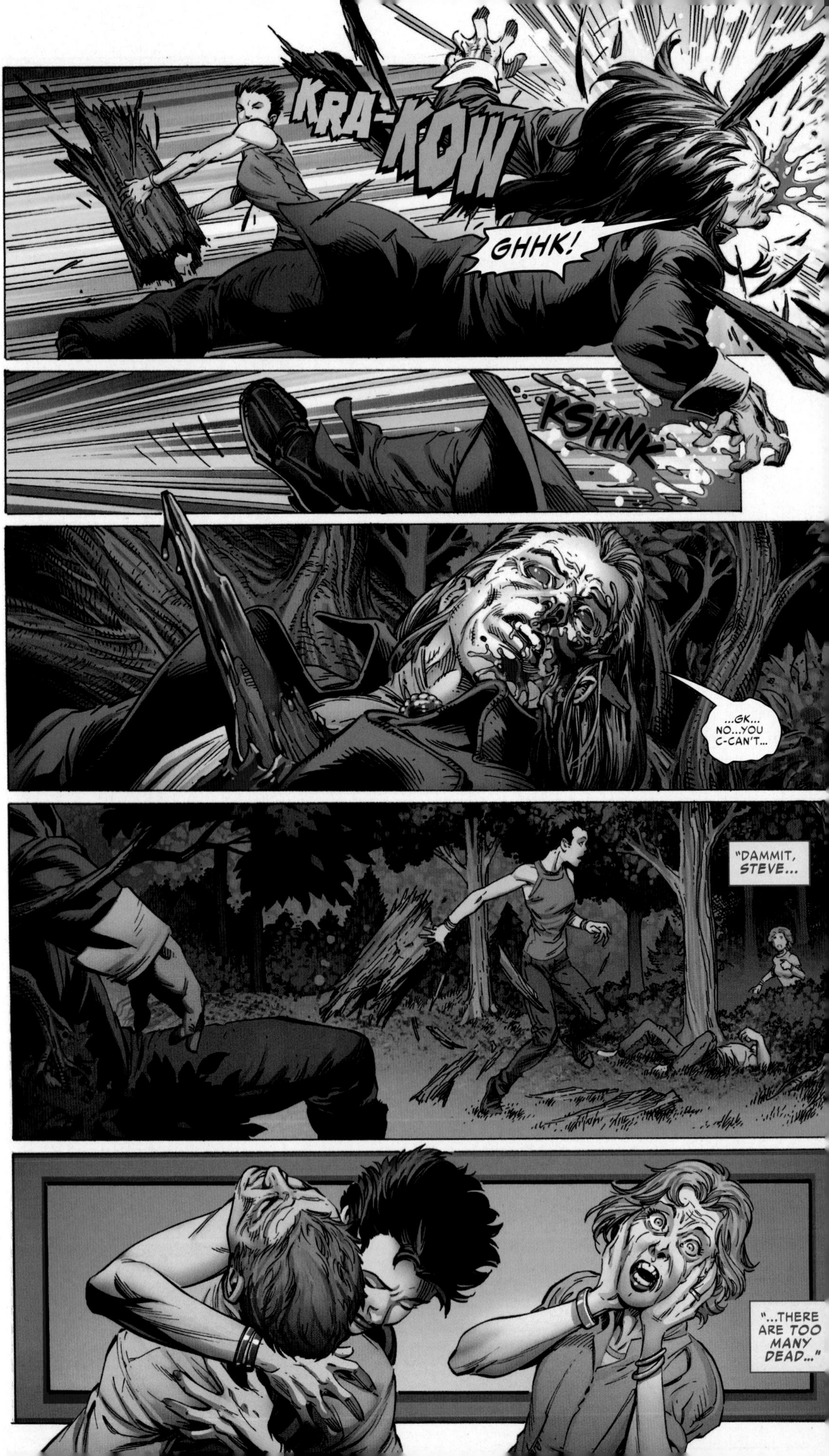
KRA-KOW
GHHK!
KSHNK
...GK... NO...YOU C-CAN'T...
"DAMMIT, STEVE...
"...THERE ARE TOO MANY DEAD..."

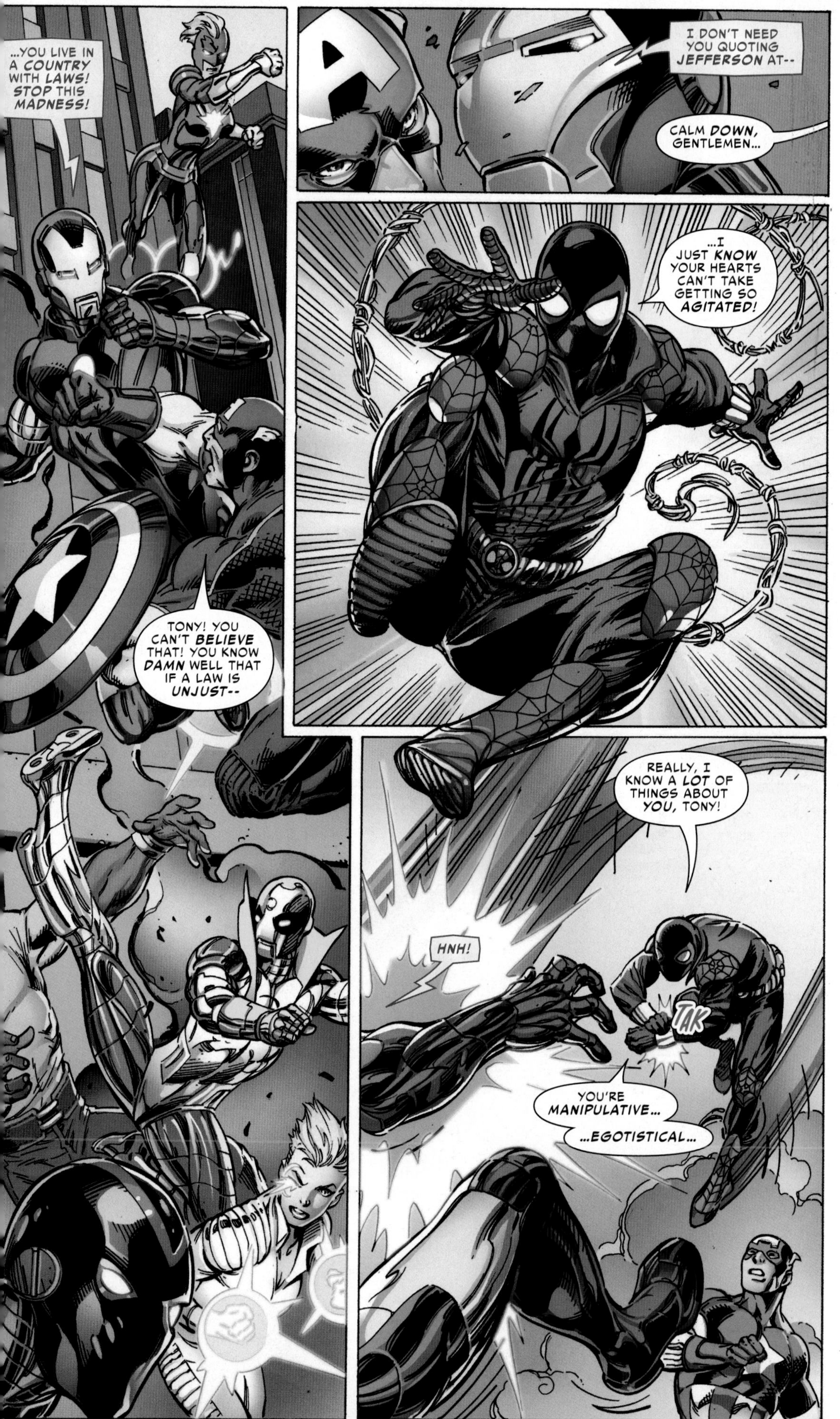

...YOU LIVE IN A COUNTRY WITH LAWS! STOP THIS MADNESS!
I DON'T NEED YOU QUOTING JEFFERSON AT--
CALM DOWN, GENTLEMEN...
...I JUST KNOW YOUR HEARTS CAN'T TAKE GETTING SO AGITATED!
TONY! YOU CAN'T BELIEVE THAT! YOU KNOW DAMN WELL THAT IF A LAW IS UNJUST--
REALLY, I KNOW A LOT OF THINGS ABOUT YOU, TONY!
HNH!
TAK
YOU'RE MANIPULATIVE...
...EGOTISTICAL...

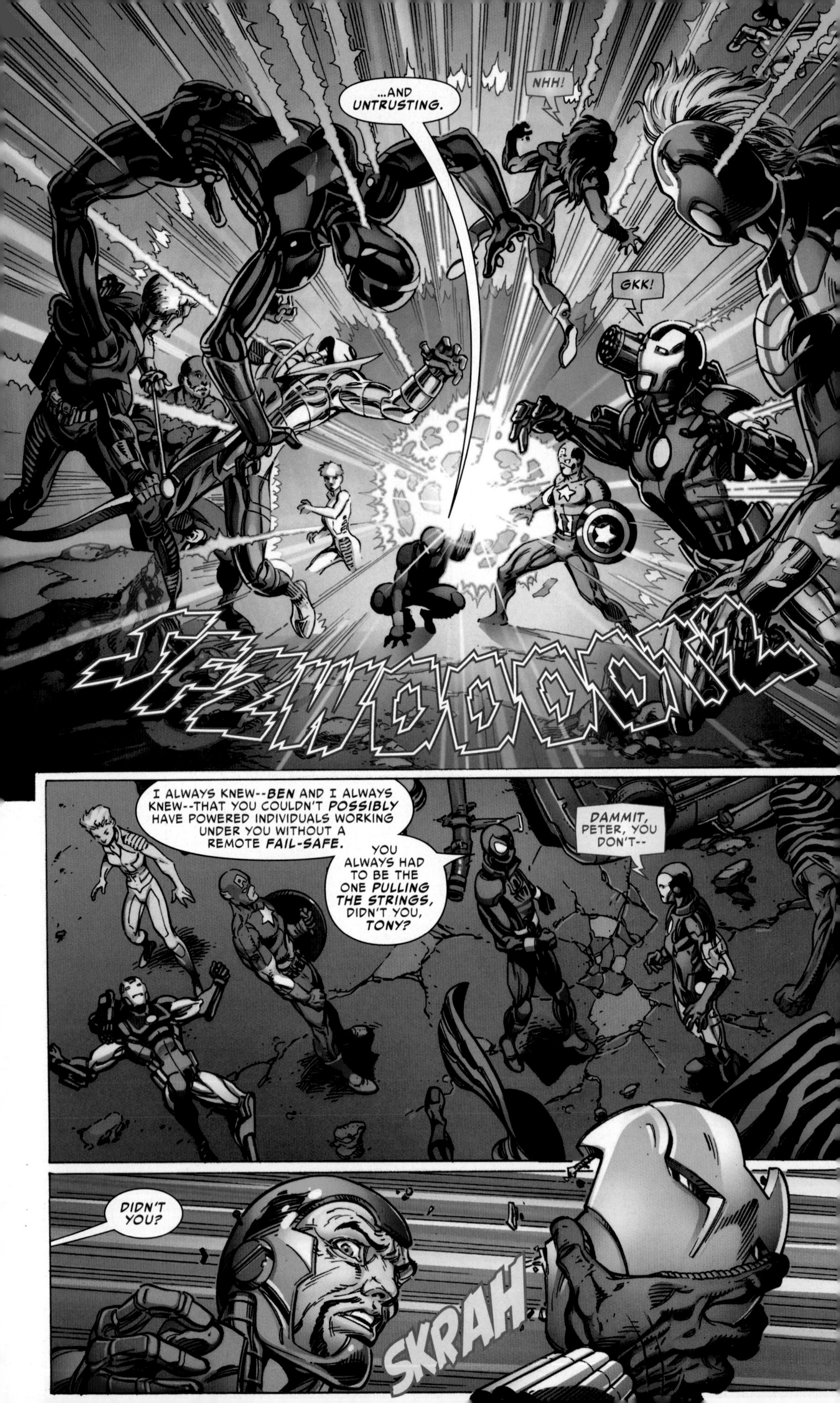

...AND UNTRUSTING.
NHH!
GKK!
SFZWOOOOM
I ALWAYS KNEW--BEN AND I ALWAYS KNEW--THAT YOU COULDN'T POSSIBLY HAVE POWERED INDIVIDUALS WORKING UNDER YOU WITHOUT A REMOTE FAIL-SAFE.
YOU ALWAYS HAD TO BE THE ONE PULLING THE STRINGS, DIDN'T YOU, TONY?
DAMMIT, PETER, YOU DON'T--
DIDN'T YOU?
SKRAH

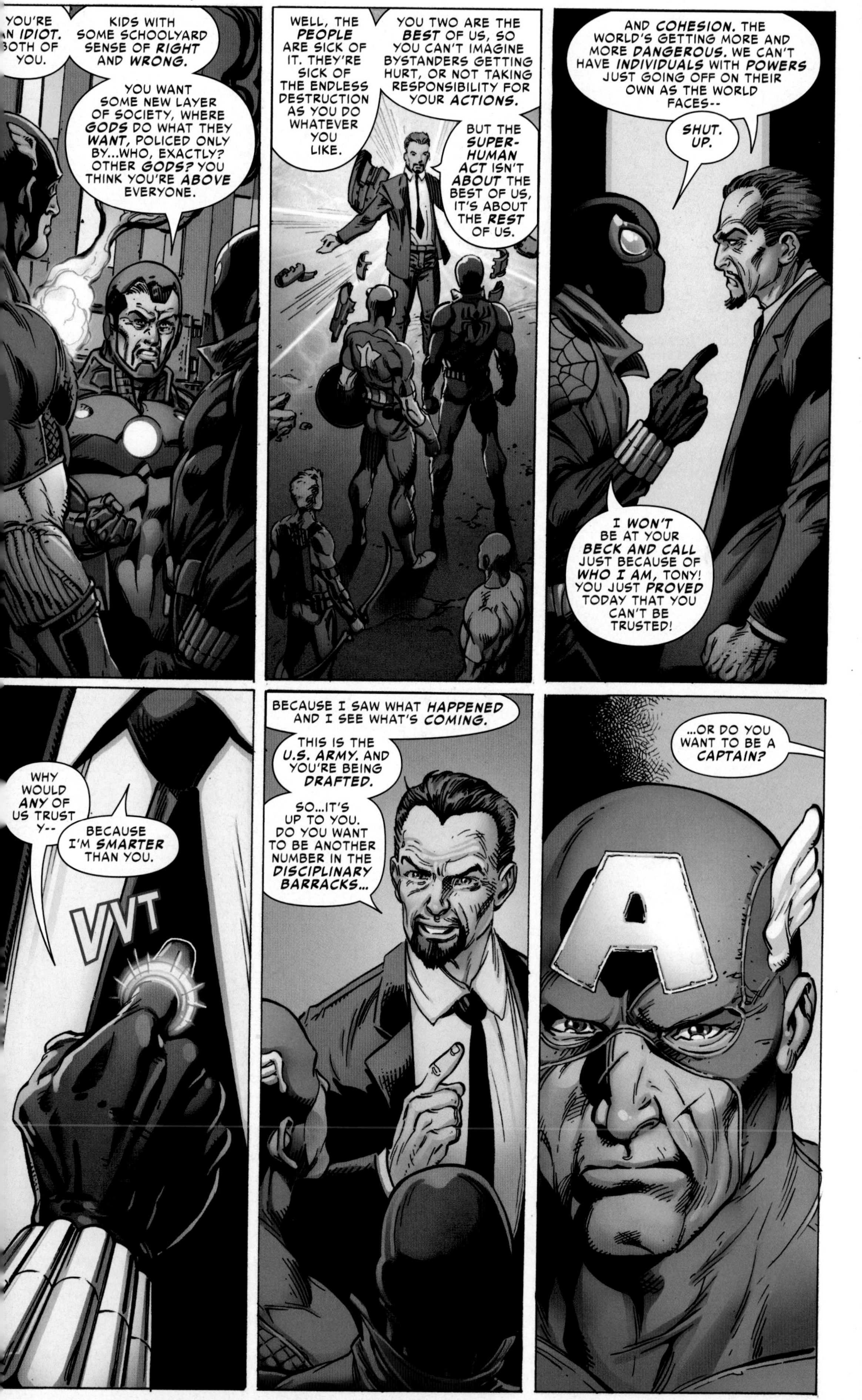
YOU'RE AN IDIOT. BOTH OF YOU.
KIDS WITH SOME SCHOOLYARD SENSE OF RIGHT AND WRONG.
YOU WANT SOME NEW LAYER OF SOCIETY, WHERE GODS DO WHAT THEY WANT, POLICED ONLY BY...WHO, EXACTLY? OTHER GODS? YOU THINK YOU'RE ABOVE EVERYONE.
WELL, THE PEOPLE ARE SICK OF IT. THEY'RE SICK OF THE ENDLESS DESTRUCTION AS YOU DO WHATEVER YOU LIKE.
YOU TWO ARE THE BEST OF US, SO YOU CAN'T IMAGINE BYSTANDERS GETTING HURT, OR NOT TAKING RESPONSIBILITY FOR YOUR ACTIONS.
BUT THE SUPER-HUMAN ACT ISN'T ABOUT THE BEST OF US, IT'S ABOUT THE REST OF US.
AND COHESION. THE WORLD'S GETTING MORE AND MORE DANGEROUS. WE CAN'T HAVE INDIVIDUALS WITH POWERS JUST GOING OFF ON THEIR OWN AS THE WORLD FACES--
SHUT. UP.
I WON'T BE AT YOUR BECK AND CALL JUST BECAUSE OF WHO I AM, TONY! YOU JUST PROVED TODAY THAT YOU CAN'T BE TRUSTED!
WHY WOULD ANY OF US TRUST Y--
BECAUSE I'M SMARTER THAN YOU.
VVT
BECAUSE I SAW WHAT HAPPENED AND I SEE WHAT'S COMING.
THIS IS THE U.S. ARMY. AND YOU'RE BEING DRAFTED.
SO...IT'S UP TO YOU. DO YOU WANT TO BE ANOTHER NUMBER IN THE DISCIPLINARY BARRACKS...
...OR DO YOU WANT TO BE A CAPTAIN?

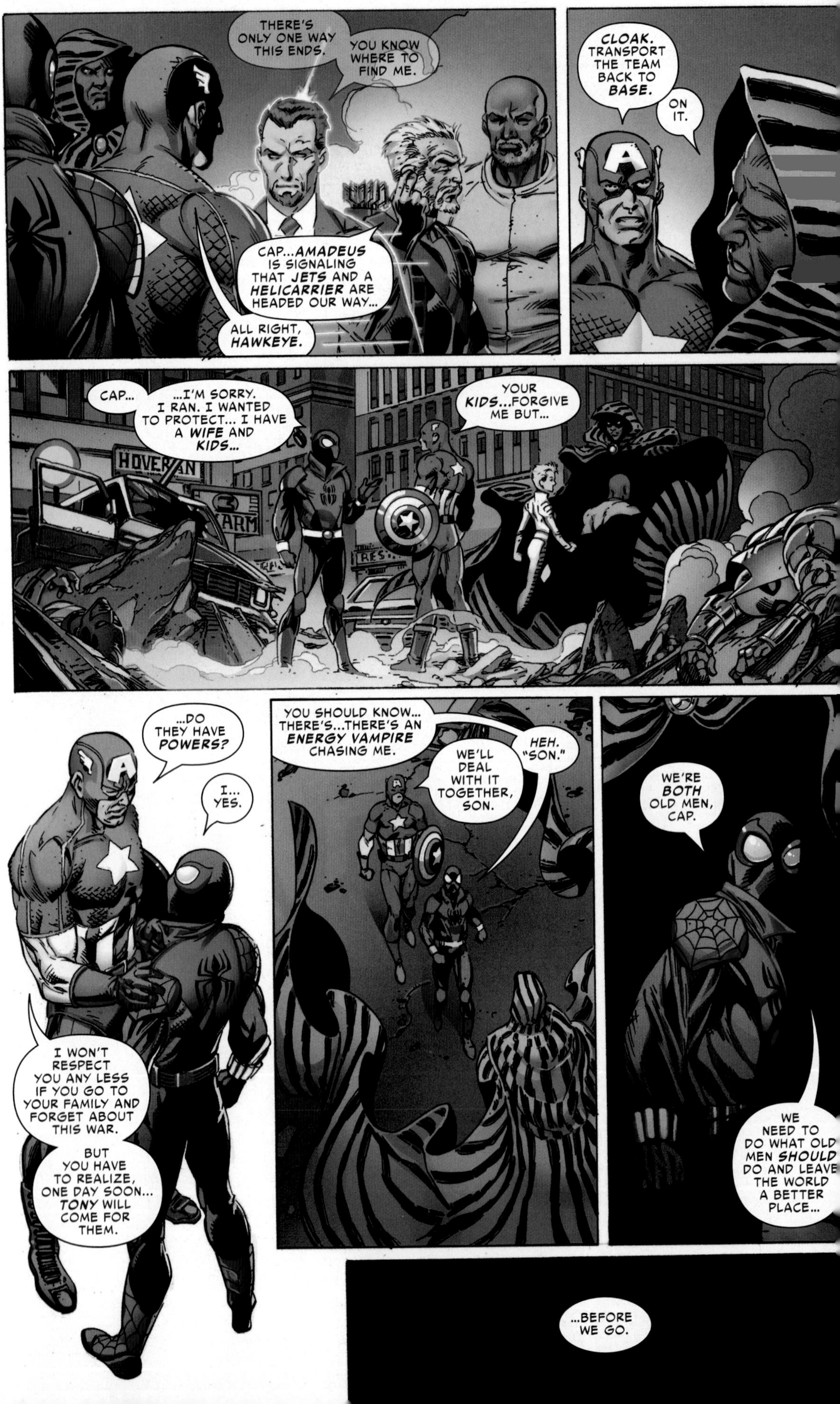

THERE'S ONLY ONE WAY THIS ENDS.
YOU KNOW WHERE TO FIND ME.
CAP...AMADEUS IS SIGNALING THAT JETS AND A HELICARRIER ARE HEADED OUR WAY...
ALL RIGHT, HAWKEYE.
CLOAK. TRANSPORT THE TEAM BACK TO BASE.
ON IT.
CAP...
...I'M SORRY. I RAN. I WANTED TO PROTECT... I HAVE A WIFE AND KIDS...
YOUR KIDS...FORGIVE ME BUT...
HOVERVAN
...DO THEY HAVE POWERS?
I... YES.
I WON'T RESPECT YOU ANY LESS IF YOU GO TO YOUR FAMILY AND FORGET ABOUT THIS WAR.
BUT YOU HAVE TO REALIZE, ONE DAY SOON... TONY WILL COME FOR THEM.
YOU SHOULD KNOW... THERE'S...THERE'S AN ENERGY VAMPIRE CHASING ME.
WE'LL DEAL WITH IT TOGETHER, SON.
HEH. "SON."
WE'RE BOTH OLD MEN, CAP.
WE NEED TO DO WHAT OLD MEN SHOULD DO AND LEAVE THE WORLD A BETTER PLACE...
...BEFORE WE GO.

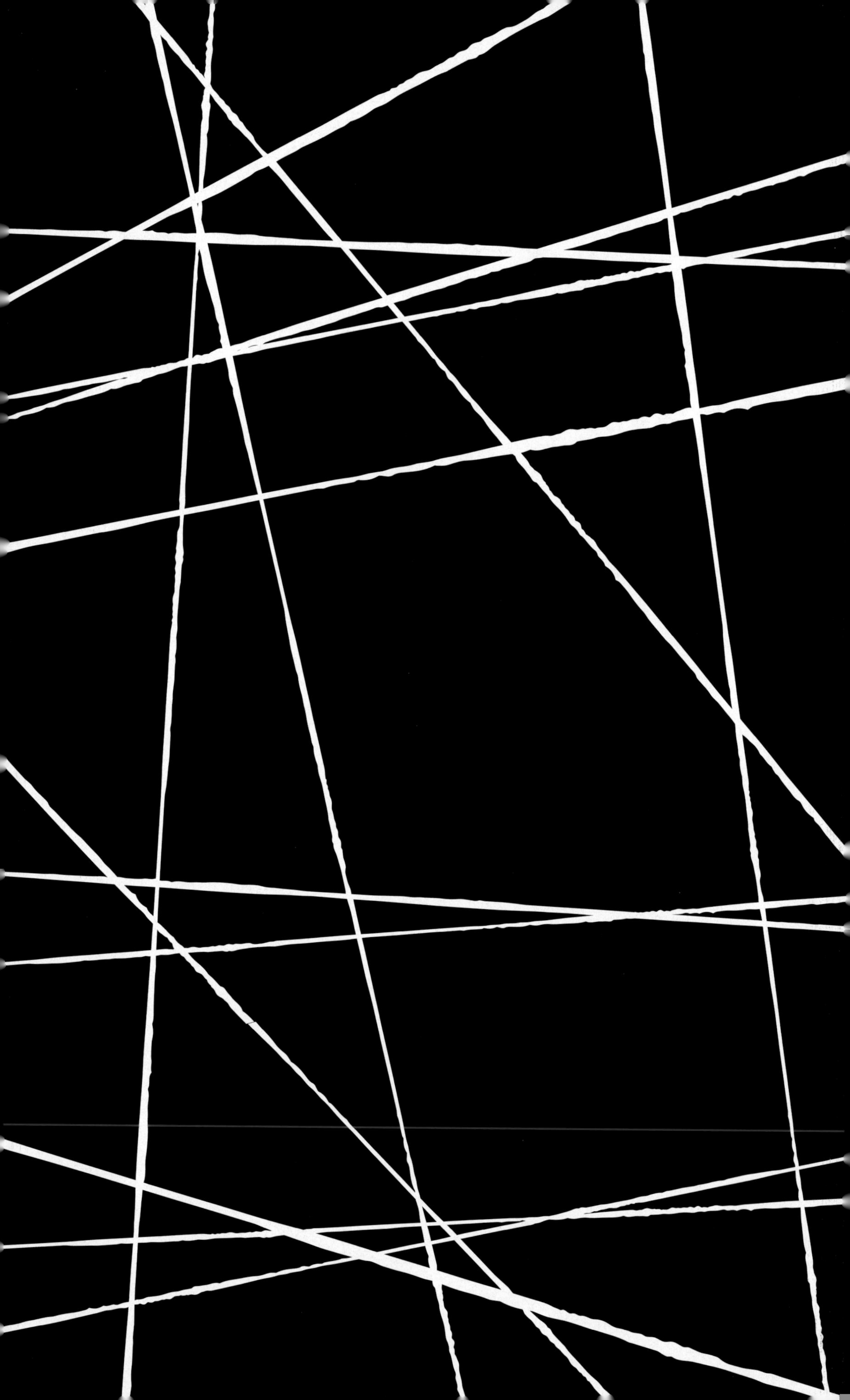

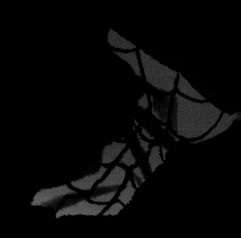

SPIDER-MAN
Life Story 6 The '10s

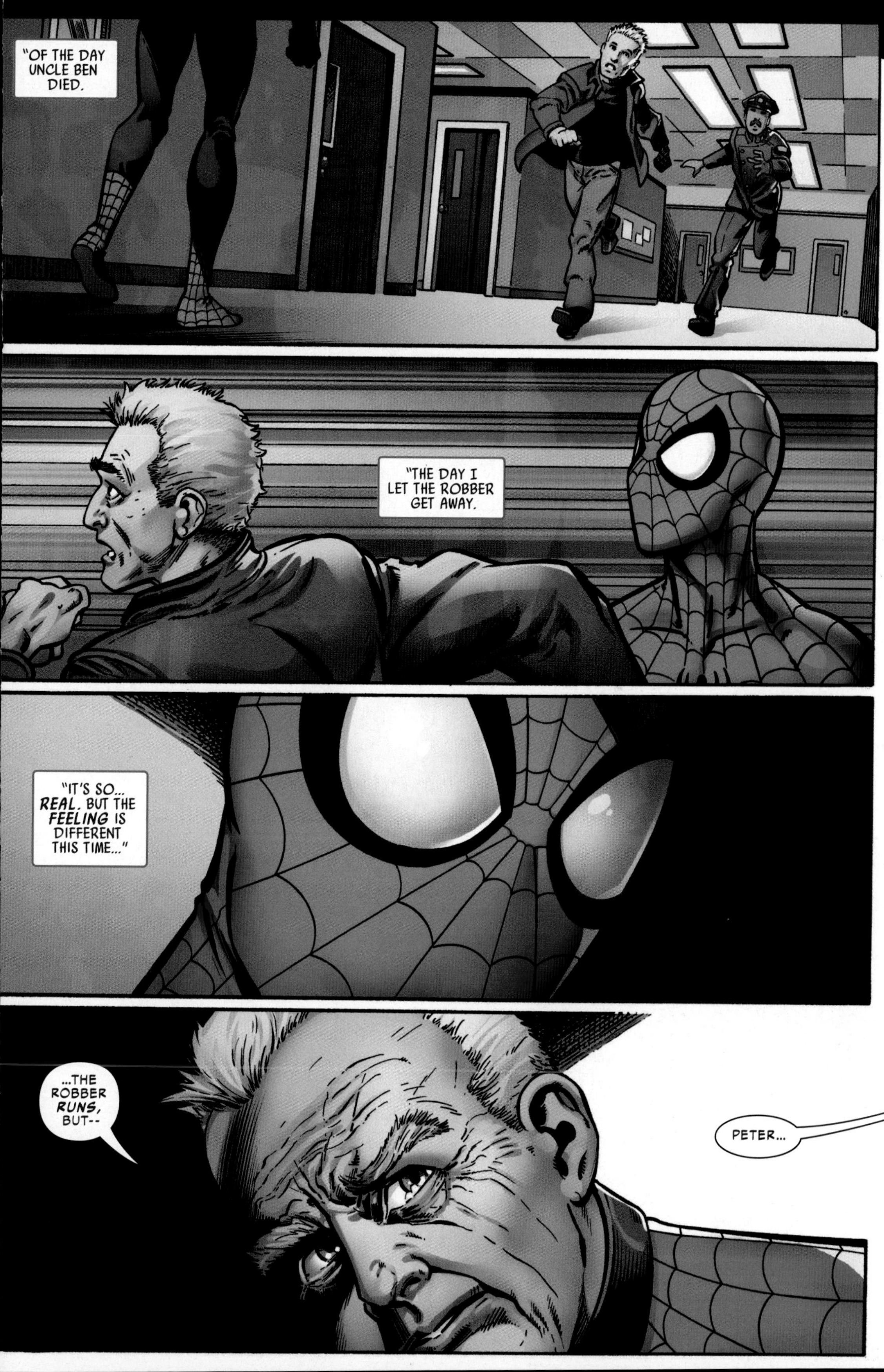
"OF THE DAY UNCLE BEN DIED.
"THE DAY I LET THE ROBBER GET AWAY.
"IT'S SO... REAL. BUT THE FEELING IS DIFFERENT THIS TIME..."
...THE ROBBER RUNS, BUT--
PETER...

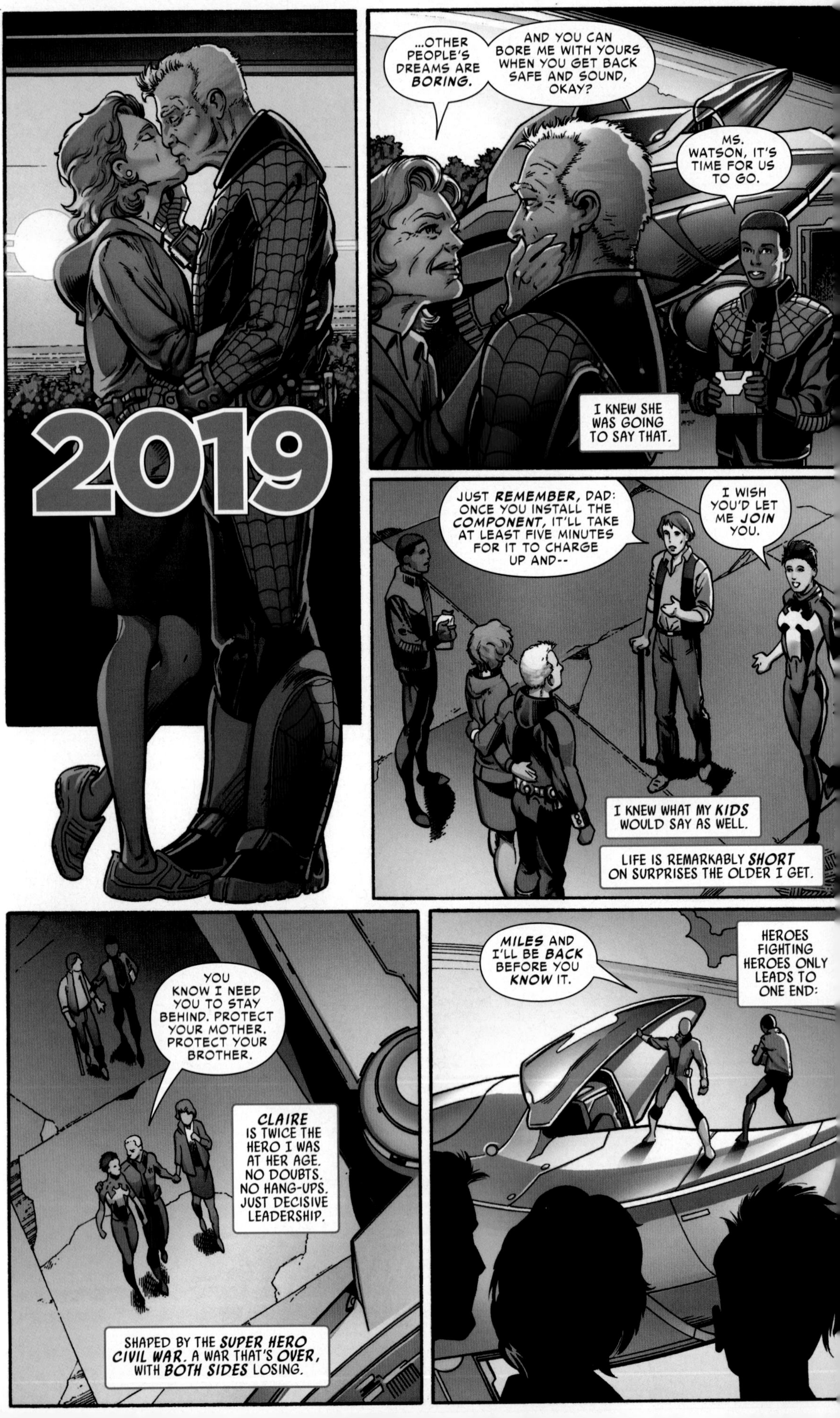
2019
...OTHER PEOPLE'S DREAMS ARE BORING.
AND YOU CAN BORE ME WITH YOURS WHEN YOU GET BACK SAFE AND SOUND, OKAY?
MS. WATSON, IT'S TIME FOR US TO GO.
I KNEW SHE WAS GOING TO SAY THAT.
JUST REMEMBER, DAD: ONCE YOU INSTALL THE COMPONENT, IT'LL TAKE AT LEAST FIVE MINUTES FOR IT TO CHARGE UP AND--
I WISH YOU'D LET ME JOIN YOU.
I KNEW WHAT MY KIDS WOULD SAY AS WELL.
LIFE IS REMARKABLY SHORT ON SURPRISES THE OLDER I GET.
YOU KNOW I NEED YOU TO STAY BEHIND. PROTECT YOUR MOTHER. PROTECT YOUR BROTHER.
CLAIRE IS TWICE THE HERO I WAS AT HER AGE. NO DOUBTS. NO HANG-UPS. JUST DECISIVE LEADERSHIP.
SHAPED BY THE SUPER HERO CIVIL WAR. A WAR THAT'S OVER, WITH BOTH SIDES LOSING.
MILES AND I'LL BE BACK BEFORE YOU KNOW IT.
HEROES FIGHTING HEROES ONLY LEADS TO ONE END:

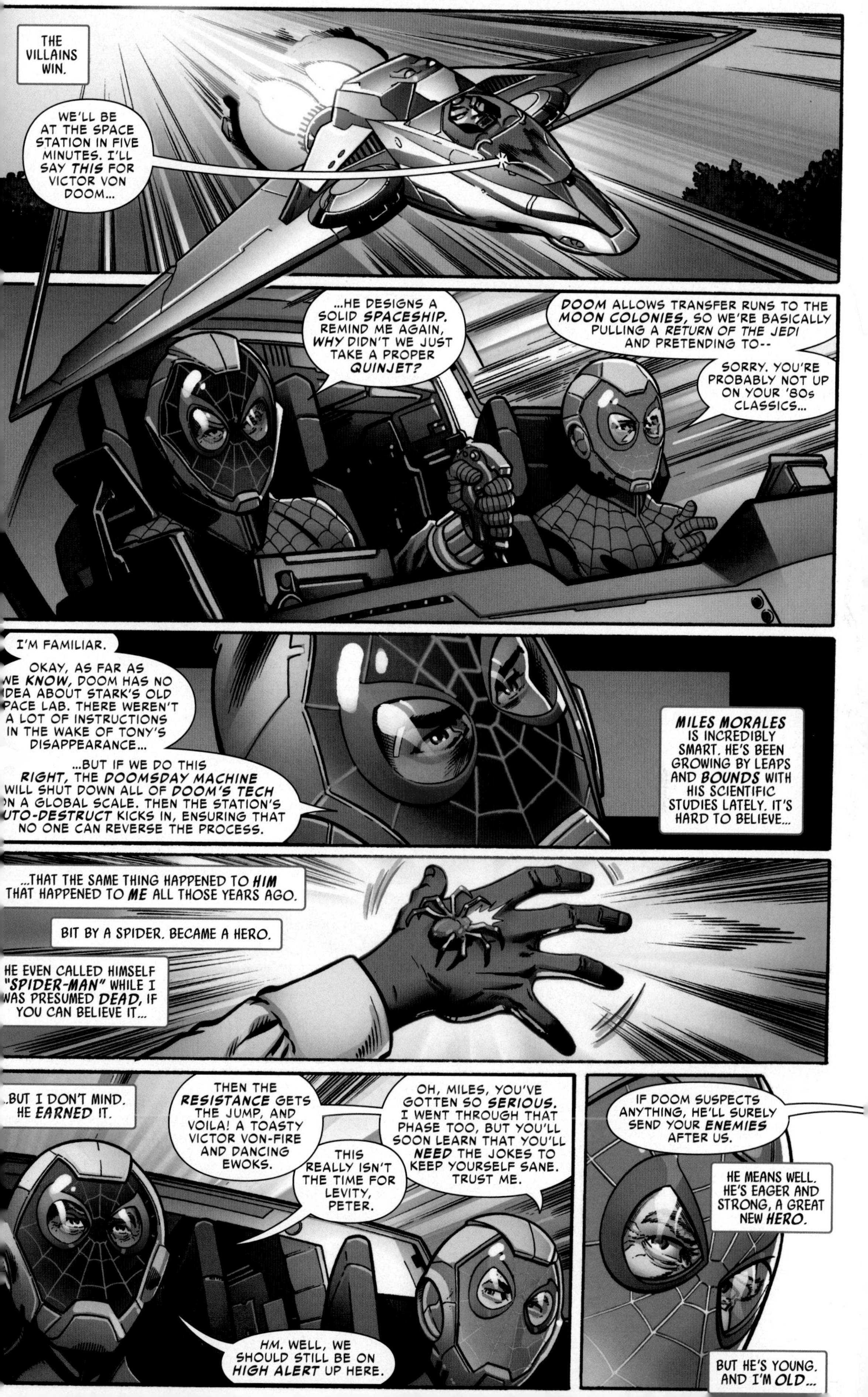
THE VILLAINS WIN.
WE'LL BE AT THE SPACE STATION IN FIVE MINUTES. I'LL SAY THIS FOR VICTOR VON DOOM...
...HE DESIGNS A SOLID SPACESHIP. REMIND ME AGAIN, WHY DIDN'T WE JUST TAKE A PROPER QUINJET?
DOOM ALLOWS TRANSFER RUNS TO THE MOON COLONIES, SO WE'RE BASICALLY PULLING A RETURN OF THE JEDI AND PRETENDING TO--
SORRY. YOU'RE PROBABLY NOT UP ON YOUR '80s CLASSICS...
I'M FAMILIAR.
OKAY, AS FAR AS WE KNOW, DOOM HAS NO IDEA ABOUT STARK'S OLD SPACE LAB. THERE WEREN'T A LOT OF INSTRUCTIONS IN THE WAKE OF TONY'S DISAPPEARANCE...
...BUT IF WE DO THIS RIGHT, THE DOOMSDAY MACHINE WILL SHUT DOWN ALL OF DOOM'S TECH ON A GLOBAL SCALE. THEN THE STATION'S AUTO-DESTRUCT KICKS IN, ENSURING THAT NO ONE CAN REVERSE THE PROCESS.
MILES MORALES IS INCREDIBLY SMART. HE'S BEEN GROWING BY LEAPS AND BOUNDS WITH HIS SCIENTIFIC STUDIES LATELY. IT'S HARD TO BELIEVE...
...THAT THE SAME THING HAPPENED TO HIM THAT HAPPENED TO ME ALL THOSE YEARS AGO.
BIT BY A SPIDER. BECAME A HERO.
HE EVEN CALLED HIMSELF "SPIDER-MAN" WHILE I WAS PRESUMED DEAD, IF YOU CAN BELIEVE IT...
...BUT I DON'T MIND. HE EARNED IT.
THEN THE RESISTANCE GETS THE JUMP, AND VOILA! A TOASTY VICTOR VON-FIRE AND DANCING EWOKS.
THIS REALLY ISN'T THE TIME FOR LEVITY, PETER.
OH, MILES, YOU'VE GOTTEN SO SERIOUS. I WENT THROUGH THAT PHASE TOO, BUT YOU'LL SOON LEARN THAT YOU'LL NEED THE JOKES TO KEEP YOURSELF SANE. TRUST ME.
HM. WELL, WE SHOULD STILL BE ON HIGH ALERT UP HERE.
IF DOOM SUSPECTS ANYTHING, HE'LL SURELY SEND YOUR ENEMIES AFTER US.
HE MEANS WELL. HE'S EAGER AND STRONG, A GREAT NEW HERO.
BUT HE'S YOUNG. AND I'M OLD...

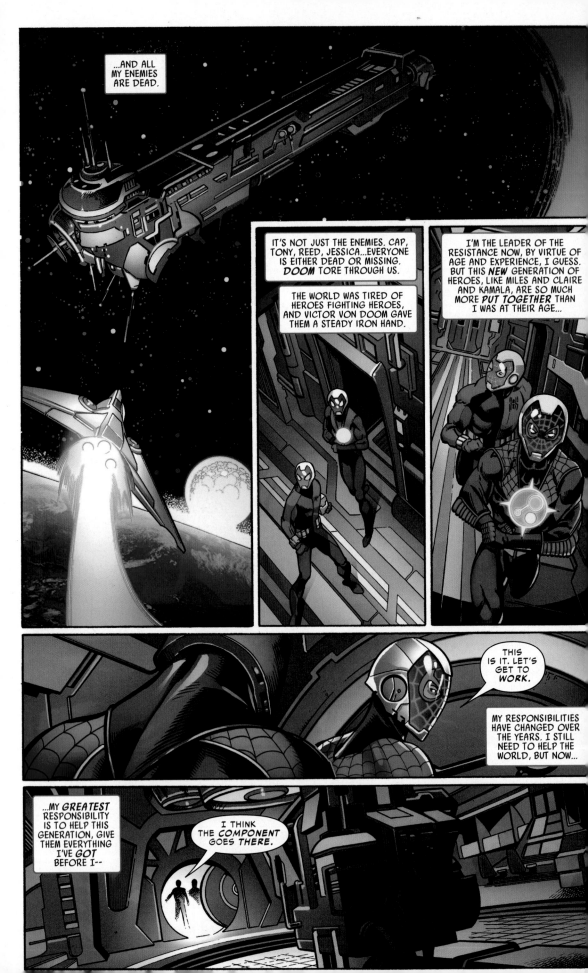

...AND ALL MY ENEMIES ARE DEAD.

IT'S NOT JUST THE ENEMIES, CAP, TONY, REED, JESSICA...EVERYONE IS EITHER DEAD OR MISSING. *DOOM* TORE THROUGH US.

THE WORLD WAS TIRED OF HEROES FIGHTING HEROES, AND VICTOR VON DOOM GAVE THEM A STEADY IRON HAND.

I'M THE LEADER OF THE RESISTANCE NOW, BY VIRTUE OF AGE AND EXPERIENCE, I GUESS. BUT THIS *NEW* GENERATION OF HEROES, LIKE MILES AND CLAIRE AND KAMALA, ARE SO MUCH MORE *PUT TOGETHER* THAN I WAS AT THEIR AGE...

THIS IS IT. LET'S GET TO *WORK*.

MY RESPONSIBILITIES HAVE CHANGED OVER THE YEARS. I STILL NEED TO HELP THE WORLD, BUT NOW...

...MY *GREATEST* RESPONSIBILITY IS TO HELP THIS GENERATION, GIVE THEM EVERYTHING I'VE *GOT* BEFORE I--

I THINK THE *COMPONENT* GOES *THERE.*

PHEW! I WAS RIGHT IN THINKING TONY USED AX INPUTS ON THE MACHINE. FINISHING THE FINAL COMPONENT WHILE THINKING LIKE TONY WAS TRICKY. HAD TO BECOME A REAL JERK AND BE WRONG ABOUT EVERYTHING ELSE IN LIFE--

GOD! ENOUGH WITH THE JOKES, PARKER! WE'RE ON THE CLOCK!

..."PARKER"?

MILES, YOU REALLY NEED TO TAKE IT DOWN A NOTCH BEFORE--

CHK

...UH-OH.

IS THE MACHINE...

NEVER MIND, IT'S ON THE BACKUP POWER SOURCE, THANK GOD. IT'LL STILL NEED TEN MINUTES TO CHARGE UP AND CREATE THE GLOBAL DISRUPTOR PULSE. I DON'T THINK THIS WILL INTERFERE WITH THE AUTO-DESTRUCT EITHER...

OKAY, GOOD. I'LL GO SEE WHAT'S GOING ON. HOPEFULLY TONY JUST SET THE STATION POWER TO CYCLE FOR CONSERVATION.

MILES IS UNDER A LOT OF PRESSURE. I NEED TO GIVE HIM SOME SLACK. I DIDN'T EVEN ASK HIM IF THIS IS HIS FIRST TIME IN SPACE.

IT CAN REALLY MESS YOU UP THE FIRST TIME.

THE FEELING OF BEING UTTERLY ALONE IN SUCH A COLD, HOSTILE...

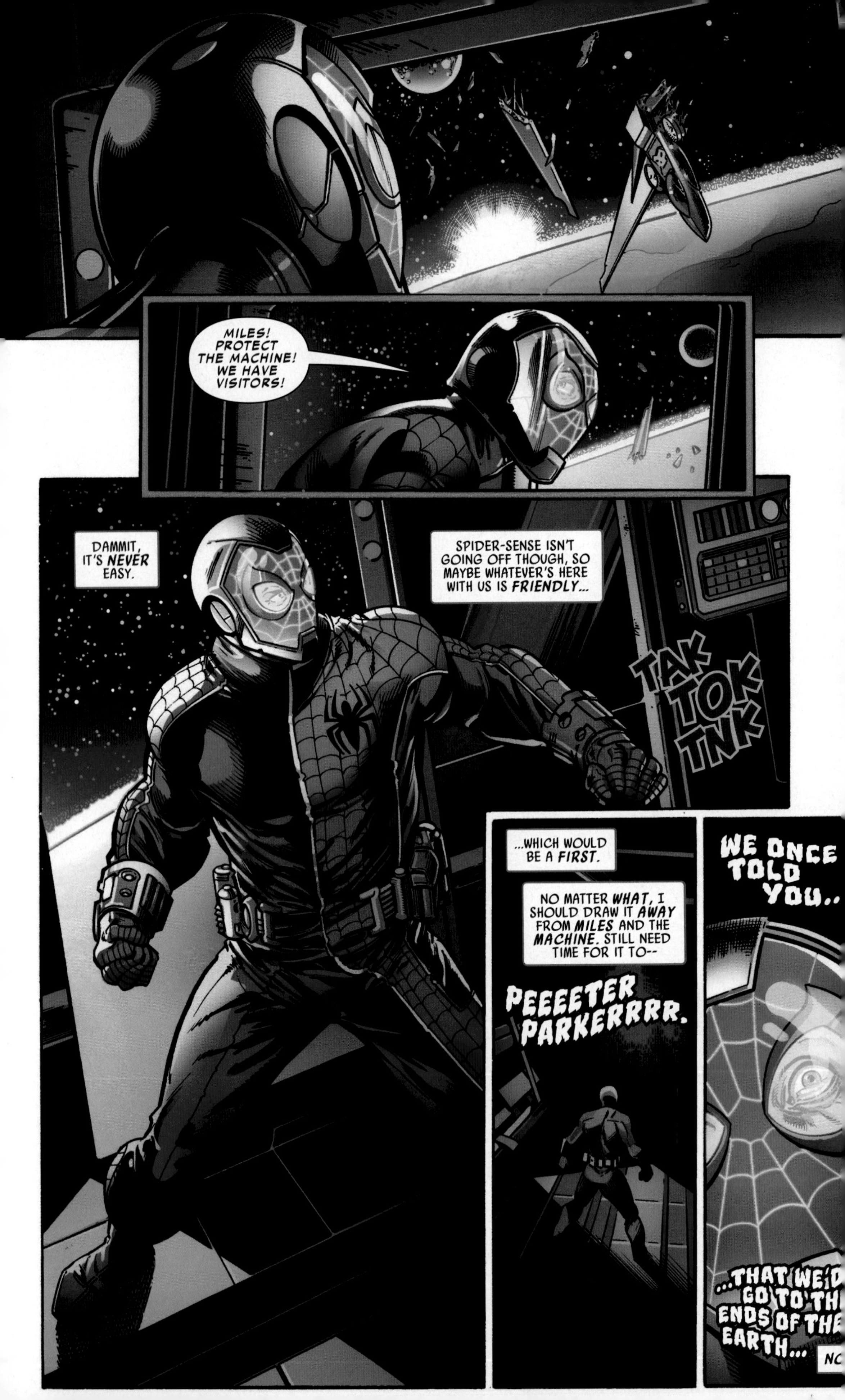
MILES! PROTECT THE MACHINE! WE HAVE VISITORS!
DAMMIT, IT'S NEVER EASY.
SPIDER-SENSE ISN'T GOING OFF THOUGH, SO MAYBE WHATEVER'S HERE WITH US IS FRIENDLY...
TAK TOK TNK
...WHICH WOULD BE A FIRST.
NO MATTER WHAT, I SHOULD DRAW IT AWAY FROM MILES AND THE MACHINE. STILL NEED TIME FOR IT TO--
PEEEETER PARKERRRR.
WE ONCE TOLD YOU..
...THAT WE'D GO TO TH ENDS OF THE EARTH...
NO

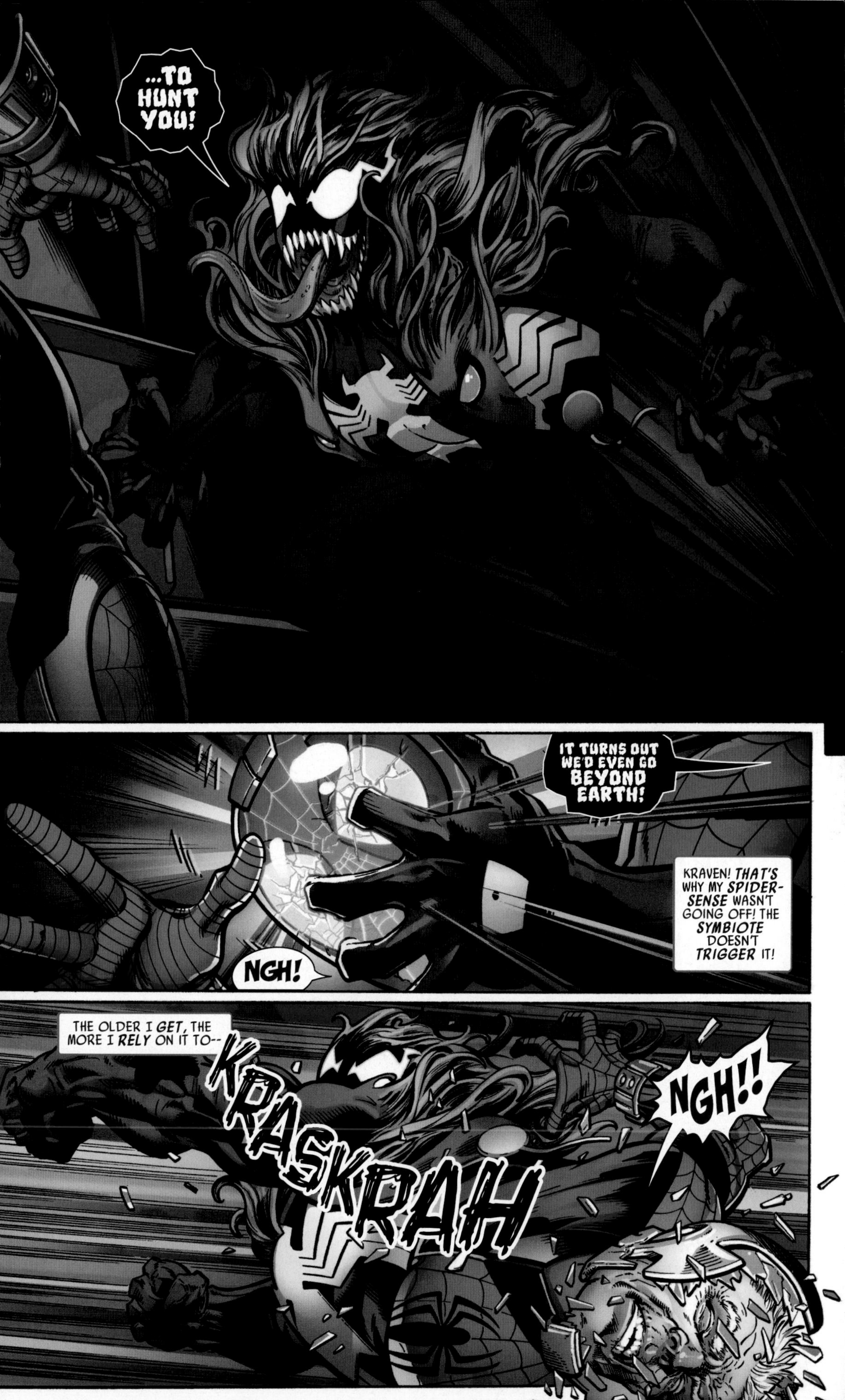

...TO HUNT YOU!
IT TURNS OUT WE'D EVEN GO BEYOND EARTH!
KRAVEN! THAT'S WHY MY SPIDER-SENSE WASN'T GOING OFF! THE SYMBIOTE DOESN'T TRIGGER IT!
NGH!
THE OLDER I GET, THE MORE I RELY ON IT TO--
KRASKRAH
NGH!!

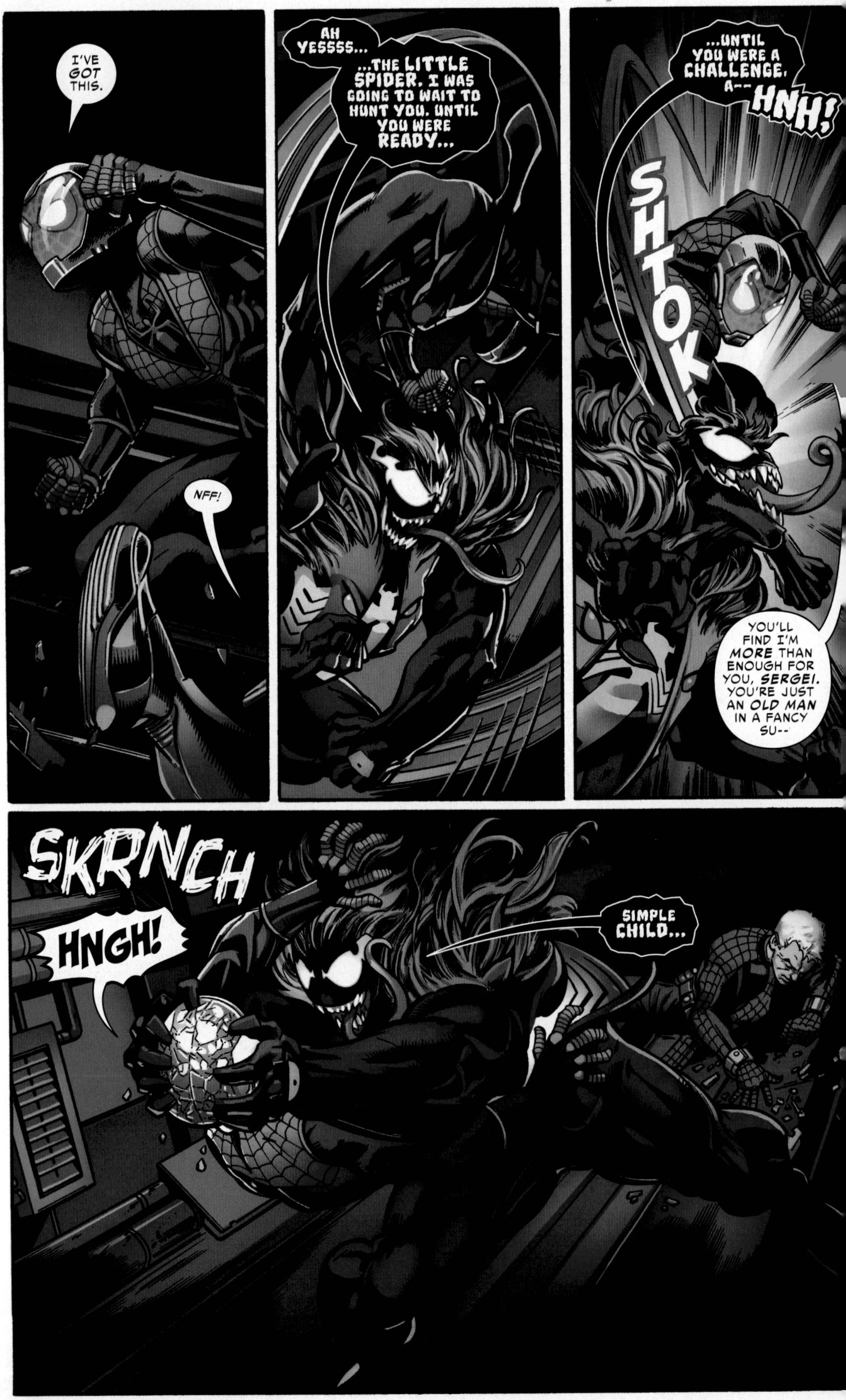
I'VE GOT THIS.
NFF!
AH YESSSS...
...THE LITTLE SPIDER. I WAS GOING TO WAIT TO HUNT YOU. UNTIL YOU WERE READY...
...UNTIL YOU WERE A CHALLENGE. A-- HNH!
SHTOK
YOU'LL FIND I'M MORE THAN ENOUGH FOR YOU, SERGEI. YOU'RE JUST AN OLD MAN IN A FANCY SU--
SKRNCH
HNGH!
SIMPLE CHILD...

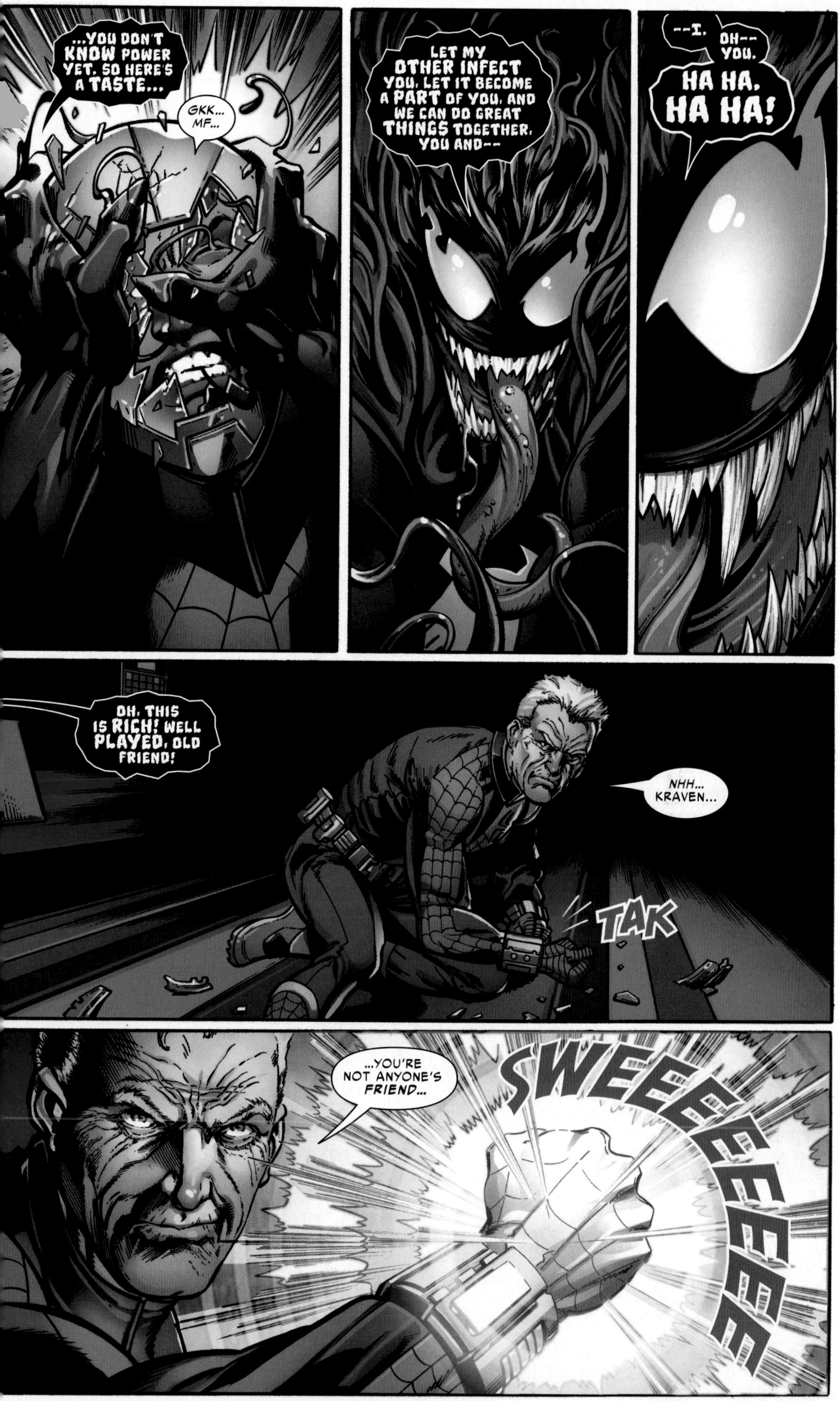
...YOU DON'T KNOW POWER YET. SO HERE'S A TASTE...
GKK... MF...
LET MY OTHER INFECT YOU. LET IT BECOME A PART OF YOU, AND WE CAN DO GREAT THINGS TOGETHER, YOU AND--
--I.
OH-- YOU.
HA HA. HA HA!
OH, THIS IS RICH! WELL PLAYED, OLD FRIEND!
NHH... KRAVEN...
TAK
...YOU'RE NOT ANYONE'S FRIEND...
SWEEEEEEEE

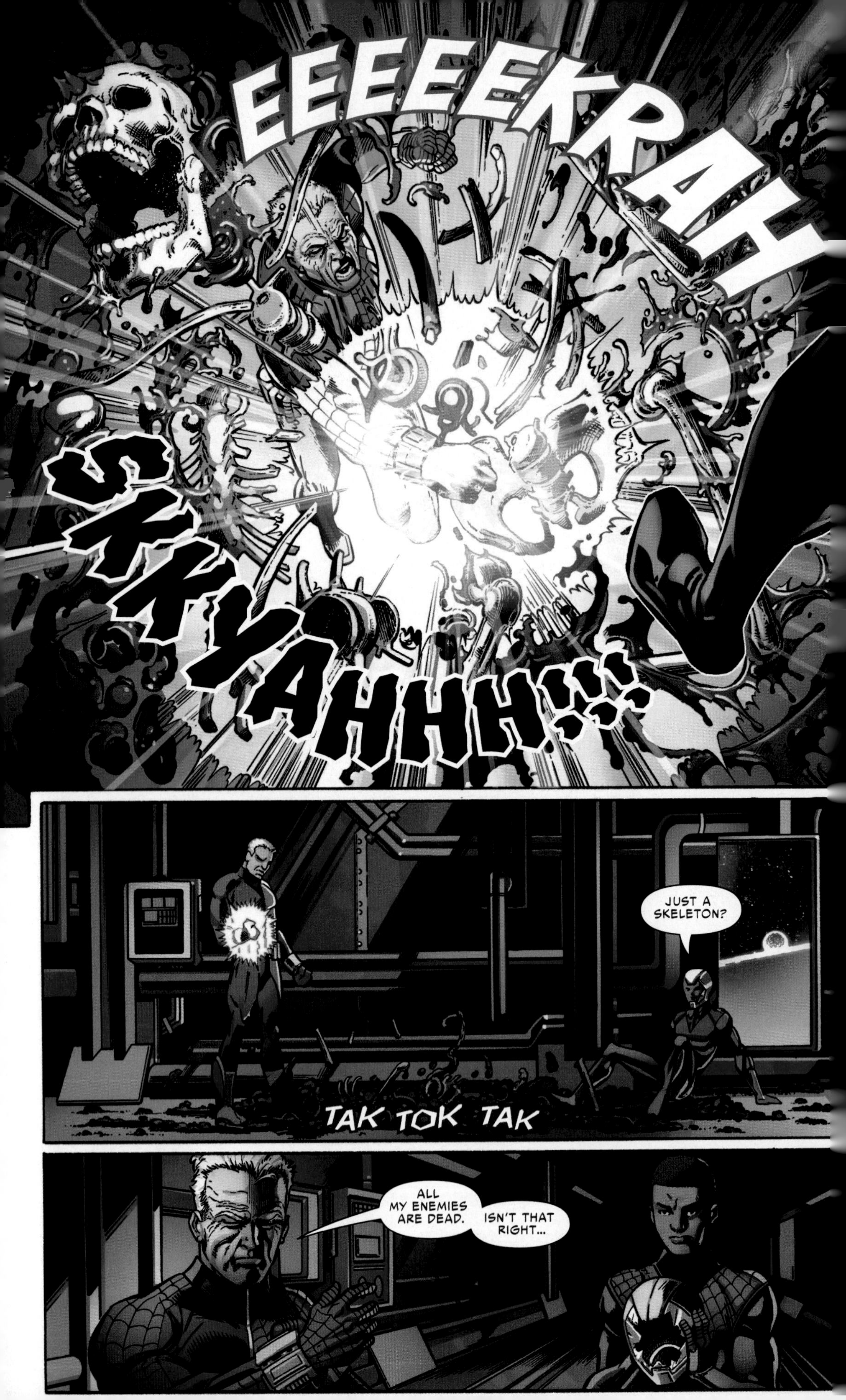
EEEEEKRAH
SKKYAHHH!!!
JUST A SKELETON?
TAK TOK TAK
ALL MY ENEMIES ARE DEAD.
ISN'T THAT RIGHT...

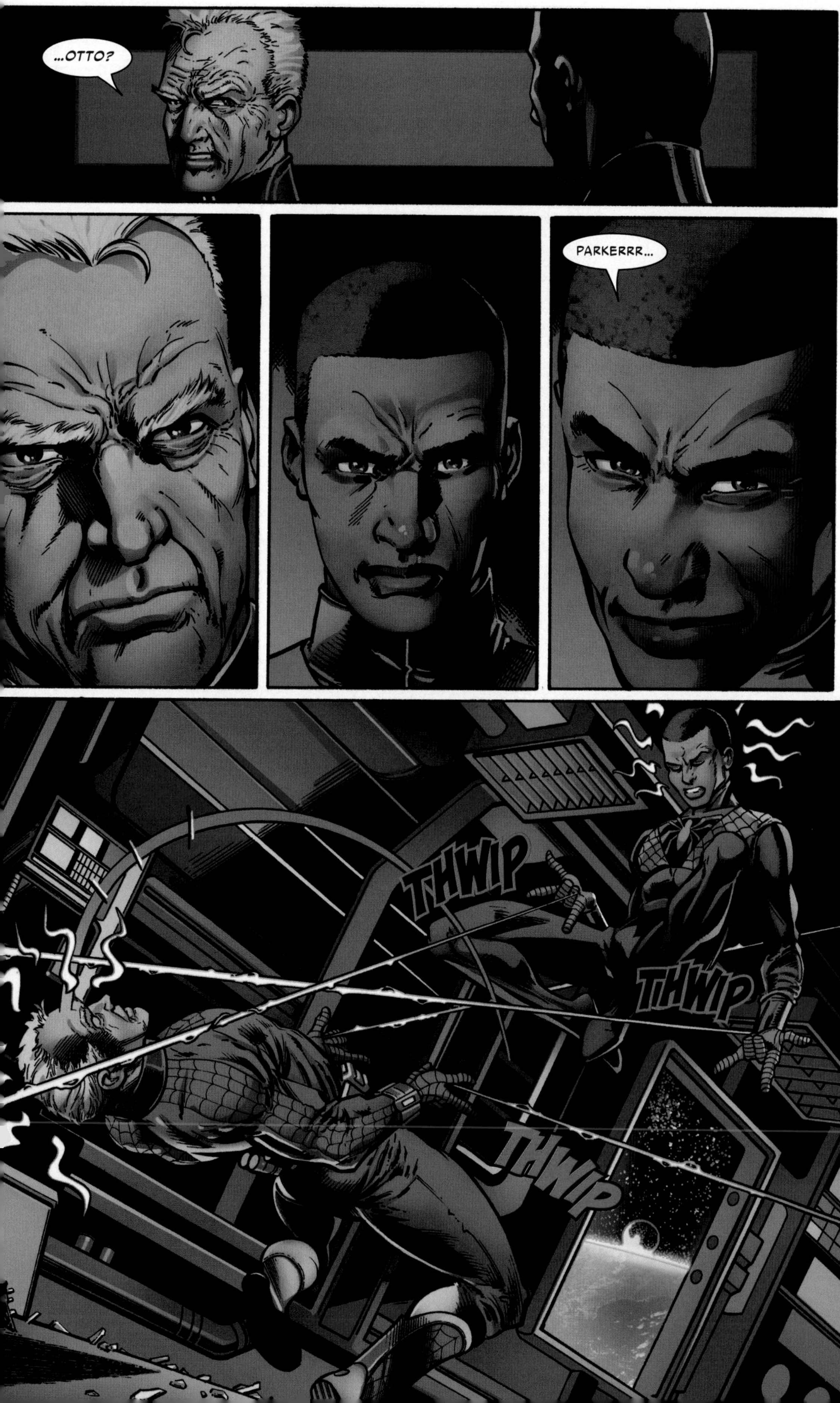
...OTTO?
PARKERRR...
THWIP
THWIP
THWIP

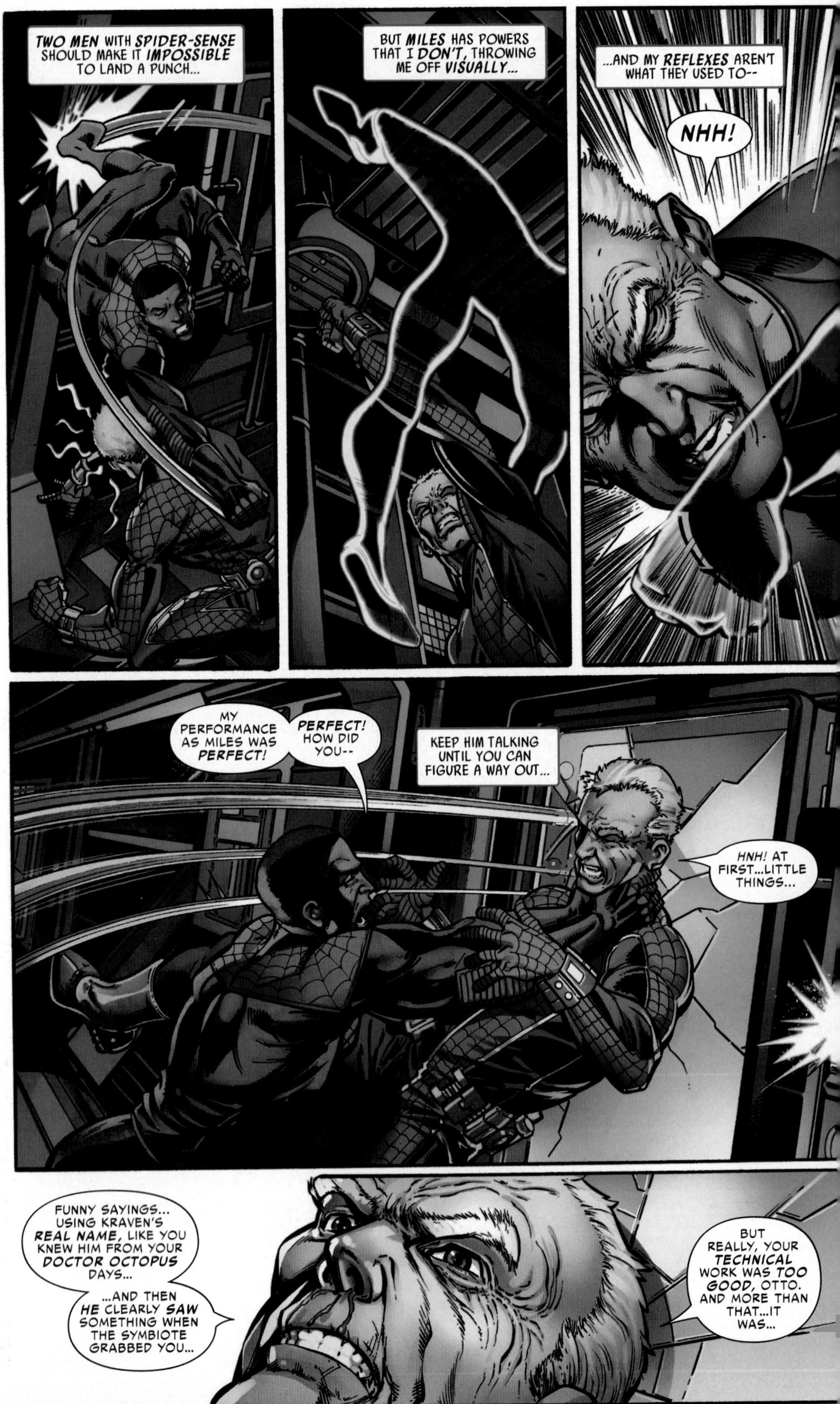
TWO MEN WITH SPIDER-SENSE SHOULD MAKE IT IMPOSSIBLE TO LAND A PUNCH...
BUT MILES HAS POWERS THAT I DON'T, THROWING ME OFF VISUALLY...
...AND MY REFLEXES AREN'T WHAT THEY USED TO--
NHH!
MY PERFORMANCE AS MILES WAS PERFECT!
PERFECT! HOW DID YOU--
KEEP HIM TALKING UNTIL YOU CAN FIGURE A WAY OUT...
HNH! AT FIRST...LITTLE THINGS...
FUNNY SAYINGS... USING KRAVEN'S REAL NAME, LIKE YOU KNEW HIM FROM YOUR DOCTOR OCTOPUS DAYS...
...AND THEN HE CLEARLY SAW SOMETHING WHEN THE SYMBIOTE GRABBED YOU...
BUT REALLY, YOUR TECHNICAL WORK WAS TOO GOOD, OTTO. AND MORE THAN THAT...IT WAS...

...OLD. OUTDATED.

LIKE Y-- NGH!

IT WAS GOING TO BE *YOU* I REPLACED! I'D PLANNED IT FOR SO *LONG!*

MY BODY, WEAK AND ANCIENT, LOCKED AWAY IN *CRYOSTASIS* AS I INHABITED MY *GREATEST ENEMY.*

BUT *YOU'RE* ALMOST AS *BROKEN* AS I AM. AND *THIS* YOUNG MAN...

...HAS AN ENTIRE LIFE *AHEAD* OF HIM, OF *US*...

H-HOW DID YOU...

DOOM WAS THE KEY. HE *UNLEASHED* THE *POWER OF MY MIND,* AND ALL HE NEEDED FROM *ME* WAS TO KEEP *TABS* ON YOU!

BUT I *TURNED* ON HIM! DON'T YOU *SEE?!* I'M A *HERO* NOW! *SUPERIOR* TO ANY OF *YOU!*

HH... S-SENTENCE A YOUNG MAN TO *DEATH*...AND MURDER AN *OLD MAN* WITH HIS BODY...

A G-GENIUS...WHO C-COULDN'T EVEN PROVE IT...JUST A *BRUTE*...

...EAL ...ERO," ...TO...

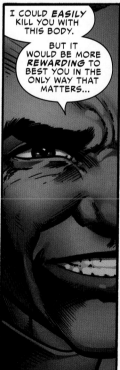

I COULD *EASILY* KILL YOU WITH THIS BODY.

BUT IT WOULD BE MORE *REWARDING* TO *BEST* YOU IN THE ONLY WAY THAT MATTERS...

...WITH MY *MIND.*

WH-- WHAT'RE Y--

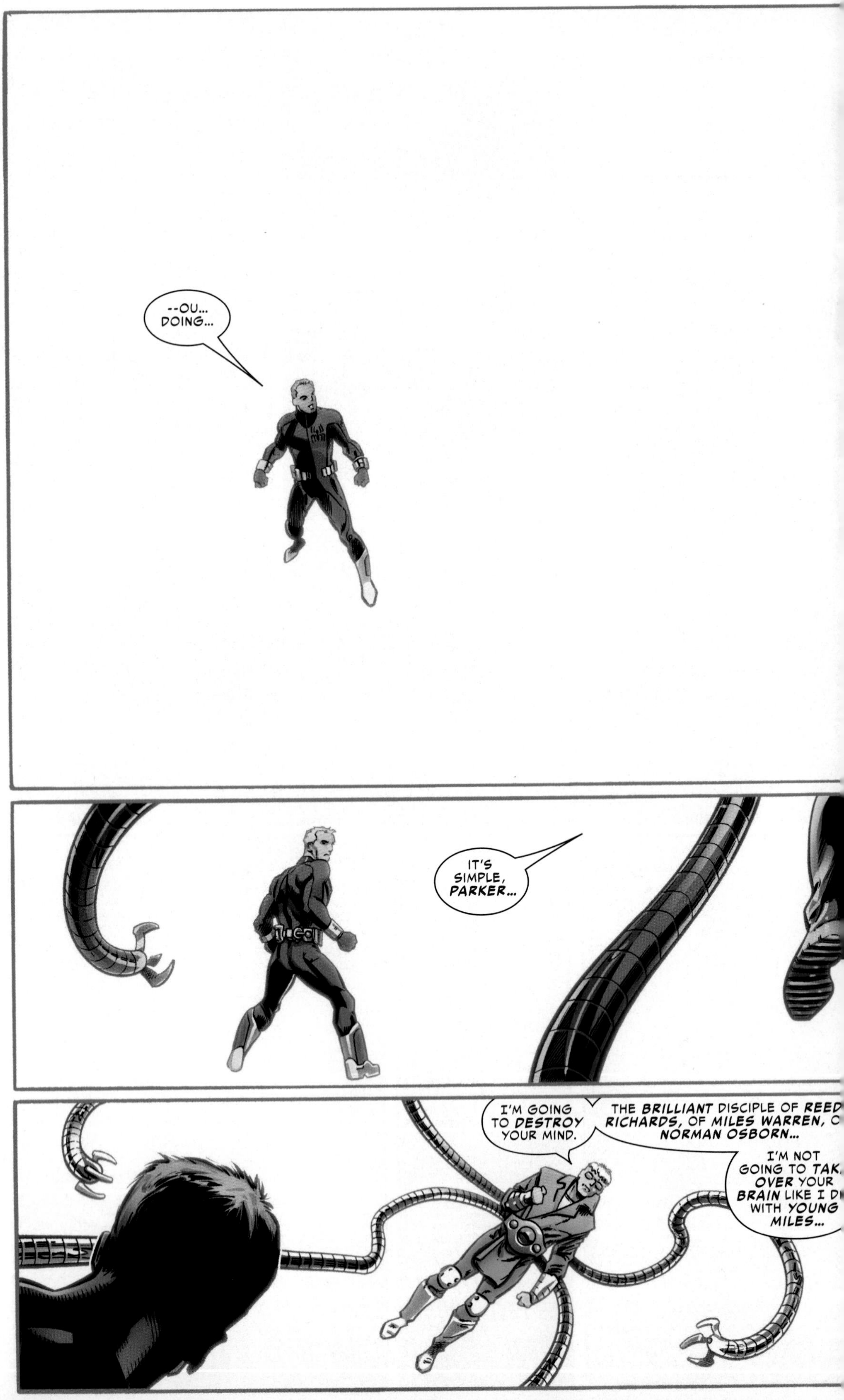

--OU... DOING...
IT'S SIMPLE, PARKER...
I'M GOING TO DESTROY YOUR MIND.
THE BRILLIANT DISCIPLE OF REED RICHARDS, OF MILES WARREN,
NORMAN OSBORN...
I'M NOT GOING TO TAK OVER YOUR BRAIN LIKE I D WITH YOUNG MILES...

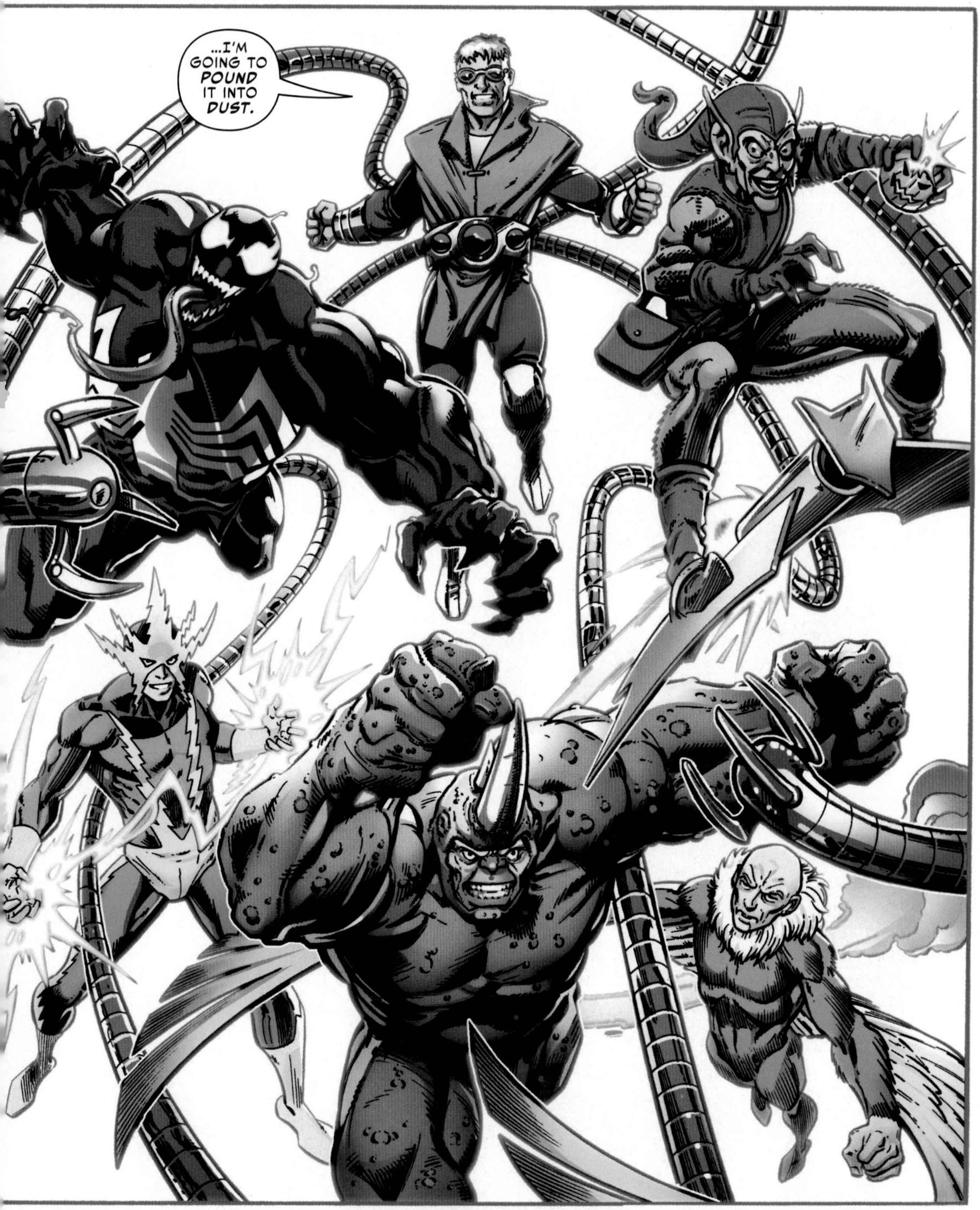
...I'M GOING TO POUND IT INTO DUST.

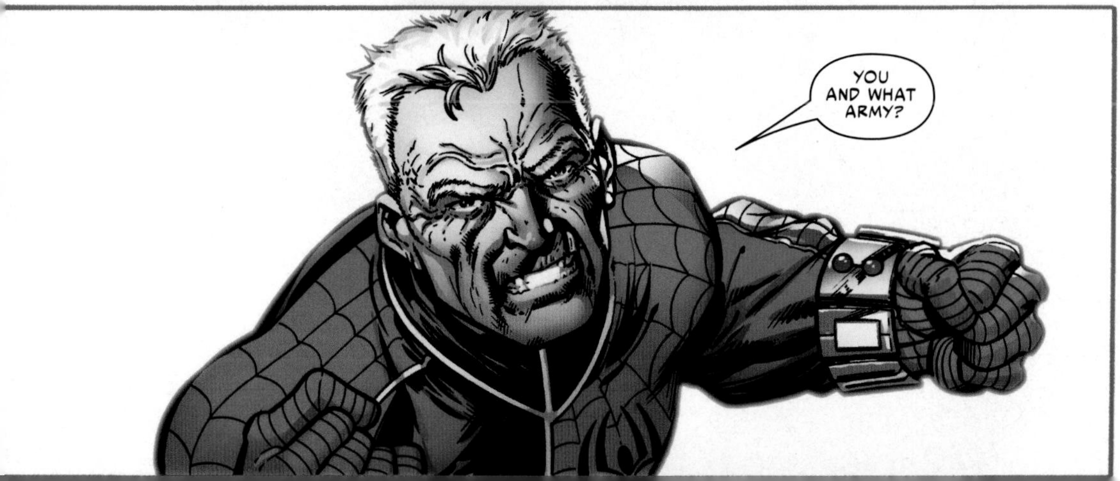
YOU AND WHAT ARMY?

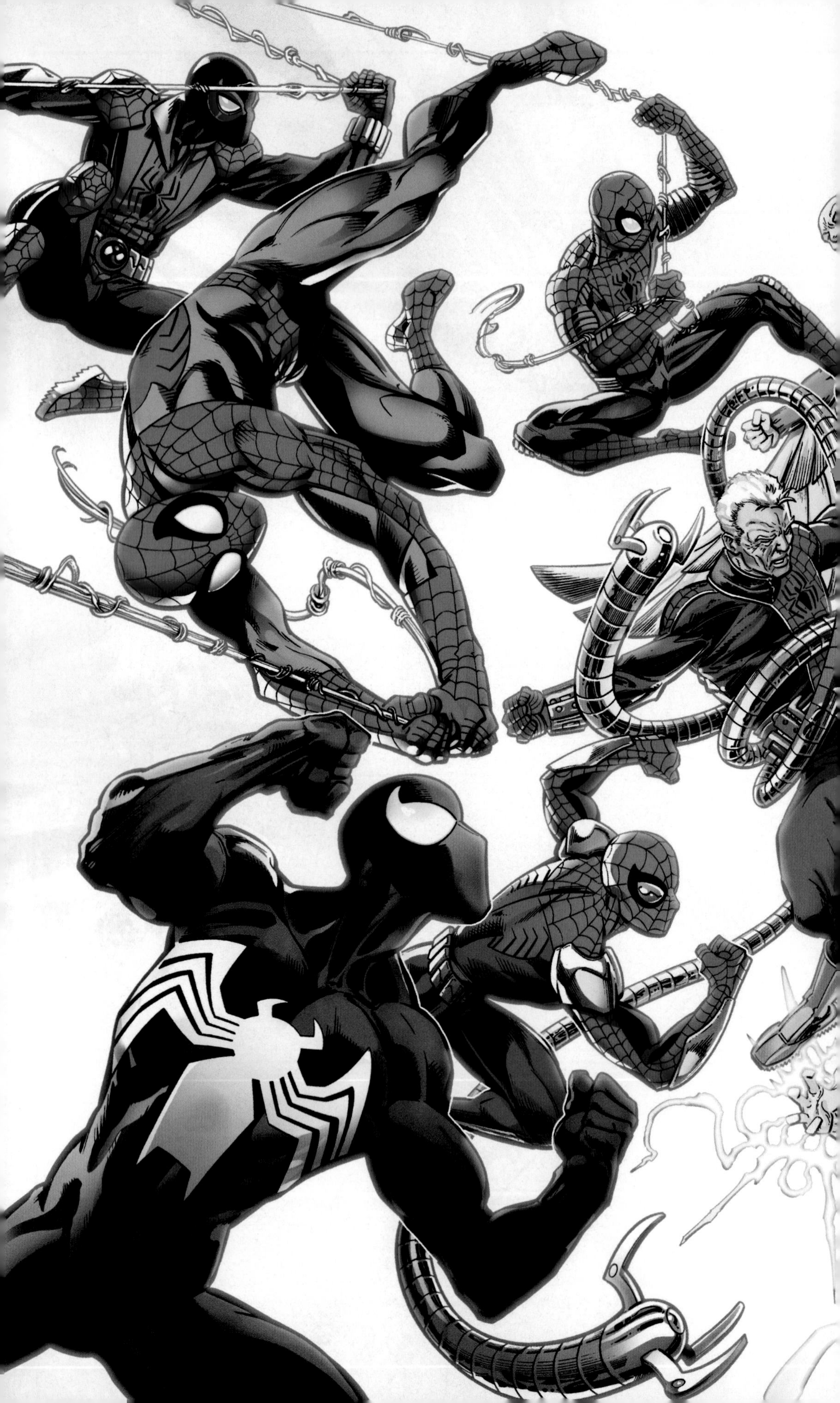

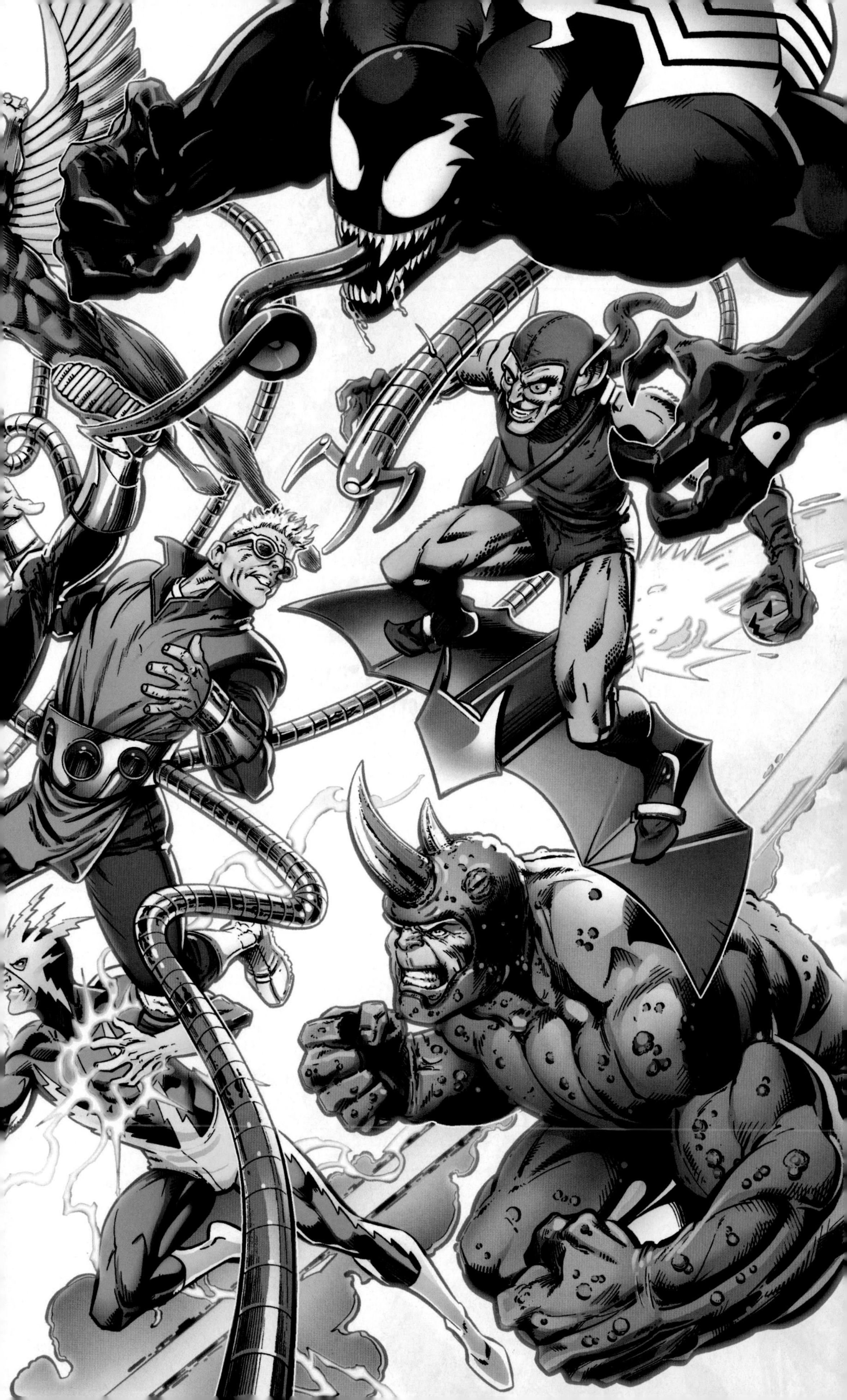

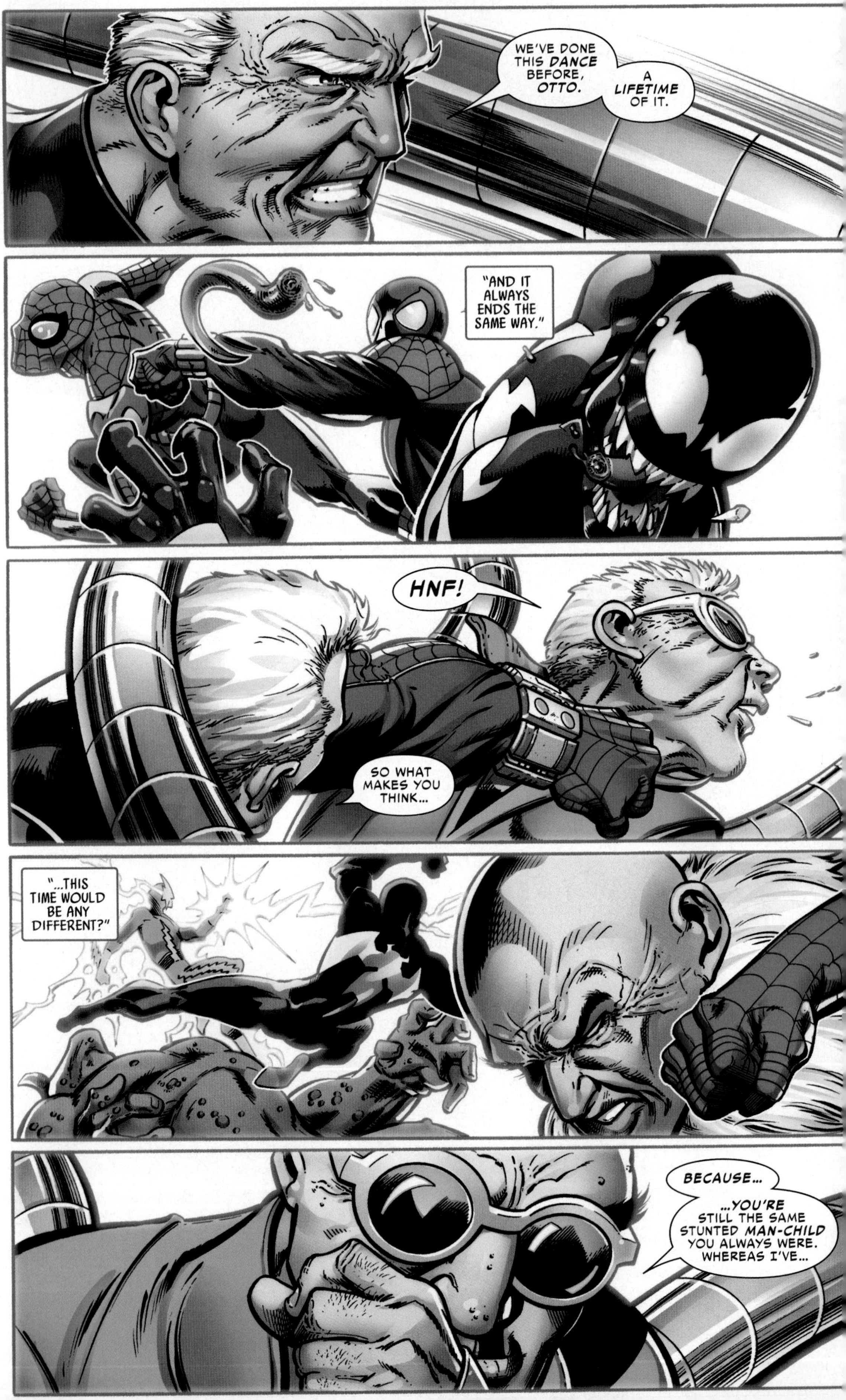
WE'VE DONE THIS DANCE BEFORE, OTTO.
A LIFETIME OF IT.
"AND IT ALWAYS ENDS THE SAME WAY."
HNF!
SO WHAT MAKES YOU THINK...
"...THIS TIME WOULD BE ANY DIFFERENT?"
BECAUSE...
...YOU'RE STILL THE SAME STUNTED MAN-CHILD YOU ALWAYS WERE. WHEREAS I'VE...

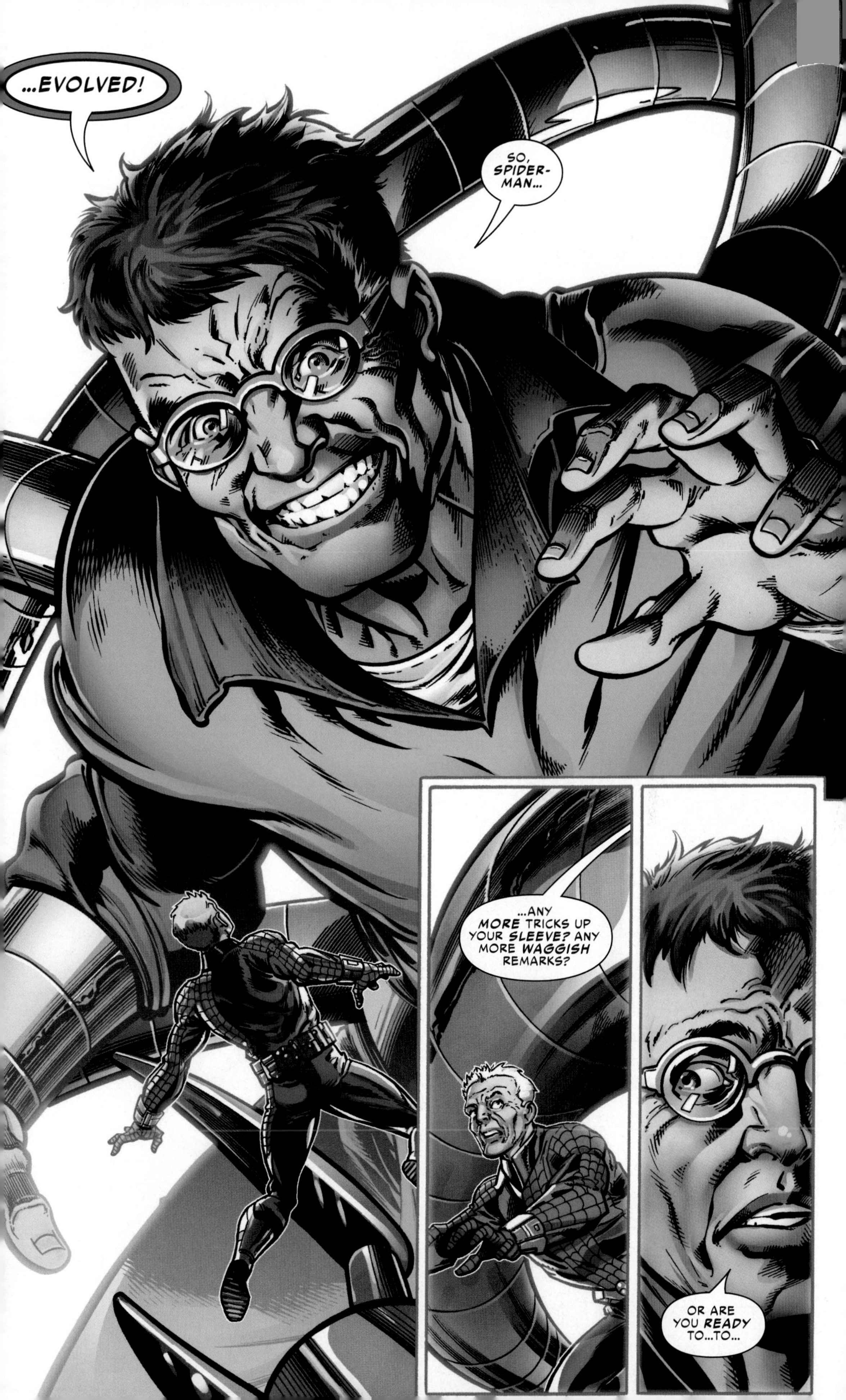
...EVOLVED!
SO, SPIDER-MAN...
...ANY MORE TRICKS UP YOUR SLEEVE? ANY MORE WAGGISH REMARKS?
OR ARE YOU READY TO...TO...

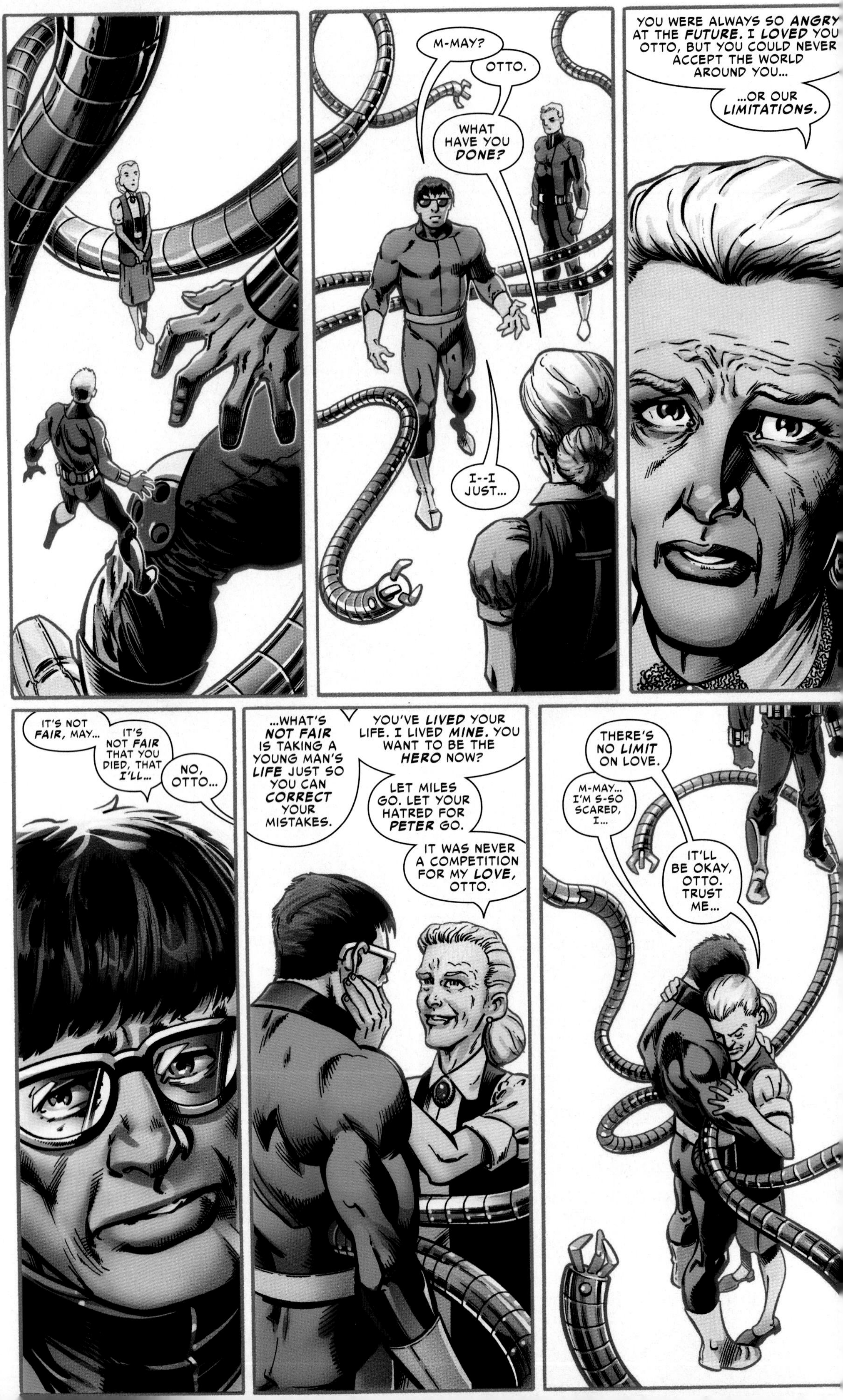
M-MAY?
OTTO.
WHAT HAVE YOU DONE?
I--I JUST...
YOU WERE ALWAYS SO ANGRY AT THE FUTURE. I LOVED YOU OTTO, BUT YOU COULD NEVER ACCEPT THE WORLD AROUND YOU...
...OR OUR LIMITATIONS.
IT'S NOT FAIR, MAY...
IT'S NOT FAIR THAT YOU DIED, THAT I'LL...
NO, OTTO...
...WHAT'S NOT FAIR IS TAKING A YOUNG MAN'S LIFE JUST SO YOU CAN CORRECT YOUR MISTAKES.
YOU'VE LIVED YOUR LIFE. I LIVED MINE. YOU WANT TO BE THE HERO NOW?
LET MILES GO. LET YOUR HATRED FOR PETER GO.
IT WAS NEVER A COMPETITION FOR MY LOVE, OTTO.
THERE'S NO LIMIT ON LOVE.
M-MAY... I'M S-SO SCARED, I...
IT'LL BE OKAY, OTTO. TRUST ME...

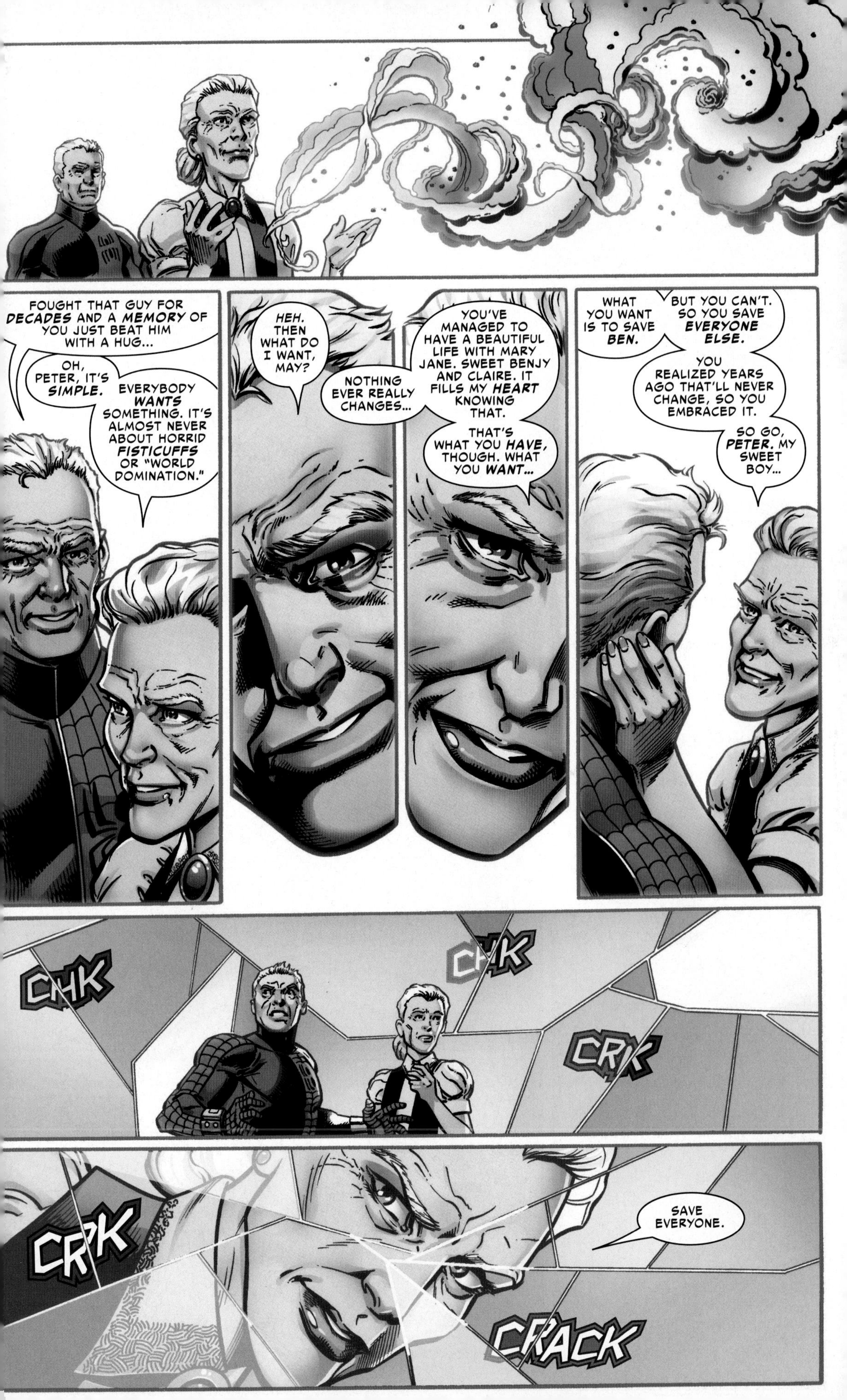

FOUGHT THAT GUY FOR DECADES AND A MEMORY OF YOU JUST BEAT HIM WITH A HUG...
OH, PETER, IT'S SIMPLE.
EVERYBODY WANTS SOMETHING. IT'S ALMOST NEVER ABOUT HORRID FISTICUFFS OR "WORLD DOMINATION."
HEH. THEN WHAT DO I WANT, MAY?
NOTHING EVER REALLY CHANGES...
YOU'VE MANAGED TO HAVE A BEAUTIFUL LIFE WITH MARY JANE. SWEET BENJY AND CLAIRE. IT FILLS MY HEART KNOWING THAT.
THAT'S WHAT YOU HAVE, THOUGH. WHAT YOU WANT...
WHAT YOU WANT IS TO SAVE BEN.
BUT YOU CAN'T. SO YOU SAVE EVERYONE ELSE.
YOU REALIZED YEARS AGO THAT'LL NEVER CHANGE, SO YOU EMBRACED IT.
SO GO, PETER. MY SWEET BOY...
CHK
CHK
CRK
CRK
SAVE EVERYONE.
CRACK

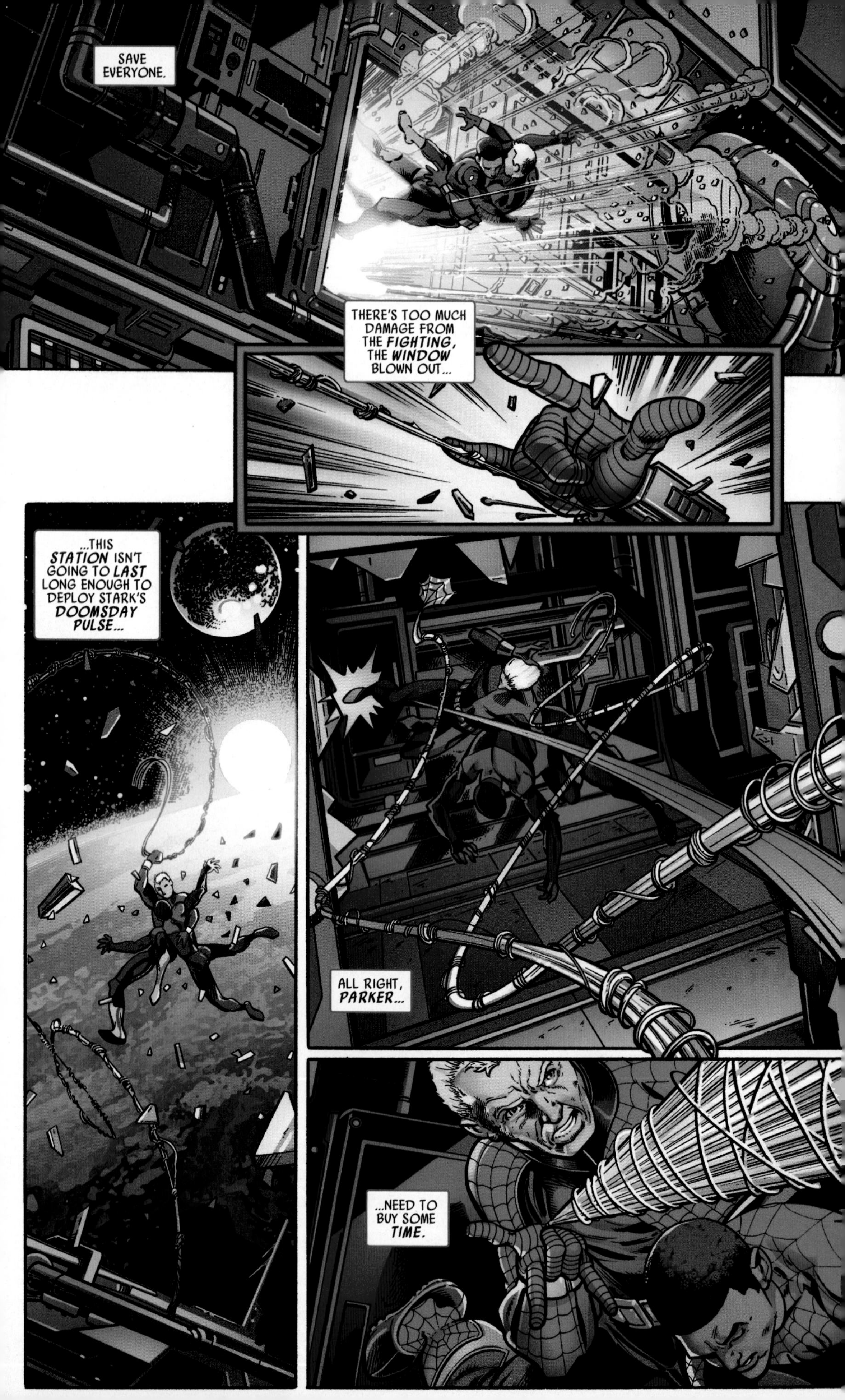
SAVE EVERYONE.
THERE'S TOO MUCH DAMAGE FROM THE *FIGHTING*, THE *WINDOW* BLOWN OUT...
...THIS *STATION* ISN'T GOING TO *LAST* LONG ENOUGH TO DEPLOY STARK'S *DOOMSDAY PULSE*...
ALL RIGHT, *PARKER*...
...NEED TO BUY SOME *TIME*.

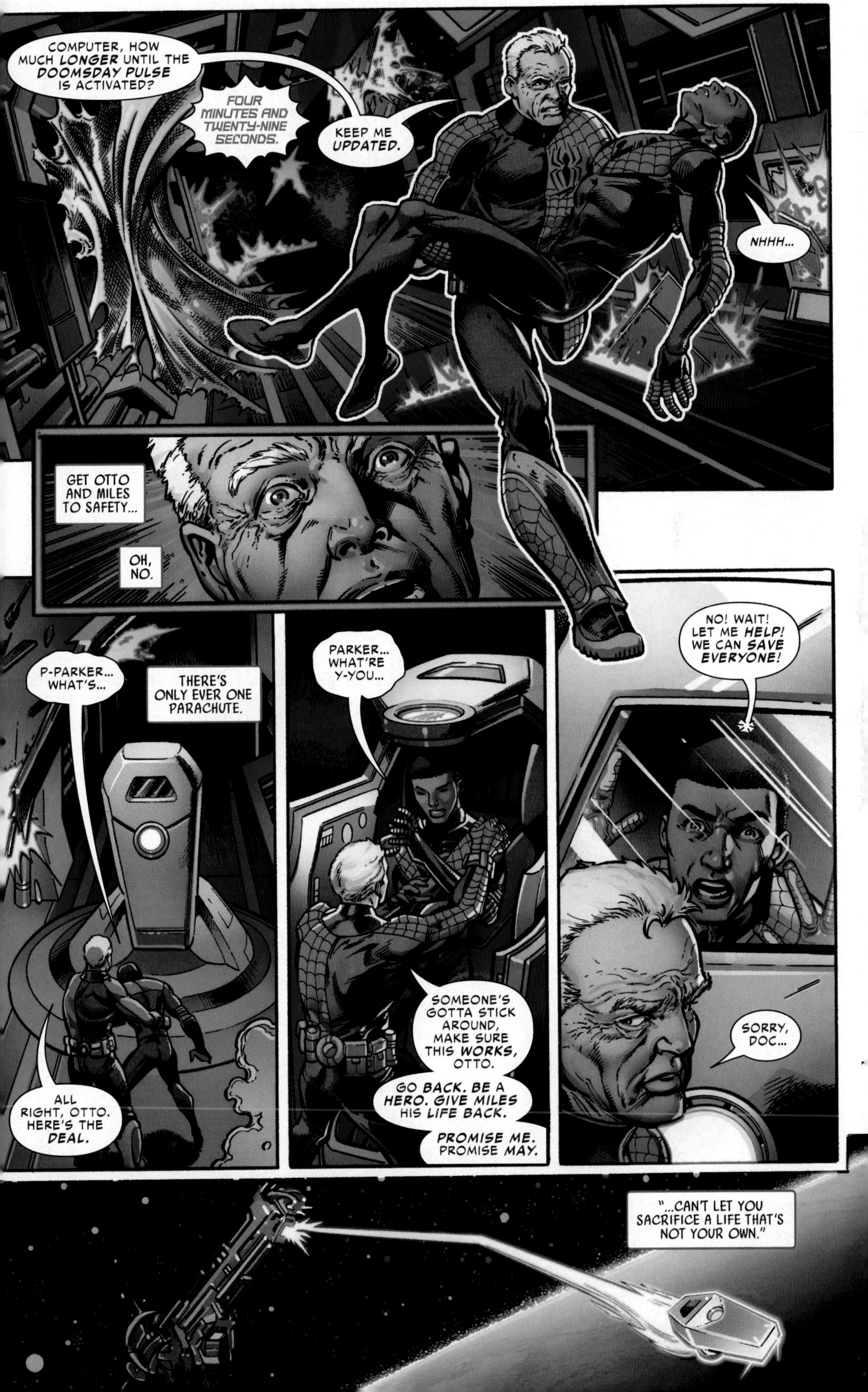

COMPUTER, HOW MUCH LONGER UNTIL THE DOOMSDAY PULSE IS ACTIVATED?
FOUR MINUTES AND TWENTY-NINE SECONDS.
KEEP ME UPDATED.
NHHH...
GET OTTO AND MILES TO SAFETY...
OH, NO.
P-PARKER... WHAT'S...
THERE'S ONLY EVER ONE PARACHUTE.
ALL RIGHT, OTTO. HERE'S THE DEAL.
PARKER... WHAT'RE Y-YOU...
SOMEONE'S GOTTA STICK AROUND, MAKE SURE THIS WORKS, OTTO.
GO BACK. BE A HERO. GIVE MILES HIS LIFE BACK.
PROMISE ME. PROMISE MAY.
NO! WAIT! LET ME HELP! WE CAN SAVE EVERYONE!
SORRY, DOC...
"...CAN'T LET YOU SACRIFICE A LIFE THAT'S NOT YOUR OWN."

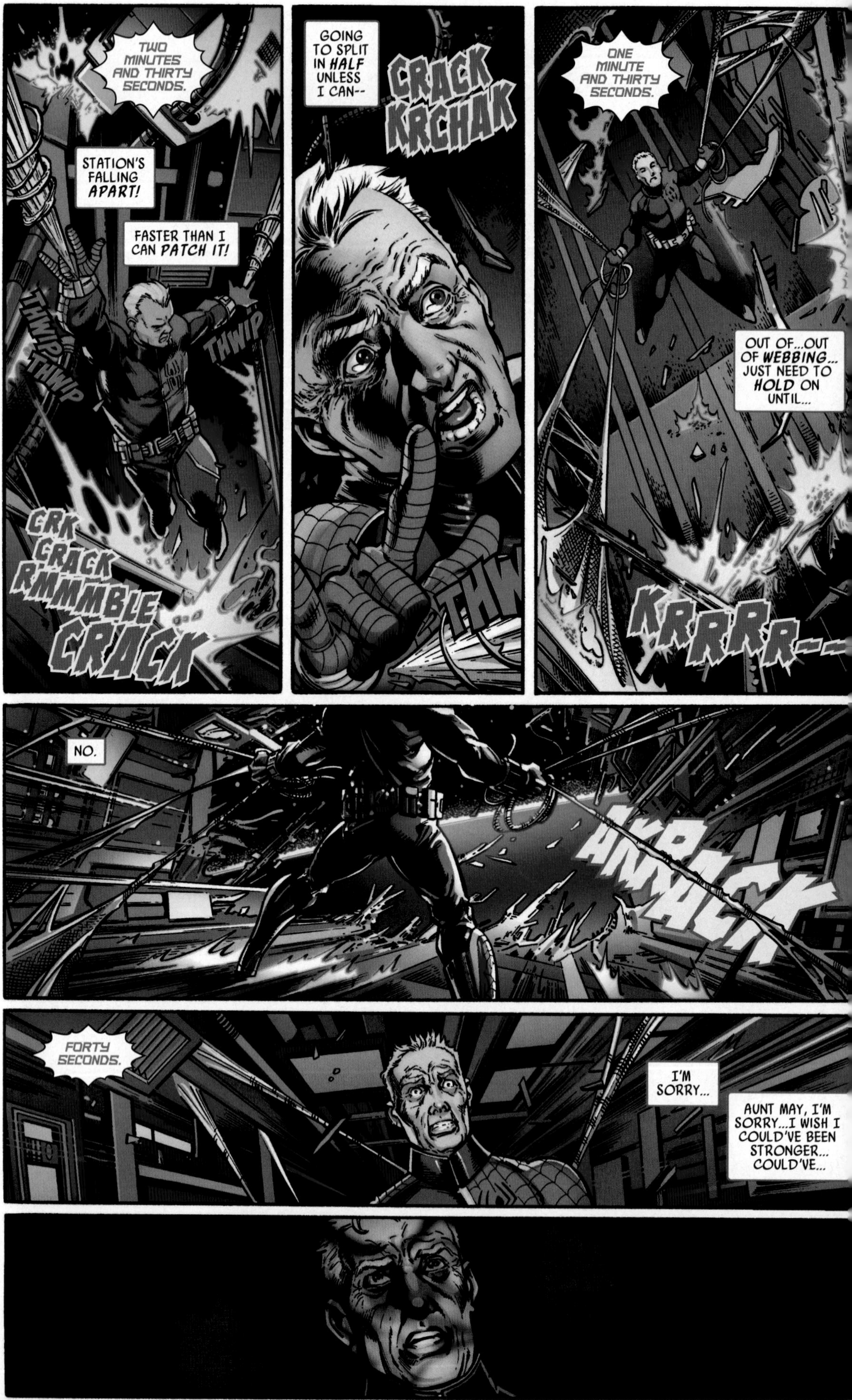

TWO MINUTES AND THIRTY SECONDS.
STATION'S FALLING APART!
FASTER THAN I CAN PATCH IT!
THWIP THWIP
THWIP
CRK CRACK RMMMBLE CRACK
GOING TO SPLIT IN HALF UNLESS I CAN--
CRACK KRCHAK
ONE MINUTE AND THIRTY SECONDS.
OUT OF...OUT OF WEBBING... JUST NEED TO HOLD ON UNTIL...
KRRRRR--
NO.
FORTY SECONDS.
I'M SORRY...
AUNT MAY, I'M SORRY...I WISH I COULD'VE BEEN STRONGER... COULD'VE...

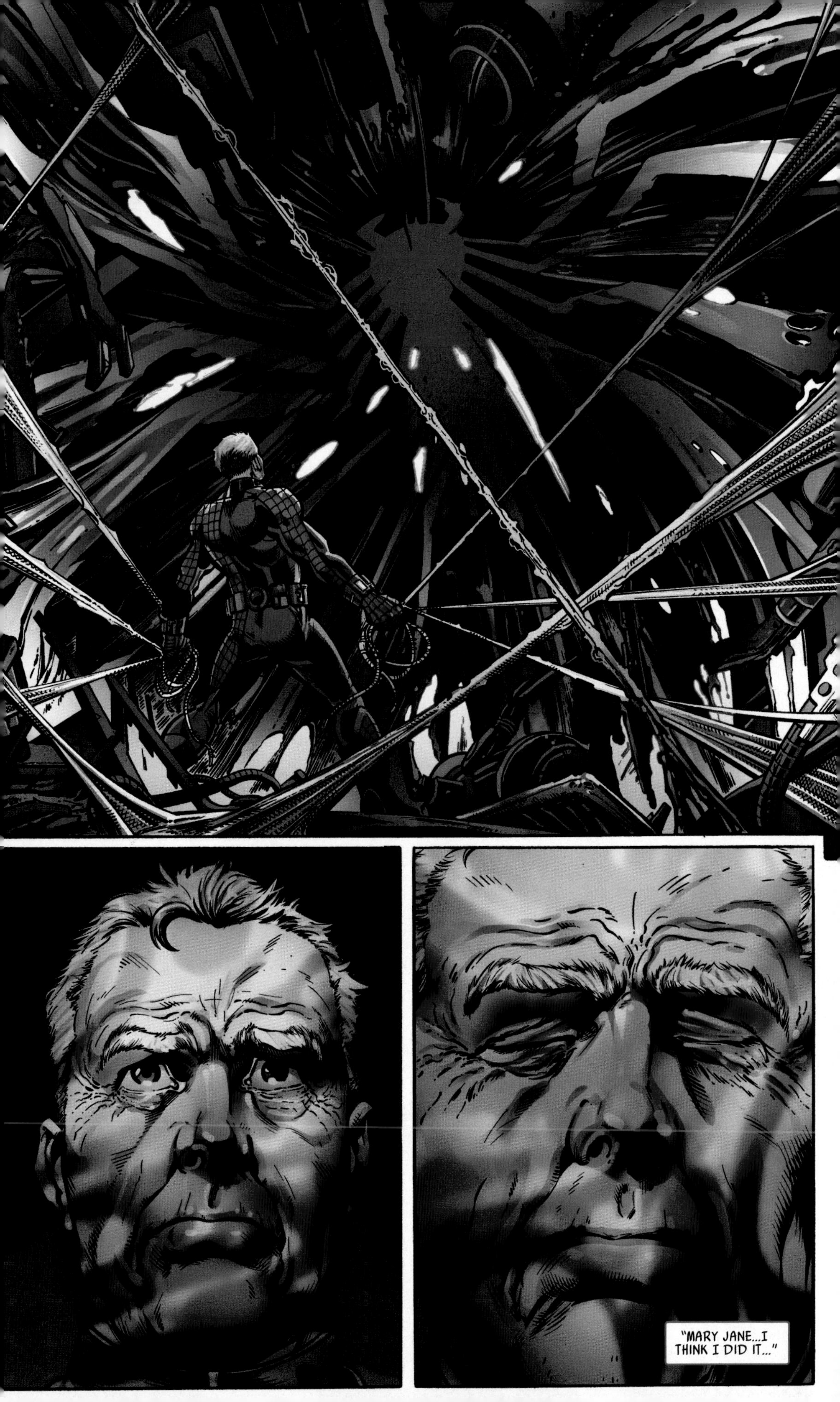
"MARY JANE...I THINK I DID IT..."

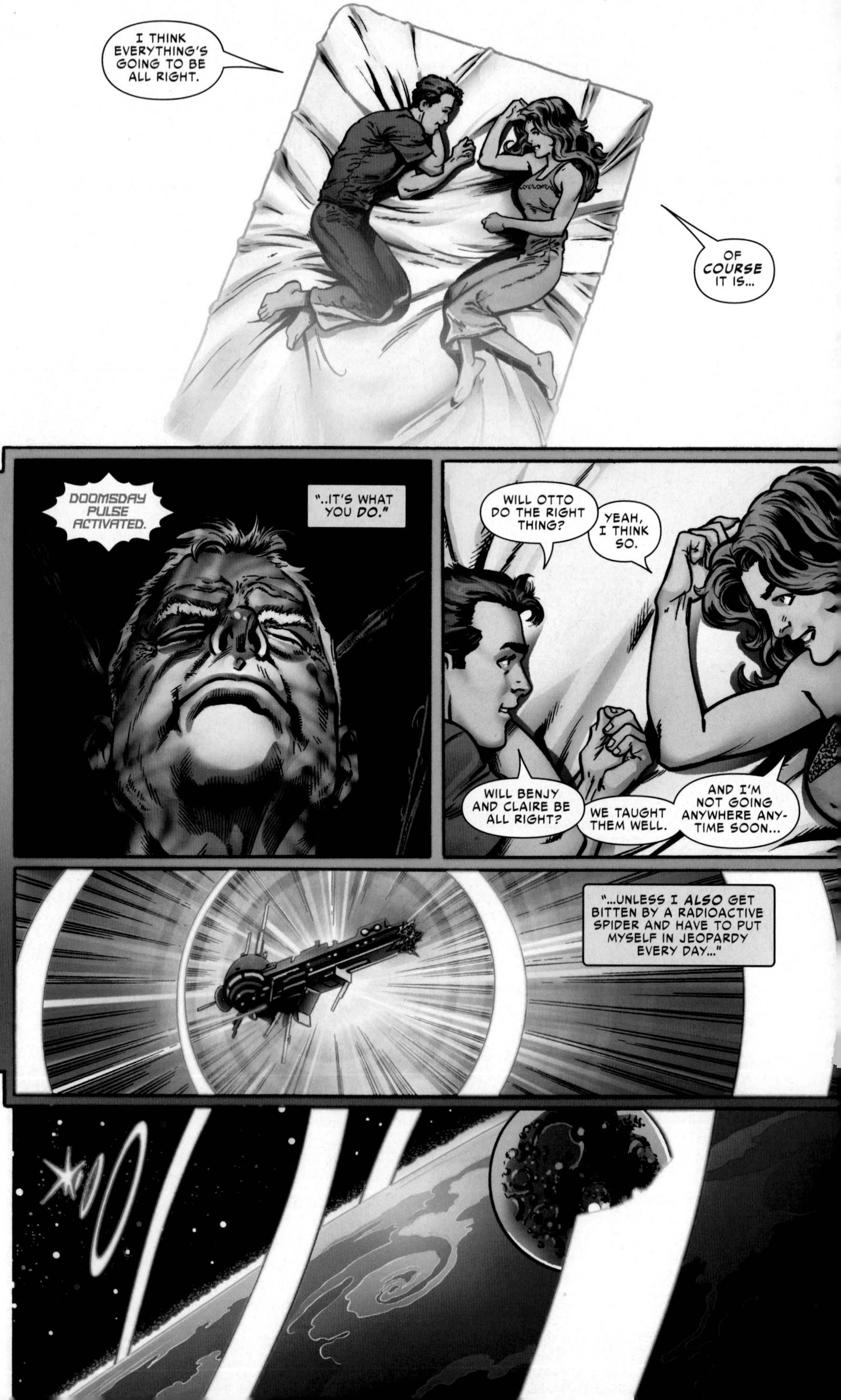

I THINK EVERYTHING'S GOING TO BE ALL RIGHT.
OF *COURSE* IT IS...
DOOMSDAY PULSE ACTIVATED.
"..IT'S WHAT YOU *DO*."
WILL OTTO DO THE RIGHT THING?
YEAH, I THINK SO.
WILL BENJY AND CLAIRE BE ALL RIGHT?
WE TAUGHT THEM WELL.
AND I'M NOT GOING ANYWHERE ANY-TIME SOON...
"...UNLESS I *ALSO* GET BITTEN BY A RADIOACTIVE SPIDER AND HAVE TO PUT MYSELF IN JEOPARDY EVERY DAY..."

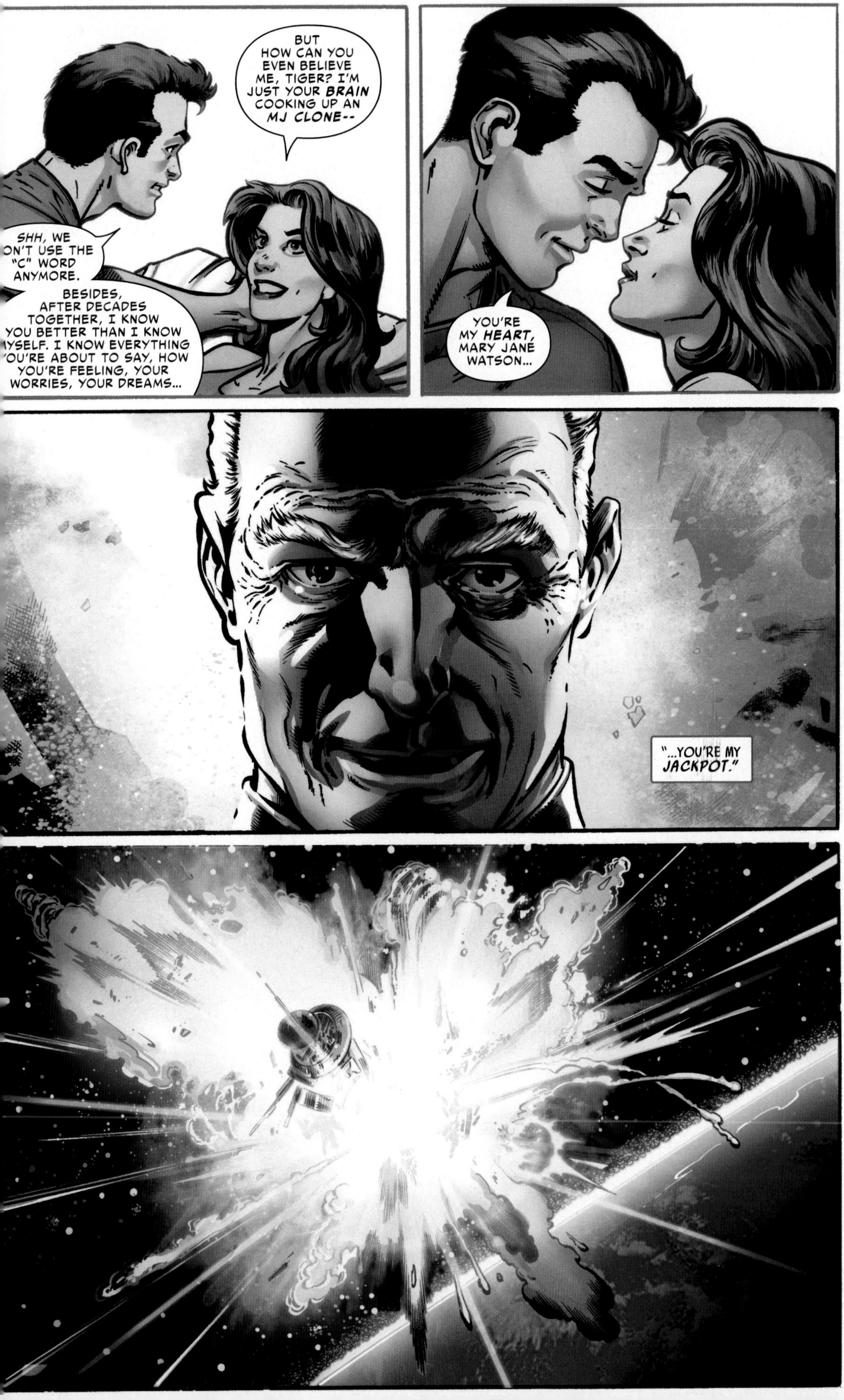
BUT HOW CAN YOU EVEN BELIEVE ME, TIGER? I'M JUST YOUR BRAIN COOKING UP AN MJ CLONE--
SHH, WE ON'T USE THE "C" WORD ANYMORE.
BESIDES, AFTER DECADES TOGETHER, I KNOW YOU BETTER THAN I KNOW IYSELF. I KNOW EVERYTHING 'OU'RE ABOUT TO SAY, HOW YOU'RE FEELING, YOUR WORRIES, YOUR DREAMS...
YOU'RE MY HEART, MARY JANE WATSON...
"...YOU'RE MY JACKPOT."

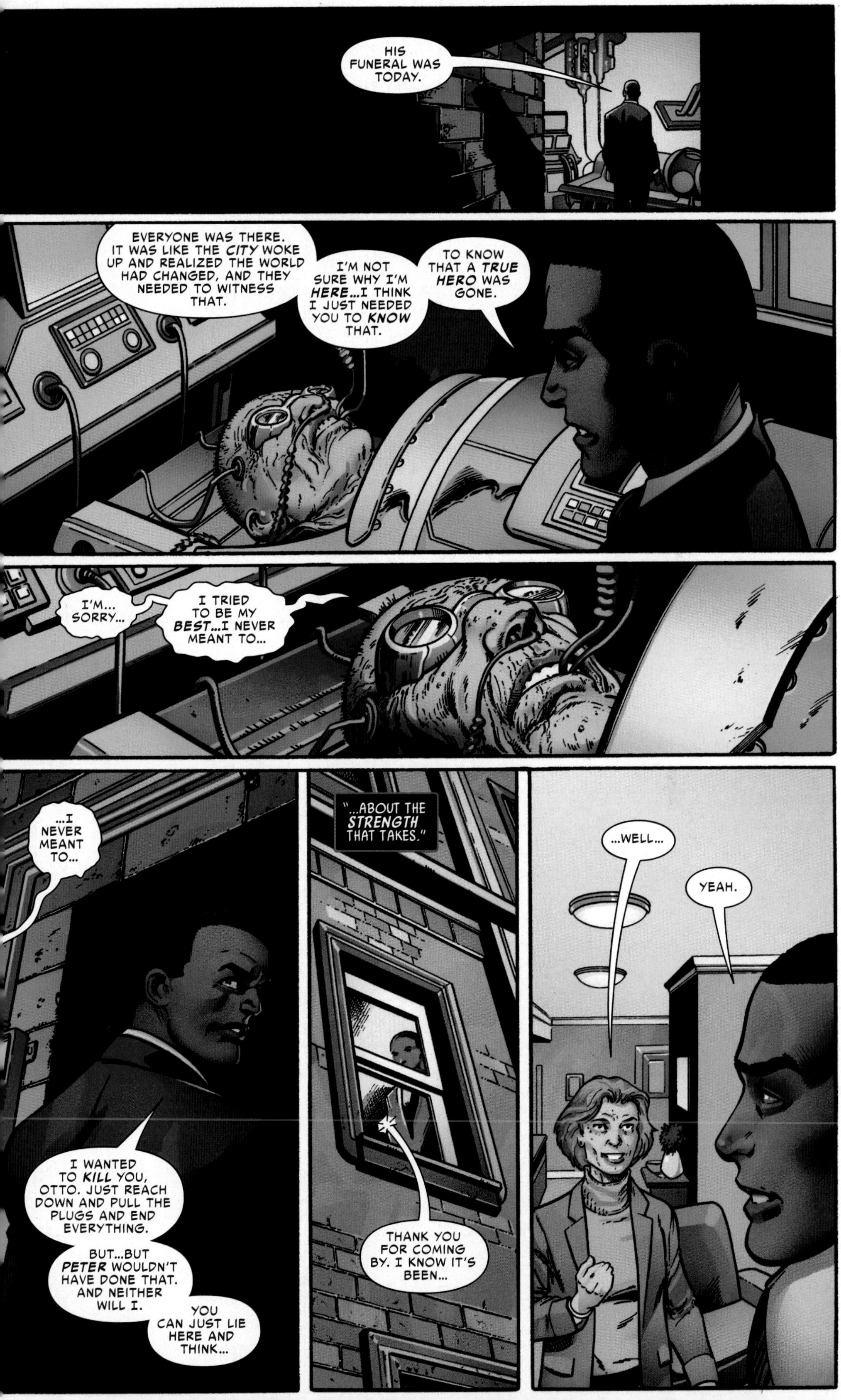
HIS FUNERAL WAS TODAY.
EVERYONE WAS THERE. IT WAS LIKE THE CITY WOKE UP AND REALIZED THE WORLD HAD CHANGED, AND THEY NEEDED TO WITNESS THAT.
I'M NOT SURE WHY I'M HERE...I THINK I JUST NEEDED YOU TO KNOW THAT.
TO KNOW THAT A TRUE HERO WAS GONE.
I'M... SORRY...
I TRIED TO BE MY BEST...I NEVER MEANT TO...
...I NEVER MEANT TO...
I WANTED TO KILL YOU, OTTO. JUST REACH DOWN AND PULL THE PLUGS AND END EVERYTHING.
BUT...BUT PETER WOULDN'T HAVE DONE THAT. AND NEITHER WILL I.
YOU CAN JUST LIE HERE AND THINK...
"...ABOUT THE STRENGTH THAT TAKES."
THANK YOU FOR COMING BY. I KNOW IT'S BEEN...
...WELL...
YEAH.

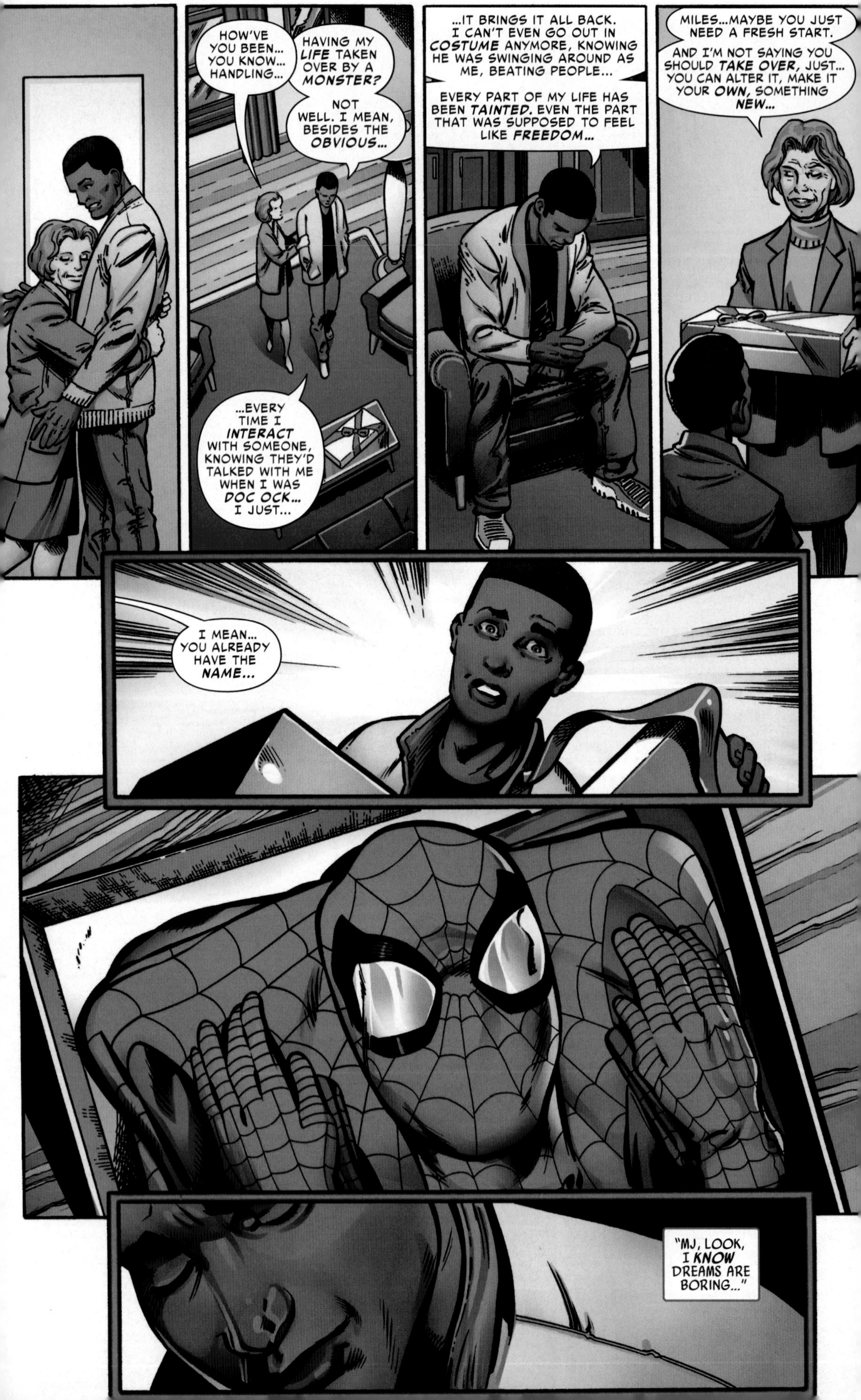
HOW'VE YOU BEEN... YOU KNOW... HANDLING...
HAVING MY LIFE TAKEN OVER BY A MONSTER?
NOT WELL. I MEAN, BESIDES THE OBVIOUS...
...EVERY TIME I INTERACT WITH SOMEONE, KNOWING THEY'D TALKED WITH ME WHEN I WAS DOC OCK... I JUST...
...IT BRINGS IT ALL BACK. I CAN'T EVEN GO OUT IN COSTUME ANYMORE, KNOWING HE WAS SWINGING AROUND AS ME, BEATING PEOPLE...
EVERY PART OF MY LIFE HAS BEEN TAINTED. EVEN THE PART THAT WAS SUPPOSED TO FEEL LIKE FREEDOM...
MILES...MAYBE YOU JUST NEED A FRESH START.
AND I'M NOT SAYING YOU SHOULD TAKE OVER, JUST... YOU CAN ALTER IT, MAKE IT YOUR OWN, SOMETHING NEW...
I MEAN... YOU ALREADY HAVE THE NAME...
"MJ, LOOK, I KNOW DREAMS ARE BORING..."

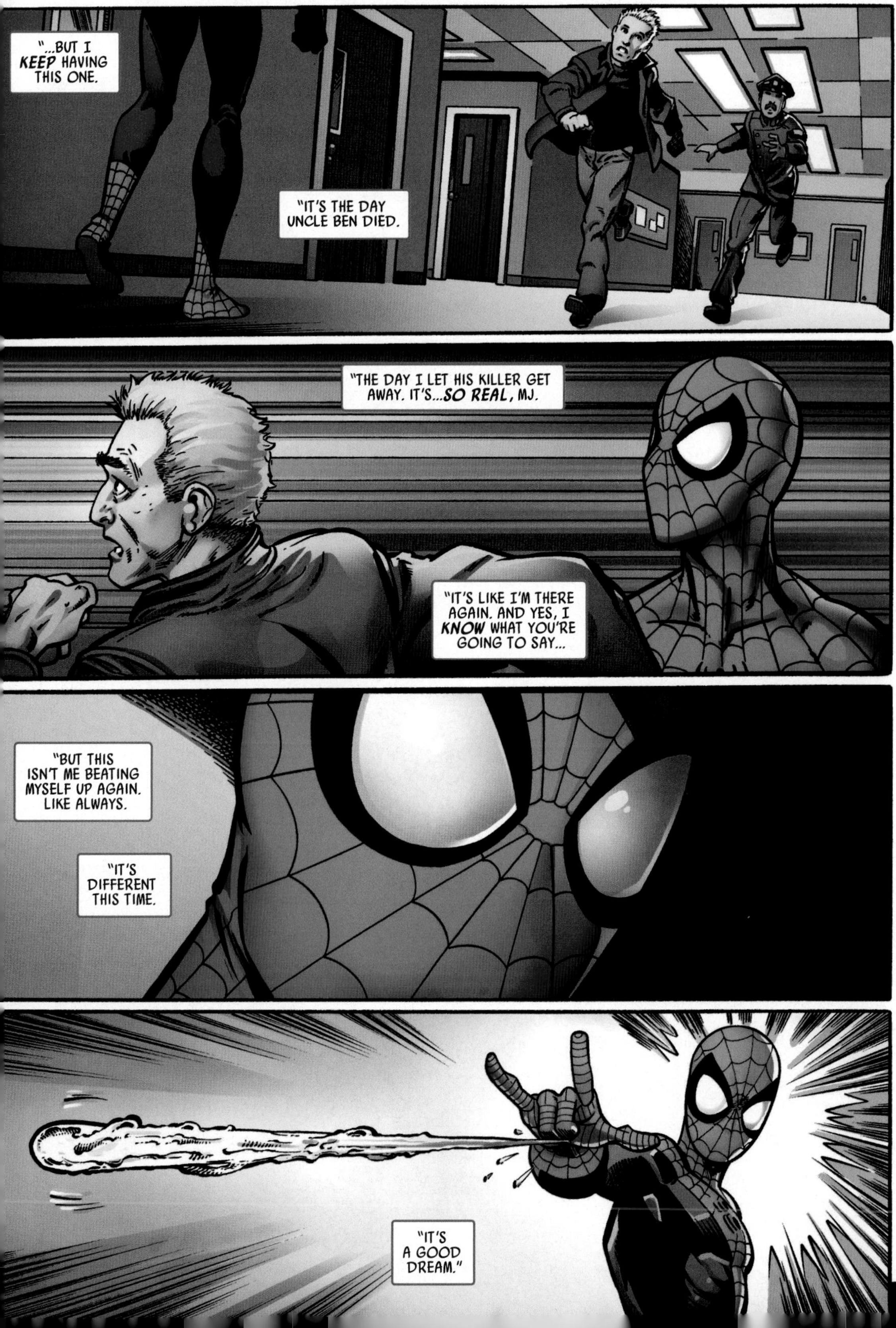
"...BUT I KEEP HAVING THIS ONE.
"IT'S THE DAY UNCLE BEN DIED.
"THE DAY I LET HIS KILLER GET AWAY. IT'S...SO REAL, MJ.
"IT'S LIKE I'M THERE AGAIN. AND YES, I KNOW WHAT YOU'RE GOING TO SAY...
"BUT THIS ISN'T ME BEATING MYSELF UP AGAIN. LIKE ALWAYS.
"IT'S DIFFERENT THIS TIME.
"IT'S A GOOD DREAM."

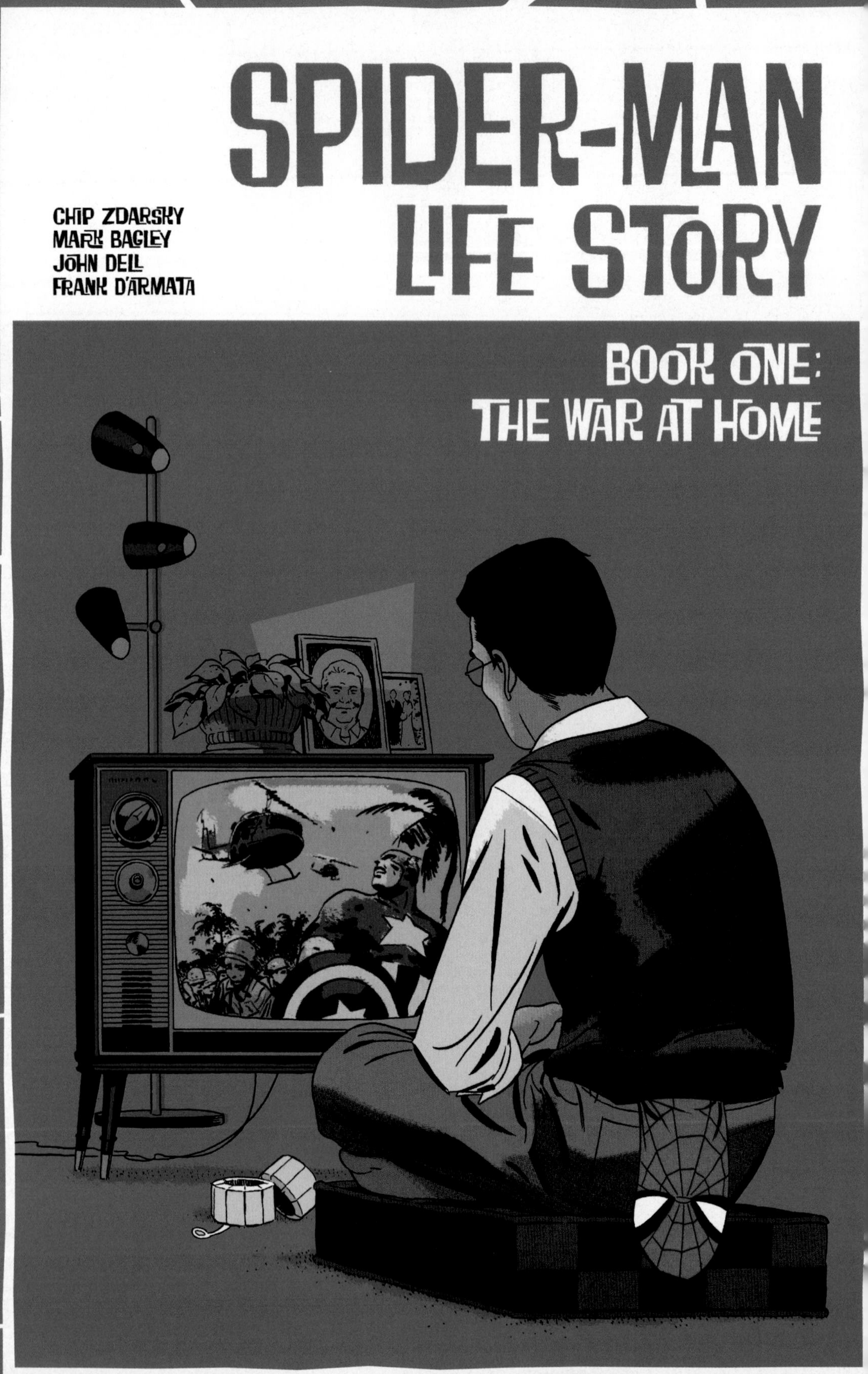
SPIDER-MAN
LIFE STORY
CHIP ZDARSKY
MARK BAGLEY
JOHN DELL
FRANK D'ARMATA
BOOK ONE:
THE WAR AT HOME

MARCOS MARTIN
SPIDER-MAN: LIFE STORY 1 VARIANT

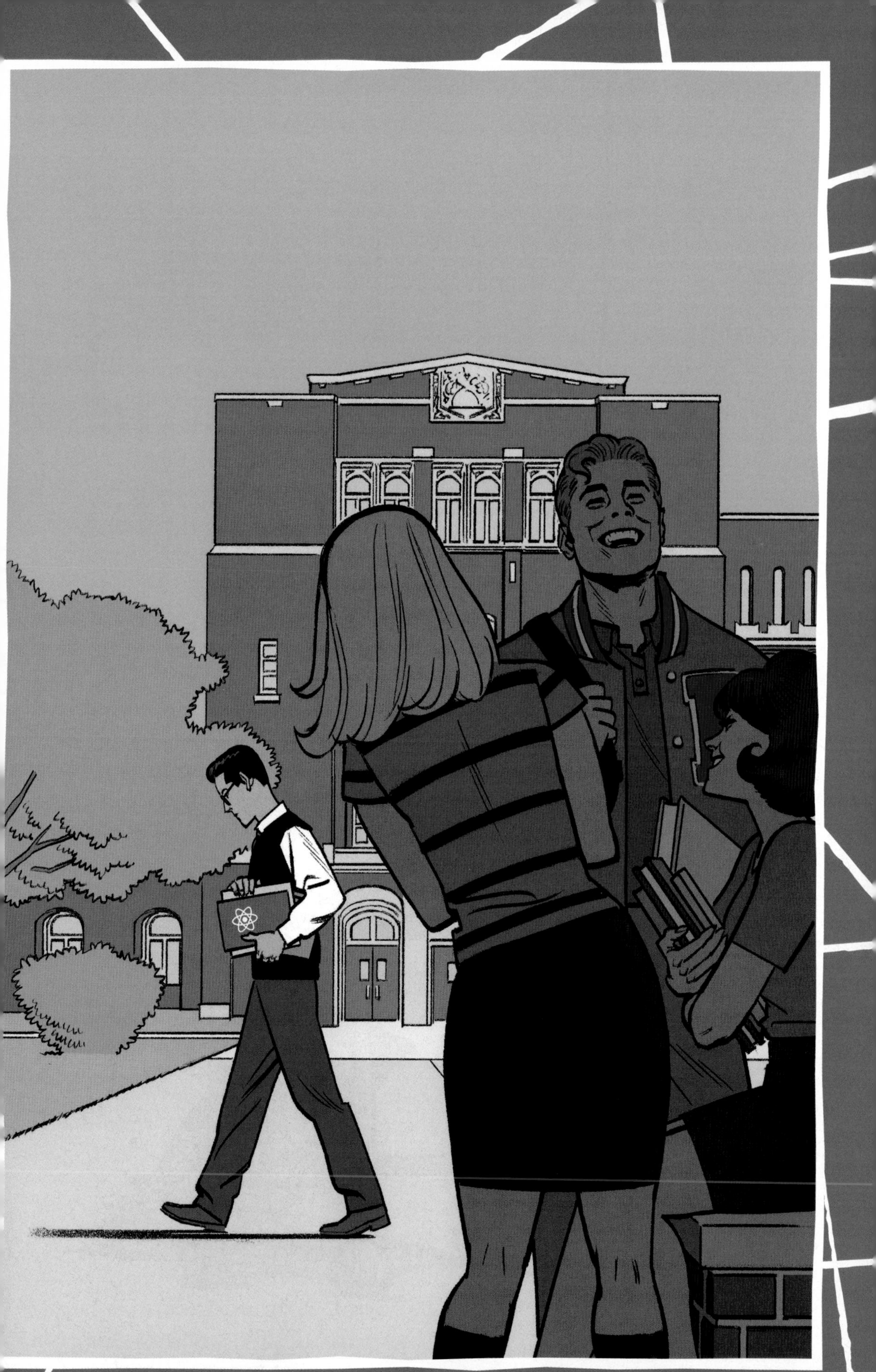

GREG SMALLWOOD
SPIDER-MAN: LIFE STORY 1 VARIANT

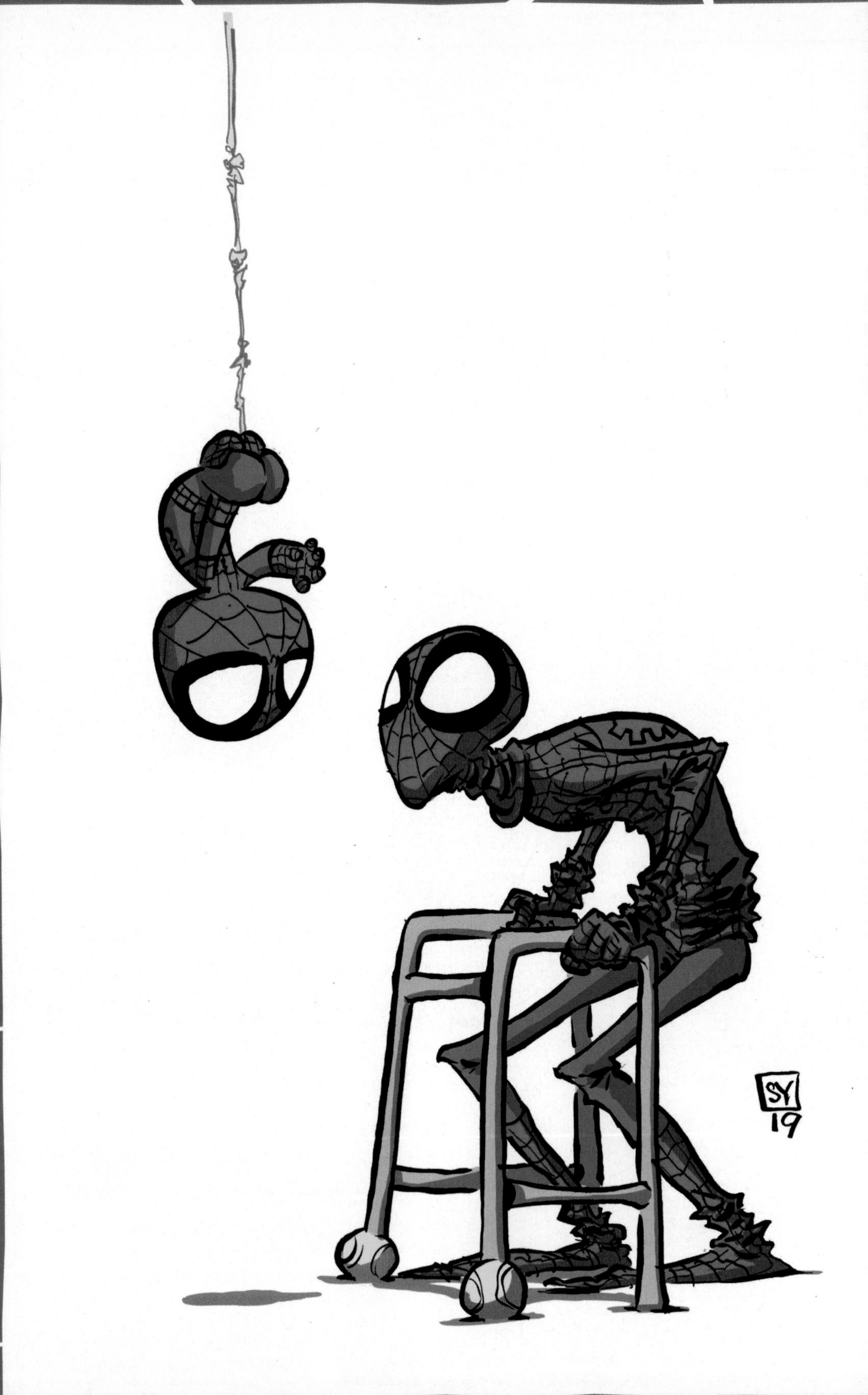
SY
19

SKOTTIE YOUNG
SPIDER-MAN: LIFE STORY 1 VARIANT

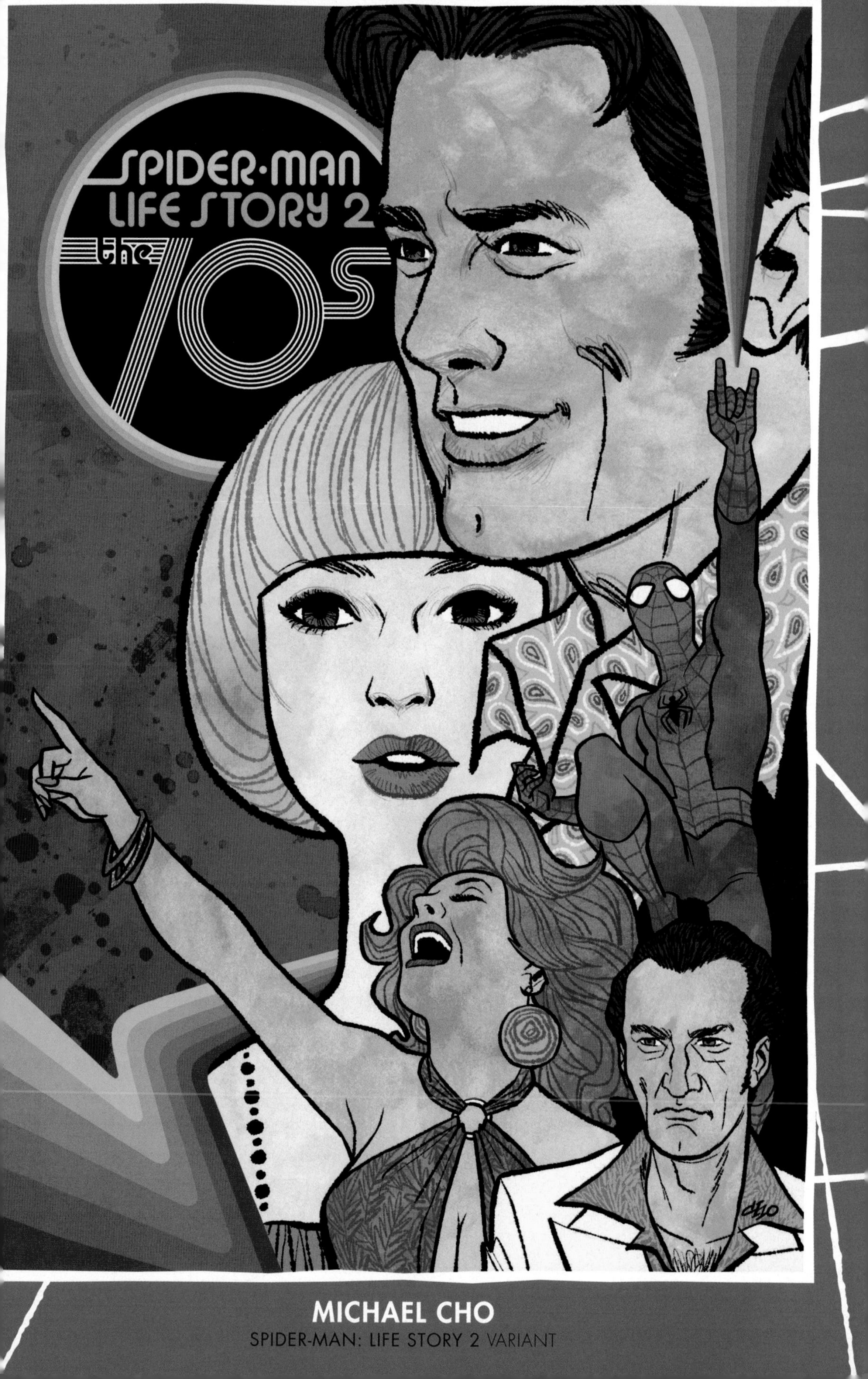
SPIDER-MAN
LIFE STORY 2
the 70s
CHO

MICHAEL CHO

SPIDER-MAN: LIFE STORY 2 VARIANT

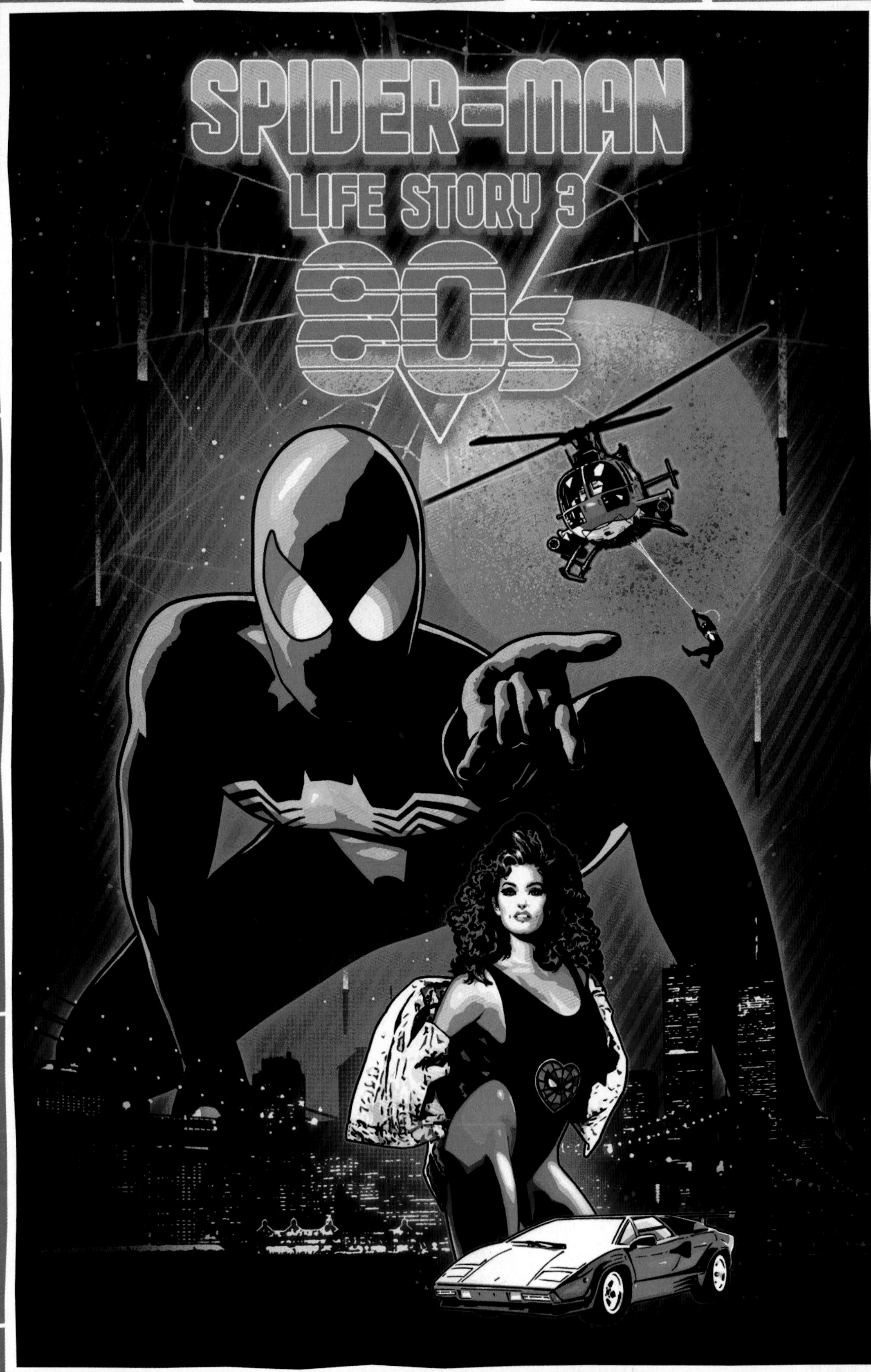
SPIDER-MAN
LIFE STORY 3
80s

ACO
SPIDER-MAN: LIFE STORY 3 VARIANT

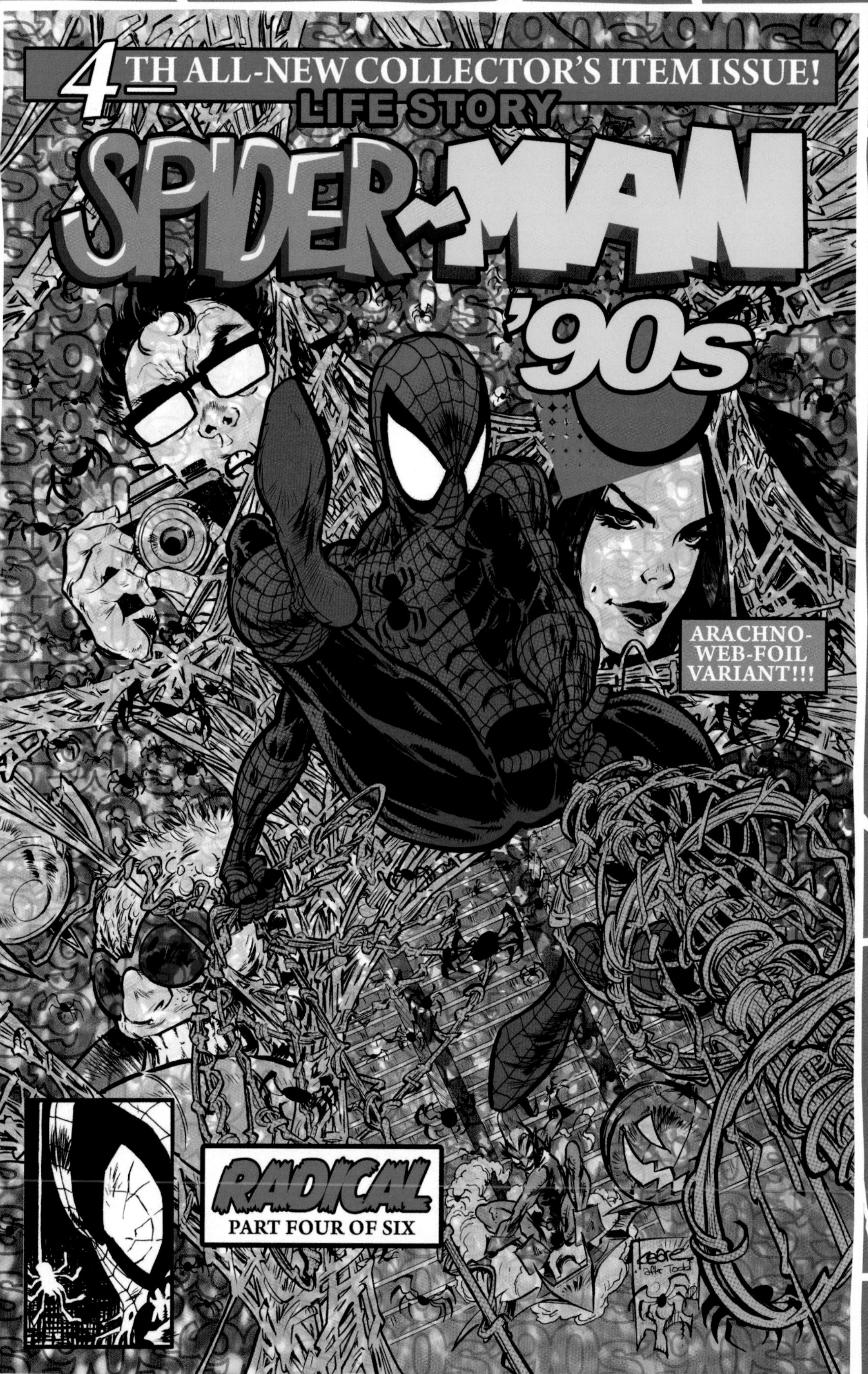
4TH ALL-NEW COLLECTOR'S ITEM ISSUE!
LIFE STORY
SPIDER-MAN
'90s
ARACHNO-WEB-FOIL VARIANT!!!
RADICAL
PART FOUR OF SIX

KAARE ANDREWS

SPIDER-MAN: LIFE STORY 4 VARIANT

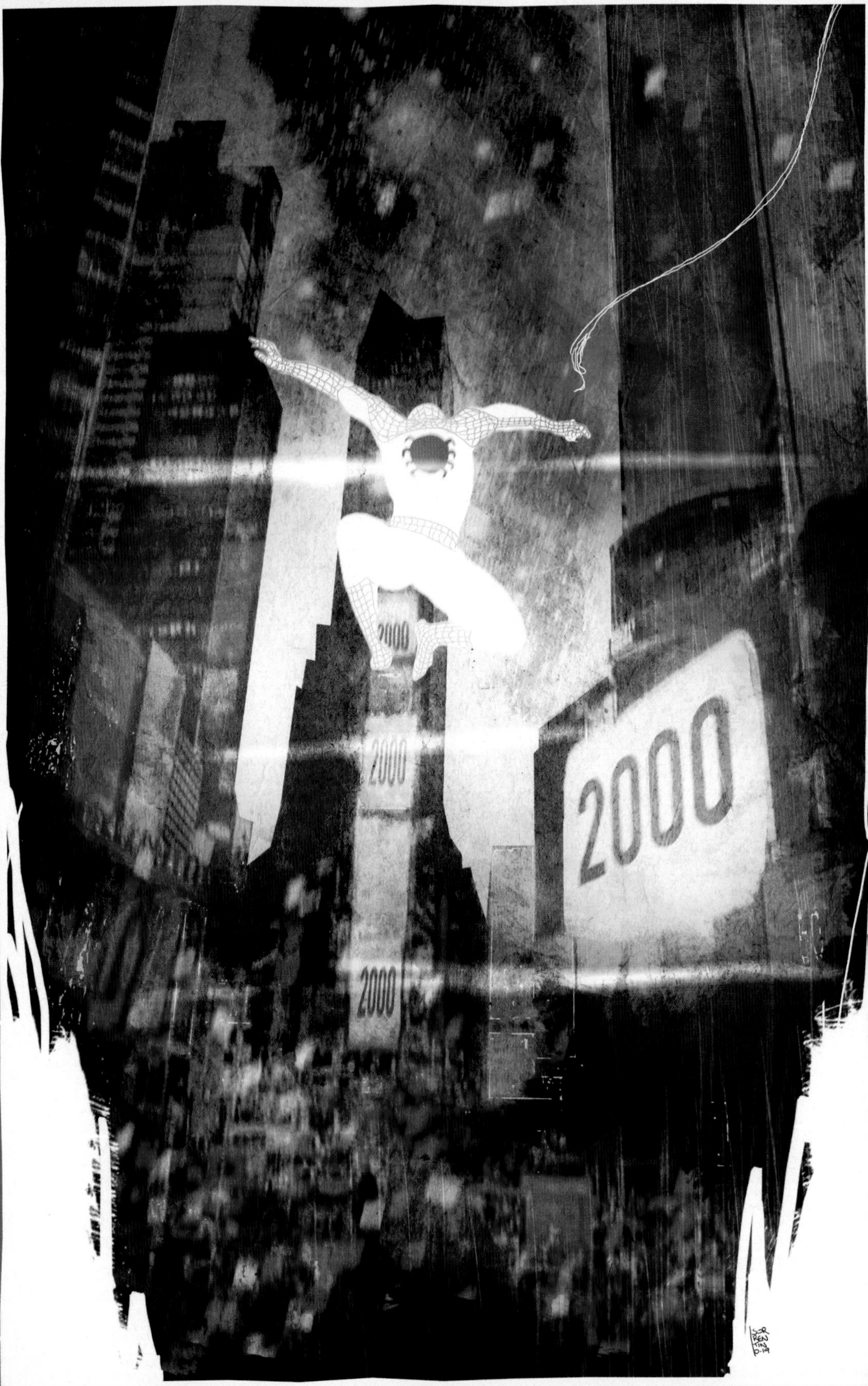
2000
2000
2000
2000
SOR REN TIN 0-19

ANDREA SORRENTINO

SPIDER-MAN: LIFE STORY 5 VARIANT

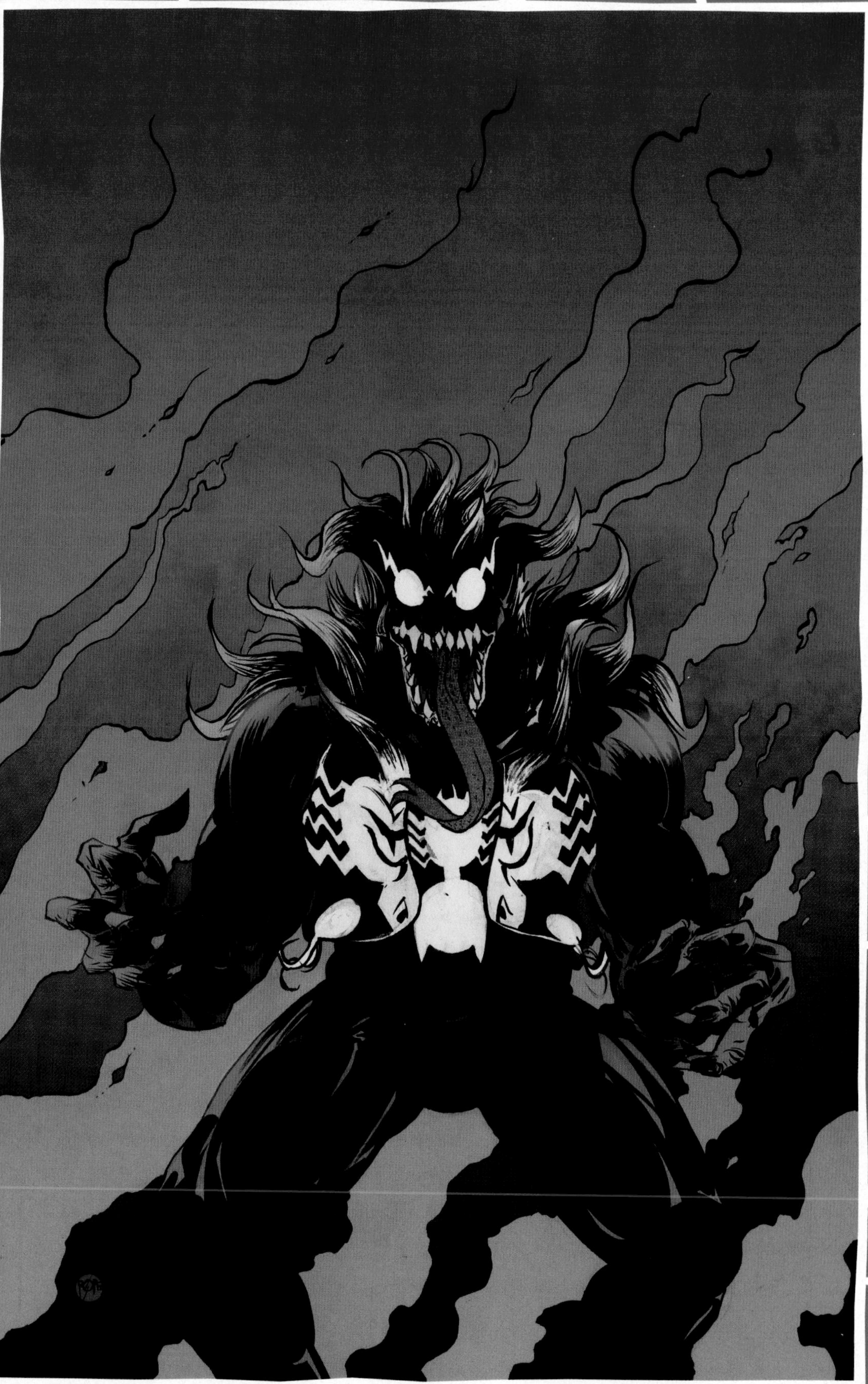

PAUL POPE & **BRUNO SEELIG**
SPIDER-MAN: LIFE STORY 6 VARIANT

COVER ART PROCESS BY

CHIP ZDARSKY

Like the fools they are, Marvel let me illustrate the covers for the series. I've long thought that we could bring in comic cover design ideas from book designs and movie posters, so this was me putting my little money where my mouth is.

MARVEL AGE
SPIDER-MAN
BOOK ONE:
All Our Wars
ZDARSKY • ARTIST • COLOURIST

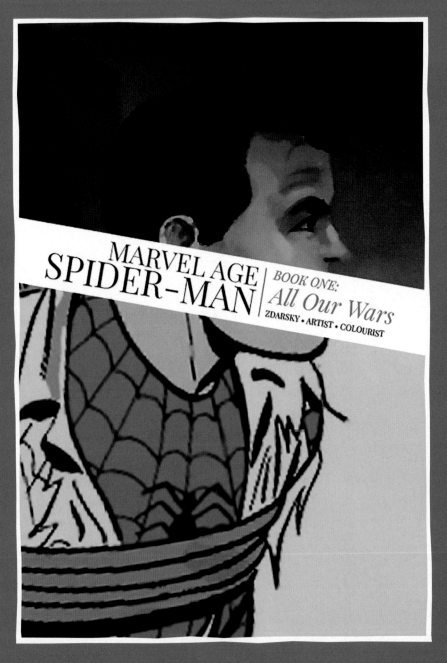

At first I attempted to use the classic comics as design elements, tweaking things so we could get the idea of a more realistic series based on the original stories. The problem with this one is that it looks too much like a retrospective on those stories.

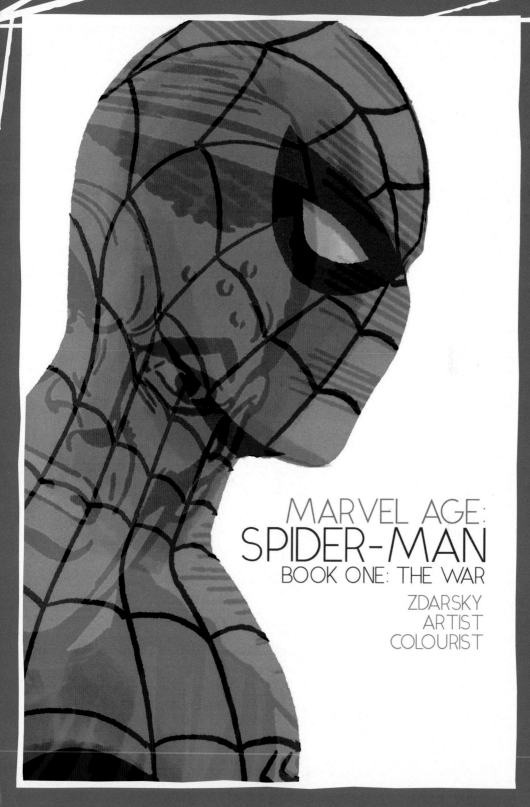

MARVEL AGE:
SPIDER-MAN
BOOK ONE: THE WAR

ZDARSKY
ARTIST
COLOURIST

My next attempt was to keep the classic imagery lighter and just focus on a proper Spidey image. Which could have worked, but I found it hard to imagine what the cover of issue #2 would be if we were to maintain the theme. But this came in handy later when trying to decide what to do for this collection, which needed an image not rooted in a particular decade.

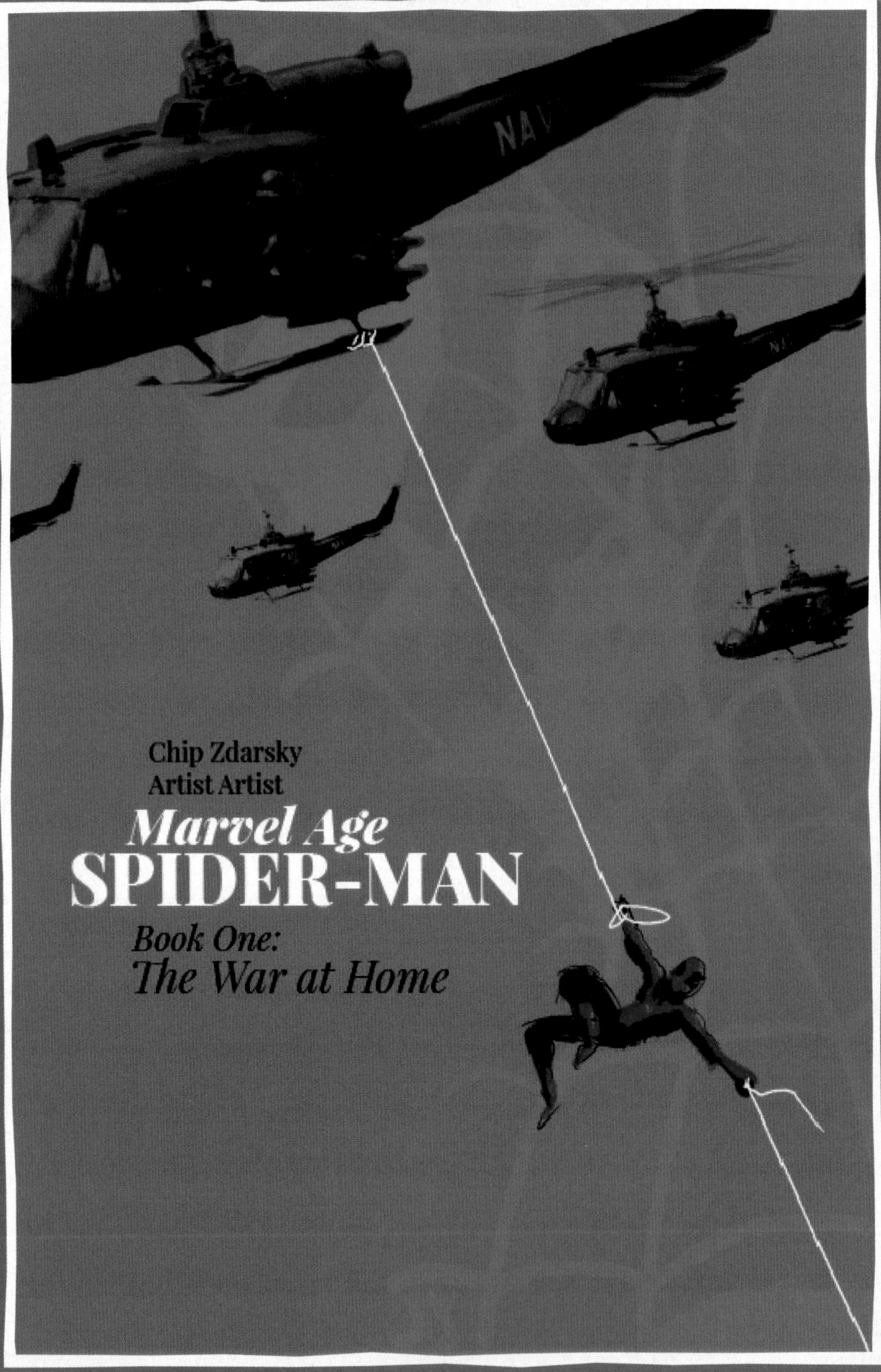
NAV
Chip Zdarsky
Artist Artist
Marvel Age
SPIDER-MAN
Book One:
The War at Home

This is where we ended up. By keeping it monochromatic we could just change the base colour for every issue. A lot of comic covers are literal, so being interpretive with the imagery from issue to issue was a fun challenge. Trying to sum up the decade in a single illustration.

Chip Zdarsky
Artist Artist
Ink Inker
Colour Colourist
SPIDER-MAN
Life Story 2 The 70s
MARVEL

Chip Zdarsky
Artist Artist
Ink Inker
Colour Colourist
SPIDER-MAN
Life Story 3 The 80s
MARVEL

Chip Zdarsky
Artist Artist
Ink Inker
Colour Colourist
SPIDER-MAN
Life Story 4 The 90s
MARVEL

Chip Zdarsky
Artist Artist
Ink Inker
Colour Colourist
SPIDER-MAN
Life Story 5 The 00s
MARVEL

Chip Zdarsky
Artist Artist
Ink Inker
Colour Colourist
SPIDER-MAN
Life Story 6 The 10s
MARVEL

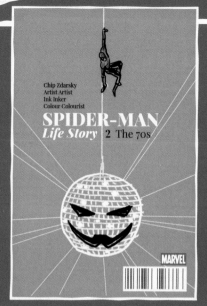

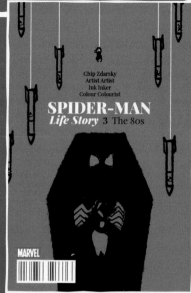

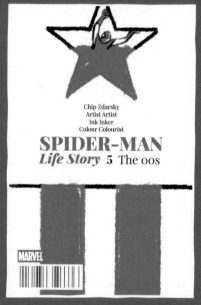

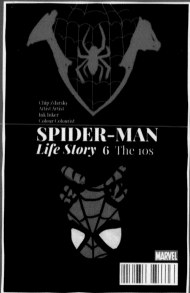

Everything ended up pretty close to these roughs, except for issue #6. Featuring the Miles costume on the cover felt like I was giving too much away.

Our editor, Tom Brevoort, suggested the blue for issue #5's cover, which was the smart way to go even though it broke my single-colour rule, damn him.

CREDITS DESIGN PROCESS BY

CHIP ZDARSKY

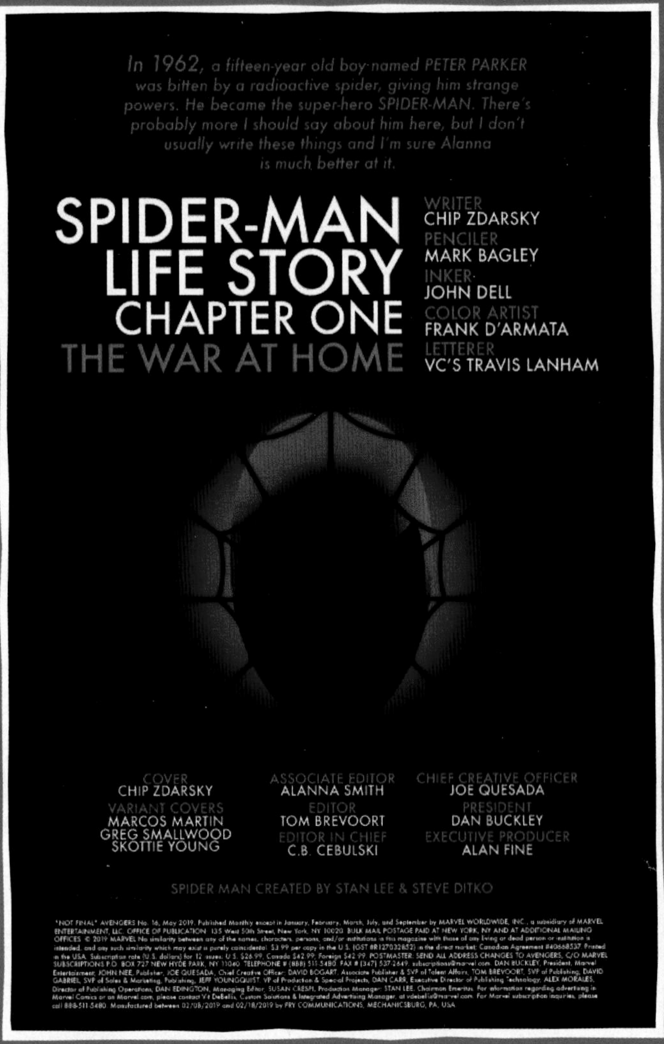

In 1962, a fifteen-year old boy named PETER PARKER was bitten by a radioactive spider, giving him strange powers. He became the super-hero SPIDER-MAN. There's probably more I should say about him here, but I don't usually write these things and I'm sure Alanna is much better at it.

SPIDER-MAN
LIFE STORY
CHAPTER ONE
THE WAR AT HOME

WRITER
CHIP ZDARSKY
PENCILER
MARK BAGLEY
INKER
JOHN DELL
COLOR ARTIST
FRANK D'ARMATA
LETTERER
VC'S TRAVIS LANHAM

COVER
CHIP ZDARSKY
VARIANT COVERS
MARCOS MARTIN
GREG SMALLWOOD
SKOTTIE YOUNG

ASSOCIATE EDITOR
ALANNA SMITH
EDITOR
TOM BREVOORT
EDITOR IN CHIEF
C.B. CEBULSKI

CHIEF CREATIVE OFFICER
JOE QUESADA
PRESIDENT
DAN BUCKLEY
EXECUTIVE PRODUCER
ALAN FINE

SPIDER MAN CREATED BY STAN LEE & STEVE DITKO

NOT FINAL AVENGERS No. 16, May 2019. Published Monthly except in January, February, March, July, and September by MARVEL WORLDWIDE, INC., a subsidiary of MARVEL ENTERTAINMENT, LLC. OFFICE OF PUBLICATION: 135 West 50th Street, New York, NY 10020. BULK MAIL POSTAGE PAID AT NEW YORK, NY AND AT ADDITIONAL MAILING OFFICES. © 2019 MARVEL No similarity between any of the names, characters, persons, and/or institutions in this magazine with those of any living or dead person or institution is intended, and any such similarity which may exist is purely coincidental. $3.99 per copy in the U.S. (GST #R127032852) in the direct market; Canadian Agreement #40668537. Printed in the USA. Subscription rate (U.S. dollars) for 12 issues: U.S. $26.99; Canada $42.99; Foreign $42.99. POSTMASTER: SEND ALL ADDRESS CHANGES TO AVENGERS, C/O MARVEL SUBSCRIPTIONS P.O. BOX 727 NEW HYDE PARK, NY 11040. TELEPHONE # (888) 511-5480. FAX # (347) 537-2649. subscriptions@marvel.com. DAN BUCKLEY, President, Marvel Entertainment; JOHN NEE, Publisher; JOE QUESADA, Chief Creative Officer; DAVID BOGART, Associate Publisher & SVP of Talent Affairs; TOM BREVOORT, SVP of Publishing; DAVID GABRIEL, SVP of Sales & Marketing, Publishing; JEFF YOUNGQUIST, VP of Production & Special Projects; DAN CARR, Executive Director of Publishing Technology; ALEX MORALES, Director of Publishing Operations; DAN EDINGTON, Managing Editor; SUSAN CRESPI, Production Manager; STAN LEE, Chairman Emeritus. For information regarding advertising in Marvel Comics or on Marvel.com, please contact Vit DeBellis, Custom Solutions & Integrated Advertising Manager, at vdebellis@marvel.com. For Marvel subscription inquiries, please call 888-511-5480. Manufactured between 02/08/2019 and 02/18/2019 by FRY COMMUNICATIONS, MECHANICSBURG, PA, USA.

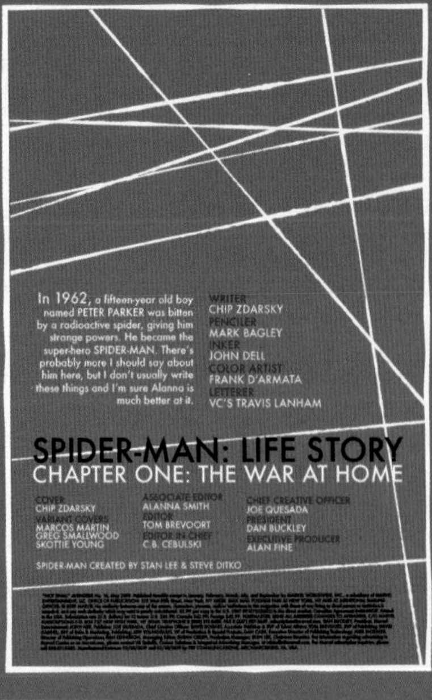

In 1962, a fifteen-year old boy named PETER PARKER was bitten by a radioactive spider, giving him strange powers. He became the super-hero SPIDER-MAN. There's probably more I should say about him here, but I don't usually write these things and I'm sure Alanna is much better at it.

WRITER
CHIP ZDARSKY
PENCILER
MARK BAGLEY
INKER
JOHN DELL
COLOR ARTIST
FRANK D'ARMATA
LETTERER
VC'S TRAVIS LANHAM

SPIDER-MAN: LIFE STORY
CHAPTER ONE: THE WAR AT HOME

COVER
CHIP ZDARSKY
VARIANT COVERS
MARCOS MARTIN
GREG SMALLWOOD
SKOTTIE YOUNG

ASSOCIATE EDITOR
ALANNA SMITH
EDITOR
TOM BREVOORT
EDITOR IN CHIEF
C.B. CEBULSKI

CHIEF CREATIVE OFFICER
JOE QUESADA
PRESIDENT
DAN BUCKLEY
EXECUTIVE PRODUCER
ALAN FINE

SPIDER-MAN CREATED BY STAN LEE & STEVE DITKO

I asked to handle the credits page as well to keep the design feeling cohesive. My first pass used an old unpublished Spidey illustration I did, but it didn't really work with the bumpy ink line and flat colour I was using on the cover. So no cohesion, which was my goal.

So I just mimicked the cover colour and kept it as abstract, rough weblines. Simple but effective, I think.